Humans, Animals, Machines

Humans, Animals, Machines

Blurring Boundaries

GLEN A. MAZIS

Published by
State University of New York Press, Albany

© 2008 State University of New York

All rights reserved

Printed in the United States of America

No part of this book may be used or reproduced in any manner whatsoever without written permission. No part of this book may be stored in a retrieval system or transmitted in any form or by any means including electronic, electrostatic, magnetic tape, mechanical, photocopying, recording, or otherwise without the prior permission in writing of the publisher.

For information, contact State University of New York Press, Albany, NY
www.sunypress.edu

Production by Eileen Meehan
Marketing by Michael Campochiaro

Library of Congress Cataloging-in-Publication Data

Mazis, Glen A., 1951–
   Humans, animals, machines : blurring boundaries / Glen A. Mazis.
     p. cm.
   Includes bibliographical references and index.
   ISBN 978-0-7914-7555-3 (hardcover : alk. paper)
   ISBN 978-0-7914-7556-0 (pbk. : alk. paper)
   1. Philosophical anthropology.　2. Animals (Philosophy)　3. Machinery.
4. Technology—Philosophy.　I. Title.

BD450.M342 2008
113'.8—dc22
                                        2007049732

10 9 8 7 6 5 4 3 2 1

*This book is dedicated to the memory of Mike Dillon,
who introduced me to the love of philosophy
and was a rare teacher of wonder, a dear friend, and a wise man.*

Contents

Acknowledgments xi

Chapter 1 Approaching Humans, Animals, and Machines 1
  Blurred Boundaries 1
  Where Are the Machines? 2
  Are Humans Not Animals? 4
  Are We Not Confused about Definitions? 6
  Doing Away with Hierarchy Can Preserve Uniqueness 8
  Ambiguity, Openness to Experience, Phenomenology, and Nondualism 11
  Embodiment as Cooperation with the Surround 14
  Meaning-Bearing Matter 17

Chapter 2 The Common Ground between Animals and Humans: Prolonged Bodies in Dwelling Places 21
  The Elusive Boundaries among Humans, Animals, and Machines 21
  Avoiding Reductive Senses of Overlaps of Humans, Animals, and Machines 23
  New Ways to See Overlaps and Differences: Living Space and "Understanding" One's Place 24
  Animal and Human Worlds and False Boundaries: Heidegger and von Uexküll 28
  The Lack of an Expanded Sense of Embodiment and Animality in Heidegger 32
  How Another Sense of Embodiment Opens These Dimensions 38
  Differing Spaces, Bodies, and Differing Worlds, but Open to Each Other 44

Chapter 3	Machines Finding Their Place: Humans and Animals Already Live There	49
	If Bodies Are Relations to Surrounds, Are Artificially Intelligent Machines Gaining Bodies?	49
	Embodied Understanding, Movement, and Meaning: Robots and Embodied Artificial Intelligence	53
	Enmeshed Worlds: Cochlear Implants and Michael Chorost's Sense of Being a Cyborg	58
	Making a Cochlear Implant Work and Perceptual Faith, Attention Flow, and Emotional Connection	64
	Indeterminacy Is Openness to the Overlap	70
	Plain Machines and How We Are All in This World Together: Humans, Animals, and Machines	75
	Dangers of Imploded Boundaries and the Need for Ambiguity	82
Chapter 4	Drawing the Boundary of Humans with Animals and Machines: Greater Area and Depth	87
	Can We Even Draw Boundary Lines?	87
	"The Rational Animal" Using Tools, Speaking, and Passing the Turing Test	91
	Thinking "Substance" and How It Feels to Meet a Thinker with a Face	94
	Human Thought Extended by Machines	99
	Humans Locate and Direct Themselves in Mood, Emotion, Feeling, and Thought	104
	"We Feel" and the Emotional Valence	109
	Neural and Material Plasticity and Open Systems	113
	Brains as Process, Emotions as Integrating, and Selves both Inside and Out	118
Chapter 5	Drawing the Boundary of Humans with Animals and Machines: Reconsidering Knowing and Reality	125
	Juxtapositions, Brain Hemispheres, Brains as Observer/Observed, and the Logic of Yin/Yang	125
	Quantum Minds and Nondualistic Reality	132
	Nonlocal Quantum Reality, "Phenomenality," and Magic in Emotion	137

Imagination, Being Moved, and the Virtual Dimension of
   Human Life   141
The Storytelling Communal Animal, Integrated Brains/Selves,
   and Human Excellence   148
Ambiguity and Boundaries among Networks   153
Inside and Outside Ourselves Simultaneously, Freedom, Interbeing   156
Humans Witness the World's Depth in Multivalent Apprehension   161

Chapter 6   Animals: Excellences and Boundary Markers   **169**
The Problem of Understanding Animals' Perspectives
   from Within   169
The Thickness of Animal Perception versus a Reductive
   Mechanical Model   177
Animals and Prereflective, Perceptually Grounded Selves   182
Animal Perceptual Sensitivity Meshes with Ecological Niches,
   Not Human Enclosures   186
Instinct as the Life of the Dream   190
The Expressive Spontaneity of Animals as Embodied Dialogue   195
Animals in the Slower Time We Call Nature   200

Chapter 7   Machines: Excellences and Boundary Markers   **209**
Machines and Solid, Impervious Materiality   209
Machines, Consistency, and the Time of the Earth   213
Machines, Power, Precision, and Machine Beauty   218
Machines, Speed, and the Lack of Place for Deeper Time   222
Machines, the Arbitrary, and Dissonant, Arrhythmic Time   227
Machines as Woven into the Fabric of the Surround   230

**Conclusion   Toward the Community of Humans, Animals,
   and Machines**   **235**
Is There Personhood for Animals and Machines?   235
Obligations to Sacrificing Animals and Helping Machines,
   Good and Bad Persons, and Guardianship   244
An Ecospirituality of Humans, Animals, and Machines   251

Notes   259
Index   267

Acknowledgments

My ongoing interlocutor and reader of works in progress, Judith Kennedy, is owed much thanks for helping me clarify many of the issues of the book. My mother, Charlotte, who has always inspired me as an example of how to live affirmatively and to pursue a love of learning and thinking, was even more helpful with this text, engaging in constant proofreading and discussions. Jane Bunker was steadfast in her enthusiasm for writing this book and her determination to see it through. She is also fun to have as an editor, as well as a dog lover. Catherine Keller and Jason Starr are also friends with whom many lengthy discussions opened new vistas on these questions. Bruce and Donna Wilshire shared their insights on many topics that overlap with those of this book. Penn State Harrisburg gave me the opportunity to teach two upper-level, interdisciplinary seminars on this topic, which helped me greatly clarify my thinking. A hearty thanks to the students in those two seminars, who at first thought how weird a topic and then become utterly engaged with it and stimulating to me. The book is dedicated to Mike Dillon because he was not only the wonderful teacher who introduced me to philosophy and to Merleau-Ponty, but his leadership of the Merleau-Ponty Circle for a quarter of a century until his recent untimely death gave me my truest home within philosophy. I always owe a debt of gratitude to the members of the Circle who have been enlightening partners in dialogue for three decades. Other friends, family, and colleagues who should be thanked for their support are Peter Kareithi, Pat Johnson, Crispin Sartwell, Marian Winik, Ed Casey, John Neill, and Joan Kuenz. Many thanks to the Dallas Museum of Art for use of the reproduction of Scheeler's "Suspended Power." Once again, I am so grateful that Bhakti, the "Zen Chihuahua," is still with us at her advanced age. She has sat at my side for every page of this book's writing, and watching the wonder of her existence over the years was certainly a source of inspiration for this book. Lastly, David Chappell's passing away during the writing of this book was a tragedy to the world's peace movement, and I hope I have captured just a little bit of his spirit with the final section of this book.

Chapter 1

Approaching Humans, Animals, and Machines

Blurred Boundaries

Life in the early twenty-first century seems dominated by systems of machines that encroach upon our day-to-day rhythms. They are often a source of anxiety, as well as a source of success, and the means whereby to accomplish many of our daily projects. They are also harbingers of national security, means to exchange capital, ways to communicate with each other, and verifiers of what is going on around us. More personally, machine systems are the heart of whether our own shelters function properly, are sometimes key monitors of maintaining the functioning of our own bodies, and are becoming virtually omnipresent in most dimensions of our day-to-day existence. Even our vital abilities to be sexual or digest food or process the air around us are often keyed into pharmaceutical or biotechnical products that are machined for us in laboratories and factories. More and more, we write, think, and dream at screens of computers like the one I am sitting at to write this book. However, it is not only that we are surrounded by machines. These beings we created seem to be crowding us out and transforming our world in ways that are unsettling, thrilling, and puzzling. More and more, it is our growing sense that they have become the very means whereby we can maintain ourselves as who we are that is so unnerving, yet we tend to keep this anxiety hidden. We created machines and now they create us, or at least they shape us in ways to which we are too accustomed to relinquish. Countless plots of horror films or novels, as well as countless philosophical theories of dialectical interplay, have been spawned by this fear in our bones about a vulnerability to a reversal of who is the creator and sustainer between humans and machines.

The process of populating the globe with machines and reconstructing who we are in their image is a number of centuries in the making, but also for several centuries we have come to understand ourselves also as biological beings, as creatures or animals, yet comprised of mechanistic systems that allow us to function in response to the world around us and in response to the various systems within us. The creaturely is often seen mechanically. Even our inner world is one of biomechanics. We are able to intervene increasingly in these interlocking mechanisms, even reading the detailed instructions in DNA codes, and so on. We have now invented machines that can even move around atoms. There are those who descry this increasing infiltration of our rhythms, our thoughts, our feelings, and our dreams with machines. Yet there are also those who dream of "storing" our consciousness in computers or machines and thereby realizing the age-old dream of many to escape the flesh—or, what is called by these advocates, "the meat." In another reversal of traditional visions, immortality beckons to these individuals, not as realm of spirit but as having become downloaded into the invulnerable shell of the machine. Whether this encroaching mechanization and love for the machine is seen as menace, as source of oppression, alienation, and disconnection, or as salvation against the contingencies of a threatening natural world, a chaotic physical realm, and an avenue to greater order, productivity, and rationality of existence, it has become harder and harder to maintain a simple "us" versus "them" mentality with our machine confreres. As we recognize increasingly that vital and vast parts of who we are as distinctively human are not possible without this mechanistic dimension being at the heart of our viscera, our genetic codes, our electronically based neural functioning, and so on, who we are becomes more insecure from this direction too. With the scientific revolution of early modernity, the divine itself has been seen by some as a machinist and the creation as a clocklike invention. In this vision, the esteemed place of the soul in opposition to this material realm seems vestigial. If the material realm is merely a grand mechanism, then the place of spirit seems merely a confused afterthought as if it were a smoke screen to keep us from settling up the score with ourselves as to who we really are.

Where Are the Machines?

This sense of becoming reduced to a mere machine, to a spiritless realm, however, may also be an outdated carryover from our tradition, insofar as the way we tend to think of machines keeps old industrial models dancing in our heads instead of savoring newer dimensions of the machine we have not fathomed yet. There is a need to see older definitions of the machine and the characteristics of mechanism as often outdated. The vision of clanking gears and cogs grinding an invasive path through the external world in a maniacal blindness might have been properly directed at the core of the industrial mechanism, and once properly dictated our assessment of the traditional machine. Yet this view might not fit what we now ask machines to do, or how we see vast portions of our physical and human reality to be machinelike. We can narrow our vision to fit these older notions of the mechanical, but they do not encompass the trajectory of where machines, and we in tandem with them, appear to be going. In looking back, we might see that we were not as discerning as possible about the varied aspects of machine beings, as well as the varied ways to be human that might overlap with machine being. Also, it has become increasingly undeniable that machine being is not just about physical apparatuses constructed by us to do certain tasks but equally concerns other dimensions of human existence.

When we look farther, social mechanisms or governmental mechanisms or educational or religious ones often disturb many who are not even as concerned about the machine as physical entity. There are other ways to be caught by machines or to become part of machines than being caught up in the gears of a factory monster, such as the famous image of Charlie Chaplain being swallowed up in the enormous metal cogs in *Modern Times*, where his being caught up in the literal mechanism of the factory is symbolic of the mechanism of industrial life measuring the worker's value in terms of productivity and efficiency. Becoming just a number or a set of statistics or a profit margin or a strategic piece in a movement or within an institution that has forgotten its purpose, or being reduced to an object to be conveyed here or there by certain procedures, or becoming reckoned upon as a set of behaviors to be managed within acceptable parameters for the overall functioning of the larger social system is a way to be incorporated into machines without becoming metal or silicon. Some of these mechanisms are truly horrifying, such as the "war machine" written about abstractly by Deleuze and Guattari, but also written home about by any grunt stationed in the modern fighting force or by those occupied civilians who live in these zones of containment, control, and devastation. Yet as in the case of the literal, specific machine, life seems improbable without these sorts of mechanisms channeling energies, thoughts, materials, events, communication, transportation, and so on. So, intrusively or invisibly, helpfully or as a mode of resistance, the machine lurks in many dimensions of human existence having nothing to do with metal or silicon. Yet what seems most striking is that we have not really thought through globally the characteristics of the machine, whether machines are evolving in their characteristics, and what exactly their relationship is to human being.

Machines and humans are often taken to be in opposition, to be at odds in a war of dominance that our science fiction movies increasingly portray as perhaps perilous for humanity, another tradition that has long antecedents but probably is most famously represented in American popular culture by the nineteenth-century specter of Mary Shelley's creature,

Frankenstein—a "machine" made out of biological "parts," or is it a creature brought to life by the power of mechanisms in turn powered by human will and imagination? It is fictional, but the grey area it opened in the public imagination about possibilities for the future is an ever-expanding one and also a zone of indeterminacy that has always existed between human and machine from the earliest myths of humankind. In Shelley's vision, the "monster" is initially more humane than its creator or the other humans it encounters, who spurn its tender feelings of wanting to embrace all beings, because of the *mechanism of prejudice* that guides their responses and behavior—an automatic response to its unsightly looks. Who is machine, who is creature, and what is human? We will see not only Frankenstein, but in many collisions of humans, animals, and machines, they are like Möbius strips—if one follows them along their apparent surface, they turn inside out and are part of another domain entirely, while still also being part of the first domain.

Are Humans Not Animals?

At the same time the boundary between the human and machine has been contested, puzzled over, and debated increasingly in the past centuries, humans' relation to the creatures around us has become increasingly unclear. In American culture, it was certainly the spread of Darwinism that brought to a fever pitch a debate whether humans were just another sort of animal, or something distinct from the rest of animal being, a debate that has only become more heated with the advent of machines allowing us to probe ever more deeply into our mutual constitution and to see that 98.6 percent of our DNA is shared with certain apes. This fact was brought home most forcibly to popular culture when Jared Diamond, in his best seller of the early 1990s, declared that "we are just a third species of chimpanzee" and titled his book *The Third Chimpanzee*. His initial sentences explaining this claim inform his readers that "the genetic distance (1.6 percent) separating us from pygmy or common chimps is barely double that separating pygmy from common chimps (0.7 percent). It's less than that between two species of gibbons (2.2 percent), or between such closely related North American bird species as red-eyed vireos and white-eyed vireos (2.9 percent). The remaining 98.4 percent of our DNA is just normal chimp DNA."[1] In this perspective, not only are humans not distinct from animals and other chimpanzees, humans "don't constitute a distinct family, nor even a distinct genus" (TTC, 25).

Yet once again it is not just on the level of our changing perspectives of what our makeup is where these boundaries cross and blur; it is in the matrix of economic, political, and social activity that we struggle to understand the ways in which a sense of animality pervades aspects of our culture and collective activity, just as these dimensions, too, analogously can be seen to be mechanisms. It would be an easy matter to digress into many issues that contest the boundaries of the human and the animal, from animal rights debates in which the shared human-animal capacities for pain or loyalty enter, to the explosion of time, capital, and emotion aimed at pets within postmodern capitalist societies, which is not only some romanticized and cute sense of fetish ownership but part of a longer history of what Donna Haraway calls the "natureculture" of "companion species" in her small book *The Companion Species Manifesto* (a supplement to her earlier, famous "cyborg manifesto"). Haraway describes our flesh and our language as a "metaplasm," as an ongoing remolding or remodeling among humans and other species, especially focusing on the human relationship with dogs: "Domestication is not creating a tool out of an animal, but a co-habiting in which both species are part of a protean, historical, obligatory and constitutive emergent process."[2] Instead of seeing domesticated animals, pets, and working animals as tools, as something external to human being, she believes species incorporate aspects of the other into what they have become. This parallels her earlier work on the way humans and machines have become assimilated within each other in their being.

Like Haraway's new work, part of my own writing has been to document the ways in which animality is constitutive of what we think of as most human about ourselves and how animals express themselves through behaviors and interactions that suggest they have intelligence, feelings, morality, capacities for relationship, and recognition of mortality in certain cases. I have made the case that these phenomena must alter our sense of the different kinds of being of animals and how we share with them dimensions of who we are.[3] Perhaps it is not mere superstition that indigenous cultures have referred to animals as our teachers if it were true that we have learned from animals or from the animal nature within us some of our finest "human" attributes.

Yet it is not altogether unreasonable that the opposite point of view, that of Descartes, Malebranche, and a host of philosophers, cognitive scientists, ethologists, and others, maintained that animals are basically no more than machines, and at the same time worried that humans were driven by emotions that in turn were driven through the blood in a mechanistic way. Perfectly expressing this blurring of boundaries, Descartes called these mechanistic forces of emotion "the animal spirits." The overlapping of boundaries may be quite apparent when the philosopher whose credo is achieving "clarity and distinctness" coins a term and a notion that wonderfully conflates human, animal, and machine. His terminology conjures up a picture of how humans are compelled in a way like an *animal* as a *mechanism* that is driven as *spirits* coursing through the blood. It is uncanny, as we will see in case after case in this book, from physiology to metaphysics, psychology to political science, mythology to physics, computer science to painting, that when one proceeds to the core of what seems to be the animal, both the machine and the human emerge into the discussion. When one proceeds to the core of the human, both the animal and the machine emerge. When one looks most deeply at the domain of the animal, descriptions of mechanism and humanity emerge. The three realms, I would contend, can only be thought through together. The boundaries of the human, animal, and machine overlap, dance within each other, and separate, or maybe they should separate at certain key moments, but these lines or arabesques have been barely drawn or even traced out for the intricacy and beauty of their movements. Cyborg being—our sense of incorporating tools, and becoming interwoven with machines within us, about us, and within the meshes of how we have organized the world—has always existed—it is just becoming more literal and extravagant. The animal within us as source of vitality, of joy at organic being, of intercommunion with the creatures around us to experience the planet, is also an ancient aspect of human existence—dimensions that I have written about at length in *Earthbodies: Rediscovering our Planetary Senses*.

Are We Not Confused about Definitions?

By often limiting the discussion to each of these boundaries with the human—both with the machine and the animal—we are overlooking possible sources of answers to many vexing questions. In order to decide when the infringement of the mechanical is becoming destructive in certain instances to human possibilities, to decide when humans have imposed a corrosive dimension onto the quality of animal life, or to understand how machines may be due a certain inclusion within the community of fellow beings that demonstrates an emerging excellence of spirit and beauty, and might have an intrinsic worth, it is necessary to understand the ways in which each dimension lies at the heart of the other, where each needs to remain distinct and still be able to speak to the others across the differences as is needed for dialogue. As Haraway says in *Companion Species Manifesto*: "Post-cyborg, what counts as biological kind troubles previous categories of organism. The textual and the machinic are internal to the organic, and vice versa, in irreversible ways" (CSM, 30). This trouble has been with us for a while—when we started cutting up humans more routinely in the eighteenth century to make repairs and now often to replace parts (utilizing the machine dimension of humans to advantage), when disabilities that are seen as simply organic but are based on the failure to achieve certain sorts of culturally established language and communicative norms that lead persons to be disenfranchised or in extreme cases to be imprisoned in institutions (in other words, defining the proper "machine function" by cultural ideals of human being that says one *should* experience the senses as distinct, for example, and not overlapping in an autistic sense), or when a history of agricultural cultivation has led to utilizing the "mechanisms" of animals as unfeeling, replaceable cogs (confusing animals with machines—like hens lined up and piled atop each other in "assembly lines" their entire lives—to the formers' acute disadvantage). The list of conflations of humans, animals, and machines in confused and destructive ways, both old and new, would go on for chapters and need not be rehearsed here. However, to mention these confusions can bring to mind the need to define these differing realms in *both* their inseparability *and* difference, in their capacities for mutual destructiveness, and in their capacities to help each other's realm achieve distinctive excellence.

At Stanford University in 1987, a conference was held to try to sketch out the boundaries and overlaps among humans, animals, and machines. The resulting presentations were published as *The Boundaries of Humanity: Humans, Animals and Machines*. When one reads the essays, it is clear that none of the conference presenters had a cogent sense of how to draw these boundaries or even to articulate what was distinctive about humans, animals, and machines. Advances in computer science, neurophysiology, genetics, ethnography, biology, philosophy, critical theory, communications, and so many other fields have perhaps made this task more plausible now, have at least given us more data and theories to consider, and certainly also have made the need more pressing. A book such as Bruno Latour's *Politics of Nature* calls for the formation of a new collective that includes humans and nonhumans in ways that no longer oppose nature and culture, matter and spirit, politics and science, and the animate and the inanimate and avoids other dualisms that have left humans, animals, and machines as adversaries, yet Latour despairs and derides any attempt to find a new way of philosophically articulating the being of these realms and their interrelations. He feels that such a task is overwhelming and unnecessary to the practical dialogue of working out the ramifications of science and technology.[4] He seems to assume, as do many in popular culture and the academy, that any attempt to really articulate the distinctive senses of being in each of these realms and in their interrelation will lapse back into some traditional metaphysical speculation that cares not a whit about the advances in scientific, empirical research, nor the practical exigencies that come from the collisions of these realms with cultural values, economic realities, and political processes.

I will assume the opposite of Latour: the only way we can proceed with sensitivity and creativity in responding to the advances in what Haraway calls "technoscience" is to have a better sense of what makes each of these realms—humans, animals, and machines—distinctive and also inseparable. I also will assume that philosophy is up to the task of returning to the concrete phenomena of the varied sciences and social sciences, as well as to the arts and humanities in their concrete articulations of data or insights of another sort, and providing a dialogue of the results of these fields, giving us insights into their significance. We can probe the identities of the realms these fields uncover, even if they are not the old eternal essences of metaphysics but are, rather, the fluid, evolving, and problematic coming together of differing perspectives that cross-fertilize and also break off in differing vectors, only to rejoin again at some later point. The image we need for these results is of a nonlinear equation's graph with its myriad branches and discontinuities, rather than the incremental, straight-line and consistently predictable Cartesian graphs that the old philosophies and sciences sought as companion models and emblems of their thought.

Doing Away with Hierarchy Can Preserve Uniqueness

In order to achieve the aforementioned task, however, we will have to leave aside preconceptions of what is obvious about each realm, and the most difficult, of course, is to hold in abeyance those self-attributions of humans that increase our self-esteem in the household of the universe. As all writers who venture over ecological terrains point out, the *oikos* that is the first part of that word ("eco"), the Greek for "household," does not mean our human domain but a much larger kinship, ordering, linking, and relating with myriad beings. For this book, we will need to leave this horizon as open as possible for a time. Humans have been persistent in varied cultures in seeing themselves as special—not just different from other beings—but somehow privileged, more valuable, a reflection or an instantiation of the divine. For more modern atheists, humans often have been considered the pinnacle of billions of years of material and biological evolution culminating in the great engineering being, destined to control the others. This sense of human superiority is not universally true, however, of all cultures or historical periods. Some cultures have insisted that humans are merely the two-legged ones in a larger family gathered under the Great Spirit of four-legged ones and winged ones, such as in many Native American tribal perspectives, or that our celebrated language abilities are part of a larger voice originating in the myriad beings of the world and universe for whom we happened to be the speaking or writing instrument.

We can be unique, as indeed all beings can be unique, without being better, more intrinsically valuable. This placing ourselves on a higher plane has taken us out of the interplay of other beings on the planet in such a way that perhaps much of what we experience has come to seem mysterious or fantastic or just not plausible. It is a strange fact that both those on the one extreme, who believe in religious views based on the divine as supernatural and as utterly certain, and those on the other extreme, scientists who feel that any talk of emotion, consciousness, or spirituality in regard to animals or the material world is somehow not properly factual, are united in keeping humanity distinct from the rest of the planet. Animals, inanimate matter, and machines must be seen as included in a differing realm by both those who claim absolute insight into human's spiritual superiority to the rest of the planet and those who deny that there are any mental, spiritual, or emotional realities that can be known. Yet I feel that our thinking must be based on what we experience, whether personally or collectively, scientifically or spiritually, otherwise we risk being ignorant of the relationships that make our lives as valuable and meaningful as they are. The dogmas of religiously inflexible doctrines or scientific theories claiming certainty, but ungrounded in our current experience, may offer worthwhile visions of possible futures, but the first order of business is seeing where we are in the variety of the cultural, historical, and material settings in which we find ourselves. I recognize that there is a problem in "just paying attention to experience." There are grave challenges to this goal, too, and I will return to consider them.

However, it is not just a problem of method and what counts as knowing or understanding that has prevented so many philosophies, religions, psychologies, myths, artworks, and scientists from exploring fully the ways we might be on a *horizontal plane* of distinct differences within an inseparable linkage with the beings of this planet—instead of *being above* other creatures and inanimate beings. This prospect of being on an equal footing with the rest of the planet or even the cosmos as miraculous and worthy of respect, as special, but also as an integral part of larger movements than the merely human, has rattled something very deep in many cultures' collective psyches.

Few have had the feeling of Siddhartha Buddha in his going forth from the palace in order to encounter reality after being sheltered from life by his father for the first time in his three decades, when he was overcome by the sight of worms and insects that had been torn apart by the plow or crushed under his own feet while walking upon the land. Few have seen the littered bodies of insects and worms on the ground at their feet and become as "overcome with grief as if he has witnessed the slaughter of his own family."[5] This radical sense of interconnectivity and lack of hierarchy, the savoring that each being is unique and intrinsically valuable, has been a rare and often seemingly rarified feeling and, many would say, merely sentimental. A sentiment is a feeling that is of our individual or collective ego's creation, propelled by an idea, and often a faddish one. Sentiments do not require a radical openness and a deep responsiveness. They are projected onto things or people. Yet, there may be profoundly sensitive emotions of wonder, awe, joy, grief, playfulness, empathy, and others that can be cultivated to the larger surround, and Siddhartha's may be among these. We may not have simple access to the deepest feelings possible in regard to the surround *without work*—the work of integrated feeling, thought, and articulation. However, this work of articulation cannot happen if we cling to a notion of being both separate and above as required by an ego insecurity built into our cultural thinking. It is not imperative to begin thinking through these issues by merely accepting intuitions such as Siddhartha's, but it is necessary to be open at least to the possibility of this interconnectedness. If we are open to feelings that suggest these insights, then we can better explore the depths and complexity of how we are related to other beings. This requires not being repulsed at the outset as if there is a contagion within the idea of our interconnectedness or a lack of revealing sensitivity in such feelings of kinship.

The contagion felt by some in giving up the first rank, the highest order above other beings, is the sense of some that to be interconnected, of equal worth, is to enter the impurity of mixing categories, an affront to clear thinking and even a kind of moral transgression to mix that which should be separate. This tradition has roots that go back to ancient times, at least to the fertile era when Plato thought one should die to the earth, its sensual pull and emotional resonances, fighting the shifting tides of the earth that would condemn the soul to lose its own purity and separate identity; echoed by the Indian sages of the Upanishads, who cautioned against getting lost on the roads of the mazes of desire by allowing the chariot of self to be pulled astray by the "horses" of the senses instead of transcending to the purity of the Atman; or modulated differently in the same era by the nonascetic message of China's Confucius to restrain, control and order the senses and the emotions through fealty to the power of law, rites, and the ancestors above. Yet the imperative of humanity to detach itself in a higher dignity from the rest of the earthly, although a global theme (and also countered by many other cultures and traditions), has certainly been transmuted into a new level of power and worldwide influence through humanism's and science's evolution into technoscience and global consumerist capitalism.

Unlike the earlier traditions, which opposed human dignity to the slime of the earth, the newer ideologies of detachment from the earth seem to imply a more equal linkage with the beings of the globe that are manipulated and used in various processes of production or within technoscience. They seem to invoke an obsession with materialistic satisfaction as the end point of humanity. However, these postmodern stances in their apparent materialism are misleadingly still detached from the material surround about us. Technoscience and postmodern capitalism focus only on the *possession* and *consumption* of *objects*—beings crafted or identified in certain socially and economically promoted categories of value—which is not a hearkening to the significance to be found in the material surround, whether of the natural world or in communally expressive projects. It is another sort of imposition upon the surround of prefabricated and insular goals. This focus on the world around us is not one of sensitive encounters and dialogue—with the richer materiality of the earthly that contains alien voices to which to hearken. Insofar as we cling to our superior purity above the animal, the machine, and the inanimate, the level of spontaneous communication with much of our surroundings remains closed.

Ambiguity, Openness to Experience, Phenomenology, and Nondualism

I alluded before that it is not so easy to say we will be "open to experience," as if that approach to inquiry is any more self-evident than any other theory. An invocation to openness of experiencing often rightfully invites the question, "Whose experience?" Experiences seem to vary so widely given personal, historical, cultural, ideological, and other differences. Scientists are right to be careful about safeguarding against being caught up in distorting culturally bound interpretations, and religions also are right that "the facts" can always be reinterpreted meaningfully in another context. In order to avoid some of the problems we will encounter in looking at animal studies, artificial intelligence (AI) research, neuropsychology, and other scientific or social scientific fields, as well as philosophy, literature, and other fields in the humanities, I am going to pursue a certain method of thinking that I will quickly sketch out here. I find myself at odds with academic writing and thinking in finding little gain in offering elaborate explanations and justifications of method. The audiences with whom I most desire dialogue are thoughtful adults of all walks of life, including, I might add, academics who can speak with other members of the community more straightforwardly, who are willing to see where one's way of proceeding leads, to what sorts of insights. I will not indulge in arcane terminology, long-winded arguments, and justifications for a method, other than to ask the reader to be patient in considering in the course of the book what it allows us to see together.

If people of many different cultures and historical periods consider it reasonable to assert that animals can feel emotions or perceive objects, and yet a philosopher or scientist says it is impossible for such and such a theoretical reason, then my bias or perspective will be to take these groups of people seriously, to hearken to their experiential sense, their perceptual understanding. If people in all cultures assume they know other people and feel together with them certain shared emotions such as love, and a philosopher questions whether we can ever know if another person is really a person or really thinks or feels like we do, then the ongoing sense of the overwhelming majority of people is the evidence I will follow. It will then be incumbent to describe how this is the case. As for the theories that deny this, I will assume that not only their philosophical point is not relevant to our considerations, but that there is something wrong with the way they are thinking that needs to be uncovered.

Given the aim of articulating philosophically the meaning and structure of how most people under identifiable circumstances experience the world, the way of proceeding that makes the most sense to me is phenomenological. By invoking this philosophical perspective, the aim is to question the relationships among humans, animals, and machines in a manner that remains faithful to the original inspiration of phenomenology as "back to the things themselves"—a cry for thinkers to rejoin the common world of experience and leave their ivory towers of theories that provide explanations but fail to articulate the texture and sense of the experience of many of us to some cogent degree. Even though the movement's founder, Edmund Husserl, initially sought to find certainty and "see essences," phenomenology soon was transformed into a never-ending attempt to describe more closely the always shifting, multidimensional, interrelated context of everyday experience among the many ways we have of encountering the world among natural and cultural inputs, among the varied ways of apprehending and expressing the world, from perceiving to imagining to thinking to feeling emotionally, and so on, and among the ebbs and flows with the beings of all sorts around us who address us indirectly in the midst of our addressing them. Perhaps most importantly phenomenological description aims to articulate the sense of people, of things, of cultures, and of relationships as they unfold within time, changing, evolving, and becoming more complicated and interwoven. Given this aim, phenomenology came to realize that to achieve rich, detailed description is a daunting, worthwhile task and is revealing of that kind of awakening to meaning and truth that philosophy seeks, as much as or even more than logically argued and abstract systems of propositions.

The approach to phenomenology that best exemplifies these points and can most cogently further this inquiry is Merleau-Ponty's. He expressed the aim of phenomenology in a way that opens philosophy: "All its efforts are concentrated upon re-achieving a direct and primitive contact with the world and endowing that contact with a philosophical status."[6] In the paragraphs following that declaration, Merleau-Ponty makes clear that there are no "bare facts" or universal experiences to which we could return, and that the best we can do is participate in an ongoing unfolding of our shared experiences of which we are all a part and about which we can only have an interpretation. However, he also insisted that ambiguity is not bad but a part of how we experience and understand things. He described how our perceptual access to the world is ambiguous in shifting rhythms of confusion and greater resolution. Our understandings based on this also continually shift and are open-ended. We do not come to "perfect" or complete answers. For example, we will see that there are ways one could interpret animal studies as showing that animals have superior memories to humans, but then we might also claim that these are not really memories in the same sense as human memories and fail to capture some of the powers of human memory. Rather than have to decide between these oppositional claims that one is true and the other false, it is more helpful to see the sense gained by considering both positions as revealing something important. This approach leads to a lack of closure to our questions, especially the wider and the deeper they go, but yields interpretations that are more suggestive. We can still see, despite the uncertainties, that some descriptions seem to open up more meaning that we can use to deepen our lives and our abilities to fathom others and our world. If some interpretations give whatever "facts" we provisionally have at that point more meaning, then they are worth trying to incorporate into a larger narrative. This deepening of possibilities and becoming more inclusive of perspectives is what I would like to achieve in this book. Certainly there are "bad" ambiguities when something is articulated in an unclear way when it can be formulated better, but there also are vectors of sense in perception and in conception, as well as in imagining and other modes of apprehension, which are unassimilable to perfect clarity and closure and yet suggest a depth of meaning.

Merleau-Ponty realized that we make sense of the world in ways in which both reason and emotion, both sense experience and memory, and both logic and imagination resonate together and among themselves in the fullness of the ways we perceive the world. One aspect of this perception of the world is shaped by the ideas and frameworks of interpretation we have been taught by our culture, family, and other institutional forces. This is part of the power of human insight that allows our historical and cultural sense—these interpretations do open up new possibilities for action and understanding. Yet these capabilities have dangers. Our perceptual life is deeper, our emotional life is deeper, and our imaginative life is deeper because of its integration and shaping by intellection and reason. However, rational frameworks also can restrict and distort these other levels of apprehension. Merleau-Ponty called the imposition of our ideas onto perception in occluding ways as screens to the particular and unique sense of meaning at the moment, "the experience error." Whitehead, another beckoning guide on this investigation, called this same distortion the "fallacy of misplaced concreteness." Both meant to indicate that gaining access to what we really experience can be a difficult task when we see, hear, touch, feel, smell, and so on, through the filters of abstract preconceptions of the world. The realm of engaged, embodied, and committed experience that has important keys to the linkages of humans, animals, and machines will have to be unearthed painstakingly as we might not be able to even see or feel it without "cleaning the mirror," as the Buddhists would put it, or finding other depths that have receded into the background, as Merleau-Ponty would put it, given that our categories may block access to parts of who we are and what our world is. These are *motivated* distortions in that they serve cultural agendas, personal defenses, ideological aims, and so on, so our blindness to their shaping power resists revelation. So, for example, when this book ends with a consideration of how human wars have disrupted elephant cultures and societal structures, we will need to abandon our tightly held notions of how institutions and cultural structures are only human structures of existence and be able to hearken to evidence of elephant culture through scientific observation, extrapolation of concepts, imagination, empathy, intuition, and a host of other ways of allowing the experience of the other being's experience as well as new ideas about the earth to emerge. We may literally see rampaging elephants but not "see" the connection to the damage we have inflicted upon their kinship structures, for example, because we do not want to be challenged to change our human ways and compromise interests that we wish to maintain.

Embodiment as Cooperation with the Surround

To examine the overlaps and blurrings of boundaries of humans, animals, and machines—the locus where all three are interdependent historically and in terms of future directions—without one-sided preconceived responses or applying naively moralistic categories entails looking at or perhaps listening to—hearkening to—the phenomena from a different perspective on embodiment in relation to materiality. To find the places where humans can be surprised and taken aback by new senses of animals and machines, and of humans in their overlap with animals and machines, as well as to see the suffering of the collisions of these realms, requires entering the depth of the meaning of the material realm "taken in" by the body that binds these beings. The binaries of matter versus mind, inanimate being versus animate, nature versus culture, body versus spirit, emotion versus matter, reason versus emotion, logic versus imagination, abstraction versus memory, self versus other, and so many consequent chains of oppositions follow from a dualistic, reflective perspective on bodies and materiality. They short-circuit attempts to think through the possible creative interpretations of the intertwining of human, animal, and machine. My method in this book will be to get beyond or beneath or to "the other side" of these dualisms, and to embrace many ways of knowing, if they seem to help us take in the world in meaningful and less fragmented ways.

These dualisms are undercut by the notions of an "earthbody" and of "dream-filled materiality" (oneiric materiality), which are notions about which I have written—where the first would make us reconsider if our embodiment, as a dynamic process, an ongoing activity, is a taking in of both information and also meaning, and then the expressing through the interrelations of ourselves with myriad other material beings. This means that as embodied beings we are enmeshed in the world with which we relate in such a way that we are woven into its fabric. If the power of abstract reflection is *to pull away* from being "caught up" in things, to think through the relations of which we are a part from a needed distance, then the body, through perception and the other powers mixed within it, is our *way into* the world. The body, in perceiving, "plunges into the things perceived," (PP, 67) as Merleau-Ponty phrases it, and enters a round dance, where each object is a "mirror" to all others (PP, 68). By being taken up *somewhat* (to some indeterminate and changeable degree) as a body in one object, like the tree beside me, the perceiver also is taken up into the bush beside it and the perspective of the leaves at the top. This articulation by Merleau-Ponty of what he will come to call "the flesh of the world" (in *The Visible and the Invisible*) is a Western attempt to say something parallel to what the Zen archery master tells Eugen Herrigal in *Zen and the Art of Archery*, when he foolishly grins with self-satisfaction that after years and years of trying, he has finally "let go" and made a good shot! The master tells him that he did not shoot the shot, but rather "It shoots."[7] The master does not mean some supernatural force or some sort of special energy, but that Herrigal's wife was part of the shot, the flowers she has learned to arrange that taught her a certain patience, responsive sensitivity, and concentration were part of the shot, the master was part of the shot, the master's teacher, the man who made the bow, the archery hall, the arrow itself, and so on. In other words, everything in its interrelation gave rise together to the shot as taken up by the way the body allows these energies and meanings to flow through it apprehendingly and expressively. This is what I meant to indicate as an "earthbody," that our perception and overlapping feelings, emotions, memories, imaginative echoes, and so on are not "our accomplishments" but "co-accomplishments" with all those beings to which we are related. Perception is a gathering together of all of these levels of meaning. Notice, however, the logic of ambiguity: we are not *one* with trees or archery halls but, rather, there are just energies, directions, senses that flow among us yet are still uniquely what each one is. It is a "knit" or a "weave" and not a fusion (or a "coincidence," to use the philosophical term).

The second notion would ask us to also forestall our traditional categorizations and consider materiality not as inert, dead stuff but as a way to give heft, to find in a certain place, to make encounterable and shapeable ideas, feelings, thoughts, memories, imaginings, intuitions, and so on in a way parallel to how the sensual perceptions of dreams become the substance of different dimensions of experience for us each night. Perhaps without the solidity of rock, we could not feel the solidity of our purpose or the calm of being secure. This book invites us to see, whenever possible, how contributions to meaning may come from many sources cooperatively. The material world with its qualities can be objectified for many important purposes, but qualities such as the blue of the sky or the lake, the slow rhythm of a gesture made by either an animal or a human, or the dark of the middle of the night also can be explored as dimensions of meaning that are passed along among beings and go beyond the merely quantifiable. Perhaps it would be better to say that there is a "material sense" embedded within all things that may infiltrate humans, animals, and whatever becomes responsively interactive with them.

Some will say that this sort of significance is merely a cultural production, a projection of a group of humans onto the world, whether the sense of blue skies or the rhythm of certain gestures, and try to break the link of human with the natural, animal, and inanimate world. Equally, in an opposite position, some will assert that the world has its inherent sense, and that we just manipulate what is given to us, but there is no dialogue, just the givenness of the world. It seems obvious that there is no "answer" to nature versus culture, nurture versus nature, because to pose these oppositions has already broken apart their interdependence that gives us the very texture of our experience. Rather than start with the traditional opposition that defies our articulable experience, we will assume a continuum and an interplay of the cultural and the natural throughout this work, unless there are good reasons to abandon it with a particular instance. As we work toward finding ways to create a collective of various beings, the terms *nature* and *culture* will have to give way to something more like Haraway's "naturecultures," since this division is unsupportable in its arbitrariness once we are dealing with the experience of beings with whom we are active and engaged and not just as conceptualized. For example, approaching a dog with the preconception that this being is merely a machine will most probably give way over time to its nuzzles and licks and frolics, as we will see, as even the dean of the Harvard Divinity School or the MIT computer scientist was caught unaware by experiencing for a moment an artificially intelligent robot as a fellow human.

Meaning-Bearing Matter

For all of the current global materialism, matter is mainly known negatively, as either that which just obstinately and mutely resists us or that which we manipulate to display properties we find useful or entertaining. Matter as speaking or insinuating into our being meanings of all sorts is foreign to us. We think of matter as inert, as dumb, as senseless, and as self-contained. Yet what a strange predicament for a material being to fall into—to become closed off to the ongoing communication with other material beings! If we can at least start being open to the possibility of materiality as *impacted* with the meaning usually thought of solely as the product of humans and their "consciousness"—impacted in the sense of having a grain, being full of or being dense and rich with significance that is insinuated to us.

Matter is an activity, too, as we are—as animals are, even as machines are. Like us, or these other beings, matter as activity can only be fully understood through tracing its contours and rhythms. Again, we seek to articulate things through time, as we actually live and experience, as the world actually exists, dynamically and evolving in myriad ways. To be open to meanings that are the interdependent *process of emergence* from the "holdings" of matter with human interlocutors in a depth of memory, imagination, reason, emotion, and intuition would mean that we ourselves as humans could be encountered as "open systems" that are partially machine and animal, even if something unique emerges in our distinctive human activity. By "holdings" of matter, I mean the way in which meaning "inheres" or "dwells in" the things around us. For example, in an explicit, personal way, we might return to a town we lived in long ago and suddenly be flooded by a series of memories about the time we lived there, the people we knew, and events that occurred. It might well be that these memories would never have occurred to us without being within that material context of the town. The memories arise from the interweaving of ourselves and the locale and have been "held" within the streets, the houses, and the roads of the place as much as within our brains as a series of traces to become active again within that encounter or energy flow. On an implicit, impersonal level, a person sitting on the riverbank may suddenly have a sense of calmness from the steady flow of the current or a sense of the movement of time or of the unfolding of his or her life. Another way to say this is that these are the "murmuring of things" about which Gaston Bachelard wrote at length—that the world has its significances in its different material dimensions and specific shapes that we can "hearken to" when we are quiet and open to their copresence with us. Bachelard found distinctive flows of sense and energy within flames, fire, in water, lakes, ponds, oceans, within the air, wind, fog, and within the earth, rock, soil, and dirt, to name a few of the myriad material dimensions of sense he articulated and found resonating within poetry and literature. The presence of other beings is neither utterly closed off, impenetrable, nor is it open, transparent, but rather it is suggestive, implied, in numerous and powerful ways that shape lives, not only our own.

The primary level of matter and human, animal and machine, may be found in a level some have called "symbolic," or something we might call more "oneiric" or dreamlike than our rational, deliberate way of making sense—something more like a primary process or processing of embodied consciousness that emerges from our taking in the world in perception. It is a level in which qualities, whether of feeling at home or at harmony, those fragile atmospheric senses emergent through the interaction among beings, come to the fore. That is how we have access to facts, whether through our senses or instruments that augment the senses, as inseparable from how we get other levels of meaning. *First*, for example, we feel amazement at the fragility and intricacy of the spiderweb, or feel its tinkling quiet suspend our calm, *then* we rationally explore the makeup of the fiber, the conditions that promote its production, and so on. I propose to explore a depth of differing layers in how the world is given to us in perceptual experience as interwoven with feeling, emotion, imagination, reasoning, memory, and the cultural. This level of the way the world is processed, or perhaps more properly identified as a process *between* ourselves and the world, will be our focus, even if it might be habitually ignored and suppressed.

This kind of engaged perceptually grounded understanding is an "embodied intelligence" that is being recognized in fields such as philosophy, psychology, and artificial intelligence science (and elsewhere). Such an understanding is not the product of a central human agency, or of a mystical entity lodged within us such as the "mind" but emerges as a process within the embodied interaction of beings with other sorts of beings in their surround through their material interweaving. However, to grasp it we need new senses for terms such as engagement, learning, place, motion, transition, envelopment, spirit, and Eros in order to find where these realms of human, animal, and machine meet. The description of this site can open new dimensions of meaning, identity, and cooperation while also providing a new sensitivity to varied senses of violation in all three realms that impact the biosphere, ethical issues, questions of diversity, and the quality of human life. However, to discover whether the descriptions can provide this meaning entails first looking at the complicated material interactions of our perceiving and expressive bodies with those of animal creatures also within this matrix of the surround and now, too, with those created mechanical beings that transform the material, perceivable world.

Hopefully this book can draw upon varied sources from Heidegger's discussions of animals to those of autistic writer, Temple Grandin, as she works with cows and other animals, from considering shifts in the studies of artificial intelligence in MIT's "embodied intelligence" project to how it stands with the hardware of human intelligence in considering work on brain science and advances in technology, from considering modern physics to older sources in philosophy, such as Kant, Langer, and Merleau-Ponty, whose poetic and phenomenological works tease out the depths of experience, and newer sources in philosophy, such as Baudrillard, and psychology and neurobiology, such as Daniel Siegel. The interdisciplinary blending of sources will run throughout the book as much as the many kinds of varied beings will be presented in finding resonances and juxtapositions among them. This is another ramification, I believe, of a fully phenomenological approach: that differing aspects of how something comes to be and thrive within its interrelations need to be brought into play from differing disciplines. It is the hope of this work that by moving from the many discussions of the boundaries of humans and machines and of humans and animals to a consideration of all three realms together there might be made possible another sort of creative redefinition. Given that most discussions of the boundaries among any two of these realms invariably use metaphors, images, and schemata that refer to all three, it seems that it is time to think of all three realms together.

Chapter Two

The Common Ground between Animals and Humans

Prolonged Bodies in Dwelling Places

The Elusive Boundaries among Humans, Animals, and Machines

It is a mistake to define humans, animals, and machines as three separate kinds of entities, for there are mechanistic dimensions of animals and humans, as well as animal dimensions of humans and, in some ways, even of machines. The machine might be called the "postmodern animal." In the twenty-first century, it haunts the images of our souls, as an unknown face of who we are and who we are becoming, as a vision of wildness and unknown territories of new experience, and as a repressed dimension harboring fears that this is what we really are in important ways, just as the animal haunted our forebear's dreams, fears, and desires, and still does in ways unnoticed by most of us. To complete our triad, attributes we may have wished to reserve as exclusively human can be seen to also permeate animals and machines. Here the nature of these overlaps will be articulated, as well as examples examined from different disciplines. The human, animal, and machine are lodged within the core of each other's being.

The cultural and intellectual legacy beginning with the Greeks and running through contemporary Western science and philosophy and the popular culture representations often have assumed that the differences among these three kinds of beings are obvious, yet the characteristics we point to as essential to each realm have paradoxical or even contradictory aspects that undercut these clear boundaries. For example, what is seen as the most animal dimension of humans grounded in shared biological aspects as organisms is the same cluster of phenomena that in other contexts is considered to indicate the most mechanical dimension of humans and may become a site of mechanical intervention through surgical and other medical practices. We are grateful that the animal being that comprises our organism is also mechanical, and therefore can be repaired by mechanical means. So, to amplify this point in another realm, "fight-or-flight" mechanisms often are cited as how humans respond to many situations that inspire fear in ways analogous to animals confronted with a predator or other threats to them as immediately reactive organisms, yet they are simultaneously considered mechanical processes governed by chemical reactions and neurotransmitters. They are "organic," or "merely animal," in the paradoxical sense of also being "mechanical"—a ground floor of our being that might be managed but cannot be altered in its "hardwiring."

To offer an example of the contradictions that have beset some of the traditional boundaries drawn among these three dimensions, machines often are taken to be mechanical in being cut off from their environment, in being self-enclosed and self-propelled, unresponsive to what is around them (especially for those machines held up as paradigmatic of the "most mechanical"). Yet in the simplest animals, such as sponges, what makes them most mechanistic compared to "higher" animals is their utter seamlessness with the environment—they are totally at one with it—and therefore not self-determining in any fashion. The kind of responsiveness we consider evidence of some sort of agency is a simultaneous distance and insertion—an "interrelation"—with the surround. Yet these simplest animals, as described by Merleau-Ponty, lack this confrontation or encounter with what is around them. As Merleau-Ponty puts it, "The behavior characteristic of these animals is that they have the air of being machines."[1] So what makes them mechanical in this instance is the opposite of what often is taken as paradigmatic of machines. Rather than having a "center" of awareness or seeming to display a kind of agency, to have a unity of action directed toward the world, the changes within these animal beings appear as merely a function of changes in their environment, whether chemical gradients or variations in temperature or physical pressure upon their skin, and so on.

Merleau-Ponty gives examples of these "animal-machines:" the medusa, whose entire life consists of "one single movement, the muscular contraction of the edge of the animal ordered by its sensory organs at the periphery," the marine worm, the sea urchin, and the starfish. For the marine worm, the organs function in eating and moving and seem to have no real unity, "as if the animal were two," and its movements are "monotonous movements," not foraging or swimming, but just as a result of contact of the sand on the skin of its back, or water turbulence, or the intensity of the sun. As for the see urchin, its motor spines fire off in contact with the surround, but "when a dog runs, it is the animal that moves its legs, when an urchin moves, it is the feet that move the animal." There is no "core" being here. The case of the starfish brings together most strikingly and concisely what Merleau-Ponty uncovers about all of these "animal-machines," as he calls them:

The Common Ground between Animals and Humans

> The starfish, it has pincers close to its mouth in order to feed itself, but these pincers function on their own account. The animal pinches everything found it its way; it would pinch itself if nature had not used a subterfuge by covering its skin with a chemical product that exercises an inhibitory effect. There is no unity of the living being which unfurls itself towards the outside. The phenomena of behavior are sewn together: it is a collective animal. (N, 169)

The animal that is seamlessly at one with its surround has its activity occur as if "all that happens . . . is produced by physical and chemical forces" or, as Merleau-Ponty puts it, as if its actions "are made up of pieces and morsels" with no central relationship to each other.

Animals are seen to have a unity, a center, whereas machines are seen as made up of parts, each exterior to the other, with no relationships emerging from these parts that give rise to a greater sense of the whole or of a whole confronting the being. However, just as frequently, the sense we attribute to animals and often use to explain aspects of their behavior is a seamless immersion with the surround that humans lack—it is the very quality that often is romanticized about animals and that humans, feeling alienated, yearn to imitate—their "oneness with nature." Yet here these creatures, although animals, are pushed into the category of "the mechanical" by being one with the environment, merely an echo of the surround. So what is seen as mechanical is contradictory, and what is seen as animal is equally contradictory.

Avoiding Reductive Senses of Overlaps of Humans, Animals, and Machines

An equally dangerous move in assuming the obvious distinctive qualities and boundaries among humans, animals, and machines without getting clearer in what ways this might be the case is to try to find their common ground too easily. Traditionally there has been a reduction of the distinctiveness of humans, animals, and machines, both "from above" and "from below." From both ends of the spirit versus matter opposition, humans, animals, and machines have been seen as actually one sort of being in a way that makes it impossible to savor and appreciate what each realm contributes to existence and to each other. "From below," it has been declared that we are merely a concatenation of chemical, electrical, and mechanical processes of the very same sort that power the most distant star to shine or make the rain fall from the sky. Then, in some very real sense, being comprised of the same stuff, there are no humans, animals, and machines as distinctive realms of being, for everything in the cosmos is reducible to a common denominator, a foundation, in the material universe. "From above," perhaps all beings are just instances of a life force or a divine creation of goals and purposes that they all strive to realize together, whether apparent or not. But then everything is just this divinity or this life force—instances of another sort of being.

This sort of conflict arising from the dualist conceptions of matter and spirit echoes the mechanist versus vitalist debate in which the universe was claimed to be either just made of impervious fragments in senseless encounters or is really the face of the final purpose of each being coming to be itself in time as part of a great and unified being. For these opposite visions, the earth was either an endless horizontal plane of energy transfers or the systematic vertical upsurge of an ascent toward realization transcending earthly existence aimed at something greater. Does the human mean anything in its own nature—in its distinctiveness—for either of these two visions? These visions render humans only a glorified machine as part of a larger material system or else a caretaker as a restless pilgrim destined for a higher realm and currently misplaced within space and time. The animal is either that which is to be tamed, herded, and cultivated before consuming, or else it is a lost being in the mire of the slimy realm that threatens to suck us down with it. The machine is either just an instance of what everything really is in its functional niche in the larger mechanism or else is an utterly soulless being of an empty realm that would only have meaning and value by participating in a higher spiritual realm to which machines have no linkage. From either of these perspectives, the seeming encounters among humans, animals, and machines, let alone the crisscross among their boundaries, are chimera, illusions of no real substance or import, for all are homogenous parts of a divinity or a hodgepodge of matter in motion.

New Ways to See Overlaps and Differences: Living Space and "Understanding" One's Place

There are other ways to see the overlaps and differences if we pay attention to the specifics of observations in each realm, allowing the boundary notions to "bubble up" from the details of activities of humans, animals, and machines, rather than from overarching metaphysical or scientific principles. In keeping with this spirit, that learning from details of specific events in the existence of humans, animals, and machines is key, let us start by attending to a certain bird's behavior as a possible source of new notions for these comparisons. Sailing above the mountain pines in the

American Southwest, the Clark's nutcracker, an eleven-inch bird of pale gray plumage, with a long, pointed, black beak and black wings, descends to find pine seeds and takes them to hide throughout that landscape. The bird will harvest pine seeds during a period of just a few weeks in the late summer and early fall and then will fly about its forest and manage to create about 2,000 places where they are hidden. The usual nutcracker cache holds two to five seeds, and a single nutcracker may store up to a total of 23,000 seeds when the cone crop is heavy. It is estimated that the nutcracker has to retrieve at least 3,000 seeds to make it through the winter.[2] Are these actions merely meaningless reactions of chemicals, electrons, and moving parts, or is there some relationship to the parts of the forest dangling in the wind with nourishment, sheltering the store of seeds through the harsh times to come? Is there an encounter between the bird and the things around it? Is there some sort of understanding about the surround, about the creature and its plight, or does the bird grind through the motion of its life and actions like the small automata we create to stand on our mantel and dazzle our children? Or is it merely a speck of spirit, the divine plan in action, and not some very distinctive way of taking in the world, of finding a place and of making a mark?

Scientists Vanderwall, Bald, and Tuck attempted to assess the sense of the landscape that guides the nutcracker to have such a highly articulated and memorable relationship to the surround. In laboratory tests, the nutcrackers were presented with eighteen cache sites, which they proceeded to use for storing seeds. They were removed from the laboratory first for eleven days and then for 285 days and were as accurate at finding the caches after the 285 days as after eleven days. The conclusion drawn by Vanderwall, Bald, and Tuck was that the bird's far greater memory ability than that of humans is due to its facility at using "mental maps." This idea of birds being guided by mental maps is one supported by experiments with hummingbird territories, chickadees, and jays. The birds seem to have a sense of the surrounding area in which they live as one that has places or zones that can be marked and used for guidance or remembering (IAM, 57–63).[3] What does that mean—a "mental map?" What does it mean to say of animals that they move through the world and encounter things within the world according to their sense of a "mental map?" There is an apparent relationship between bird and world such that the surround has an immediately recognizable set of sites that stand out in relief as having a certain meaning for the bird's existence. This meaning has been created by its past actions in response to beckonings of the surround and this significance has been inscribed into the appearance of the landscape for the bird.

In order to see the deeper implications of this idea of animal mental mapping, it is instructive to look in comparison at perhaps the most famous philosophical analysis of the twentieth century of "human existential structures," as Heidegger called them in *Being and Time*, first published in 1927. In that work, Heidegger described in detail how our sense of space, our sense of time, and our awareness of finitude were interwoven and shaped what was most human about us. He articulated at great length these structures of existence that allowed for the human sense of "dwelling" in a surround that seemed to him uniquely human and determinative for our sense of being. Heidegger, like the artificial intelligence scientists of the 1980s and 1990s, realized that unlike the Kantian and Newtonian perspectives, humans do not understand their way through space from some centralized and universally cogent rational grasp of space, as a system of arithmetically consistent, measurably laid out coordinates. Rather, Heidegger said that in lieu of finding ourselves in a rationally laid out space, we are enclosed in a space made up of the places to which we are related in an immediate way, because they mark those aspects of the surround with which we are concerned for our nurturance and getting the things done that we need to do. He states that instead of a centrally conceived space, "in each case the place is a definite 'there' or 'yonder' of an item of equipment which belongs somewhere."[4] In other words, there are only arrayed around us distinct places that are the sites of that which is useful or needful for us to continue our lives and to get done what we have to do.

Equipment, as the term is used here by Heidegger, indicates whatever things have a practical role to play in getting something done of necessity for that being. They all have a place within our surround, or context, of work and concerns. This is why Heidegger says that we are inseparable from the world as context of all these practical engagements, that there are worlds nested within a larger horizon toward which we are implicitly directed by an "understanding" (*verstehen*) that is not reflective but rather "lived" as a sense of belonging and feeling immediately vectors of direction around us. He calls this kind of human being "being-in-a world" and makes it one phrase (*innerweltsein*) in order to indicate that we are inseparable from the relationality to all these spots around us. By articulating this sense of human space, Heidegger has given us a different sense of how building relationships with what is around us may be our most basic sense of "understanding" our world. I think this idea of a "lived space" and an "understanding of implicit relationship" could be useful in seeing our overlap with the being of animals.

One could easily see how this "hodological" space, as others have called it—a space of practical doings and being caught up in the flow of life toward projects—could be taken to be analogous to what Vanderwall, Bald, and Tuck designate as the space of a "mental map" for birds and other creatures. A mental map, after all, is a space that is comprised of places of practical import that are immediately "known" as the sense of having a surround. In addition, what is analogous is not only the sense of space as this network of places of practical import implicitly lodged with significance for memory, future actions, and intuition of possibility but also *the way* such mental maps are "known" or understood by humans and animals: in an immediate way that is evidenced through action or behavior, through a "feeling of rightness" about going here or there to this or that entity. Despite the unfortunate use of the term *mental* map, we see here an instance of what this book will find as most cogent in reconsidering humans, animals, and machines: a bodily level of understanding that is more primordial than deliberative, reflective understanding and that underlies it. I believe this understanding was called a "mental" map by ethologists because of our cultural bias that anything cognitive is mental, whereas this "understanding" by birds and other animals can be seen to flow through the body's sense of its surround once we abandon that prejudice.

This analogous spatiality and mode of understanding that accompanies it could be seen to be further grounded in the additional parallel of animals and humans as being caught up in a primary way in relations of use and investment of varied energies. Animals have a sense of place in which food, prey, rest, refreshment, play, dangers of varied sorts, and so on, are all arrayed around them at certain directions and distances, immediately felt by them in hunger, fear, rest, joyfulness, and so on. This is parallel to humans being inseparable from their particular "world" or context of involvements that has unique directions and attachments felt in an orientation and affectivity with what is within that surround. The farmer senses the presence of the sun above his fields after days of rain, or the nurse the quiet on the floor late at night as she watches the monitors in patients' rooms in ways distinctive to their embeddedness in a certain situation, and for each there is a calm relief at these different events in different contexts. Both animals and humans have to be distinguished from inanimate objects as not merely physically located within a space as a mere chunk of matter externally related to what is around it (Heidegger called this aspect of things as being merely "presence-at hand") but rather as having this sense of the surround an essential component of their being. The sense of the world is "felt" in affective currents that Heidegger calls "attunement" (*Befindlichkeit*) that are at the core of sense given to us in perception.

This being at one with the space around it, being immediately related to the beings within this space and gaining direction, orientation, and an immediate kind of "understanding" from this spatiality, is a fundamental overlap in the being of animals and humans. Yet Heidegger draws the exact opposite conclusion, as many scientists, philosophers, and psychologists often do, even when an empathic response would seem to beckon otherwise. In arriving at this conclusion, Heidegger is following Jakob von Uexküll's work with animals and his original descriptions of their "around world," or Umwelt. Von Uexküll took these phenomena as evidence not of kinship among animals or between animals and humans but as evidence of their utter difference. However, I think we must ask of von Uexküll and Heidegger: Why take a sense of space and a different kind of knowing that seems so similar in the lives of humans and animals and use it as another wedge of absolute difference between them?

Animal and Human Worlds and False Boundaries: Heidegger and von Uexküll

This section is entitled animal "worlds" to signal disagreement with Heidegger's refusal to grant animals a "world." Heidegger's misinterpretations are instructive for helping us further modify the way we need to think about humans, animals, and machines in this book. If we do not, we will not see the creative overlaps possible among these realms or be able to draw needed boundaries among them. Both many ethologists' work with animals and Heidegger's description of the structures of human existence drew upon the ideas and concepts of the founder, in many ways, of animal behavior studies, Jakob von Uexküll, whose work in the late nineteenth century and the early decades of the twentieth century was contemporaneous with breakthroughs in quantum mechanics and movements such as cubism in art. Heidegger's commentator on his understanding of the relationship between humans and animals, Giorgi Agamben, points out that all of these movements were articulating ways in which human beings were not the center of everything, unlike the preceding emphasis of humanist philosophies and cultural practices. Uexküll's work was part of this abandonment of anthropocentrism that appealed to Heidegger's project of placing humans back into a larger context of meaning, rather than humans' self-satisfied sense of being the measure of all things.

However, von Uexküll and Heidegger could not follow out these implications that would lead humans to see themselves within a more enmeshed relationship with animals, nor could they abandon a logic of insular individualities that had been the problem with the opposing physicalistic approach. Heidegger was aware that animals were not machines in important ways when he states "but the other things in question do not stand in a mechanical relation to the animal."[5] He also denied the stance of Descartes, that the bodies of both animals and humans were simple mechanisms in the sense of being self-contained in awareness, driven by external factors, and dumb to meaning. In Descartes's famous example in *The Meditations*, he speaks of a pain in the foot of a human as the result of mere physiological factors that has no indication of any relationship to the world or even to the person feeling the pain, other than the meaning that can then be derived by the interpretation of the mind through intellection. Heidegger, however, counters any simpleminded stimulus-response model by declaring, "It is easy to see the extent to which this customary interpretation of stimulus and the various relations into which it enters is all too clearly oriented around a comparison with mechanical relations. Yet even disregarding this fact, the interpretation is false" (FCM, 256). For Heidegger, it is false because the animal is clearly *related* to the things around it before it is stimulated and acts.

Heidegger also wished to get beyond another Cartesian legacy: the isolation of minds that only knew themselves while denied comparable access to the being of other people or even of the world at large (except mediated through intellectual interpretation and the certainty of quantification). Whether Heidegger successfully articulated how others are given to us as fundamentally as we are given to ourselves is questionable, despite his attempts to articulate a "Mitsein" among humans—that the other person is "with me," is "being-with" me in my own very sense of self. Despite coining this term to designate our co-being with other humans, given Heidegger's framework for discussion, he struggles to describe how this sense permeates the sense of our lives. The missing insights for Heidegger are not in probing further the depth of sense of perception and embodied understanding. What is clearer, however, is whatever intrinsically shared being he envisioned at least conceptually among humans, he did not see any possible overlap in the being of humans and animals: "The animal is separated from man by an abyss" (FCM, 264).

It might seem ironic that von Uexküll and Heidegger developed an idea of the "around world" of animals and for Heidegger the "in-the-world" sense of humans that literally could give a *common* ground for humans to find themselves more interwoven in community, both with other humans and with animals and even the inanimate world, yet they could not affirm the possibility of this new plane of encounter. For von Uexküll, the very idea of *Umwelt*—literally, the "around world"—within which each animal was embedded, forerunner of a key idea of the "environment" in ecological discourse, that each creature is what it is and thrives within a web of relationships with what surrounds it, meant instead for him that each creature was confined within its separate "world." This insight of "around world" did allow him to avoid the mistake of seeing animals as being reducible to a common physicalistic denominator (the reduction "from below"), as merely a concatenation of chemical, electrical, and mechanical processes in a unitary world of cause-and-effect chains of relation by distinguishing the environment-world of a context of significance for each creature (*Umwelt*) from the objective world (*Umgebung*). However, without a differing notion of the body, not as separate object but as a medium of interbeing or as a way of becoming incorporated into the process of an always unfolding world or as part of the ongoing processing of meaning from within the material environment, there is no site of interconnectedness with animals or, even more fundamentally, with other humans.

For von Uexküll, as for Heidegger, and as now also for philosopher Giorgi Agamben, explaining and agreeing with them both: "The fly, the dragonfly, and the bee that we observe flying next to us on a sunny day do not move in the same world as the one in which we observe them, nor do they share with us—or with each other—the same time and the same space."[6] It is interesting that Uexküll, Heidegger, and Agamben see these worlds as "unknowable worlds," as isolated from one another, when the analogy Agamben uses to show how the flower's calyx is a different and an unknowable being in differing environments for the girl picking flowers, the ant reaching nourishment, the larva of the cicada, or the cow who chews it is to compare this difference through an analogy to the human experience of a forest by differing humans among "a forest-for-a-park ranger, a forest-for-the-hunter, a forest-for-the-botanist, a forest-for-the-wayfarer, a forest-for-the-nature-lover, a forest-for-the-carpenter, and finally a fable forest in which Little Red Riding Hood loses her way" (OMA, 41). Agamben believes it is obvious that among the animals cited and between the girl and the animals, there is a gap of experience that is not present among the humans who approach the forest from such varied human contexts. However, in a way we may normally fail to appreciate, these differences in context among people make for great differences in what we experience, as attested to by the famous controversy about spotted owls between loggers and environmentalists in the Pacific Northwest and Western Canada begun in the 1980s and still raging. For one group, these birds are irreplaceable sources of wonder and for the other a pest in the way of their livelihood. Aren't these gaps as wide as those among differing species of animals?

It does seem plausible that the gaps in the sense of the context may be as wide in the way varied humans experience the forest, even given their basic overlaps. If this is so, despite the possible wide gaps between differing animals or with humans, there might be basic overlaps too. Is an animal looking for a stream to find a source of coolness on a scorching day utterly in a different context than an overheated hiker looking for a stream in which to soak? If humans do live in a more consistently shared world, if they identify sources for these commonalities, then might they not find overlaps with animals? The naturalist's and the logger's contexts may differ in a wider way than the deer and the human both looking for shelter in the driving snow, or of the elephant and the trader looking for the oasis in the parched desert for drink.

What might be most telling would be to question more deeply the ground of commonality among humans and animals versus that among humans, and then to assess the amount of overlap possible for each.

The gap among humans would seem to occur when the categorical dimensions of interpretation—for example, in the case of the ecologist and the logger, a whole set of concerns about industry and labor, about livelihood and family anxieties, or a set of concerns about knowing the planet is losing ecological niches and suffering species extinction—are interwoven with our more immediate perceptual access to the world. Our distinctively human concerns as reflective knowers of the world are inseparable from our perceptual experiences and leave us walking through different surrounds within the ostensibly same surround. Yet despite these differences—the commonalities of the ranger and the wayfarer, and even of Little Red Riding Hood (or logger and protestor), on the level of prepersonal or prereflective, perceptual, embodied beings, where the percept is given more as sensed, felt, affective, and imaginative—the overlap of experience is great. Each of these very different persons could feel the open depth of the night in the forest, or the uplift of the sun streaming through the leaves and bathing all in golden light on a crisp, but warm, day, or the fecund feeling of the forest floor beneath footsteps and the hushing peacefulness of the centuries old trees. On this level of more straightforward perceptual and affective engagement, at a level "below" the structuring of ideology, personal concerns, and vocation, there is a more common matrix from which the surround emerges, but to which our postmodern culture pays less heed.

Perhaps if we were just some purely willed and immaterial project of employment or conservation or longing to see grandma, we would not find ourselves shifted to other meanings within each embodied moment within the forest, as when the perception of the streaming white-green sunlight through the trees suddenly pervades us with the bright feeling of sunniness, or within the chilly, windy, limb-swaying pitch darkness, the foreboding of the midnight forest suffuses our body for a moment when going about very different business. Then we are no longer loggers or wayfarers per se but human creatures embraced by the natural surround. As embodied beings, we are pulled in so many directions by each perceptual experience, even if our willfulness chooses not to pay attention. Each of these directions opens up many pathways of apprehension, some of which are merely personal and fleeting, some of which are cultural and indicative of shared aspects of our situation, and some of which are others ways to take in the factual sense of the environment. It is on this level of perceptual engagement and attunement that the "world" of the alien might not be as alien, which supports the idea that the gap between the experience of the logger and the conservationist may at moments be greater than that between human and animal. For it is on this more primal level of sensed experience with broad affective currents that humans and animals may be seen to overlap.

The Lack of an Expanded Sense of Embodiment and Animality in Heidegger

Many of us who read Heidegger's work wanted to read it sympathetically and say that his analyses of how the surrounding sense of place, of being emplaced within a set of relationships and his plea that we are to approach the idea of "understanding" differently in order to grasp the sense of direction, of connection, and of an affective attunement between human and context as key to this "lived" understanding imply shifting the locus of subjectivity from an abstracted consciousness to a power of embodiment. However, Heidegger does not bring embodiment into his exhaustive descriptions in *Being and Time* and, with few exceptions, elsewhere either. He *struggles* to show the ways in which we are inseparable from other humans and with the earth and world, and like the rest of our intellectual and popular culture heritage, this lack comes from a limited sense of embodiment's possibilities.

Heidegger's lack of development of the idea of embodiment and of the differing levels contained within a depth of perceptual richness shows in his dismissal of animals as "captivated" by the surroundings to which they are drawn in relation. By using this term, Heidegger agrees with von Uexküll, that the animal is inseparable from what is around it, but this being caught up in an "around space" (*Umwelt*) is "impoverished" to the extent that "Beings are not manifest to the behavior of the animal in its captivation." He adds, "Neither its so-called environment nor the animal itself are manifest as beings" (FCM, 248). Because the animal is "driven directness," it is suspended between itself and the environment, but without being able to encounter either. Instead, the animal is "possessed" by things in such a way that "it precisely does not stand alongside man and precisely has no world" (FCM, 269). For Heidegger, there is a "ring" of these instinctual drives encircling the animal that makes it "incapable of ever properly attending to something as such" (FCM, 249). The animal is inseparable from all of the entities within the ring of the environment that surrounds it, but "in a fundamental sense the animal does not have perception" (FCM, 259) as it is "self-encircled" by the things around it, which it does not encounter. The beings that make up the context or the "around world" (*Umwelt*) of the animal stand in relation to it of powers that allow the "disinhibition" of instinctual drives and actions toward them, and in that sense Heidegger acknowledges that animals are not like the rock that lacks relationships (from within itself) to that around it. Yet this disinhibition is far from having any sense for the animal of what it encounters from the world. For Heidegger, animals are as unable as rocks to really encounter other beings: "The animal in its captivation finds itself essentially exposed to something other than itself, something can never indeed be manifest to the animal as either a being or a non-being" (FCM, 273). Only humans can encounter beings. Only humans have relationships that have sense at their core. Animals respond to needs for food, shelter, or safety, but without sense or recognition.

In holding to the assertion that "the animal is poor in world," Heidegger not only denies that animals can encounter objects, other animals, or even light and sees all reactions to light and other objects according to models of tropism (FCM, 250–51), which are cause-and-effect reactions and involve no "encounter" between animal and other beings. He even denies that animals can have any sense of death. He states that animals can "only come to an end . . . but cannot die in the sense in which dying is ascribed to human beings" (FCM, 267) insofar as humans are always aware of their impending end and of the nothingness that invades life through death. For Heidegger, this is what makes humans distinctive in *Being and Time*. This seems like an increasingly dubious statement as ethologists show us how often animals are deeply affected by the death of other animals and may well have a sense of the fragility of their own lives. They certainly are capable of grief. Whether it is a group of elephants trying to nurse a dying member of their group, then resuscitate her, then bury her, and then stand vigil for the next night, as reported by Cynthia Moss and others, or whether it is Koko, the gorilla who was taught American sign language and cried for a week after her kitten companion was killed, after howling at the time of the car accident. Koko responded both then and later when she was asked online about how she might describe the nature of death that death is "sleep forever."[7] Of course, Koko's responding to questions online seems like a different universe of animals' ability and even desire to encounter other beings, let alone to engage in expanding the sense of things, than Heidegger's portrayal of animal existence. However, we do not have to resort to the case of such a "highly developed" mammal or highly structured situation to see what is wrong with Heidegger's ideas, which are all too close to current "common sense."

Despite Heidegger's intention not to see the animal as a machine, and to find a distinctive sense of animal being, he falls back upon a mechanistic sense of animals because he retains a mechanistic sense of embodiment in general. The animal's embodiment is seen by Heidegger as a site of drivenness by instincts in a straightforward cause-and-effect manner. Acting from this center, the animal is rendered a machine in the most reductive, unknowing sense. Heidegger's interpretive stance becomes most obvious not in the theoretical part of his lectures but when commenting on specific scientific experiments—one of the only times he does so in his long career. Looking at some of the early experiments with bees that will later help give rise to the idea of "mental mapping," and even the speculation of some sort of consciousness among bees by some ethologists, Heidegger makes more obvious his inability to think his way into the possible experience of animals and its overlap with humans.

In these experiments to which we will return again in this book, it is noted that bees seem able to reckon on a flight path from the hive to food source or back by taking into account the angle of their flight from the sun, as well as the traversed distance by reference to landmarks in the surround. When their hives have been removed, bees can return to the spot where they had been by using such reckoning with the aspects of the surround. However, the reckoning by sun happens only in an empty landscape, whereas when there are trees or houses, bees seem able to refind the locations of food sources and their hives by making use of these landmarks to orient themselves toward the direction and distance they need to pursue. Heidegger notes this fact but then ignores for the rest of his discussion that bees seem to take note of trees, houses, and other landmarks. Heidegger disputes the bees' apparent relationship to aspects of the surround by reckoning on the angle of the sun and the distance of the flight. He also denies that when the bee arrives back where the hive should have been that there could be any sort of "knowing" that this was the proper location. Hediegger must admit that the bee stops its flight at the spot where its hive had been and starts a searching behavior until it finds the relocated hive. However, Heidegger insists: "The bee is simply given over to the sun and to the period of its flight without being able to grasp either of these as such, without being able to reflect upon them as something thus grasped. The bee can only be given over to things in this way because it is driven in its fundamental drive of foraging. It is precisely because of this drivenness, and not on account of any recognition or reflection, that the bee can be captivated by what the sun occasions in its behavior" (FCM, 247). When Heidegger asserts that the bee is "given over" to the sun, what does this mean? That the sun is a gear and the bee a cog? This does not make any particular sense. Yet to say the bee reckons with the sun, encounters the sun, and uses the sun for guiding itself according to a sense of direction within the surround seems the more sensible and parsimonious explanation.

It is most important to notice that Heidegger conflates the terms *recognition* and *reflection* in his statement of interpretation about the bees' lack of encounter with the sun "as a manifest being." To assert that the bee does not *reflect* about the sun and its relationship to the sun seems perfectly plausible, for we have no evidence of a kind of reflection taking place. However, to say that the bee does not *recognize* the sun is to deny something else altogether. When we consider Merleau-Ponty's formulation of recognition, it is a perceptually integrative experience that combines feeling, memory, intuition, and the relating of different entities to one another in an existential flow of directness and energy within the surround, and it does so in an immediate or a "felt" fashion registered in one's body and from within a "perceptual field" (as Merleau-Ponty calls the overall sense or matrix of significance of an environ that forms around us in perception as an extension of our body "infiltrating" the surroundings). It is not to make any claims about reflection or a deliberative and thoughtful type of "recognition." Instead, an immediate perceptual "knowing" seems like the most plausible description of what is happening, yet it is not considered by Heidegger or by many scientists and philosophers. By holding animal experience up to the standard of "reflection" and then claiming that this is missing is to discount evidence of other ways of understanding by claiming that it does not match some "higher" or quite different level of experience that is a deliberative, intellectual operation. Heidegger's speaking as if the two kinds of encountering another being were the same—reflection and recognition—is sloppy and does not attend to the animal, insect, or other creature in terms of the flow of its existence.[8]

Equally surprising is Heidegger's use of the experiment in which a bee is placed before a bowl with so much honey that it is unable to suck it all up at once. Normally, the bee will stop sucking and fly off at a certain point, leaving the remaining honey in the bowl. Heidegger says it might seem plausible to say that the bee "recognizes the presence of too much honey for it" (FCM, 242), but he does not believe this is the case. Citing the experiments in which once the abdomen of the bee is "carefully cut away while it is sucking, the bee will simply carry on regardless while the honey runs out of the bee from behind," Heidegger declares, "This shows conclusively that the bee by no means recognizes the presence of too much honey." His explanation for his assertion is that the drivenness of "being taken by its food" impels it with no awareness. Yet Heidegger then discusses how normally, if the bee's embodiment has not suffered this traumatic destruction, the bee will feel a sense of satiation that leads it to stop sucking honey. For Heidegger, like "being taken by the food," this satiation is seen as some "counterdrive" that blindly forces the bee to stop. However, for any thinker with a sense of the importance of a lived understanding as an embodied being, the feeling of satiation is a recognition of one's body about one's current state of being, as well as a recognition of one's current relationship to the food. It is precisely what Heidegger denies of the bee: "There is no self-directing towards these things" (FCM, 243). Yet what else is this feeling of "satiation" than an immediate, bodily awareness of the bee in regard to sucking and the honey? It is precisely through the bee's bodily sense, another way of understanding other than disembodied intellection, that the being directs its behavior in regard to the honey. The utter lack of such thinking leads to an even more distressing aspect to Heidegger's interpretation in his not being struck by the horrid mutilation of the bee's body.

These types of experiments that have been perpetrated upon all sorts of animate creatures—invasive, destructive, and mutilating alterations of their embodiment—follow a logical vicious circle, besides the ethical objections that should be raised to causing another feeling creature such harm. It is assumed by the experimenter that knowing or understanding is a purely mental, cognitive act, usually centering on logical and intellectual discrimination. Therefore, the bodies of the creatures that are the objects of the experiment may have their embodiment devastated in all sorts of traumatic ways, because they are not essential to knowing as the experimenter prejudged the case. It is no surprise then that as Heidegger does here, the experimenter or philosopher can now safely judge that the experiment demonstrates an underlying and ongoing lack of understanding in the life of the creature, when the experimental procedure itself has in all likelihood destroyed the way most creatures "know" through their bodies' immediate relationships to their surroundings, which would be true of humans also. If we inflicted massive trauma to a human subject's body, such as cutting it in two, taking it as an insignificant alteration to processes of knowing as long as the brain had been left intact, then we would not take the subject's perceptions and understanding of her or his situation, whether she or he still desired more food or not, for example, under these conditions as revealing much about the subject's normal way of taking in meaningfully her or his surround. Yet, we persist in doing this to animals.

If Heidegger's own work might lead us to envision a combination of prereflective understanding of the world felt in the body through the depths of perception and affective attunement to the context, within a kinesthetic meshing with things about us and perceptions of one's own body in these relationships (proprioception), then traumatizing the body, even going so far as to destroy its integrity and normal functioning, surely will not show us how creatures or even humans come to understand the world. What makes more sense in assessing what and how animals might understand in ways that might overlap with humans is to attempt to transpose ourselves as imaginatively, intuitively, thoughtfully, empathetically, perceptually, and so on, into the embodied world of the animal and the ongoing practices of sustaining its life in a significant environ. This kind of "transposition" into the context or "world" of another is what Heidegger envisions as the way of investigating humans. He claims humans can only be understood in how they make sense of their existence by exploring them within a nexus or matrix of prereflectively "lived" relationships to all that is around them. These capacities, however, may be capacities based on felt connection, sensual perceptions, images born of immediate interactions, and so on, and not based on a reflective distance (even though these reflections may expand and deepen this other sort of understanding for humans). The "world" of the animal and of humans where we may meet either is not seen from "above" or "outside" in abstracted reflection. What is needed for the work of interspecies' comprehension is to expand these capacities as philosophers, scientists, and thinkers.

The body of the animal, in Heidegger's thought, as in many others, is seen to act propulsively from within according to a determinate mechanism called instinct. The relations with other beings in the environment that are part of the animal's actions are components of a functioning constellation that is utterly opaque, or what Agamben aptly calls "the zone of nonknowledge—or of a-knowledge" (OMA, 91). The animal's relation to its surround, its *Umwelt*, is barred from any sort of lighting up in revelation of that world. For Heidegger, the revelatory moment occurs through the power of language to open up the earth, or as Agamben puts it, "Only with man can . . . beings become accessible and manifest" (ibid.). For Heidegger, this is a path of recognition inseparable from reflection and the power of the word and occurs only in the human. We do not need here to follow the details of how, for Heidegger, humans encounter beings truly—that is to say outside of their usually being distracted and unaware—by opening up to the "gathering-together" of the poetic power of language and the ability to be called to an encounter with all the beings in the world in their wholeness and as pondering the mystery of the difference between specific beings and the sense in which there is a greater whole of which they are part. This is a lot of effort on behalf of the few humans who achieve this and is certainly beyond animals' capacity. However, what is crucial is to note that in failing to give evidence of these abilities, since animals are unable to fathom any "a as b," an "encounter" with any being "is refused to the animal" (FCM, 287). Heidegger may seem to have a very different perspective than the so-called "analytic philosophers," those philosophers who insist that logical assertion is the sine qua non of "mind" and cognition, or than scientists who rigidly cling to the purely logical and abstract as the only objective knowing, yet in regard to animals, Heidegger is making similar judgments and disqualifications. To make the poetic use of language the standard of real understanding is no better than taking the logical propositional use of language as the sole way of knowing. Both embody excellences of insight possible for humans, but they might not exhaust all the possible ways for the world to come to be encountered or revealed. If they are taken this way, both become presumptions of anthropocentrism.

How Another Sense of Embodiment Opens These Dimensions

For Merleau-Ponty, the body is not an object but rather the human way of being intertwined into the world's ongoing weaving. Humans' embodiment is a piece of the fabric of the world, but one that is torn away from the seamlessness within it, inseparably a part and yet having some distance. Perceiving is not a sensing from afar but is rather a "certain possession of the world by my body, a certain gearing of my body to the world" (PP, 250). We have the world, and the world has us as embodied beings. Later, Merleau-Ponty will articulate a new language to say that humans and the surround are of the "flesh of the world" [*la chair du monde*], or that humans and surround are "interlaced" [*entrelacs*]. It is not my intention to give an exhaustive or a scholarly analysis of how Merleau-Ponty construed the body in a rather unique way that has not been largely seized upon by philosophers or scientists until rather recently through their own independent discoveries, despite Merleau-Ponty's writing and speaking widely from the end of World War II until his sudden and early death in 1961.

Scientists still shy away from seeing the body as being the site of ways of knowing other than the traditional emphasis on intellection or reflection, as do philosophers of all sorts, from Daniel Dennett, an analytic philosopher, to even Heidegger, a phenomenologist. They fail to appreciate how limited traditional ideas of the body as object are, as the unfolding subject of physiology or traditional neurobiology, of anthropology or evolutionary theory, computer science or psychology, and so on. As Donald R. Griffin says in *Animal Minds*, after examining evidence of animals cooperating, communicating, and projecting future outcomes, for example, in the cases of lions hunting wildebeest and of other predators, such as hawks and otters, "As in so many other cases of versatile animal behavior, one can always argue that it is not absolutely necessary to infer even the simplest level of perceptual consciousness. But the weight of accumulating evidence tips the scales so strongly that the rigid exclusion of any possible consciousness has become stretched to the breaking point."[9] In looking at how various types of predator fish and prey fish make intricate moves in response to each other, Griffin comments on the attempt to reduce the bodies of animals to unaware physical parts in lockstep motion: "One can postulate a complex network of instinctive reflexes to account for observed behavior.... But the 'ad hocery' of such schemes increases in proportion to the completeness of our understanding of the natural behavior. It becomes increasingly plausible, and more parsimonious, to infer that both pike and minnows think consciously in simple terms about their all-important efforts to catch elusive food or to escape from a threatening predator" (AM, 66).

What is important here is not to survey or document these mistakes, nor to give a history of the notion of the "body subject" and "the flesh of the world" as first articulated by Merleau-Ponty, but to sketch how these ideas give us a very different sense of the body than that assumed in the philosophical tradition of classical Greek to modern European thought and in much traditional scientific thought. In the latter decades of the twentieth century, the larger American and global culture has responded to the prior dismissal of the body as a mere vessel of mind or spirit, and in many ways embodiment has been glorified and made into a fetish of the modern, economically rich societies, marked by an explosion of cosmetics, fitness, fashion, plastic surgery, and the like, as well as the proliferation of academic literature about aspects of the body. However, these events do not really signal a recovery of the deeper sense of embodiment, any more than rampant materialism hearkens to the deeper sense of matter. As Timothy Morton puts in *Ecology Without Nature*, registering his surprise at the current cultural and academic fascination with "the body" as new metaphysical theme, "The body stands for what we think we've lost, a little world, a floating island."[10] The body is still seen as an object of a special sort and as part of a dualistic way of framing the world.

This other sense of embodiment will help us interpret experiments dealing with the "knowing" of animals, machines, and humans in a different way. Embodied ways of knowing have to be seen as comparable to and perhaps even more primary than intellectual ways of knowing, and both seen in their value and coordination. If a bee with an abdomen that has been severed by the experimenter can be used as the subject of an experiment in order to understand a bee's way of knowing or recognizing the world and to assess its relationship to it, then there is something as blatantly amiss as destroying or radically rupturing a chimp's nervous system or brain and then expecting to see how these creatures know or recognize. For Merleau-Ponty, our embodiment, and the embodiment of the animate beings around us, is not the mere housing or hardware or tools of consciousness or any other faculty of knowing. Our embodiment, which is an ongoing fluid meshing with things, people, and events around us, is the way into the world, and the way of having a world, and the primary way of being human or animal. It also means we are *of the world*, that our relationships with animals and machines, as well as other beings of the surround, are echoed in the depths of who are, what we do, and how we experience.

Merleau-Ponty opened his first book, which expressed this sense of embodiment, with the statement "There is no inner man, man is only in the world" (PP, xi). He means by this that the act of perception is not a "taking in from a distance" but rather "to look at an object is to plunge oneself into it" (PP, 67). If in perceiving something, I am "in" it in some way, then this is because during the time of that perception I partially live the world *through the vantage point* of that object, or as Merleau-Ponty put it, "To look at an object is to inhabit it" (PP, 68). So when I look at the stone, I am that stone for the moment, or at least I live the world through that stone for the moment. This is an element of our experience that we may notice or not, develop to a greater degree than others or not. This is why stately rocks are placed in a Zen garden to engender the unmoving, serene, stable sense they instantiate for us when we gaze upon them. Within that gaze, if we open ourselves to its power through concentration, then the stable serenity and stillness of the rock can become part of who we are at that moment. To some lesser extent, it will happen for all.

However, even this provisional way of trying to expand the body and perception is still tied to a sense of isolated objects rather than the energy fields of various sorts, from those that are electromagnetic to those that are made up of sense or meaning. When we plunge into an object or commune with an object in perceptual consciousness, we are entered a linkage among objects, events, and beings through our shared material being. Merleau-Ponty states, "Every object is the mirror of all others" (PP, 68). By this he means that the lake over there is seen by us as it is seen by the sky above it and by the fish within it and by the trees beside it, because our body is not "here" where I physically stand but is dispersed within the process of perception throughout the sensible landscape. We do not have to think about these other aspects of the lake; we "see" them from within whatever perspective we "literally" see the lake, because to have a body is to inhabit the sky above me, the birds over my head, and the bushes beside me in a circulation of sense or "perceptual understanding." Again, this is how embodied perception works and may go unnoticed. Of course, the top of the tree is given to me with a different degree of determinacy—that is the view as seen from the sky above or from the vantage point of the bird flying over me—but it is still given to me nevertheless as one of the layers or levels of my perception. Not everything about me is perceptually given with the same degree of determinacy and certainty, which is the power of reflection and intellection to isolate, examine, and maximize, but there is still rich meaning and understanding all around me.

This is the power of having a body that flows through the "perceptual field" around me. The body, when it sees or touches something, "synchronizes with it" in order to come to a greater sense of what had been an instant ago "nothing but a vague beckoning." In an example he offers, Merleau-Ponty talks of turning toward the blue of the sky not as set over and against it but rather as "I abandon myself to it and plunge into this mystery, it 'thinks itself within me, I am the sky itself as it is drawn together and unified' "

(PP, 214). My embodiment allows me to enter the things of the field and pull them together.

To really think of the body in a different way is to think differently of the space around us and our relationship to beings around us. Merleau-Ponty states: "I am not in space or time, nor do I conceive space and time; I belong to them, my body combines with them and includes them. The scope of this inclusion is the measure of my existence, but in any case it can never be all-embracing. The space and time which I inhabit are always in their different ways indeterminate horizons which contain other points of view" (PP, 140). As infiltrating this space through my body, and its time, other vantages enter and intermingle with my hold on the world. Merleau-Ponty goes on to say that this is because my body as kinesthetic literally moves into and through the world and is projected into all those movements that it may never literally make, such as soaring in the sky as the bird or cloud above, but that nevertheless inform the sense of the scene for me and reverberate through my body. Merleau-Ponty shows in his detailed study that "movement is not a particular case of knowledge" but "has to be recognized as original and perhaps as primary." The energy around us, the vitality of its sense for us, is a kind of movement that is inseparable from the ways in which embodiment in perceiving "moves" through its world, not necessarily literally but virtually. This means that unlike the traditional idea of knowing, "my body has its world, or understands its world, without having to make use of my 'symbolic' or 'objectifying function'" (PP, 140–41). The sense of things is partially given to us by the things around us, which is why Merleau-Ponty calls them part of the "flesh of the world" or a shared sense of "Visibility" with the things around us, as we "move" into, through, and from within them in perception. Another way to say this is that humans and other beings are processes and incorporate the elements with which they are in relationship into the unfolding movement of who or what they are. In this way, the perspective of phenomenology agrees with the ancient wisdom of Buddhist and Taoist philosophies, that everything is in process, that even the seemingly at rest flows, changes, and incorporates other processes into it.

In another essay, Merleau-Ponty shows how our bodies, and how they come to experience, are not solely "mine" but rather are shared among other humans, for example. This phenomenon is more obvious in the young infant, what Merleau-Ponty calls "syncretistic sociability," or the "transitivism" of embodiment. He cites how in a group of infants if one infant's hand is struck, then all of the infants howl and cry. This happens because in some sense "the hand" of all of them was struck in a shared sense of their bodies flowing through them.[11] As adults, as self-reflectors, and as possessors of ego boundaries, our response is more measured, but we still feel the pain of someone hit in our presence echo in our own bodies, and we can feel the reverberations in our bodies of the pain of other creatures around us, as well as feeling crackling presence in our bodies of the flow of the vital, bubbly joy of playing cubs or puppies in front of us. The transitivism of the infant subsides into the background but is not utterly lost to adults. This is the normal circumstance of embodiment as moving and becoming in a circulation or flow of sense throughout the space and things about us.

To attempt to be brief at this point, I will cite just two more ideas of the later writings of Merleau-Ponty, which might help in the "gestalt switch"—like suddenly seeing the two faces instead of a wine glass in the silhouette drawing—of going from identifying the source of human knowing with intellection to shifting to recognizing another more primary level of knowing through embodiment, through a kind of resonance with the world. Right before Merleau-Ponty's sudden death, he was writing of the "flesh of the world" in which he struggled to find a way of saying that the relatedness of our body with the environment formed a kind of connective tissue like the element of flesh that has many distinct beings within it, yet these are inseparably related in one functioning matrix or medium, so this is how our bodies are with the world: "That means that my body is made of the same flesh as the world (it is perceived), and moreover that this flesh of my body is shared by the world, the world reflects it, encroaches upon it, and it encroaches upon the world."[12] We feel the heat of the 100° afternoon infiltrate us, and we tend to become hot tempered, not just an empty figure of speech, unless we can modulate its presence within us. The flesh means we sense, because we are *of the* sensible itself. We can *see because we are seen* by others, whether in the vision of other humans, the dog at my feet, the fly buzzing around me, or *as if* the tree had a certain vantage point over me sitting at this table, which it does, that would reveal my thinning hair seen from above and my squat figure like a trunk. Touching is even a better paradigm for this aspect of perception that Merleau-Ponty called "reversibility," since in touching whatever we are aware of, we are touched back by it: the other's smooth or rough skin touches me back, as does the grainy texture of the tree against my smoother palm.

We have learned to make a sharp division in our conception of subjects confronting inert objects, and the flesh of the world is a notion that puts us into the world in such a way that we are never above or outside of it but come to ourselves and to everything else only by emerging from within its matrix and therefore never having final closure or clarity: "The flesh of the world is indivision of this Sensible Being that I am and all the rest which feels itself in me . . . a mirror phenomenon" (VI, 255). The wovenness of ourselves as bodies with the bodies of all those around us yields a kind of sense that is always greater and richer than our later thoughts about experience, because we come to ourselves through the world in this "reversibility." Not all of the world's meaning is our articulation; some of it is a gift of other beings. Artists have always been particularly aware of this dimension of perception and their bodily relationships with things and others. Merleau-Ponty was interested in their experiences as key to a dimension of perception others ignore. Cezanne spent ten years painting different canvases of Mount St. Victoire and claimed that the mountain was painting itself through him. Michelangelo said the same of a piece of marble—the statue he was to carve was already in the stone, and he had only to follow its sense. Valery spoke of writing poems that were given to him by the voices of the forests. Merleau-Ponty takes seriously these artists and others who said the earth and its objects communicate a sense that in perceiving them gives the artist what she or he then finds a way to bring to expression.

Another famous example of this palpably felt sense of reversibility helps explain the fact that Steiglitz photographed the same tree in his backyard for five decades. He did not feel that the tree was literally looking back at him, but he could feel the vision of the world as it was shaped through the tree by paying greater and greater attention to his perception of the tree through this long and intimate relationship. Yet reversibility is not a fusing or a "becoming one" with something or someone. It is important for Merleau-Ponty that the perceiver remains the one seeking the sense of the tree, which withdraws as well as overlaps, or in his example of the one hand touching the other, the hand touches and is touched back but does not fuse with the touched. Neither with ourselves or other beings does this interplay cease. Not only is there no overarching and static oneness, but the back and forth that finally blurs the boundary is not symmetrical. The perceiver never loses the priority of his or her perspective and has a better sense of his or her own registration of the world than how it might appear to other beings. As Merleau-Ponty put it, "I am always on the same side of my body" and not on "the side of" trees, mountains, other people, or birds. Yet my hold on what I know is always indeterminate, open, and I do somehow, to some degree, "escape myself" through the body into the sense of these other beings, but only hauntingly so, with rich feelings and suggestions but not any determinate grasping.

As Merleau-Ponty put it, we are "in one another" as having a body that resonates, reverberates, extends, and infiltrates but "which is not a group soul either" (VI, 174). We must break down the categorization of the body as either subject or object. As embodied beings caught up in the flesh of the world, the material pulp of each perception could carry us to myriad interconnections of sense, remembrances, imaginings, and so on, that trace out the inexhaustible context of relationships. The shade under the tree is not only an invitation to coolness but a remembrance of this gathering with friends, of the spot under the trees at another favorite place, which is like the imagined oasis that flits across the mind during the blazing trek, and so on, indefinitely. A Proust or a Joyce, or many other authors, poets, and painters, makes manifest some of the weave of relationships that could be entered into at each node of the nexus we are within as embodied with others. However, what is most relevant for our exploration is that as far as we can tell, the creatures in the surround with us, as the nutcracker we mentioned earlier, or the bees, turtles, or elephants, live within a surround in which they are pulled this way or that by senses similar, such as spots of nourishment, to places where food is hidden, or where coolness awaits, or where danger might threaten from a predator—a surround of myriad senses woven into its context of which its body is part of this larger fabric.

Differing Spaces, Bodies, and Differing Worlds, but Open to Each Other

Merleau-Ponty empasizes in many of his writings the indirect nature of access to many philosophically important insights. When we compare animals and humans as objects stripped from their contexts as static themes' of study, their differences are highlighted. For example, the differing kinds of barks made by prairie dogs may seem to have no resemblance to the words uttered by humans in communication with each other, if placed side by side outside of the living contexts of prairie dogs and humans. It is only by observing how these barking sounds are uttered in the unfolding context of the approach of predators and seeing how other prairie dogs seem to distinguish from differing barks what sort of predator is approaching and even what size and color. Seeing the set of relationships within which the prairie dogs live and also how humans live opens up places in which our senses of things may overlap. The overlap of humans and animals is "in the world" of crisscross spaces and energies running through them. Merleau-Ponty asks, "Why not the synergy exist among different organisms, if it is possible within each? Their landscapes interweave, their actions and passions fit together exactly: this is possible as soon as we no longer make belongingness to one same 'consciousness' the primordial definition of sensibility, as soon as we understand it as the return of the visible upon itself" (VI, 142). If our understanding is primarily embodied through perception's many layers of sense, its feel, its emotional pulls and pushes, its kinesthetic trajectories, its images, and its rhythms, and so on, then our focus and revelations may emerge from shared sites of sense with animals with analogous roles within our surrounds.

Ed Casey builds upon Merleau-Ponty's insights in his exhaustive work about place and space. He agrees that we have to understand the human grasp of space in terms of embodiment: "The human body that brings with it what has recently been called a 'spatial framework.' " By taking human embodiment as the guiding theme, Casey suggests it can be registered how "places ingress into bodies in enduring and significant ways," and that "body and place are *congruent counterparts*."[13] To be embodied is to be "emplaced" in the sense that bodies are drawn to spots around them, related viscerally by ties of concern, familiarity, and urgency, whereas a pure mind is "above" or "outside" being drawn into the material surround. Embodied beings judge from within a circle of engagement. Merleau-Ponty demonstrated that perception is inextricably interwoven with the sense of action within an environment, drawn into the objects around it as vectors of possible actions, responding to puzzles presented to its body to be resolved through further activity. A body is a network of place ties. It is only on the basis of this "communication with the world more ancient than thought" (PP, 254) that we then can institute the directions and orientation of a clear and deliberate thought. At this more primary level, we may meet other sorts of beings in ways not articulated.

Surely birds and other animals do not have a projected, deliberative sense of a map, a conceptualized array of coordinates, directions, and distances. For this reason, from Descartes to modern ethologists to cognitive psychologists to contemporary thinkers such as Daniel Dennett, animals have been discounted as not being aware of their environment and themselves within the environment, given a rational yardstick of "knowing" being considered a conscious, deliberative grasp of facts. However, we may shift our sense of possible kinds of knowing and instead see that animals more plausibly have a "felt understanding," a beckoning within their bodies of spots to which they are related and drawn, just as Merleau-Ponty had asked us to reconsider our primary knowledge of the world to be a sense felt by our human bodies: "Our own body is in the world as the heart is in the organism" (PP, 203). Like the heart in the body, our body in its surroundings gives them a felt sense of unity and vitality. This knowing is not of distanced reflection but of *lived relation*, expressed by Merleau-Ponty in a metaphor that is at once human, organic, and machine: "What counts for the orientation of the spectacle is not my body as it is in fact is, as a thing in objective space, but as a system of possible actions . . . a certain possession of the world by my body, a certain gearing of my body to the world" (PP, 250). For Merleau-Ponty, "The thing and the world are given to me along with the parts of my body" as a lived sense of being in a place in a "living connection comparable, or rather identical, with that existing between the parts of my body itself." The body is a connectedness to that around it, a felt beckoning and a being directed or oriented as a visceral pull toward those things that matter to me, that I have feelings about, and that are experienced as part of a larger tissue I am with the world— a more fundamental level of "understanding" the world and oneself.

So to have a sense of my hand is to have a directedness and connection to the rock at my feet that I might pick up or throw, or to have blinking eyes and sweating skin is to be aware of the beckoning shade under the trees there, or as in Merleau-Ponty's famous example that takes us outside of nature and back to machines, to be having a sense of my torso in the seat of my car is to equally have a sense of how to squeeze the car between those other ones without reckoning or thinking but through a kinesthetic sense akin to that of my own body, since the car's body has been incorporated into my own sense of embodiment (PP, 143). This felt orientation, connection, and directionality are more akin to how the nutcracker, hummingbird, bumblebee, turtle, chameleon, or chimpanzee has within its body a lived sense of the "mental map" of what surrounds it, calling out to it for action. In finding the overlaps among the human, animal, and machine dimensions, we will have to allow the key terms we use to characterize them, such as "acting," "knowing," "expressing," "behaving," "communicating," and so on, find new articulations that do not prejudge how these phenomena can be manifest in ways that do not fit the classical assumptions of the past few centuries based on the subject-object duality, the corresponding valorization of abstract logical reasoning, and the overlooking of how we are primarily embodied subjects of the world. Both creatures and humans "dwell" in spaces, to use Heidegger's repeated phrase, or as Merleau-Ponty concurs, "We must avoid saying that our body is in space . . . it inhabits space" (PP, 139). Using this sense of embodied and lived space, all of these terms mean something new.

When we take the immediate experience of the world and allow it to suggest its own sense and not impose abstract prejudgments upon what we perceive, then that undivided sense of people, things, and creatures may reveal the most constructive and deep overlaps among humans, animals, and machines. I say most constructive in the sense of allowing each realm to find its own echoes and possibilities for wider functioning in the others. Looking at our overlaps with birds and chimpanzees, turtles and bumblebees, and so on, in a way that makes us hearken to what appears to us even if it does not fit our schema of the "chain of being" (in which the human mind is the pinnacle on the earthly plane) or the exclusiveness of rationality allows us to comprehend dimensions of ourselves that may give us more meaning from our world and more ways of knowing to understand parts of it that seem foreign. This approach contrasts with the rationalist approach first made influential in Western intellectual history by Descartes, which still has a firm hold on much of our current "common sense." Maybe part of the way a chimpanzee, turtle, or nutcracker takes in its space and understands it through its body will point to ways that we in a differing space of concerns and objects have analogous understandings.

There is an arrogance of taking our way of understanding ourselves in terms of one or two capabilities such as reason or logic, saying they are the highest powers attainable on the planet, and then measuring other beings in that light. A famous example of such an interpretation in animal studies, so often quoted, which Radner and Radner, in their book *Animal Consciousness*, call a "fable" at this point in history,[14] in its constant retelling by philosophers, scientists, and psychologists, is the denigration of the capacities for knowing of the yellow-winged Sphex (*Sphex flavipennis*), a hunting wasp. The wasp was the subject of a famous experiment in 1915 by French entomologist Jean Henri Fabre. As Fabre observed, the wasp "lays her eggs in a nest provisioned with a cricket for food. The wasp stings the cricket in a way that paralyzes it, but does not kill it. She brings the prey to the mouth of the burrow. Leaving it there, she goes to the burrow for a few seconds. Then, she reappears, drags the cricket inside, lays her eggs on it, and closes the cell" (AC, 174). Fabre found out that when the wasp went inside her burrow, if he took the paralyzed cricket and moved it a few inches away from the burrow, she would come out and drag the cricket to the mouth of the burrow and then go back inside again to check the burrow, only to return and find the cricket moved. Then she would again reposition the cricket by the mouth of the burrow and then again go back into the burrow (AC, 175).

Fabre found he could repeat this drama forty times and that the wasp would not figure out that the cricket was being taken and instead try to safeguard the cricket by just dragging it in the burrow with her. Fabre found this failure to respond to be evidence of the "ignorance of instinct" that allowed the wasp only to repeat a mechanical sequence of actions even in changed circumstances. He did find that not all wasps in all colonies responded this way, but nevertheless stated, "I conclude therefore as I began: instinct knows everything in the undeviated paths marked out for it; it knows nothing, outside those paths" (AC, 174). Radner shows how this conclusion on the nature of the comprehension of the wasp and the nature of instinct relies on the imposition of human prejudices upon the situation, in the sense that for a human to repeat something forty times would be onerous in a way that it is not for a wasp, and furthermore that in the world of humans, repeating something forty times probably does not make a lot of sense or yield productive results (AC, 178). However, to enter the world of the wasp, its way of being in its own set of relationships with the things and beings around it, repetition may be a part of its continuing activity that is part of its particular melody of life and makes up the core rhythm of how it gets most things done. In the wasp's world, repetition may be quite efficacious, given its different tasks and circumstance that it is enmeshed within.

The idea of seeing humans and animals within a space that is part of their embodiment allows us to see differences within different contexts without judging them as superior or inferior, but it also allows us to see on a level of anonymous embodiment that many of our relationships overlap. To deal with the cold, to find something to eat, to want to romp with other members of our species, to want to avoid dangerous others at a distance or across the river, to take account of the sun in reckoning how to get back to where one lives, to make it over the mountain on a hot day, and so on, are problems, posed by the surround, that call for bodily responses and immediate assessments that may cross boundaries to shared powers of locomotion, stealth, deception, reconnoitering, remembering, navigating, or planning. The phenomena of embodiment are meaningful but indeterminate, not the yes or no or one or zero of mathematical binary functions, and they allow for both difference and overlap.

Chapter 3

Machines Finding Their Place

Humans and Animals Already Live There

If Bodies Are Relations to Surrounds, Are Artificially Intelligent Machines Gaining Bodies?

If it is true that both humans and animals live out a direct bodily relation of direction and connection with myriad parts of their surround that has been called a "mental map" (and that we should start calling a "body map," reflecting more clearly the embodied nature of the phenomenon we explored in the last chapter), then we can see how through this "being out there together" within the byways of the surround, there is an overlap between humans and animals, but what of the machine? Surely this is what makes the machine a "mere object"—it has no relationship to its environment. Yet in our current era, machines are transforming and entering a more mature age of their development. We could cite the host of machines that now function as tied into "feedback loops" with their environment, a relationship in which events in one play back into the other in a mutual manner, from the simplest thermostat-driven heater or central air-conditioning unit to the most sophisticated medical prosthesis or even to the most prosaic newly marketed vacuum cleaner that moves around the room redirecting itself until it has covered all of its space. More complex machines are moving into more complex feedback loops with the surround. In this chapter we will look at different sorts of machines insofar as they seem to have some part in these information loops.

However, the most instructive area to look at first in order to see machines' current development and their potential is the shift that has taken place in "artificial intelligence" projects. If humans and animals are marked by some sort of "understanding," then we should see if machines can be said to be developing this capacity at all. However, traditionally we equate a kind of awareness or reflexivity of oneself and one's actions as being the norm of "understanding," at least as we often use the term in both intellectual history and in popular culture. We often assume that to understand is to first understand oneself through self-consciousness. For Descartes, it was this self-certainty, knowing that one is thinking and then being able to rationally and willfully direct one's thinking, that safeguarded our sure path of knowing the world. Yet we have already seen that there is a question of whether there are not other sorts of "understanding"—as a mutual relating that accommodates two or more beings in adjusting to each other and working together without deliberate self-reflection—that might be said to be part of human "knowing" in other ways. This sense of knowing as being more akin to the way animals "know" aspects of their world opens possibilities that other beings who are not self-reflective may still be part of a "coming to know" as a co-contributor with humans. Even inanimate materiality may have a place in a dialogical relationship of knowing, so that there might be differing senses of an inherent "knowingness" possible, in material objects. If there is a circulation of the sense of things in relationship to each other, then humans may be attuned to this emergent sense that arises from the network of relationships without being the sole author of that sense, as Merleau-Ponty's work would lead us to appreciate.

Ever since computers began to store information, do calculations, and reassemble inputted data in new constellations, there has been the dream that these kind of machines could have an "intelligence" that was "artificial" in the sense that it was created by human engineering and not the product of "natural evolution" among animate creatures. In Ann Foerst's book *God in the Machine: What Robots Teach Us about Humanity and God*, she describes the shift of focus of many within the artificial intelligence and robotics research community away from constructing the "classical systems" that relied upon a central computer control unit and were modeled on the idea that what intelligence was about was some sort of disembodied intellect that laid down an intelligible, stable general framework upon the world in order to interpret specific phenomena that arose within experience. This perspective, which envisioned the central data processing system as being the agent that imposed order upon the inputs of the environment to make sense of it, and also to control the mechanical parts or "the body" of any robotlike sort of construction, insofar as the intelligence was to be harnessed to any material components to achieve tasks in an environment, has been discarded by many researchers. There has been a shift from the idea of creating an agency that dominates a chaotic world to see how intelligence emerges "while the new systems learn to be stable through dynamic interactions with the outside world."[1] In other words, now the stability that marks understanding in making sense of something is not prefigured and imposed upon an environment supplied by the central agent but is the result of the surround and that which encounters and interacts with it. Order and sense emerge from the network of relationships. It would be from the dynamic unfolding of interactions with the artificially intelligent agent that meanings grow and evolve.

To replicate human intelligence, it was realized, meant being able to find the ways that embodiment as a fluid state of interaction with the environment and the events within it transformed the body's grasp on its surroundings. Stability was achieved gradually and through changes in the relationships to those corresponding changes in the surround. What was fathomed by M.I.T. scientists in a parallel insight to Merleau-Ponty's is that the heart of human thought is the way humans take up the world through the body and learn the way through space and about things within space through the varied rhythms and unfoldings of embodied interactions. This shift in artificial intelligence research and robotics moves away from the logic-centered principles of cognitive science toward an approach called "embodied intelligence." Philosophically, it means that computer scientists are making the same sort of turn away from the Cartesian idea that humans are basically disembodied intelligences merely using a body as a vessel and tool, to seeing that as embodied beings, humans distinctively "take in" and understand their world, as had been articulated by Merleau-Ponty and other phenomenological philosophers. This is not to claim that intelligence as cognition, abstraction, and logical ordering is not incredibly powerful, but only to say that it takes place after the organism already has taken in the "lay of the land" in a certain context, and that this initial "taking in" of relatedness, directness, and connection is both significant and an achievement in its own right. This is the fundamental level of relationship and learning between embodiment and world that makes more distance-taking rational reflection possible and efficacious.

According to Foerst's sense of things, ironically it may have been the seemingly greatest moment of triumph for cognitive science's approach to artificial intelligence that made apparent the limitations of this notion of intelligence as something to be replicated through a centralized agent of abstract reasoning, mathematical calculation, and following determinate rules. When in the early 1990s the supercomputer, Deep Blue, defeated the then world chess champion, Garry Kasparov, in its rematch, instead of proving how machines had come to realize intelligence, the computer had only produced such a limited capacity to function in this one arena that its disparity with true intelligence became obvious to many:

> These chess games between the two helped us to see the limitations of this traditional understanding of intelligence. When Deep Blue beat Kasparov, there was still no robot that could actually butter a piece of bread because it is so difficult. You have

>   to know the consistency of the butter, how hard the butter is. You have to know about the knife. You have to know about the consistency of the bread. You have to have very strong feedback loops between your arm, the knife, the butter, and the bread. You have to know a lot about the world. Otherwise you just have bread crumbs. (RHG, 71)

"Understanding" within the world of chess takes place in a highly constructed, logical realm of determinate relations and goals, unlike the world of humans and animals, which is always changing, fraught with new relationships and meaning. The kind of "knowing" referred to at the end of Foerst's passage in buttering bread is not a distanced or an abstract or a categorical knowing, but a "knowing of the hands" (again, a phrase invoked by Merleau-Ponty and also by Heidegger in one interesting passage) or a "knowing" of the body in general that is nuanced and dynamic in ways that are not obvious at first glance.

The abstract logical knowledge of the rules of chess so masterfully programmed into Deep Blue—although "an incredible engineering and software development"—became apparent to those observing the match as "so limited in its capabilities and so useless for everything but chess, they lost respect for it." Whereas buttering bread, which is an action that for someone like Descartes or other traditional rationalist philosophers seems meaningless and mechanical, actually if attended to carefully makes apparent that we live in relation to the world of qualities around us in such a way that in perceiving the subtle qualities of these objects we learn a varied and subtle sense of ourselves. "Having a feel" for the things around us, their qualities, and how we might relate to them productively is already a significant understanding—the body's kind of understanding taken for granted for centuries of Western thought.

Not only did computer scientists realize how complex the knowledge gained through perceptual and kinesthetic interaction with the environment is, but also that it is learning *through* the material reality of being an embodied being. Such knowing is not accessible to an encapsulated immaterial intelligence but opens up for an interactive one that loops within the relationships of its surround. This means that the body is not incidental to knowing, but central. As Rodney Brooks, then associate director of the M.I.T. Artificial Intelligence Lab, which began in 1992 to construct robot intelligences, explained, "If AI researchers attempt to build intelligent machines, they ought to build embodied entities that interact with the real world. One might not need abstract thought in the beginning, since after all most animals survive pretty well without it and newborns don't have this capability either" (GM, 4). The site of this sort of knowing is the body. The body provides a primary understanding of the world that is fundamental to other kinds of knowing, such as intellection, which only take place on the basis it provides through a relationship with the environment and a perception of the embodied self in this interaction. These insights led the Artificial Intelligence Lab at M.I.T. to undertake in the 1990s the project of building robots in a humanlike form, so that in dealing with problems of gravity, grasping, and moving, they would be forced to learn and to develop an evolving, open-ended understanding of the world. The idea is that robotic intelligence would develop in experiencing the world in analogous ways to the way we build up the capability for intelligent thought from the perceptual, kinesthetic basis that Merleau-Ponty had articulated decades before as our primary level of understanding the world—a "motor intelligence" in dialogue with the world.

The M.I.T. researchers also knew that in human development, the young child develops self-awareness, motor control, intentionality, visual acuity, and coordination through *interaction* with the environment and caregivers. Abandoning the prime assumption of traditional approaches to artificial intelligence—the assumption that there is some central "I" or intellect that "runs" the body as tool—the M.I.T. investigators became convinced that the human interacts with the environment finding its way about through embodied experience. The implicit experientially gained "understanding" of body and world would later become integrated as the robots learned to master certain tasks that confronted them. Rather than centralized control systems, the robots were made up of "distributed" systems that were to learn from the environment through an equivalent of human embodiment. For example, the arms of the robots were constructed with several "degrees of freedom" of movement (the possibility of moving in several ways), as were other parts of its robot "body," just as humans are able to move various parts of their bodies in different directions and angles. These different possibilities of kinesthesis were to become geared into specific tasks facing the robots and corresponded with various motherboards in their "brains," which were not directly connected but would come to interact within the experience of the robots in coordinating several motors in reaction to the demands of a specific task (GM, 97). Without a preset plan, the robots would try gestures or movements of their arms and hands in varied ways until the successful solutions were arrived at. There would be a give-and-take between the robot "body" and the world about it.

Embodied Understanding, Movement, and Meaning: Robots and Embodied Artificial Intelligence

This notion of significance grasped through movement, through meaningful gestural response to tasks, exactly parallels how Merleau-Ponty articulated consciousness as being first and foremost a phenomenon of the body: "Consciousness is being toward the thing through the intermediary of the body. A movement is learned when the body has understood it, that it, when it has incorporated it into its 'world,' and to move one's body is to aim at things through it; it is to allow oneself to respond to their call, which is made independently of any representation. Motility, then, is not, as it were, a handmaid of consciousness, transporting the body to that point in space of which we have formed a representation beforehand" (PP, 139). Rather, says Merleau-Ponty, the sense of things, their meaning for me as a being for whom things have significance and their place in my world, as well as other people and other creatures, is first and foremost grasped in its significance by my body in "the motor grasping of a motor significance." So, for example, as I move to hit the shuttlecock floating down from the sky, I must ignore the voice of my mind that is telling me to "hit" in a much too preremptory fashion and instead learn to dance with the tumbling object, my taking its movements in all my limbs, torso, and legs, and gaze and flick my wrist at the last moment just as it almost kisses the racket. I only learn to do this with learning a new rhythm of moving in time with the shuttlecock's flight and softly dancing across the lawn and in time to the movement of the other player across the net, and so on.

Movement for humans is not the dumb moving of parts but rather is the expression of a comprehension of things around it and the person's relationship to those things without ever having to become reflectively conscious. This is shown partly, Merleau-Ponty says, by the fact that "the subject does not weld together individual movements and individual stimuli but acquires the power to respond with a certain type of solution to situations of a general form" (P, 142). There are no actions that are meaningless in themselves combined to form behavior, but rather the body first resonates to the landscape to grasp an overall significance of the situation. Movement occurs as meeting and meshing of the intention of the organism expressed through the body and the taking in of the possibilities of the surround. For example, as my body feels its way into a situation, such as the general feeling of caution and observation I have in stepping onto my roof to investigate a leak that calls for me to stay balanced, to be about to reach for the tools I need to fix it, and to keep my vision in a scanning of the tiles in front of me to see what else might be wrong, each of these tensions felt in my legs, my back, or in my crouched posture is a grasping of the slope, the perilousness of gravity, and the subtle complexity of the problem of leaky roofs, which also has elicited this scanning behavior of my gaze. My body has certain postures that are implicit recognitions of these relationships, even if I never consciously focus on any particular one. Another example is the one written about by Donna Haraway and referred to at the beginning of this book concerning her human-dog obstacle course running competitions in which one might feel a sudden repulsion on one side of the body, which is an implicit recognition to swerve that side from an oncoming obstacle or a sudden pull down on one's torso that is an implicit grasp of the dog seeing the need to get lower and crouching that has not consciously registered with its human partner yet. The interspecies obstacle partners dance together in a fluid rhythm and weave of movements. We are not machines of the old sort of conception where there is first programmed a certain movement, followed by another planned movement, but rather we are spontaneously "reading" bodies caught up in a situation that is being revealed as calling for this swerve, that jump, or this burst of speed. As we run and scan with diffuse attention to these cues in the surround, the body "takes in" in one sweeping arc what is offered to it, which results in the responsive movement.

Unlike the traditional approach to AI, which conceived of intelligence in terms of a central computer processor controlling the peripheral movements of the several parts, so that "when an arm movement is needed for the execution of a specific command, the controller makes a plan about what motors, sensors, and so on, it should move and sends the specific commands to specific parts, and they move, hopefully as quickly as our printer starts to print when we give it the command," these robots "interact because through experience they 'learn' motor control and coordination of several motors in reaction to the demands of a specific task" (GM, 96–97). The analogy is made to infants who first wave their arms about aimlessly until they learn to focus on the object desired, as does the robot wave aimlessly at first and learn through trial and effort how to grasp something. As Foerst summarizes: "It has no abstract understanding of space. Instead it learns to coordinate its arms though feedback loops that register the weight the joints have to carry in a specific arm position." The sensors and actuators that react to the environment are connected in such a way that the system can react flexibly instead of following some set internal plan. The overall sense of what occurs is "The system's body is situated in the environment, interacts with its environment, and creates new and complex behaviors out of simple interactions. This philosophy gives this AI direction its name, Embodied AI" (GM, 99). This means seeing embodiment differently—that the body is a way of knowing or incorporating many ways of knowing in a fluid, interactive unfolding.

Movements of the body are ways of inquiring and then dialoguing with the environment in a nondiscursive way—that is, in a way that is not linguistic at that moment (even if prior words and thought have helped shaped the environmental relationships with us), and they literally move into a deepening sense through bodily avenues. As Foerst sums up the experiments of Adele Diamond of M.I.T., who shows how a certain level of use of the body is necessary for certain concepts to make sense, and thereby reverses Piaget's insights that certain mental capacities must develop first in order to move foreword in understanding the world: "It seems that intelligence develops through motor control and not the other way around, that is, if the body does not develop, there will be problems in mental development" (GM, 103). Embodiment is an interactive process with the surround that opens up new levels of understanding. As Rodney A. Brooks explains in *Flesh and Machines*, to attempt to create intelligence comparable to human understanding required moving to constructing robots, since the most important aspect of these artificial creatures "had been their bodies in the world. . . . Having a body provided a natural grounding. All the computations that might be done on the robot were in service of the robot in the world."[2] Contrasting this with the older approach to artificial intelligence, Brooks comments, "Researchers who worked on abstract reasoning got abstract reasoning as their result. There was no way to tie it into a physical robot after the fact." So, in other words, it is the same problem that had frustrated Descartes philosophically: disembodied, abstract reason cannot be reinserted back into the world where humans dwell and make sense of things in a more primal way. There are not two pieces that could be reassembled but rather a dynamic process, which must be undergone or emerges in continuity. The understanding of embodiment as we have articulated in this book—as an enmeshment in a surround—is the way that understanding and meaning emerge for humans, and this is what the building of robots, as conceived by Brooks and others, to gain artificial intelligence aims to achieve: "The physics of its very embedding in the world provided a rich dynamics of interaction. In order to make it act intelligently, all we needed to do was nudge the dynamics forward in the right direction" (FM, 66). The body is the medium for an unfolding give-and-take, for a nondiscursive dialogue with the world that is a level of primary understanding. This understanding does not come from previous principles now applied but rather comes from an openness to the surround that allows for spontaneous evolving of apprehension.

    This is the tie that is bringing humans closer to these new developments in robotics, artificial intelligence, and technology—they are now becoming bodies in a shared space with us, finding their way about and learning to react. This kind of understanding is not represented adequately by purely quantitative, abstract, or logical propositions. Representing the ways through embodiment that we make sense of the world is largely metaphorical, as we say when we speak of the "warmth" of the connection of those we love or the "cold" of corporate competitiveness. Computer scientists such as Brooks realized that even higher-level concepts through which we understand the world are ultimately rooted in this more primal metaphoric understanding, such as the future is a time "ahead of us," or the present is "where we are," or that time "flows." Concepts also are metaphorical in character in a way that relies upon the body as both enmeshed in the surround and as kinesthetically exploring this surround. Brooks states, "Higher-level concepts are built as metaphors that are less direct than the primary metaphors but nevertheless rely on bodily experience in the world" (FM, 67). The sense of these ideas is a result of the structure of the world, and the physics and material characteristics of the things we encounter about us, but only insofar as we can take them up perceptually through our bodies and work with them. If there is to be a true intelligence or understanding that emerges from computers and machines, it will be from robots that take on a certain kind of embodiment analogous to our own, for this is the way understanding emerges: "If we take this seriously, then for anything to develop the same sorts of conceptual understanding of the world as we do, it will have to develop the same sorts of metaphors, rooted in the body, that we humans do" (FM, 67). The "warmth" of love cannot be measured as a temperature but only sensed in the nuances of relationships and what they mean to humans and other creatures. The sense can only be fathomed by beings able to feel physical warmth, but also the sense of the belonging of relationship, and be caught up in a world or surround as a network of relationships where both are vital.

Brooks had concluded at the end of the 1980s after experiments with an insectlike-looking robot, Genghis, that robots that could develop understanding would be both *embodied* and *situated*—the same sense of humans and animals expressed in the ideas of embodied "being-in-the-world," as we have discussed. The robots were to be "embodied" in the sense that it "has a physical body and experiences the world directly through the influences of the world on that body." A robot was said to be situated if it "is one that is embedded in the world, and which does not deal with abstract descriptions, but through its sensors with the here and now of the world, which directly influences the behavior of the creature" (FM, 51–52). This understanding accords with what we have said of animals and humans in the previous chapter—that their perceptions of the world are already responses that make sense only within the context and give a reality to the animal or human that is inseparable from the context. Humans, in ways we will explore, may have abilities to project beyond their context to imaginary or conceptualized virtual contexts (as may animals to a lesser extent), but the initial ground for humans, animals, and now even for these machines, insofar as they begin to relate to the world, is from the surround.

Other computer scientists agree and also have projected that for machines to ever achieve real intelligence they will have to "develop mental capabilities through autonomous real-time interactions with its environments by using its own sensors and effectors."[3] Weng, McClelland, Pentland, Sporns, Stockman, Sur, and Thelen look to how human infants and animals learn and see a parallel with robots in that possible learning would have to take place in a process in which "sensory data are used to modify the parameters of the redesigned task-specific representation." It is through the feedback of sensory data that could allow the machine to become responsive to the environment around it. They agree that the artificial intelligence would need to be embodied in an interactive relationship with the physical environment around it in an "open-ended cumulative process," which means instead of a closed program its "programming" would develop through the relationship with the environment. In a way parallel to humans as described by Merleau-Ponty, all actions would have to have an improvisational dimension that altered in response to what is around it, or in other words, these robots would have to perform "on the fly" (AMD, 602). Not only that, but these embodied machine intelligent beings would have to be "mentored" into their meshing with the environment through the instruction provided by being "raised by" humans, just as infants are able to find the sense of the world around them through other human beings, who are perhaps the most powerfully meaningful dimension of the surround for them.

What emerges as common in understanding humans as beings-in-a-world who first comprehend themselves and the world through the embodied sense of a situation, animals as having a sense of their surround, which leads them to take specific foraging and navigating actions, and intelligence in machines, insofar as it might emerge from being embodied and learning through meshing with an environment, is that the three realms can be seen as inseparably part of what is around them and taking in this larger sense of the world. To look for animals and machines to begin to become a community with humans through achieving abstract, logical reflection is to look in the wrong direction for a direct connection with them. The first meeting ground of these three realms is in a certain material flow of energies and meaning that comes from each being enmeshed in an environment or a surround, being inseparable from it. Each has to comprehend its many relationships with that surround in a way that is not of the intellect but stems from the body's ability to relate to things comprehendingly. As Merleau-Ponty was to state several times, to begin to fathom human existence and the reality of the world around us as becoming manifest on the level of the body, perception, affect, and so on, the approach must be to savor the indirect, or what he called "lateral relations."

Enmeshed Worlds: Cochlear Implants and Michael Chorost's Sense of Being a Cyborg

As we proceed through this meditation, we need to acknowledge that there will not be perfect symmetry in the ways we find that humans, animals, and machines overlap and are bounded. In the first dimension of overlap that has emerged in focusing on *emplacement within a context*, the meaning to human and animal identity is not parallel in the same manner as it is to machines. We speculated earlier that machines of a sort, robots that are integrated with a developing artificial intelligence, might follow a direction of engaging in a give-and-take with their surrounding environment in a more analogous sense to that we have found between humans and animals. However, there are other *less perfectly analogous* but still important ways to conceive of the overlap of machines as woven into the surround with animals and humans.

Before moving to the kind of machines that we more ordinarily encounter and how they might be woven into a context, however, we need to consider a newly burgeoning relationship that captures contemporary imagination: our relationship *as cyborgs* with our component parts and the surround. Since cyborgs are themselves an overlap between humans and machines—a hybrid kind of being, we will focus on what persons so intimately conjoined with machines have discovered about the machine's way of taking in an environment. We are fortunate to have the moving, sensitive chronicle of Michael Chorost's *Rebuilt: How Becoming Part Computer Made Me More Human* in considering cyborgs from a more experiential level. Chorost was thirty-six years old and a recent Ph.D. graduate in educational computing when suddenly he went from being hard of hearing, but able to hear fairly well with hearing aids, to becoming deaf. He was offered the chance to hear again by having a cochlear implant. In people with hearing, the conducted sound from the eardrum and the three tiny bones of the inner ear is further transmitted through the fluid of the cochlea, which in turn stimulates the 15,000 cell-size hairs in the cochlea. Each of these hairs connects to a nerve ending that sends sound messages to the brain. The implant simulates the action of the hairs with a limited number of nerve endings by using electrodes to stimulate the neurons.[4] A microphone picks up sound waves, attached to the implant by a magnet, and converts them into an electrical current sent down to a computer processor at the waist, which turns them into bits of data, and then sends them by a wire through the skin to computer chips in the implant and fires electrodes, to stimulate the neurons. In Chorost's chronicle of his first four years with this computer implant in his skull, his thinking about the relationship of humans, animals, and machines undergoes profound changes.

Although the term *cyborg* was first used by Manfred Clynes and Nathan Cline in 1960 to describe a technologically enhanced human who could survive extraterrestrial space flight, and one of the first combinations of the organic and the mechanical was in an animal—a white lab rat implanted with an osmotic pump to continuously inject chemicals into it—Donna Haraway's usage of the term in the 1990s became widely discussed as a "fusion of the organic and the technical forged in particular, historical, cultural practices." As the term was used by Haraway and other cultural critics, it seemed that it was not only the literal physical fusion of the organic and mechanical in particular, cultural historical practices that made people and animals cyborgs, but that cyborgs were created by the kind of identification invoked at the beginning of this book, in which we seem unable at times to be who we are without technological intervention and dependence and can only function through mechanical systems of biotechnology, media manipulation, and other technological systems. For example, many people in industrial nations lead lives shaped by cars that determine their range of activities, employment, need for income, and so on. Even the structure of world affairs might be seen to be shaped by the automobile to such an extent that nations might assume many lives are worth losing if the conditions allowing for auto use were to be seriously threatened by another nation, for example, by the withholding of petroleum products. Another question that plagues many is to ask whether we have been shaped in ways that change who we are and that might be damaging to other capabilities by our continual interface with computers. One dimension of the cyborg topic I explored in *Earthbodies* was that many people's involvement in the Internet might be catalyzing a "flattening of affect" by allowing them to substitute sentiment for deeper emotional involvement, which requires a face-to-face involvement (EB, 163–68).

At the beginning of his book, Chorost makes it clear that he is disconcerted by the fact that the term *cyborg* is being used in such a loose way when "cultural theorists often claim in this day and age, *everyone* is a cyborg—that technological society has worked its will on all of us" (RB, 41). It is understandable, given his ordeal of having computer-driven machinery placed into his sensory system, that he does not want to dilute the forcefulness of the idea of being a cyborg. In his definition, "The essence of cyborgness is the presence of software that makes if-then-else decisions and acts on the body to carry them out" (RB, 40). Chorost's point is that some people's bodily functioning and experience will be dictated by a machine. He disputes that having silicon chips implanted in one's body for various functions that *enhance* its capabilities or allow one to do what other humans normally do is to become a cyborg, nor is it a cyborg existence to be like Steve Mann, who wears a portable computer with a constant video stream in front of his right eye. In Chorost's terms, Mann is only a "fyborg"—a functional cyborg choosing to change his experience—"whereas cyborgs are physically fused with equipment" and *have no choice but to live through the computer's programming* or else sacrifice vital functions. However, by the end of the four years of learning about his implant, Chorost is not as adamant about the physical fusion of technology and flesh as being definitive of cyborgs, nor does he feel as different from others. Instead of feeling so isolated from the norm, he realizes that *most of us are cyborgs in the way technology has altered who we are and how we exist.* He also has seen that there is a positive power in being a cyborg, insofar as we are displaced from an objective world of set realities to a shifting one that gives us choices of ways to be. Cyborgs, for Chorost, and I agree with him, are beings who have become changed in who they are in some way, which is not merely optional anymore, so having silicon chips that do not change one's relationship with the world or others, or merely enhancing an ability, is not to be a cyborg. To be a cyborg is to experience a transformation of one's sense of existence in such a way that one cannot be fully human or fully oneself outside of the *link* to certain machines; however, notice that this link does not require literal physical fusion.

Cyborg existence teaches us the same point, again, that humans combine with other humans, animals, machines, and objects only *indirectly* insofar as they look at the sense of their functioning and experience as it is transformed. In creating cyborgs, we may directly implant a mechanism into our bodies—connect the "hard wiring"—but the "combined functioning" and shift in experience are not achieved so directly. Human and machine are joined together in concerted functioning through conjoint enmeshment in the world around them or, in other words, by both of them "gearing into" or "taking up" together the rhythms of the flow of energies and sense moving through the surround and experienced by the person. The expectation that it is just a matter of "direct hookup" becomes a driving frustration and obstacle, since it is fighting the being of humans and now increasingly machines that work as part of a "field" or a surround. A unique perspective on the ties of machines and humans to the environment can be achieved by looking at Chorost's experience of how the machine and the computer gave him a "world" or context of experience that was unique, and how his relationship to the places, people, and creatures around him necessarily had to change in the process.

Given the Cartesian notion that one's body is a mere vessel of the spirit, it is hard to fathom why putting a computerized organ into one's skull should be so threatening. Yet Chorost's initial fears about the operation are entirely understandable, given the notion of "embodied understanding" that we have articulated, in which we *are* our bodies. Chorost realizes on the eve of his operation that the way we are embodied is the way we are inserted into a world, and he is haunted by the transformation he is to undergo. Merleau-Ponty's insight that our embodiment is the way we are part of the fabric of the world hits him with full force. It is not his direct union with the computer that is so frightening as his sensing that this fabric of the world, of what is around him, will be transformed. He realizes he will have a different body, a different world, and, ultimately, a different life. Scary . . .

Chorost realizes that his hearing loss is more deeply about the body's power to "be-in-a-world," to be enmeshed with the things around him: ". . . the sense of hearing immerses you in the world as no other. . . . Hearing constitutes your sense of being *of* the world, in the thick of it. To see is to observe, but to hear is to be enveloped" (RB, 9). Hearing, perhaps even more acutely, and yet also like the rest of perception, is not about registering the world distantly but "plunging into it"—being incorporated into it. Chorost realizes that in some very real sense the world will be different for him: "The world mediated by the computer in my skull would sound synthetic, the product of approximations, interpolations, compromises." There is a sense in which, as we have said, we are machines, biological machines, and the world is a result of that operation we consider "normal," of how sound waves are translated into phenomena that are heard by the most common biological machinery. To be a cyborg is to have one's world altered. This in turn means that how one feels to be part of one's surrounding world will probably change. This was Chorost's fear before the implantation, and it also was his experience afterward. Sometimes the feeling was more acute than others: "I could hear clocks ticking across a room, but I did not feel like a hearing person. Hah! I was the receptor of a flood of data" (RB, 73). Embodiment allows us *to be what we are hearing* and not take it in at a distance as data. So at first the implant/machine disrupted Chorost's embodiment. However, *embodiment is a process, a matter of time and evolving relationships with the world.* Chorost knew this before the implantation when projecting this cyborg body: "My body would have bewildering new properties and new rules, and it would take me weeks, months, even years, to understand them fully" (RB, 9). His chronicle is a moving testimony to how embodiment changes in relationship to the world around it.

If the sense of the world will change through the mediation of a computer, and if the world will be connected to him through a different set of relationships, then as a cyborg he will no longer be the same body. Chorost realizes this also: "But this technology would make me a cyborg from the inside out, because the computer would decide what I heard and how I heard it. It would be physically small, but its effect on me would be huge. It would be the sole mediator between the auditory world and myself. Since I would hear nothing but what the software allowed, the computer's control over my hearing would be complete. . . . In a sense the process would be a reconstruction of my entire body." Following this logic, which is that qualitatively perceived experiences dictate the sense of the world, that this book has been articulating, it is fair in some way to say that even though quantitatively Chorost's body is largely the same, he is right to claim that he is now living in a cybernetic or machine body—a cyborg body. Embodiment is a way of being woven into a world, and that can change in differing sorts of meshings.

This power to shift us away from a past norm seems at first a destructive aspect of the machine that tears us away from the "natural" human and animal life. If the world has been altered through computer mediation and consequently the body has been altered by having a different sense of the world, then what has occurred to Chorost or anyone in his position is that one is prevented from "going back" to some previous sense of hearing taken to be the norm. Now the only choice is to keep moving on to a new sense of hearing, one that emerges from a new world and a new body. In some way, Chorost found himself with a new kind of hearing, one that was hard to translate into what he had experienced before with his hearing aids. He had to give up on the sense that there was one way to be in the world, one way to experience the world, for his hearing through the implant would be different: "It would not *be* hearing. It would be the *equivalent* of hearing to hearing" (RB, 79). As he realizes this, Chorost says "goodbye" to reality, for he assumes, as most of us have been taught, that there is one reality to which we all aspire with objectivity to reveal and impact. From this perspective, he could only assent to the idea that "I learned that my hearing had not been *restored*. It has been *replaced* with an entirely new system that had entirely new rules" (RB, 81). Yet what may seem to us at first as the rising up of the "artificiality" of the machine's power to change the flow of our existence, that which tears it away from overlap with animals and other humans in some sort of "natural existence," may be the very factor that promotes joining up more fully among humans, animals, and machines. For this to be true, however, we would have to appreciate more fully how the human being, in both its physical being and its relationships to the world, is a process that evolves inexorably and inseparably from those around it with which it is engaged. The machine may help us see how our embodiment and our sense of meaning is always transforming as creatively engaged with new possibilities.

Although bodies may have been seen as stable structures until this past century, it is now part of common sense to realize that the physical body is a process whose cells are continuously replacing themselves in ongoing intervals. The physical body is a flow phenomenon. It is now widely known that even the brain is capable of remapping itself by weighting inputs differently through its networks of neural connections, and that it can reorganize its structure over the longer term by growing new connections between neurons, the brain's so-called "neural plasticity." This was a discovery that soon came home to Chorost: "Thanks to neural plasticity, the neurons in my auditory cortex were slowly reorganizing themselves to handle the bewildering new input from the implant" (RB, 88). Disturbing sounds and aberrations changed in their significance or disappeared, because as Chorost relates, "Over the weeks and months my auditory cortex obediently refined its topography, making physical distinctions where none had existed before. The implant was literally reprogramming me." For us it is important to note that when the computer, the machine, is intimately joined with the human body, it is in dialogue with the physical makeup of that body, and especially with its neural network. In the neural network's plasticity, it adapts to what is around it through feedback loops that incorporate new pathways. Insofar as our own body has a mechanical dimension, it is one that adapts, that comes to meet the world around it or inside it to attempt to find a way to thrive and to make sense of experience. If the autonomic, the organic, the visceral, is that biological dimension of our existence that is seen as mechanical, then the mechanical has been miscast as the purely invariant, the unresponsive, and the unrelated.

Making a Cochlear Implant Work and Perceptual Faith, Attention Flow, and Emotional Connection

Beyond the physical adaptation of the body to the direct input from the machine are more *existential shifts* that are required of Chorost in order for the implant to facilitate full functioning in the world. Through his experience, we see that the existential and the physical are not separable. Chorost is startled when one day he realizes that his way of being concerned about other humans must change in order for the machine to be able to function as mediation with the world. Merleau-Ponty documents how perception works to give us a maximal sense of the world only when the person perceiving is invigorated by the "perceptual faith" of our sensory being. This "faith" is comprised by our openness to the richness of our experience and our plunging into its vitality in order to hearken to what calls us from all corners of the world to be experienced by us. It is the immediate sense that there is meaning to be discovered by allowing the flow of the unfolding of one's perceptions to capture one's attentiveness and care so that one becomes committed to working through what can come to be understood through this effort. When we "pay attention," for example, we are not throwing an inert, indifferent "searchlight" onto the scene about us. We are actively looking at something that promises to mean something for us. If we are more attentive, more expectant, and more engaged in finding whatever as yet muddled sense it has first presented to us, then it will yield more meaning. It develops into a "positive" feedback loop. In some way, whatever we perceive "beckons" to us and is therefore an invitation to enter a dialogue with the promise of further meaning. However, it can only become such an invitation if we sensitively meet it and enter into the depth of its sense and thereby allow a true encounter to occur.

This kind of faith in the potential unfolding of meaning of what surrounds us is profoundly lacking in our current American cultural landscape, where we often pay so little heed to the surround that many of us are at a loss to remember how we got to work, even if we were the ones driving! This faith in meaning has a moral thrust: it obliges us to hearken to things, to other people, and to other creatures, or else who and what they are will escape us, as will the fullness of our own identity to be gained through the encounter with them. We are responsible for the fullness of the world and ourselves becoming manifest. For full perception to occur means opening and working at opening our bodies to perception's depth of possible meaning, allowing ourselves to feel "the tensions which run like lines of force across the visual field" and so allow our bodies to meet up with them to resolve further meaning. If we fail to experience the deeper sense of things, other creatures, people, and ourselves, then we have not seized this responsibility. As Merleau-Ponty ends the *Phenomenology of Perception* with the declaration that human freedom "is always a meeting of the inner and the outer" (PP, 454) and it can only find its responsible use by coming alive to the fact that we are "but a network of relations, and these alone matter" (PP, 456).

Even when tuned out to our world, we feel these beckoning lines of tension in a vague, implicit way, like the buzzing of gnats around us. Yet this ordinary disposition is far from taking up in concentration and appreciation the beckonings of the environment. This is one way that our reflective ideas shape our immediate experience. If we look at the world and the sense of our lives as existing "objectively," as brutely just "there," instead of seeing that the fullness of reality emerges through dialogue with the world, then we easily fall into our culture's current quasipresence to the world. We do not think of the world as requiring our cooperation to shine forth in its full effulgence and significance, so we experience it only as a vague presence. However, if we could have the realizations that Chorost comes to through his experience with his implant, then perceptual faith could be increased by becoming aware of dimensions of meaning to be opened through deliberative insight that then can motivate and direct us to return to perceptual experience with more attention and openness. Unfortunately, in our culture, this openness and attentiveness is more often ours as children, as sadly our adult ideas, distractions, and preoccupations make most of us less open to embodiment's trajectory toward maximal sense.

At one frustrating point in Chorost's attempt to adjust to his cochlear implant, he has avoided speaking on the phone, especially with his mother, because it is too frustrating to want to hear and to not be able to hear. As he started to have positive experiences with his new implant, Chorost made the call to his mother with a new attitude—believing there was something for him to hear. To his amazement, he realized that he understood her, that he heard her. He was struck at that moment by an insight: "And yet I was understanding her. Believing that I could do it seemed to be half the battle. That let me extend myself into the sound and let it sink into me. If I didn't believe I could do it, I became a wall rather than a sponge: the sound bounced off me without penetrating. It was like the difference between looking blankly *at* an object and *seeing* the object" (RB, 99–100). On an immediate level, Chorost had started to change his relationship to the auditory world. He is leaning into it now with the expectation beginning to dawn that it will open for him in a meaningful way. He has started to believe in its sense for him, as an effulgence of significance that could be garnered. Once we are oriented, both on the level of our immediate hearkening in an emotional attunement to the perception of things and consciously turn toward them, we are able to swim into the sense of their presence. Allowed to plunge into the depths of perception, to be engaged and attentive, to become attuned, the world sings to us in a different way or shines or touches us. However, there are at least two more dimensions to this openness that allows the interweaving of embodiment and the world to be perceived that Chorost discovers in order to allow the input of the machine to become both fully functional and something more significant.

Believing in his ability to work with his hearing to add sense to his life was not Chorost's first breakthrough, even though I have presented it this way, since belief in the richness of what we could perceive is perhaps the initial prerequisite to finding the link among humans, animals, and machines, and also to returning to the deeper significance of the perceptual world. However, the cultivation of "perceptual faith" is needed primarily as a corrective to our cultural sense that perception is automatic and not necessarily an art that allows for greater levels of significance. As our childhood experience demonstrates, embodiment is a force that does not need to be directed by a distancing mind to have a spontaneously open understanding of the world. However, the mind's reflections can help us in achieving a reorientation back to the openness of a perceptual spontaneity as a road back from our cultural alienation.

This level of experience also can occur spontaneously in the midst of our alienated struggles in some situations. Chorost was surprised at an earlier moment in his struggle to make sense of the garbled sound he was experiencing in the months after the implant had been installed. One day, on the way to work, he was taken off guard by a sudden ability to hear and make sense of his car radio. At first, trying to hear what was being broadcast, he was frustrated by hearing only "pseudo-English," something that sounded like English, but only came to him as very reasonable-sounding nonsense. However, as his attention drifted off to concentrating on driving and thinking about the Halloween costume that he was going to get, he realized that parts of the radio broadcast were being heard and understood by him perfectly. When he was surprised to realize this and tried to listen to the radio again, it again sounded like nonsense. He was puzzled but realized that he had not really been paying attention to the radio and that is when he suddenly heard it. He allowed his attention to wander back to being absorbed in the road and driving, and also to still thinking about his costume. Sure enough, the radio started to resolve into understandable bits again!

So as he thought about it, the answer was one that did not fit the dominant Western yes or no, one or zero, binary logic. The key to really hearing seemed to be to Chorost that, "I had to pay attention. Just not too much attention." He tested this out further and found that indeed the radio drifted in and out of focus as he "played with different levels of attention" (RB, 90). He thought of it in the apt analogy of finding "the sweet spot" on a tennis racket, which like listening requires some sort of attunement, being in a flow with things around one, not willing, not trying forcefully, but alert in an unfocused way. As Chorost said, it is hard not to try to explicitly focus, and then refrain from forcing it, when it starts resolving, but that will destroy the attunement and perception. Chorost concludes, "You have to be calm, open, relaxed alert. Poised at exactly the right mental place between idleness and tension" (RB, 91) This description fits the lived sense of the sort of embodied understanding that we have been articulating in this chapter. Merleau-Ponty described how as the body attunes itself to the environment as a whole, it takes in the sense of the surround in a way in which items form a constellation or a gestalt, an overall organization, which reflects our felt and habitual relationships. There is no need for a deliberative, reflectively directed focus for this sort of "lived" or "embodied" understanding. Actually, it dissipates as we turn our reflective focus upon it or will ourselves to the same sort of relationship. Yet even though it cannot be forced or willed, this spontaneous upsurge of the sense of the world in perception has to be *allowed* by a belief that it can occur. In addition to this belief, however, the world must be hearkened to by allowing it to flow out to meet us, but not wrestled into our grasp. We have to let our attention be captured, not willed. We have to be open to the world as a partner in dialogue that has to be given the space to form.

Merleau-Ponty makes the analogy between attuned perception and sleep, where we have to let it happen, to "come over us," or if we *try to will* sleep, it will not happen. Similarly with the fullness of perception and its relational understanding with the qualities of things, one *has to let go into* the perception. This letting go is an art that can be learned. Again, to give the more startling example from another cultural context, it was this lesson that for seven years the Zen archery master tried to share with Eugen Herrigal in various ways, as related in Herrigal's chronicle of this experience, *Zen and the Art of Archery*. Whether it was Herrigal's incredulity that he had to stop trying to snap the bow and just let it happen, like ripening snow falling off the branch, or whether instead of trying to aim precisely and guide the arrow, he had to just be open to the shot and the target, and the arrow would go toward the bull's eye, or whether it was the final indignity that he had to stop trying to shoot the arrow and just let the shot happen, the master's invocation was the same one of allowing the body to be captured by the surround in a kind of unfocused thrall. The master summed it up one day quite well when he challenged Herrigal, "You think what you do not do will not happen" (ZA, 63). Herrigal could not see how he could let go of being in charge of acting. However, as Chorost said, it was not simply doing nothing, but a kind of open alertness of the body in tune with its entire surround that allowed the spontaneous activity to occur. Again, in another cultural context, the Taoists have a term for this concentrated yet relaxed "letting happen," called *wu wei*, translated usually as "not-doing."

The third part of this "letting be" of the surround is that it is not only a matter of modifying the will or ego and also the kind of attention we immerse ourselves within, but in addition the emotional relationship to what we might understand is vital. The space within which we are interwoven is not just a set of factual occurrences or indifferent objects. This space is crisscrossed with vectors of sense about which we have feelings. Part of our connection to this space through embodiment is affective. For example, we are anxious about being in this part of town because there has been a series of crimes in this locale lately, or we are fond of this neighbor and pay more attention to him than someone else who lives next door on the other side, or this chair is a comforting presence at the end of the day, since it offers rest and has associations of many books read in its confines, or that set of eyes glowing in the forest on my nightly walk is a scary, disconcerting presence that gives me a panicky feeling. These feelings make us oriented and connected to phenomena in different ways that will enable us to know them in different ways. So in the examples just described, I might learn shortcuts in the streets in the threatening neighborhood, or I notice things about the neighbor I care about, such as he is quietly sick or lonely, or I notice that a chair needs some minor repair. I apprehend what I might otherwise miss if it were not for the emotional pulls I experience. Merleau-Ponty gives a striking example of being in the south of France during the war and being utterly immersed in village life until he hears that Paris has been bombed. Then his worry orients him utterly to Paris, and he feels disconnected from where he literally is located. The small details of village rhythms and surroundings that had fascinated him become inapprehensible as he is riveted to Paris by his worry (PP, 285). Fear makes some objects heightened and makes us closed off to others, just as love makes us able to perceive aspects of another person that had been hidden, but perhaps not able to see others. With indifference, however, much of our perceptual, affective lived understanding glides by in the background unexperienced by us. This lesson is important for teachers: if students do not first care about a topic or enter into an emotional relationship with it, then they will not be able to learn about it with the same efficacy.

Things are not all felt to the same degree, so therefore they do not register with us to the same degree, and they are not the focus of our directedness, connectedness, and ability to explore them to the same degree. Emotional orientation to something or someone is the "glue" of the person and the surround as one becomes immersed through feeling in an affective space. It is not surprising that emotional openness is part of the indirect way machines are joined with humans to gain access to parts of the surround. Chorost realizes this throughout the four years of adjusting to his implant. It is a discovery that he had made earlier with his hearing aids. When he had been part of a group therapy meeting during the late 1990s as a graduate student, he had the experience one night, after having been in the group for some time, of having his radio transmitter go dead that had previously broadcast to his hearing aid and helped him hear the members of the group. To his surprise, unlike other times his batteries did not function, he could still hear people on the other side of the room. What he realized was that through the therapeutic process, he had overcome his emotional isolation and had begun to feel an emotional kinship with these people and their problems. As a result, as Chorost put it, "What had changed, I suddenly realized, was my ability to listen. Not to hear, but to listen" (RB, 78). As he meditated on this, he realized that if he become a more caring person, concerned about what others were saying and able to feel his connectedness to them, then he could hear them better. He recalls this lesson and now with his implant he knows in order to become able to hear with the potential that the machine has provided him, "I would have to become emotionally open to what I heard" (RB, 78). The machine is part of his context, both internally and inescapably, as allowing him to be woven into what is going on around him in an auditory way, but for the machine to work, it needs him to develop a closer relational bond to people and events around him. To experience the way machines can open parts of the world to humanity and become more kin to us will require an emotional relatedness to things of which they can be a part. We think of machines as functioning through indifference, but insofar as there becomes a partnership, a possible overlap of human and machine, it requires care from the person toward that in the world to be better revealed and understood.

Indeterminacy Is Openness to the Overlap

Finally, there is even a further lesson in looking at the conjunction of machines and humans in cyborg existence, which has been emerging in the descriptions of this chapter and builds upon the discussion of "the world" of animals and humans in the previous chapter. Chorost had been exposed to Haraway's writings about cyborgs in graduate school and confessed that they did not mean anything to him. After his experiences with the implant, he started rereading her, and now her main point that the world itself in how it appears is indeterminate took on a new significance. The world as revealed through Haraway's analysis of the encroachment of the biotechnological across the realms of human, animal, and machine is indeterminate to all perceivers, *as well as* to perceivers directly meditated by the power of machines. Animals, too, are caught in the shared web of indeterminacy in which biopower is constantly altering how we species and objects collide. Their existence is rendered malleable through the interventions of technology and may not resemble what we thought their "natural" life was. For Haraway, this has many destructive outcomes to the thriving of humans and animals, but it also represents new possibilities. Rather than the traditional idea that the overlap between humans and machines and between humans and animals will be discovered by "digging deeper" toward the level of the most determinate building blocks—to find the "hard wired" that yields the invariant and determinate information about the world—the most startling overlaps in these three realms may come through the open-endedness of how all three realms are evolving.

Chorost had run right into the indeterminacy of machines' functioning when he discovered that his emotional relatedness changed how and to what extent the implant could create a replacement for "natural" hearing, as well as how the quality of attention also altered the implant's ability to function. He changed what it could do for him, as had also been the case as well with his earlier adaptations to its functions. For Chorost, and for all of us, this cooperative input in functioning may frustrate, given the cultural myth that machines determinately function with the proper material construction. How our efforts at self-transformation can be required by machinery to allow it to be successful does not fit the traditional separation of the realms of human, animal, and machine, nor fit the model that humans legislate for themselves exclusively what constitutes their well-being. If many have a difficult time accepting the truth of intersubjectivity—that others often understand us and impact upon us as much as we know ourselves and determine ourselves—and resist taking input from other humans, then it would be even harder to accept that a machine "taught" us something about ourselves that made us a better person as well as higher functioning, as happened to Chorost. Ultimately this is an exciting discovery for Chorost, as it should be for us, because it means that "upgrades" to ways of being human will also augment the machine's functioning. However, if our functioning and the machine's functioning are to become this coordinated, then it also means we may have tied our fate to upgrades in machinery in realizing our own potential as humanity. Is this compromising our dignity as humans?

Chorost was forced to realize that the hardware limits and the software upgrades to his implant alter the way the world as heard appears to him. He, like all of us, was faced with either fighting this further imposition of finitude or seeing its deeper and possibly redemptive meaning. At the moment these limitations really struck him, Chorost came to a creative level of acceptance of the open-endedness of humanity and reality that was empowering: "Becoming a cyborg infects one with a certain rueful irony, because it overturns the blithe assumption that one's sensory organs deliver a truthful representation of the universe. They don't; one's most basic relationships to reality can be amended and edited and upgraded; reality is ultimately a matter of software" (RB, 147). This truth of the world as we experience it is what Merleau-Ponty kept stressing as the key to greater freedom, meaning, and creativity: we must learn to accept the indeterminate as a positive phenomenon. This does not mean the world is merely relative, since there are more successful upgrades than others, differing emotional responses that allow the machine to yield better results, and there are better interpretations that make the aspects of the world more accessible. Rather than mere relativism, the world in its interconnectivity always has more possibilities for articulation. Relativity is not relativism. As Haraway puts it, "To be a construct does NOT mean to be unreal or made up; quite the opposite. Out of each of these nodes or stem cells, sticky threads lead to every nook and cranny of the world."[5] Since everything can be seen in relationship to other aspects of the surround, there is always more meaning to emerge from differing relations and perspectives, yet this bringing together and seeing of connections is not just what I make of it but what these beings bring to the fore in the situation of their interconnectedness. Yet Haraway, like Merleau-Ponty, Rodney Brooks, Andy Clark, or anyone dealing with embodied meaning within a surround, uses words such as "stem cells" or "nodes" as metaphors to express how in relationships that are dynamically unfolding through new interconnections, identities and meaning continue to alter. It is not the case of having a definite sense of who I am and what

I perceive or none at all, but rather there being a richness of sense offered by the world that we can access and shape in differing ways.

The other side of this truth is that we, as perceivers, have differing possibilities that we can enter, some of which are through the power of machines and increasingly sophisticated technologies but have always been available to us in other ways, at least to some extent. When Chorost tries another operating system software, his perspective on the world as heard alters. The machine shifts his sense of the world. However, anyone's sense of the world might shift from writing a poem about something one takes for granted or really seeing the situation from someone else's opposing view or trying to experience the world as a bat might experience it—something declared impossible in a famous philosophical article but actually only indeterminate, inexhaustible, and capable of only partial, but meaningful, success. As Merleau-Ponty said in looking at the variety of ways that humans perceive the world given differing physical and psychological makeups, "There are several ways for the body to be a body, several ways for consciousness to be consciousness" (PP, 124). Some perspectives yield helpful or revealing insights about certain aspects of a situation, and other perspectives reveal other aspects.

This sort of insight takes us beyond the dilemma posed to us in grade school, that if we all refer to something as red and yet have differing experiences, as someone does who is "color blind," for example, then we can no longer have confidence in a "shared reality" but may have merely been trained to use language similarly to represent very different experiences. The dilemma centers on either having direct and knowable access to reality or else being in the dark as to that which we really refer. The problem is created, however, by how we frame the dilemma: it is a choice between two determinate situations—one of fullness of understanding or positivity contrasted to one of lack or nothingness. Embodied understanding in humans, animals, and now machines shows us our reality is shared, but that it is open-ended, not fully determinate, and has more depths than we could fathom. It can be shaped. It can evolve. There are modulations, varied angles, or different kinds of melodies that can communicate and find resolution together but also can gain from a richness of differing sorts of participation. There are times we can make the focus so narrow, ruling out all sorts of factors that make the input wider and more varied, in order for certain purposes to get a more determinate answer, but that is always liable to be open to a wider focus with another sort of question about another sort of meaning or to go further into those depths.

Not being able to express his insight in exactly this manner, this gathering sense of openness to other ways of apprehending, first through his implant and then in communication with other sorts of beings, gradually takes hold of Chorost:

Haraway's essay now struck me as a straightforward description of my life. I experienced joint kinship with animals and machines, feeling oddly affectionate toward my robot vacuum cleaner yet also reveling in the smells and lusts of my animal body. I was permanently and pleasurably adrift in eternal uncertainty about teapots and microwaves. Cyborgs "have no truck" with master narratives because there is no single story running through their bodies. My sensory universe is now constructed by squadrons of programmers, not the garden fields of my ear. Unitary identity? Not anymore, if ever; there are two minds in my skull, one built by genes, the other by a corporation. I am a walking collective, a community of at least two. The x-rays of my head are riveting, a stark juxtaposition of sensuous biology and angular computational power. The computer invaded the sacred domain of my body, yet to my own astonishment we learned to work together as a total system, mutually changing each other in the process. I fed it lithium batteries; it fed me electrons. I altered its software; it repatterned the dendrites in my auditory cortex. We have literally reprogrammed each other. (RB, 155–56)

As Chorost rightly articulates, as a "total system" or what Merleau-Ponty meant by "the flesh of the world," differing sorts of beings can jostle against each other in their difference yet come together in an exchange of inputs or perspectives to keep moving ahead in an evolving becoming of communication and apprehension. It means articulation and apprehension do not come to a final rest but always have "more room" or are "inexhaustible," and that there are no finished subjects confronting static objects. Input from engineers, shifts in conditions of perceptions, and ties to other creatures can open or shift the register of what we fathom or can express. Instead of conceiving of an isolated subject in an internal and eternal realm of spirit or a hard-wired, brain-producing intelligence, we can envision subjects who also are altered by the perceptions of other subjects and by means that they grasp or internalize or manipulate or ingest or implant, and who also are changed by what they are perceiving. Chorost ends up feeling in his bones the kinship of human, animal, and machine by virtue of his powerful experience of this indeterminacy and interweaving of perspectives. His experience with the machine has changed his sense of who he is.

Chorost, through his four-year transformation of learning to work with the machine, both learns about himself and the world. He has come to feel a kinship with even mundane machines, because in their solidity they also have a certain plasticity that humans can work with to open up aspects of their environment. Both externally and internally (as biological machines which we are in part), machines can give us new ways of making sense of the surround, for interacting with other humans and previously inaccessible parts of our world. For both those who have suffered a deficit of functioning or for all of us seeking other capabilities, machines are extensions of our embodiment. Chorost came to feel how the deeper background of the surround in which he and all of us are embedded as embodied beings is crisscrossed with the senses of both animals and machines that move through our flesh. Chorost's realizations bring us also to an articulation of a theme that has been implicit in this chapter, but building with each page: the "manyness" of our being, as many sorts of "subjects" within our subjectivity, as being pulled in many directions and as moving out into the world in many modalities. In this manyness is how there is a mixing of human, animal, and machine. Neither immaterial spirits, nor mere chemical or electrical chains of cause-and-effect events, we are material beings embedded in a larger context of relationships. Materiality does generate sense in its relationships.

Not surprisingly, even the more applied scientists who use the power of technology and computer science to envision new products for humanity realize that machines are becoming more adept because we are beings that are open-ended sites for enhancement in how we function. Human cognition has traditionally been growing and changing for millennia as taking into itself technology and, as a result, changing its very structure. When Descartes sat in his dressing gown by his wood stove declaring that "I think, therefore I am," he took this to mean that he was a purely "thinking substance." In declaring that this immaterial substance was utterly distinct from his arms, legs, senses, and all of the material surround, Descartes was choosing not to see most of what was part of his own process of cogitation. That he could not have thought of most of his thoughts without language giving shape to them, recording them, and extending the lines of reasoning and description, that books had contained for him many of the ideas that were building blocks for his thought, and even the pen and paper onto which he wrote his ideas allowed him to mull over those thoughts and revise and shape them in a way that would not have been possible otherwise. Thought unfolds, extends, and proceeds through material means.

Traditionally, philosophers have thought of words, language, and writing as emanations of the human mind, but now many in differing fields realize that we should start thinking of how the materiality of language, words, writing, books, and a host of more literal information and perceptually related machines comprise the ways we think through our surround and the ways in which the surround comes to shape the way we think in the process. In a phrase Andy Clark uses as his book title, "natural-born cyborgs," he expresses well how our grasp of the world has always been mediated through tools that extend our scope of apprehension, and that we need to understand embodied mind as "human cognition subsisting in a hybrid, extended architecture."[6] The "information revolution" has always been occurring, in that these more wonderful inventions have augmented the sense we have explored already of how the surround "holds" memories, insights, and feelings for us and for animals. As Clark states, "It just doesn't matter whether the data are stored somewhere inside the biological organism or stored in the external world. What matters is how information is poised for retrieval and for immediate use as and when required" (NBC, 69). So Clark agrees that we have been cyborgs throughout our long human speaking and writing history: "With speech, text, and tradition of using them as critical tools under our belts, humankind entered the first phase of its cyborg existence" (NBC, 81). The key is that the final form, structure, and rhythm of what we express and apprehend result not just from us but from the complex ways our thought interacts with these other media (NBC, 75).

However, Clark distinguishes this capacity for extension of mind into the landscape and artifacts that we have created from animals. Although the way in which we create things through which we can extend this external scaffolding and the kinds of information that we can store there may differ from animals, in ways we explore in the next chapter, what is also true is that this capacity is grounded in the shared sense of embodiment with animals in which the surround is part of embodiment and its powers. So in this regard, I disagree with Clark. For example, the Clark's nutcracker, discussed previously, who stores thousands of seeds in caches throughout its environment and is able to "read" the surround throughout the winter to retrieve the seeds, is building on the same capacity of embodied understanding to have an "external scaffold" to extend its power of emplacement and recall into the surround. Humans, animals, and now, increasingly, machines have all become more highly self-supporting by extending themselves throughout the surround. This paradox of gaining self-support through becoming extended into what is around it is common to all three realms of being.

Plain Machines and How We Are All in This World Together: Humans, Animals, and Machines

Machines are largely tools. There are some machines, most famously, "Rube Goldberg" machines, that have no practical function—although that could be debated, since their very elaborate uselessness is meant to delight us, and so to entertain and fulfill a function. The original and most simple machines were pulleys, levers, rollers, and ramps that helped humans overcome resistant physical forces. Insofar as they are devices to help humans perform some task, machines make our work easier in some way. However, machines no longer primarily function to decrease the amount or duration of physical labor involved in a task but often aid mental or imaginative efforts: they perform calculations beyond human's ken; they store, organize, and retrieve information; they detect presences beyond our acuity; they make all sorts of communication possible; they perform tasks that take greater speed or sensitivity or responsiveness than humans can achieve; and they guide or perform an almost incalculable number of other sorts of jobs. As with the other two realms, humans and animals, we will define machines in detail and look at their unique characteristics in the next chapters when we shift from drawing overlaps to drawing clearer boundaries among humans, animals, and machines. However, to bring up this more traditional sense of machines as tools is to land us back in the heart of Heidegger's ideas, explored earlier, since tools were at the heart of his description of how objects around us refer to each other and to the tasks we seek to perform. For Heidegger, tools functioned in a way that opens the interpenetration of human and what is around it through a shared being as caught up in tasks. Tools are those things he calls "ready to hand" that make up the sense of context or environment by forming a nexus of references to each other in terms of human tasks.

By calling tools "ready to hand," Heidegger means they are beings that become an extension of our body, almost part of our hand, something immediately within our grasp in a certain place already aimed at another part of the environment. If this were true of tools in general and machines as mere tools in this sense, then machines at this point in our cultural and technological evolution that can directly *respond* to our intentions in many ways through electrical impulses might be seen to be "super tools"—intensifying the relationships that Heidegger had in mind in a simpler age of more straightforward mechanical tools. In *Natural-Born Cyborgs*, Clark describes the performances of Stelarc, who performs using his two arms in various graceful dance motions and then has a third prosthetic arm with microprocessors to guide it, but the third arm is attached to his body, which he controls as fluidly and "naturally" as his two other arms through electrodes and processors attached to four muscle sites on his body. Stelarc also paints with all three arms, with equal facility. Here again we are discussing a machine that some might be tempted to call a "cyborg" being, yet as we have defined the term it is not, since the sense of who the person is and the sense of the person's world have not been transformed or altered in such a way that cannot be undone, and cyborgs are not just the mere fusion of biological and humanly manufactured, inorganic parts. Stelarc has made literal Heidegger's sense of "ready to hand," but this is not perhaps as radical a shift in our overlap with machines as other senses of our co-presence.

These boundaries are shifting continually, as a year after I wrote the sentence above the *New York Times* today reports how stroke victims who cannot move their arms are being assisted by the "Myomo e100," a robotic elbow brace that "senses" weak electrical activity in patients' arm muscles and provides enough assistance so the person can perform a movement such as flipping a light switch of lifting a box. As a stroke victim, such as Mary O'Regan regains motion in her arm for the first time in twenty years, there may occur rebuilding and strengthening of neurological pathways in the brain. Her sense of the surround, its possibilities, and even her brain structure may be shifting with this machine interaction.[7] However, what is important about the idea of "tools" as part of the unity of "the person as embedded in the surround" is not the meshing of literal body parts with inorganic materials but the idea that there is an emerging seamlessness of intention of which the person and the machine as tool are inseparable parts, and both cue each other into the person's projected act toward a goal, find ways to contribute to its unfolding performance, and modify each other in a web of relationships.

Unlike the case of cyborgs, in which the machine has literally become another organ or part of the body, there is another, less literal sort of "incorporation" that happens with machines and other sorts of tools. The body is lived in immediate relationship to the surround and as incorporating machines into its "body schema," as Merleau-Ponty calls it. In using this term, Merleau-Ponty means to indicate that the phenomenological key idea that all consciousness is directed toward something (what is called "intentionality"), whether toward another person, a task to get done, an event that has evoked an emotion, or even imagining a certain state of affairs, if it is taken into account in regard to embodied understanding, then points to how the body has a "virtual sense" of emplacement, direction, and connection in a visceral way with the surround. For example, if I intend to quickly get to the store in five minutes before it closes to get a carton of milk, then my car keys, starting the car, driving down Front Street to Market Street, traversing further turns, parking in the lot, taking my wallet, paying, and so on are all implicitly given to me as the "path" or "intentional arc" carved out of the surround and implicitly called upon by starting this action. A series of objects is the means, the "equipment," of getting this task done, sketched out together in a "pathway" for me to follow. Even more so, in this action my embodiment is not just made up of my explicitly defined body but "takes in" all of these objects as its matrix for this action. Just as the car is given to me as part of my extended sense of my body, or as part of my "body schema," as mentioned previously, and we can "fit it through" a tight space, just as I fit my literal body through a space, so all of these other things around me are my "extended embodiment" at the moment. Machines in our world are often incorporated into our embodiment in this way.

As "ready to hand," Heidegger describes how the tool or machine is given to us as immediately and seamlessly as any part of the body inscribed into the intention we are aiming at achieving. If we consciously notice it, then it is not working well. Through incorporation, the tool becomes like another limb, as does the cane for the blind person, another of Merleau-Ponty's examples. The body is "expansive" and returns to itself from within the surround with parts of it "incorporated" into its "expanded" sense of how it will get things done. So even straightforward machines external to us are an immediate part of the apprehending structure of our embodied consciousness and part of the context without which we have seen there is no human existence. However, the difference that is accelerating for machines in relation to other tools is that our newest machines directly "respond" to indicated intentions in order to "perform" or "facilitate" actions. They are not an inert part of the context, like a rock or the sidewalk. It would be quite a stretch to say that the sidewalk "facilitates" our walking, even though it is useful for us in walking. It does not have any way to carry forth our intentions in a way similar to the activity of contemporary machines, as when a moment ago I misspelled a word, but the computer corrected it for me as I typed further the sentence. The computer has not "communicated" with me to see what I intended, but it can detect the "intentional arc" of the words emerging through the sequence of typing events, and it "acts" to safeguard its remaining on course, as it also suggests improvements in grammar, some of which are appropriate and some are not, given my "nonstandard" use of words and syntax at times to fit my style. Even our example of the car as a machine that is a tool has shifted recently. Now when I attempt to navigate around a curve, the car will differentially activate its "drive" to each wheel or modify the force differentially to the four brakes to make it more likely that it will get around the curve as my initial steering or braking has mapped this maneuver as a goal that is not explicitly "recognized" as such by the brakes, hydraulic system, or differential, but nevertheless, they become "engaged" in the actions unfolding and initiate further supplementary events that make my initial intention more likely to be fulfilled. In other words, our intentions, as we have described already, have a material path and set of relationships among beings inscribed into the surround, and this "map" can be used to engineer machines to "join up" with the process of carrying out those intentions.

We have already described how whatever is in the "around sphere" of humans and animals is in a "reversible" relationship with humans as embodied, meaning they always "speak back" to us in an indirect way. It would seem to be much more the case with beings like current machines in their increasing facility, called "user friendliness," that actually "act" or enter into our actions as facilitators or "co-actors." They do not have a self-reflexive sense of the activity or a sense of what they are doing, but they immediately "join up" with the intended goal of what we are doing and initiate other events that make this goal possibly realized. In the early phases of the Industrial Revolution, many were intoxicated with the potential for machines to greatly increase productivity, for machines to accomplish tasks that could not be done without them, and to open up new areas of human endeavor. They were to be our drones, whether with the initial physical tasks, such as moving large masses, for which Hobbes saw that civilization was in great debt, or later feats that would have been fantastic, such as flying, let alone being transported to the moon. However, the human was the mind, the intention, the being who was the agent and motivating force. Yet at this point in history, many *intellectual* tasks are not just achieved through computers, but even what to do next might be suggested through the results of their projections, depictions, or calculations. This relationship seems to make intentionality not just the human shaping of the course of action and event but something more complicated and cooperative, where the human initiative can be modified, added to, corrected, or facilitated by machines.

At first, especially in Europe, after the scientific revolution, given the way of looking at the world that predominated in these cultures that developed machines at an accelerated rate—that of the distanced subject versus objects rationally defined mathematically and logically—it seemed as though the proliferation of machines was something that did not alter the being of humans, or of animals, or the rest of the surround. Machines were "there," in the environment, but they could not get "inside us" psychically, as they were all "mere" tools. Of course, the cause-and-effect relationships between humans and machines could be seen to proliferate, but not deeper or "internalized" relationships. However, in the nineteenth century, writers and thinkers began to articulate how machines could alter the way we experienced human reality, created values, and made sense of things, with Marx being perhaps the most famous theoretician and Shelley the most famous novelist. Marx sounded the alarm bell that who we are might become produced in ourselves by the machines we had originally produced: the same reversal of creator and created that Shelly saw in her Frankenstein vision in how humans might become the ones who were reduced to machines in their lack of fellow feeling. It is the human lack of pity for the Frankenstein creature that is monstrous, and not the creation's inability to deal with the human's indifference and then subsequent unfeeling aggression toward it. Frankenstein's horror at what he has done evolves into a cycle of hurt and injury initiated by the unfeeling humans, following in the footsteps of the creator, the scientist, Frankenstein.

What is important for our study here is to realize how this collapse of relational distance between humans and machines makes sense given what we have seen in this chapter. It is not merely a collapse of physical distance in the sense of implantation but is a psychical distance, a distance of consciousness, where who and what we are and what the world is becoming are transformed. Machines are increasingly at the heart of the surround, which in a very real way actually comprises our bodies. Yes, some individuals have pacemakers or cochlear implants with computers embedded into their biological flesh, but they are not in a different situation than the rest of us, Chorost finally came to realize. If our bodies do not even work as sense-determining beings without being of the flesh of the world, then machines are "under our skin" in ways that have great potential for both violation and augmentation of "taking in" of the world knowingly and creatively. We are all somewhere on a continuum (or on many positions on this continuum), which runs from the "cyborg" experience of one with a computer implant within one's skull, to the blind individual wearing a camera for a video feed with neural interface, to a patient within a scanner for hours so the machine will make visible the flaws in the functioning of biological machinery, to the person whose continued health depends on chemicals machined in labs as a result of the readouts of other machines that explore his or her makeup, to the problem most industrialized populations face of having toxins and other chemicals produced by machines as part of their own bodily tissues, to all of us who see the world make vital and mundane decisions on the basis of a view of reality provided to us by machines that tell us of ozone holes, the earth's molten center, the age of dinosaurs, the dangers of radioactive materials, the makeup of cells, a hurricane approaching, the proliferation of weapons by other nations, and so on.

If, as we have said, we see the world through the way the world sees itself, so that its soaring quality is transmitted to our bodies by birds, for example, then think of how much more staggeringly true this is of how we see faraway galaxies, the electromagnetic spin of particles, the weather patterns sweeping the globe, and the fractal geometry of particles "seen" and apprehended by us only because this has been "seen" by machines used to detect, image, or measure phenomena to display them to us. It is interesting that the example of seeing the world by our bodies echoing the embodiment of birds in a soaring way from above, as we walk below, through the "extendedness" of our bodies throughout the surround in its resonances with other beings was first suggested in Merleau-Ponty's work but was also written about beautifully in the final pages of Susan Griffin's *Women and Nature*. In writing a feminist critique of how women and nature have been seen as "the other" to the male, reason, order, and the quantifiable, Griffin also articulates a perspective in which each object and living being has its integrity but is interwoven with each other through the body in the surround. Griffin writes about the sense of soaring "through" the bird flying above, experienced as through the sense of her own body being in flow with the bird.[8] Both she and Merleau-Ponty describe how our embodiment gives us this dual sense of being on the ground and above simultaneously through emplacement within the surround. They have complicated the boundaries of the human and the natural. Now, however, startlingly, technology has *literalized* and made explicit this specific and implicit bodily experience, and has made it accessible to the public as an art work that brings these boundaries further into question. Now the machine possibility of the same boundary overlap with human and animal is intensified as an aesthetic experience.

The idea discussed throughout this work so far, of the *enmeshment of embodiment and surround* in humans, animals, and now, in some ways, with artificially intelligent machines and cyborgs, is key to developments in the technological improvement of all machines. Clark, in *Natural-Born Cyborgs*, explains, "The larger lesson then is that embodiment is *essential* but *negotiable*," but what matters are all of the complex feedback loops between body and surround, that can now be mediated by technology, and ultimately "it is the flow that counts" (NBC, 114). In one of his examples of the kind of flow of perception that can be created, Clark refers to the interactive installation set up in the Nexus Contemporary Art Center in Atlanta in 1996 by Eduardo Kac. In the installation, the viewer is confronted with an aviary with about thirty flying birds in it—along with one robotic bird. The viewer of the installation puts on a virtual reality headset that receives a video feed from two digital cameras that are the robotic bird's "eyes" (NBC, 95–96). The sense that permeates the viewer is of being both aloft with the birds and below at the front of the cage. Suddenly there is the dual input of being situated as literally standing on the ground and feeling the ground beneath one's feet and simultaneously having the video feed provide one with the sense of living through the sight of soaring above—the literalized, technologized input of being both simultaneously human and akin to the birds. When I read this example, it made me gasp, since it is the technological reproduction of the example of the power of embodiment I have used for decades, drawing upon both Merleau-Ponty's work and the ending of Griffin's book, *Women and Nature*. This articulation of experience has been delivered to the viewers of this art/media exhibition through technology, demonstrating the power of the machine to insert itself into the circulation of meaning of embodiment within the environment.

What had been implicit in the way the body inhabits the surround or has this "external scaffolding" is now made explicit and intensified in its palpability through the work of machines. Another less exotic and startling example might be the global positioning system (GPS) that more drivers are having installed into their cars or that come as standard equipment on some models, which offer a view of where the car is viewed from above on a projected map grid to complement the driver's and occupant's sense of location from within the car. Again, if Merleau-Ponty is correct, then we have always had an indeterminate, implicit sense of where we are on a grid as seen from above in the sky, but now technology has made this explicitly accessible to us. Both of these instances are clues to how machines are becoming part of a dialogue with us about the sense of our experience—making what was implicitly available as richer complements of the meaning lodged within the surround that now can be technologically offered to us by machines, in enhanced and explicit ways—by keying into the body's "understanding" as being embedded within the surround.

Dangers of Imploded Boundaries and the Need for Ambiguity

It would be misleading to cite Haraway and only refer to her embracing of the enmeshment of human, animal, and machine. Another way to conceptualize the way in which human, animal, and machine overlap or even "morph" into each other is Haraway's notion in Modest_Witness@Second_Millennium. FemaleMan©_Meets_OncoMouse™ in which she claims these realms are "constituted and connected by recursive, repeating streams of information" (MW, 134). She fears that human, animal, and machine are imploding in a dislocating hyperspace. In this space, in which beings and objects seem to be circulated everywhere and nowhere, and at speeds that are quickening, there is a burgeoning access to everything. As information, humans, animals, and machines refer to other aspects of each other, give a sense of the patterns that might make up each, or open for understanding the ways in which each has been shaped that might illumine the others. As information, each of these realms can be key to the others, opening them up for greater knowledge. So a lab rat might help us see something about the human physiology of immune systems. A bird might allow us to see a new aerodynamic possibility for airplanes. A hydraulic system on a machine might reveal something about human circulation. However, this information as key to the other two realms is usually reductive and manipulative—pulled out of context as a way to grasp the correlative dimensions of these beings for specific purposes of exploitation and domination.

To see beings as information flows can screen out any context in which ethical and moral questions might occur. A particular information flow creates the leitmotif of Haraway's book that interrogates the implosion of nature and culture, the political and the technical, under the reign of a globalized technoscience, where biopower is a high-stakes economic venture and is symbolized by the recurring image of OncoMouse™. This name stands for the transformation of an animal into a morally questionable product. OncoMouse™ is a new "model" of an animal that has been machined by humans for the purpose of being created and living out its existence as a breast cancer sufferer for human research needs and also as a profit-generating object by the corporation that produces it (MW, 79–83). Genetically engineered, patented by a biotechnical company, advertised, sold, and distributed, the mice, however many are produced, are significant in this global trade of technoscience as bearers of genetic, biological, and bioengineering information. Haraway provides advertisements and other texts in which it is clear that these animals have no other status than these information flows.

Humans also can be seen this way, reducible to certain information caches, say, as genetic texts that could be altered or copied for varied commercial, consumer, or political purposes. The lives of the creatures of the "model line" of OncoMouse™ are a testimony to the possible horror of the overlap of human, animal, and machine. Here is an animal that is viewed as an invention, a mechanism with a certain function, a true Frankenstein of manipulated, manufactured biology, patented as such for profit and distribution to the science industry, the purpose of whose existence has been defined utterly by human needs and desires, condemning myriad creatures to some sort of engineered, hellish existence of suffering, disease, experimentation, and foredoomed early death. There are already several popular culture films, such as *Island* or *Coma*, that foresee possibilities of human beings used as spare parts or now to be engineered as clones and kept for "harvesting" for organs when needed by their rich clients. However, the reduction of humans to parts of mechanisms or as usable data does not have to be so overtly grisly and can be quite subtle but powerful in the case of genetic information. In the biotechnical harvest of products, the mapping of the human genome and the further gathering of data about genetics might represent a more perfect achievement of Bacon's idea of knowledge as power: "Control of the genome is control of the game of life itself" (MW, 150). Since the genome can be seen as "an information structure that can exist in various media," there is a gain in efficiency, manipulability, and potential profitability to take the genome out of the person and store, retrieve, and work on it within the cyberspace of computers. Genomes can then be redesigned to help produce other models of organisms, potentially including humans.

There already have been efforts, such as those of the Human Genome Diversity Project, to collect gene samples from over 700 targeted groups of indigenous peoples on six continents by collecting hair-root, cheek-tissue, and white-blood-cell samples. The effort been contested by the so-called "subjects" of these studies, who objected to having their genetic information patented by others or having this powerful information potentially used in ways against these people. A particularly upsetting case of this "vampire project," as some called it, was the removal of blood from a twenty-six-year-old Guyami woman with leukemia, who carried a unique virus with antibodies that might be important in leukemia research. The woman was said to have given her blood with "informed consent," yet one cannot imagine that she was presented with all of the possible ramifications of what was being done to her and how her genetic information was being "biopirated." The U.S. Secretary of Commerce had applied for a patent for this biogenetic information until he was pressured into withdrawing the application in 1993 after a protest made by the Guyami General Congress after a third party informed them of the United States' actions (MW, 249–51). This is exactly the kind of "overlap" that might better be described as the "implosion" of boundaries about which Haraway means to warn her readers. Through very subtle means, technoscience can turn us into machines or animals into machines, or use humans as another sort of animal in studies or production planning with a kind of speed and dissemination of information that is difficult for one to assimilate into one's own sense of the world.

Notice that information as a key to manipulating others parts of the environment by grasping onto a key pattern of that being's makeup is akin to Heidegger's notion of "tool," in which he claims that each object as a tool is a reference to other parts of the environment providing us access to them. So we might say that in Haraway's more postmodern description of technoscience, she is showing unthought-of ways in which everything in our world, including our genetic makeup, or the genetically controlled metabolism of mice, can be made into a tool. Heidegger, too, was prescient in this regard to see the connection with technology as it was developing in the twentieth century. In a lecture to his hometown of Messkirch, he foresaw the day when technology might come to dominate the way we thought about everything—humans, nature, and all of the beings around us. He said that at that point everything, including humans, would be "on call" and would become part of a "stockpile" for energy needs and the consumption of raw materials. He even said that the world was in danger of becoming seen just as a "gasoline station"—in 1956![9] What is interesting in terms of this chapter is that this movement to make everything into information or energy or raw material for a globalized machine of scientific and postindustrial production is happening simultaneously with the machines becoming developed through information technology in ways that surpass their traditional roles as mere tools, making them cooperators with humans in new cognitive breakthroughs. Hence perhaps these two trajectories help explain the polarized reactions discussed briefly at the beginning of this text: the screeds of those who can only see evil in the machine's increasing sophistication and ubiquity and the manifestos of those who see this same development as our salvation and the opportunity to escape mere humanness and become an immortal machine.

Merleau-Ponty also saw far beyond his time to consider the boundaries of humans, animals, and machines in his lectures about the status of nature at the College de France in the late fifties, and he specifically saw both the danger and promise of considering these realms as "information." He saw the promise of the new field of cybernetics and information science, but he projected a dire possibility in which taking humans, animals, and machines as a circulating system of information, humans could embark on the program of constructing a seamless and self-replicating system in which information would not be lost in this circulation, nor contradicted. Quantities of information would be put into circulation and maintained as such. As an example, Merleau-Ponty pointed out how computers can "automatically indicate the law of a series of numbers by eliminating the anomalies" (N, 158). Merleau-Ponty's point is that we need to embrace both—the ordering and synthesizing possibilities of seeing beings as information, but also the ways in which any being also eludes this reduction as seen from other perspectives. To see the ways simultaneously that all beings have inexhaustible meanings, aspects that are anomalous to the flow of data that can be wrested from them, is to keep alive a mystery and depth of meaning we could endanger with what Haraway labels "informatics."

The way in which humans, animals, and machines can be a key to the others as information is powerful in grasping, manipulating, and understanding key functions and behaviors. Yet if limited to that, it makes humans, animals, and machine into a kind of mechanism comprised of equal parts of all three realms. Holding in mind the anomalies as we work out the transferable data allows us to see beyond a reductive implosion of boundaries that Haraway sees in the postmodern world of the twenty-first century. Mice can be grasped as biological and genetic mechanisms to be manipulated and probed for more data and thereby key tools in fighting cancer or other diseases. However, they also can be seen as part of an ecosystem and existing in another realm and way of being that has to be understood and respected for its own kind of meaning—not to mention that mice can be pets or gentle visitors to the house and garden or objects of myth and story, such as Stuart Little going down the river in his little canoe, and so on. The danger of appropriating the world and overlooking the integrity of other beings does increase in the implosion of boundaries of humans, animals, and machines.

In order to have real communication among realms, there has to be seen both overlap and boundary. For many previous centuries, we could only see great disparity between humans and animals and between humans and machines. Given that disparity in being, we felt justified in exploiting the other two realms as mere raw materials for human need, since they were mere "brutes" and "inanimate things" with which we could feel no connection or kinship. Now we see ways in which we are animals and machines, and how the boundaries among the three realms are overrun in many ways. We need a common ground to understand fully the other two realms, but we also need the distance that allows for recognition of difference. We are at this point in global history very uncertain about what it is that makes humans distinctive or animals or machines. If we can see the unique excellence that each can bring to our interconnectedness, then we might avoid the implosions of boundaries that are violating to these beings, whether of livestock taken as cogs in a food production machine and made to exist in suffering and disease, or of humans seen as livestock to be harvested for parts or seen as machines to be reengineered into efficient producers at the cost of the meaning of their experience, or of machines treated as one undifferentiated mass of mere matter with no gradations of aesthetic, moral, or meaningful dimensions. If we can recognize the differing excellence distinctive to humans, animals, and machines, and at the same time their interconnectedness, then we can create an enhancing encounter among all three.

Chapter Four

Drawing the Boundary of Humans with Animals and Machines

Greater Area and Depth

Can We Even Draw Boundary Lines?

If we are to draw boundaries among humans, animals, and machines, then we face the daunting task of trying to define each kind of being. The history of philosophy is replete with such definitions, especially of human being, and usually the formulation given is tied to some driving purpose in undertaking the meditation. Often it has been to justify a religious revelation that human being has been defined, so humans are seen as made in the image of the divine or in relationship to some activity of the divine, who in turn is defined in a certain way. So if the divine is the forgiver or redeemer of sins, then humans can be seen as the being who sins. Sometimes, human being is defined to fit a culture's specific political aspirations. Thus the Athenians saw themselves as the beings who had a certain linguistic capacity and a certain kind of community that fit their sense of the kind of political system they should preserve and hold up as the norm that others, "barbarians" were not capable of achieving. These "barbarians" were non-Greek speakers and considered not fully human. Often, in the modern world, human being has been articulated in its boundaries as part of a scientific project, so the definition is then focused on that aspect of human being that fits that project. In terms of the work of modern geneticists, humans may be defined as the bearers of DNA of certain parameters. This sort of definition is what led Jared Diamond, as quoted earlier, to reclassify humans as a third type of chimpanzee, since only 1.6 percent of human DNA differs from chimpanzee DNA, and "the remaining 98.4 percent of our DNA is just normal chimp DNA."

Of course, even to attempt to define human or any other sort of being is most apt currently to draw snorts from any academic reader, especially those in the disciplines of the humanities in America and Europe. In the postmodern world, we seem doomed to declare only what any being might look like in some ways given a certain "subject position" of the describer in relation to the described in the nexus of politics, power, economics, media, and so on. We seem often in the humanities to feel that no common ground is possible among perceivers from different ethnic, gendered, economically placed, ideologically indoctrinated variations of perspective, while we live in a world in which science and technology shape all of these conditions by assuming that despite the myriad possibilities for any phenomenon to appear in differing ways, we can delimit enough parameters for certain purposes to fight cancer, restore people's hearing, find new food sources, improve the capacities and speed of computers, design safer automobiles, discover new sources of energy, and identify other commonly given phenomena. I do not doubt either that when one of my theorist friends is diagnosed with cancer, he or she expects the physician to have some sort of answer to how to best fight the disease, and not an endless permutation of possible approaches. If the doctor were to say "cancer" is an unnamable phenomenon that serves differing purposes in differing ideologies, then my friend would be enraged at the doctor for not knowing the "essence" of cancer, despite the theoretical ban against knowing any essences. It is vital to be able to identify what we mean by ozone depletion in the atmosphere in terms that we can agree upon or what an animal is, even if there are many ideological overtones and possible manipulations surrounding any definition. We can investigate and deal with both.

It is embarrassing to me that philosophy as a whole does not take into account what is happening in the sciences—and I do not mean in the specialized area called "philosophy of science"—but in the larger sense that whatever philosophy articulates as a way of making sense of the world must somehow be resonant with our scientific and technological breakthroughs. So, for example, throughout this work I have proceeded without calling attention to it, that if I find Merleau-Ponty's philosophical analysis of embodiment and perception to be cogent philosophically, then I had better be able to use it to make sense of artificial intelligence or cochlear implants or other contemporary scientific findings. If computers can learn through "embodied intelligence," or ethologists find that animals do have linguistic capacities, then our philosophical perspective is challenged to make sense of these findings and to help provide a framework for further exploration.

I also admire how science tends to deal with older theories. It does not condemn them as "wrong," as if they were some sort of sin against thought, but finds a way their results can be incorporated into new perspectives. They had the truth of their state of development or particular task at hand. I feel the same way about philosophical theories. Other philosophers are not wrong. It is up to me if I find another perspective to find the way in which the other philosophy somehow still works to make me see certain things, but perhaps from another point of view and with another role to play. So, for example, I do not think that the philosopher whose ideas I criticize most doggedly is "wrong" but, rather, that Descartes described one possibility of human experience that he took as exhaustive. One can live in ways that Descartes described so that mind is opposed to body, or in ways that reason and emotion are at odds. Looking at Descartes's descriptions can be vital to understanding the experience of one who does process the world in that fashion as a result of the particular circumstances of one's personal history, culture, physiology, and so on. The philosopher's task is to provide a framework in which the understanding of the world from within the unity of mind and body can be described and augmented for its particular advantages. Similarly, the world can be reduced to mere extension and mathematical quantities, not to guarantee absolute truth, as Descartes hoped, but to get certain things done, such as having my car's ignition system set properly or the circuits in my computer repaired, yet this does not exhaust the ways in which the world can come to appear. If we want to better understand our human or animal neighbors in the wider context of their concerns, or the possible ways in which machines can add to the depth of the meaning of the world, then we will have to have ways of articulating how the rational, logical, and quantitative can work with the imaginative, emotional, memorial, gestural, and intuitive in a deeper sense of perceptually grounded understanding.

I will try throughout this book to show why a certain truth fits a particular investigative situation cogently, for that is what I expect a philosophy to be able to do: to find truths in a way equal and parallel to science, but like science, for them to be taken within certain specified parameters in regard to certain articulated problems. Philosophy has not always bothered to contextualize its insights. For the purposes of this book, it seems vital that we be able to find a way of defining humans insofar as they differ from animals and machines, but also in ways that take into account the challenging new parameters that an increasing understanding of animals and machines poses to us today. We need to see how by using their differences and their common ground, these realms can augment the capacities of the other two.

In this sense, I also am American in being a pragmatist in the manner of a William James or a Charles Pierce. Philosophically, this does not indicate that truth claims are measured in a utilitarian way as giving the most practically useful or pleasurable outcome to the most people, as pragmatism often has been loosely understood. Rather, pragmatism requires the outcome of an inquiry to be seen in light of what sort of meaning it opens in the world, what kinds of possibilities for the thriving of the whole its insights allow, and how relevant its consequences are to the very motivations that inspired the inquiry. If belief in a purely disembodied spiritual realm gives people a level of meaning to their lives unachievable in other ways, then there is no reason to reject it as a possible religious tenet, unless by assuming that this as true absolutely leads these believers to disallow the meaning of other dimensions of life equally meaningful for themselves or others. When I am about to die, or if I am being held in a prisoner of war camp and having my body mutilated every day, then a belief in disembodied spirit separate from embodiment might make sense, whereas the opposite philosophy may weaken my resolve, and I may certainly be quite grateful that many of my comrades have this resource at their disposal. What seems evident, however, is that to be human, and to use language for thought, means that truths can only be the result of a certain perspective and cannot be proven as absolutely true—even this assertion itself. The drawing of boundaries of humans, animals, and machines will be articulated in this light: whatever allows for more human thriving in terms of significant priorities for many people, whatever allows animals to also thrive and lead lives that seem to meet their needs and avoid suffering as best we can discern, and the ways in which machines can develop their potential and come to be most respected as part of a larger earth community in having a key role to play on this community's behalf, will be the motivating force behind this inquiry and its yardstick. Whether in the tradition of claiming insight into the absolute or in the equally long tradition of a skeptical refusal to allow definitions to be drawn because they are uncertain, there is a fidelity to certain commitments to oneself, others, and the global community that underlies these assertions, and it is on the basis of these commitments, as stated here for this inquiry, that we can proceed to draw boundaries.

Given this approach, I am not going to give the reader a detailed history of the definitions of human being that have occurred in Western or other philosophies or within related fields such as psychology or anthropology, but I will instead briefly comment on some of the traditional answers that still pervade the global culture in places that bear upon the current juxtapositions of humans, animals, and machines. Certainly the sense that the human's boundary from all other creatures is drawn by its being essentially an immaterial substance that is not really confined to space or time and is part of divine realm to which humanity seeks to return has been central to the Judeo-Christian tradition, as well as to the Platonic tradition, and to other religious and metaphysical systems. Even a modern revision, such as Hegel's articulation that humans need to work through history and materiality but are still destined to be the beings who realize the ultimate in the rational idea, does not really differ if we look at it in the context of our inquiry. Whether or not these answers might embody an ultimate, transcendent truth cannot be known as humans, but we can see that they are not descriptions of human being that help us see the concrete relationships among humans, animals, and machines. Given this frame of reference, the common ground among the three realms would be removed, and neither could each ultimately harm the other or augment the distinctive excellence of the others, if the essence of humans were on some other plane of reality. As a religious or spiritual belief, this line drawn around humanity might be vital to some or many, but it will not advance the ways we can work with animals and machines in the material details needed for mutual thriving.

"The Rational Animal" Using Tools, Speaking, and Passing the Turing Test

Two very related definitions of human beings that have had a great impact on the philosophical and even religious traditions of the West and other cultures draw a definitive boundary between machines and animals. Many thinkers, as well as many pervasive cultural traditions, have focused on the idea that the human is "the rational animal"—a definition often attributed to Aristotle. This boundary was taken for a long time to separate humans from animals, but it now has shifted in recent years to in many ways include animals on the "same side" as humans, but to still exclude machines. Animal studies came to question what was meant by "rational." If it meant the ability to reason and make strategic plans, or the ability to use tools, or the ability to navigate through the environment in a way that was directed toward a specific location, then we have already provided examples that undermined that distinction. Even if this means the ability to count, then the distinction is called into question by many examples of animals counting, but most colorfully by the Chinese cormorants raised by and working with fishermen, who reward them with every seventh fish before they have to dive again. If the fisherman miscounts and does not give up the seventh fish, then the cormorant will wait until the fisherman realizes his mistake and hands over the fish, and then the cormorant will dive (IAM, 85–86).

If it meant that to be rational was to be "the speaking animal" that was closer to what Aristotle really said about humans, then it also turns out that other animals may be included with humans. If the boundary is about the ability to use a language to communicate, then the work of animal scientists succeeding in communicating with animals, such as Irene Pepperberg, with her African grey parrot, Alex, or Francine Patterson with the ape, Koko, made these boundaries less clear, as well as the many examples of sophisticated animal communication that may be outside of language per se, such as the "waggle dance" of the bees, indicating where a food source is located, or prairie dog warnings of different types of predators. However, these examples may not eradicate this boundary insofar as the operation of human language uses the "metalanguage" of speaking about language itself or includes speaking about absent or imagined or virtual objects. Some would say that these sorts of language uses would have to be found among the types of animal communication in order to expand the linguistic boundary to include not only humans but also animals.

Yet even these aspects of this definition excluding animals can be argued by those studying animals in two ways. First, there is new evidence that animals, such as the European starling, can recognize patterning rules of a language syntax and distinguish them from other patterning rules, something thought to be only within a human's purview. Led by Timothy Gentner, assistant professor of psychology at the University of California, San Diego, a study published in the April 27, 2006, issue of *Nature* demonstrates that starlings have the capacity to classify acoustic sequences defined by recursive, center-embedded grammars. This sort of syntax is one in which words and clauses are inserted within the middle of the flow of the communicated message of the sentence versus those sentences that contain the sequence of components of a message with the others tacked on before or after. Using a set of differing "warble" and "rattles" vocalized by the starlings in communicating, it was demonstrated that they could recognize both sorts of patterns as being different as well as those that were "ungrammatical."[1] We could discuss this in greater detail, but it might not matter given the other objection to this sort of manner of deciding whether animals "have" language: we are not looking for language or communication in exactly the human-centered paradigm, as if other types of communication and language could not be comparable and as vital to animal being within the particular context of each animal's existence. This is the issue we discussed in the closing section of chapter 2, in which animal differences in what makes sense or is tolerable should be understood from within animals' own way of being in order to give us a true comparison among humans, animals, and machines, rather than insisting that they "be like us." If we are to learn from animals and machines, then we have to appreciate their own manner of being within their contexts. Here this means that their ways of "languaging" or communicating within their worlds are achievements of their own distinctive excellence.

Also, this is a moment where taking the approach of looking at *all three realms together* may offer us new insights. Even if the boundary of humans with animals is blurred regarding capacities for "reason" and even more so for "language," it may help to introduce the other term of our comparison, machines, and look at the issues engendered by this traditional boundary of being human taken to consist in reason and language. In the comparison of a human's thinking and/or intelligence with machines, especially with computers and other "artificially intelligent" machines, there has been a half-century history of intense debate about whether computers could ever think or be intelligent. In not wanting to rehearse this too-often-told history, only a few positions will be brought into our discussion as still being key reference markers. Any discussion of machine intelligence refers to the original essay, by A. M. Turing in the journal *Mind* in 1950, "Computing Machinery and Intelligence," which has shaped so much of the speculation about these questions. At the beginning of the essay, Turing declared that it was "absurd" to try to define either what a "machine" is or what "thinking" is or what "intelligence" is. Instead, he proposed a scenario that became referred to as the "Turing test," and it has since been either used or disputed by almost any philosopher, scientist, or inquirer of any sort into the question of whether computers can think. To summarize the upshot of Turing's essay, if we were to be connected to something—either computer or human, not knowing which—by a teletype without any perceptual access to our interlocutor and could ask as many questions as we liked, and it seemed to us that we really could not tell if we had been conversing with a human being or with a machine, then we could not ask a machine to demonstrate anything else beyond this capacity in order for it to be considered intelligent and thinking.

Now, decades later, there are Web sites that might pass the Turing test, and even in 1963, when Joseph Weizenbaum wrote ELIZA, the program intended to seem like a psychiatrist, some people—to his great dismay—started to dream of the day when such programs could replace humans in doing some sorts of therapy. Currently, Web site designers have had to scramble to find a way to tell the difference between "bots"—fully automated computer programs impersonating humans—and actual visitors to Web sites. The answer discovered by Henry Baird was to protect entrance to the Web site by requiring users to distinguish words that are displayed visually on the Web site with their letters distorted (e.g., twisted) and placed within an enmeshed visual field (with conflicting lines or figures), relying upon the embodied visual powers of humans engaged in a linguistic and cultural context to pick out words—even nonsensical ones—in such a setting.[2] Being creatures who intend to see letters, our perceiving bodies gear into the situation in such a way that we ignore those visual aspects that are not essential to the appearance of a "password." So the Turing test has become a practical necessity in the struggle with spammers and others in the electronic world of cyberspace, where human identity is already tenuous and can easily be manipulated and simulated by programs. Much debate has occurred whether passing the Turing test does mean that thinking has occurred, that there is no other essential aspect to thinking as a human mind or intelligence other than producing a certain sort of conversation that is engaging and stimulating, or that the Turing test might succeed just because interlocutors are becoming insensitive to true thought. For the purposes of our inquiry, the answer to this question is irrelevant for two reasons, which will now be discussed.

Thinking "Substance" and How It Feels to Meet a Thinker with a Face

First, unlike Turing, it is the assumption of the approach of this book that thinking, that being a human, and that being a machine can be articulated and not assumed to be some sort of unanalyzable given, of which we know when we are in its presence, but has no core characteristics that can be described. This articulation may have to use poetic phrases, stories, descriptions of context, and other linguistic devices that are not quantifiable characteristics or categorical in a rational taxonomy, but language can be evocative and render key themes and depths of meaning, if used creatively. Part of the reason for taking this other path is that the insistence on settling for only a "functional definition"—if it produces the same effect as one, it is one—seems a despairing resignation that we cannot, on principle, get to some core meaning of being human and being machine—even if the meanings have some ambiguities. However, this faith in the possible description of the core being of humans, animals, and machines does share with Turing a principle of perceptible evidence versus other claims about the "essence" of humanity. What is valuable in Turing's stance is that his test was formulated in part to avoid having to debate with those who said there was some ineffable "self" or "soul" or "light" within human presence that could not be described in any other way than by pointing at it—that it escaped material manifestation and observation. Instead, Turing assumed we could experience the difference, but only, unfortunately, functionally. My optimism is greater—that we can experience and point to concrete, perceptually grounded aspects of the core being of humans, animals, machines, and even thinking. They can be described in a way that others can identify, even if they cannot quantify them.

On the other side of Turing's openness to the possibility of machines being called thinking or intelligent has been the decades-long opposition of Hubert Dreyfus, since the publication in 1972 of *What Computers Can't Do*, and reasserted in 1992 in the newer edition, *What Computers Still Can't Do*. Dreyfus made objections that computers would never be able to do certain things with their formal and disembodied use of rules of reason that hurt his credibility since they have proven to be false, such as claiming he could not be beaten at chess by a computer and was in 1967, that a really good player could not be beaten and was, and finally that a world champion could not be beaten by a computer, and then Gary Kasparov was in 1997 (right around the year that several computer scientists had earlier predicted that this would happen). Some of Dreyfus's concerns are ones we have raised and will have to be addressed, but one possible mistake in his approach was to articulate how if computers were to play chess, the way they would think through their problems would be different than humans, and therefore doomed to defeat. He declared that they would never have the same incisive ability to solve certain problems that the human approach does through judgments not tied to exhaustively "trying out" moves and evaluating the results. Yet, the human way turned out to not be the only way to solve this problem.

In the comparison between these two positions, Turing's approach in a way had the advantage in that it kept open what might be differing ways that still could be considered thinking, if comparable results were achieved. Unfortunately, Turing avoided really looking at what thinking is about, or what machines or humans are. However, the openness to different ways of arriving at comparable results might allow us to see how different ways of being might be comparable. Then there is an opportunity to make sense of differing cultures, cognitive abilities, or perspectives among people. Even differing humans may think through some issues through radically divergent ways: some mythically, some quantitatively, some deductively, some intuitively, some poetically, and some in a cultural perspective where gorillas are the height of evolution or some from the perspective of varying information processing such as Temple Grandin and others whose cognitive manner we call "autistic," and yet we can find common ground among them. By considering other ways of having a world and understanding it as "differently abled," rather than "dis-abled," we open ourselves to see multiple ways of making sense and existing, opening other depths of sense. There is a need for a balance of being concerned with comparable results with an openness and appreciation for the differing ways of getting to those results. If there is some striking similarity in results, then we can possibly compare the varying means as making sense within varying contexts without invalidating them. We might have to recognize that computers' "thought" might always have some differences from human thought, just as animal "understanding" has differences of style, purpose, and abilities yet also has important parallels to embodied human "understanding" that might revise and enrich our sense of possibilities for both humans and machines.

This consideration of the context leads to the second reason for the irrelevance of the answer as to whether a machine passes the Turing test and thereby erases the boundary between humans defined as "the thinking being" and machines. Turing assumed that the key to intelligence was some sort of functioning that could be isolated from all other human functions and aspects of its being and was detectable by an observer not distracted by any other aspects of human presence, interaction, or expression. In other words, in the long tradition since Descartes's idea of "thinking substance," Turing was speaking as if thought was objectifiable, localizable, and separable from other human capacities. He also used Descartes's method of inquiring about something as being best achieved by isolating it from all other factors, if possible. Yet just to start to address this set of assumptions, we have to keep in mind that our analysis so far indicates that the human mind is not something separable from embodiment's other modes of apprehension, and that the human body is not something even separable from its surround, and that human being is a flow or process whose characteristics are part of that unfolding with others humans, animals, and parts of the surround. What if there is something about human thinking that is unique, but *only because it is not separable from other aspects of human being that will transform its character*, such as being an embodied being that understands the world kinesthetically, that is a being of imaginary worlds, that is an emotional being, and that might be able to develop its thinking only when enmeshed with other capabilities? What if "thinking" is an evolving activity that happens in and through other human beings? What if thinking happens in an evolving process with various parts of the surround in addition to other human beings? To assume that thinking is an isolable activity short-circuits drawing out these possibilities.

The image of the Turing test of someone typing a dialogue to someplace behind a screen was first formulated when this was a far-fetched scenario, yet now it is enacted countless times a day on the planet by myriad people all over the globe typing on keyboards or speaking to the voice-recognition programs of computers to Web sites, instant e-mail sites, to postings, and chat rooms hosted anywhere on the Web. As a widespread phenomenon and part of daily life, there is a doubled-edged reaction to these encounters that parallels the Turing test. First, there is a growing pervasive skepticism that has infiltrated these ongoing daily contacts in cyberspace of millions of people about the identity of anyone contacted in this mediated fashion. Are they male or female or transgendered, from the Northern Hemisphere or a remote island, sane or scrambled, criminal or friendly, a corporation or really a long-lost relative, let alone machine or human? So Turing's question is real, part of daily life. Yet what may be more relevant after Deep Blue's triumph over chess champion Kasparov engendered less respect for computers as artificially intelligent logic machines is the reaction of both experts and nonexperts to robotic intelligences who know the robots are "mere" machines and yet cannot help feeling and acting as if they were in the presence of other persons. If we expand this to automated interactions with the Web, then many may have come to seek these interactions, whether machine or human, as the fare of their daily intercourse with the world.

In Brooks's and Foerst's books, there are many anecdotes of computer scientists and other experts who know the exact mechanics of how the artificially intelligent robots Cog or Kismet follow the steps of visitors to the M.I.T. lab with their gazes, make facial expressions, or burble with a certain emotional tonality in reaction to the analysis of the prosody of the visitor's voice pattern in certain recognizable emotional categories, or seek to look into the face of a visitor when under the sway of its "loneliness drive," and yet the visitors or scientists cannot stop themselves from responding to these gestures *as if* communing with another being. This is more to the point as a clue to what human intelligence is about and what makes thinking *matter* to a human as the attribute of an encounterable being. What we see here is the "lived understanding" of thinking, not its abstract formulation. The responsiveness of the robot driven by fifteen or more constituent computers acting in combinations strikes observers with the uncanniness of intelligence in a way that more resembles human intelligence than does Deep Blue's defeat of the chess world champion, because it has the appearance of the "face" or "gesture" or "engagement" of thinking as we experience it with others. Deep Blue achieved the opposite effect, making us wonder if a power of ours that we took to be creative and bringing honor to humanity was not more of a mechanical process, because the kind of "thinking" it achieved was in some sense so incomplete as to almost be a parody.

Kismet's and Cog's responsiveness, as crude as it still is at this stage of development, either mimics or starts to achieve an intelligence that permeates gestures, the gestures of some sort of embodiment, and strikes a chord in us, a flicker of recognition. The movement of the head taking in our movement by visual input is not just a random action but a sort of "dance" with our own movements and body that strikes us as being with a "partner" on a prereflective level. Even the strange gestures of Kismet or Cog, who do have facial features, limbs and hands, and so on, make us disbelieve what we know intellectually, and start to feel as if they must be real presences, aware and somehow intelligent. Their gestures evoke in us resonances, since it is the case that as part of the flow among other people or creatures, our gestures are woven into matching movements and feelings with others. Thinking, embodiment, feeling, gesturing, moving, and other aspects of who we are as humans weave together in more complex and more holistic identities to which we have not paid much attention. We need the sense of the whole to have the sense of the parts, since they emerge from the whole—thinking from gesturing, feeling, remembering, imagining, and so on, or any of these from the whole weave. Artificial intelligence as "embodied intelligence" in robots is different than "intelligence" as evidenced by Deep Blue, since as Foerst says, "The power of robots lies in their physical appearance." Having even awkward bodies, gestures, and actions creates a bonding through the material interacting in a physical space (GM, 8–9), which is a lived, existential space. Thinking "without a face" may not be thinking as we perceive or understand human thinking.

The phrase "having a face" points in two directions. First, to have a face is to invite a response from another face. As the protagonist in Kobo Abé's novel, *The Face of Another*, discovers when he loses his face in a lab accident, "without a face you'll be consigned to oblivion."[3] The problem with the original approach to creating artificial intelligence in creating a bodiless, faceless, logical, computing force was like Turing's intelligence behind a screen: it would be utterly absented from the regard of humans. It was the Turing test scenario brought to life and found to be somehow beside the point, trivial. Rather, to be intelligent in any sense comparable to human intelligence is to manifest a quality that is *engaging* to other humans. Turing made the Turing test purely cognitive—whether the person assessing could figure out whether the agent was machine or human from the seeming intelligence of its responses. Whether the person involved in the test was engaged or impressed or provoked by the responses was not relevant. Yet in the presence of human intelligence we do have some of these responses and others. Is this accidental, and does it have anything to do with what demarcates human intelligence? Is utterly abstracted intelligence human thinking?

Foerst's *God in the Machine* builds on the drama of the description with which she begins her book—the meeting of Harvey Cox, a professor at the Harvard Divinity School, and Cog, the humanoid robot of the M.I.T. AI Lab. She describes Cox as someone "who had devoted his entire life to bringing Christian theology into a dialogue among people with different worldviews, and he didn't want to stop at a robot." She then relates that when Cox saw Cog's eyes following him around the room, he made eye contact and "tentatively extended his hand, and Cog, after some trial and effort, grasped it." The crowd of scientists and Harvard theologians gasped at witnessing this (GM, 1–2). For Cox, and for others who were witnesses, a gesture of welcome and an encounter carried out in the heft of bodies, whether of human flesh and bone or metallic parts, echoed in their embodied understanding of what they experienced in some other way, not yet definable. This being "touched" in some way that has no clear thought to encapsulate its sense is in contrast to Kasparov's scornful reaction to being defeated by Deep Blue, when he takes delight in the fact that Deep Blue could not enjoy winning and would take no satisfaction from the victory. Kasparov felt no sense of awe.

At the M.I.T. lab, people could not refrain from feeling some sense of encounter and even concern for the robots, seeing them reach toward them, seeing them move around the room, seeing their features, gestures, and differing tones of voice. With Deep Blue, in the face of an astounding feat, playing chess at the highest level, there was indifference to the computer, Deep Blue, although admiration for the computer scientists. The answer lies in the other direction of the face. We are drawn into faces and respond to them, because they are turned toward the world and ourselves. The face indicates the regard of the being directed toward things, creatures, and events in the world around it. In seeing embodied robots with multiple computers find ways to walk around the room, reach for an extended hand and grasp it, and respond to a depressed tone of voice in a soothing tone cannot help but evoke in us a response, because the kind of cognition that is part of these actions and responses is one that appears to seek to make connections with the world. It follows a trajectory of movement toward others probing the surround that buzzes with all sorts of living beings seeking out others for varied purposes. Deep Blue is turned into itself and is palpably cut off from the world, presenting a wall of sorts in its facade. It does process input from the chessboard, but only the bare minimum of the world's information enters into its processors that it needs to go through myriad permutations within its own algorithms and calculations. Not only does it not have a literal face, or even like Kismet's, with its seventeen different kinds of identifiable expressions, ranging from "anger" to "happy/perky" to "tired/depressed," but its seeming intelligence is all "internal processing" and not a give-and-take with the environment. It is questionable whether an intelligence disengaged from its world would be called human intelligence, or certainly, even if some of us might reach this level of withdrawal and isolation—it would be just that, a diminution of what we take to be standard human intelligence, a deviation of some sort, maybe caused by trauma or something else. Simulated catatonia will never yield human artificial intelligence.

Human Thought Extended by Machines

Another way to look at human thought is that in its most rational, most logical dimension, it needs help—to extend itself and to develop. Descartes said that when we arrive at clear and distinct thought, we humans have achieved our distinctive excellence as reasoners. He takes it as self-evident that this achievement is the pinnacle of human self-sufficiency. However, to achieve this excellence truly may entail going beyond the isolated "I" of Descartes's "I think." This might mean that instead of Deep Blue's victory over the world champion of chess erasing the boundary of humans as the thinking being, it was only feeding the illusion of helping humans move farther in the direction they had always taken as somehow being beyond the rest of the world through feats of abstracted reason. The more computers of various sorts have achieved proficiency in calculation, mapping, predicting, taking in the environment, information storing and retrieving, and so on, they seem to have allowed us to strengthen our sense of being humanly intelligent far in advance of anything else on the planet. We see them as our tools and as an extension of the genius of human being. We have not paused yet to consider in what ways they might outstrip us in these more narrow senses of intelligence.

Given the nature of human thinking, it is not surprising we have not rethought whether we are the highest example of logical and abstract reasoning on the planet. If we were to consider the history of human thinking then we might see that there never has been an isolated human thinker, and our excellence may have never been just "our doing." It is true that instead of losing our identity as the sole true thinkers on the planet, by externalizing these capabilities into silicone-based constructions within the surround, we have only deepened our abilities, as part machine, part animal, that make us human, and we have not lost the part that was distinctive, even the thinking part. Perhaps our minds could never have achieved that sort of logical, calculative, categorical type of intelligence except as a cooperative enterprise with machines in the world, from beads to count with, to the invention of language and numerical systems, to paper and writing instruments, books, and so on. Maybe this human type of intelligence was always cyborglike and is just deepening. Rather than taking the fact that computers are now better at doing symbolic algebra than are human scientists and mathematicians, better at laying out circuits for fabrication, better at scheduling complex events and exchanges (FM, 169–70), and so on, as a defeat for us, this may just better shift the focus on what was always most distinct about our thinking and intelligence—that we cannot do it well, at least for ourselves, but only with and through the world!

So perhaps computers have given us a chance to see ourselves better—not as "pure" thinkers but as part of a cooperative enterprise. Descartes seems wrong in declaring, "I think, therefore I am." What fits our experience is the idea that we continually deepen who we are as thinkers through other entities. Abandoning Descartes's logic is to give up the logic of individualism and isolated minds. If Descartes had been a better phenomenologist, then he would have said, "We think, or we think with all sorts of things and through all sorts of things, so therefore we exist, and we exist as spread out amongst all these things, especially as intelligent or thinking beings." This would be far from the material world being utterly opposed to mind and thought. Matter is the very way that thinking happens. Mind and matter are not opposed substances but differing moments of an integrated process that can be abstracted from a deeper, moving flow of realization of sense.

Jettisoning the awkward dualism of mind and matter is occurring with many fields, such as in the work of how Andy Clark defines human intelligence in his working with new technologies, "for what is special about human brains and what best explains the distinctive features of human intelligence is precisely their ability to enter into deep and complex relationships with non-biological constructs, props and aids" (NBC, 5). As Clark articulates this, the human brain dovetails with all sorts of technologies in the surround, and these become similar to our neural components as additional resources of the biologically given brain. Instead of being a thinking substance to which I have private access, Clark sees humans as "reasoning and thinking systems distributed across brain, body and world" (NBC, 33). This is also exactly what Merleau-Ponty meant by describing the "flesh of the world" and the way that we are "reversible" with it—that it "extends" us and expresses itself through us. When Merleau-Ponty says we can see only because we are visible, he means to say that there is a larger dimension of visibility that works itself out in what we call matter and mind, which are really part of a larger weave or interplay or field. Vision, touch, thought, and feeling come to be through the material world as having a sense that is more than matter, but inseparable from it.

Technologists can design new technologies by realizing that this interplay has always been at work in the human coming to a greater awareness by working with the world around them. Clark contrasts the newer, "more responsive" technologies with "the old technologies of pen and paper" and suggests what I also have alluded to—instead of thinking of language as somehow an emanation of our spirit or reason, it is a material reality that we created as a tool or even as a machine in certain ways—with complex rules of operation—that has extended the reach of our thinking. The letters on this page, the paper on which they are printed, or the book in front of the reader is not "spirit" but a material reality made to display sense. As Clark continues speaking of these "aids and props" to thought, "such tools are best conceived as parts of the computational apparatus that constitutes our minds" (NBC, 5–6). Clark makes the case that language as speech, and then especially as text, was an invention with which "humankind entered the first phase of its cyborg existence" (NBC, 81). In other words, as explained by Clark, having certain words and certain constructions within language does not just record or communicate our thoughts to a receiver but instead is a process that, as it unfolds, allows us to think new thoughts and in new ways, forming part of "the apparatus of the mind."

Even though Clark uses the word "tool" for language, I think his claim is correct that when humans turned to language they became "cyborgs." The human ability to "think" became something else as it flows through and is shaped by, extended, and made more complex by language. In this sense, language was never a mere tool but has always been more like the modern machines we have described by taking our original intention and adding to it and modifying it. Language, at least at its most creative and powerful, takes a vague intention, a stumbling forward in a certain unknown direction, gives it shape and direction, and "fills in" the intention. So the definition of humans as speaking creatures may actually be seen more precisely to indicate that humans are the animals who think things through in extending the range, scope, and structure of their thought by using machines—first language itself, then books, calculators, geometries, computers, and other extensions into the environment that feed back into their thinking.

We said that thinking has to have a face or, in other words, to address the world around it to be human thinking. Now we also see that human thinking may only happen at its higher levels, as humans have developed and evolved with and through their surround. In this manner, thinking is only following the pathway of human perceiving, which *happens through* all that surrounds it (being part of its "flesh") or, rather, as humans being part of the "world's flesh." We see from our own vantage point, but simultaneously *through* the vantage point of the bird above, the tree beside the house and the person at the end of the street. This movement from "out of the head" and into the world regarding human thinking should cause us to reconsider thinking as something that occurs independently of other ways the human takes in the surround. Chief among these ways, other than the perceptual level that we have already discussed, is the emotional level. This is fascinating in regard to our particular question of what humans are, especially in relation to animals and machines, given the various twists and turns that the status of the emotions has taken in relation to the boundaries among humans, animals, and machines.

Originally for Plato and Aristotle, and then reinforced by the scientific revolution and Enlightenment, humans were seen as distinctive in that they were *not* defined by their emotions—humans transcended the emotional pushes and pulls upon them, unlike the "lesser brutes." In current cultural interpretations, we are beginning to see the fact that animals are driven in ways similar to our passions or "basic emotions," where these are taken as those "that have been found universally throughout human cultures, such as sadness, anger, fear, surprise or joy."[4] Analogous emotions are a ground for seeing the fruitful overlap of humans and animals. Yet for the rationalist like Descartes, this possible identification led him to label the emotions as forces within us that were driven by "animal spirits," as if they were alien forces to overcome. The rationalist dismissal of emotion was more complicated, however, since these emotional forces were seen as *"animalistic" because* they acted so *mechanically*. In meditations upon the human and animal boundary, it often is recognized that animals do think in several ways, such as using language, creating tools, counting, planning strategies, and so on, but in the end, it often is concluded that humans still think in ways more powerfully abstract than animals, and so are unique. Part of this ability to abstract is to remove insights from their emotional matrix. Emotions were somehow infected with the brutishness of animals. Paradoxically, it was the grinding determinism and heartlessness of machines that were central to machines being seen as inferior to the human rational transcendence of this realm.

It is therefore startling that in recent decades, the emotional life of humans has been elevated to a status of what is unique about humanity than can never be achieved by a machine. In many recent meditations upon the human and machine boundary, it is reluctantly admitted that artificially intelligent robots are encroaching upon emotions, however, "It is all very well for a robot to simulate having emotions. And it is easy to accept that the people building robots have included *models* of emotions. And it seems that some of today's robots and toys *appear* to have emotions. However, I think most people would say that our robots do not really have emotions" (FM, 158). Given the contemporary uneasiness that information processing machines might usurp our status as unique beings, suddenly emotion has taken on the role as the defining and distinctive aspect of humanity that is humanity's secure possession. As Rodney Brooks of the M.I.T. AI Lab puts this popular sentiment, "We may have been beaten out by machines in pure calculating and reason, but we still have our emotions. This is what makes us special. Machines do not have them, and we alone do. Emotions are our current last bastion of specialness" (FM, 171). Unlike machines, humans are said to truly feel, to care, and to be able to be passionate—the very attributes it was their duty to resist and supersede by power of the will guided by reason, first championed by Plato, and taken up by Descartes and others of the Age of Reason as humanity's distinct destiny and excellence.

However, if what we have said in this chapter is true, then machines have not yet beaten humans in terms of achieving human thinking, and we may not have to prove that humans are different from them by turning to emotion. Yet in a sense we do, since the way we have redefined human thinking is not as abstracted logical deduction. Part of what makes human thinking distinctive cannot be understood without considering its inseparability from emotions. We have said already that it is in human thinking being directed toward the world and in proceeding through the aspects of the surround, including the elaborate "architecture" of machines, that it is different—that it is the product of no one agent but a myriad of cooperating sources. Humans are unique, not in their power of abstract calculation but in bringing together differing registers. Yet another aspect of this same description is to see the way in which unique human thinking not only follows the paths of perception but also the movements of emotion. To follow out this path of thought may demonstrate in greater depth what human thinking is like but also may begin to reveal how human feeling or emotion also is distinctive, despite its numerous similarities to many animals' experiences. Again, it might be that looking at humans, animals, and machines at once instead of in pairs gives us a somewhat different and telling perspective.

Humans Locate and Direct Themselves in Mood, Emotion, Feeling, and Thought

There is a potential coming together of phenomenological philosophy and brain science that has only been made possible through advances in technology in the past few decades—another example of machines deepening thinking and making possible the connection of ideas. In Heidegger's *Being and Time*, discussed previously, we saw how Heidegger defined human being as inseparable from its context—what he called "being-in-the-world" (*Innerweltsein*). This sense of "world" or context was made up of tools that bespoke our immediate—but not deliberately conscious—sense of how all of the things around us are related to one another in terms of the meanings they have for what we care about and how we have implicitly projected the paths of our daily projects. In this 1927 work, Heidegger stated that two of the main ways we "take in" the world as context is through "mood" (*Stimmung*) and "state-of-mind" (*Befindlichkeit*). Only recently have these insights been corroborated by brain science.

Mood, as articulated by Heidegger, is an emotional sense of the world that is not specifically focused on any particular object. It is a felt sense that is diffuse, that reaches out to the surround as a whole. If we are creatures who can only exist by feeling located within a surround, then we are given a sense of being "here" in the place we dwell through an immediate sense—the mood we are in—of how it stands with this, our particular world, as a totality. As I have tried to show in my book *Emotion and Embodiment*, all affective experiences have what I call an "e-motional sense"—that is, we are "moved" this way and that, not in literal physical space but in our sense of direction and connection of the "belonging" within a surround. The prefix "e," in *e*motion, designates a "movement" out of ourselves as contained beings and into the world. All emotions register *how* we come back to ourselves from this sense of the embedding context viscerally registered. However, the sense of a mood (without yet being put into words) tells us about our relationship with "the general lay of the land" of the surround. We feel loved or threatened or abandoned or serene as a "background" feel to what is going on at the moment.

In trying to conceive of mood, we could think of it as the widest circles in which we are moved through our world and then back to ourselves as it is felt by our bodies. So in a lighthearted mood, there is a felt glow emanating from all things and everywhere, a buoyancy that wells up from ordinary things, fills the air itself, and is exhaled by the gestures of others, and that suddenly delights us. We are caught in a circular groundswell of a smiling burbling coming from all corners. In depression, however, the mood is heavy, somber, and too dense, leading to obscure and perilous depths, with a jagged, hurtful aspect that presses against us. As Heidegger described moods:

> A mood assails us. It comes neither from "outside" nor "inside," but arises out of being-in-the-world, as a way of such Being. . . . The mood has already disclosed in every case, Being-toward-the world as a whole, and makes it possible to be directed towards something. (BT, 176)

For Heidegger, a mood is not about either the subject or object but the interrelation of everything within the context of one's world, and the mood's "feeling tone" is the palpable registration of how it stands for that person in the midst of this nexus. The way we are "in" a world is not just physically located somewhere but how we are directed toward that situation in terms of how it feels at that moment, "mood-wise."

Mood itself relies on an even deeper sense of how we are related to the context of our lives at any point in our history. Heidegger calls this "state-of-mind" (*Befindlichkeit*) and has the sense in the German of the state of how it is that one has found oneself. For example, I find myself in a situation of despair or desperation as I wake up to my country torn by war with needless death and destruction occurring every day, or, in a happier alternative, I find myself in a contented state of mind with my family, my job, and the place I live and of which I am part of a community. Another way to say it would be that we are all "attuned" to our surround in ways that reflect "how it goes with us" in our lives of myriad relationships to people, things, events, and so on. It is only on this basis of having a "place," a "here" where we are, that is immediately felt washing through our body that we can then think about our lives and what we encounter. There is this emotional "taking in" in a very implicit way of moods within the more general "states of mind," as when I am in a happy mood today within the more general context of despair or anxiety about the war around us. Heidegger says, "The fact that this sort of thing can 'matter' is grounded in one's state-of-mind; and as state of mind it has already disclosed the world—as something which can be threatened, for instance. Only something which is in a state-of-mind of fearing can discover what is environmentally... threatening." There is a resonance of our embodiment with the surround that makes our categorical thinking possible. In my fear I see the oncoming car and then realize intellectually the identity of the threat to me. For Heidegger, this emotional "understanding" of the world is "the primary discovery of the world" (BT, 176). It is on the basis of finding ourselves faced with a surround that has presented itself to us through a state of mind and mood manifest to us at all that we can explore it further or think about it categorically.

However, it is Merleau-Ponty who is the phenomenological philosopher who focused on embodiment and perception as comprising our ongoing sense of ourselves and the world and followed through on describing how we apprehend the world through the body in such a way that "my body is the fabric into which all objects are woven" (PP, 235). We are connected to everything in the surround to which we are related through embodiment. Perception itself is a richer, layered experience before we explicitly focus on aspects of what is present to us. As such, Merleau-Ponty sees the body as not in space like an object but as *being space itself* insofar as "... the body is essentially an expressive space" (PP, 146). The body is a give-and-take with a flow of energy and connection with the surround that uncovers meaning in the surround. Merleau-Ponty declares that space is alive with "directions of significance" that are emotional pulses running through space so that "it rises and falls with the existential tide running through it, or again it is the pulse or my existence, its systole and diastole" (PP, 285). The distance between us and things on this embodied level cannot be measured and captured by the literal physical distance on a grid but rather is the distance of emotional connection: "Besides the physical and geometrical distance which stands between myself and all things, a 'lived distance' binds me to the things. This distance measures the scope of my life at every moment" (PP, 286). In the second chapter we focused on how we perceive only within a surround, but this idea has to be elaborated further with the sense that this scope of things to which we are "connected" and initially "directed" within the surround occurs through the emotional attractions, repulsions, and other ways we are "moved."

Merleau-Ponty gives an example based upon his own experience to demonstrate that although we are usually "located" emotionally in the same space that we are physically, this is not necessarily the case—that emotion first binds us and directs us to place. Rather than our sense of location being built up from bits and pieces of "objective reality"—that is, what we distinguish from a distance by placing it within a category, making assertions, following logic—our primary or initial sense of space is more similar to what we find in myths or dreams: "In dreaming, as in myth, we learn where the phenomenon is to be found, by feeling that towards which our desire goes out, what our heart dreads, on what our life depends. Even in waking life things are no different" (PP, 285). Objects as they are first lived by our bodies are not neutral objects but things that draw our desire, or repel us in fear, or lure us in curiosity. Merleau-Ponty elaborates on his conception of "lived space" with the story previously mentioned about how he has settled into life in a small village in the French countryside. He is feeling happy and relieved to be on vacation, to have left behind his work, and to be outside of his usual surroundings. He becomes absorbed in the context of village life. For these weeks "it becomes the center of my life," he tells us. During this time, the longtime Parisian is now interested in the "low level of the river" and in "the maize crop or nutting," as if these are the big events of his life. He has been absorbed into the "existential space" of the small village and its affective rhythms (PP, 285).

However, this interlude is during the Second World War. Despite the web of these feelings, Merleau-Ponty realizes that "if a friend comes to me bringing news from Paris, or if the press and the radio tell me that war threatens, I feel an exile in the village, shut off from real life, pushed far away from everything." If there were to be this sudden emotional upsurge of fear or concern for those he loves, then Merleau-Ponty knows he will be "really" within the surround of Paris for those moments, no matter where he is physically located. As he sums up, "Our body and our perception always summon us to take as the center of the world that environment with which they present us. But this environment is not necessarily that of our own life. I can 'be somewhere else' while staying here, and if I am kept far away from what I love, I feel out of touch with life." So as much as Merleau-Ponty based his analysis of human understanding on perception, it is equally true that at the heart of perception, before it becomes explicit, as part of the "depth" of perception, there is a give-and-take with the surround that places us first in what Merleau-Ponty called an "existential space." So our sense of directedness, of being located, of above and below, is first anchored in this sense of space run through by emotional vectors. In this sense of space, "directions and positions within it are determined by the residence in it of great affective entities" (PP, 285). To offer an example outside of the European culture's sense of the objectivity of space, Merleau-Ponty alludes to the spatial sense of indigenous cultures that have not yet learned to rely upon maps and the division of land into grids. He observes that their "knowing the whereabouts of the tribal encampment does not consist in locating it in relation to some object serving as a landmark—it is to tend towards it as towards the natural abode of a certain peace or a certain joyfulness" (PP, 285). For Merleau-Ponty, this is the most primary sense of space.

The relationship between this immediate felt sense of the space of the body and the reflectively registered space of objectivity is interdependence. As he admits, this felt sense of things and emplacement "has a non-thematic or implicit meaning," but "this is not a lesser meaning" (PP, 289). Given this primary sense of the surround, "objective thought itself draws on the non-reflective consciousness and presents itself as an explicit expression of non-reflective consciousness." In other words, rather than saying our initial experience is clear and distinct and gives us the building blocks of existence and understanding, Merleau-Ponty shows how the initial sense of things is more akin to the child (studied extensively by him), to our immediate experience and feelings, and to the mythical sense of things. Myth, childhood, immediacy, and other cultures often have been dismissed by Western philosophy and science, but Merleau-Ponty sees them as describing a deeper level of grounding in the world. Yet this is not the complete picture. He also was clear that the emotional was structured by the rational and logical, as much it gave them their deeper sense: "If we think about the mythical experience of space, and if we ask what it means, we shall necessarily find that it rests on the consciousness of a single objective space, for a space not objective and unique would not be a space." We might tend toward home drawn by a feeling of comfort, security, or belonging, but these feelings are still anchored in that objectively describable space where the wooded structure stands beneath the trees by the river and could be mapped by a cartographer. The texture of emotional direction and connection is grounded, has a substantiality that is nurtured by also being an objectively knowable place, object, person, or event. Merleau-Ponty goes on to develop this idea that an experience may be the founding level, and yet it too is constantly restructured by what it founds. There is a constant interplay and inseparability. So, in this case, emotions may turn us toward a person, place, or object in friendship, or in excitement, or in appreciation of beauty, but these feelings are modified by the encounter with the objective dimension of these objects of our feelings, which in turn might make us feel somewhat differently, and then subsequently see differing objective aspects of them, and so on.

Actually, unlike so much of our philosophical tradition that chooses the objective over the subjective and then rebels and chooses the subjective over the objective, or the same with reason versus emotion, Merleau-Ponty, in describing experience carefully, finds that it is the tension between the two, the fact that both are inseparable and yet different, that gives us meaning and reality. This undecideability is not a defect of being human but rather that which gives human experience depth, which Merleau-Ponty defines as "being simultaneously present in experiences which are nevertheless mutually exclusive" (PP, 264). The two perspectives might seem to portray different realities, but reality is precisely that tension of their going together in a deeper sense of the world. Merleau-Ponty gives a wonderful example of a bouquet of flowers given by a character, a young man, in a Balzac novel to a woman with whom he is love. It is obvious that the bouquet is an expression of love, yet objectively considered it is only a number of flowers gathered together in a bundle. Yet Merleau-Ponty says "Love *is* in the flowers" (PP, 321). In analyzing what makes them so, Merleau-Ponty points to cultural and historical contexts, but also to the quality of the color of flowers and the rhythm of the shapes, the soft texture, and so forth. The objective takes on meaning within the cultural or subjective context, which in turn is transformed by the objective nature of the flowers' characteristics.

What gives us the sense of love from the flowers will never be decided, because any such meaning is perceptually grounded, culturally signified, and it has to do with personal history and echoes in the natural world. As a matter of fact, as his discussion continues, it becomes evident that "psychological definitions" cannot be separated from "the very organization of its sensible aspects," and that any attribute only gains its meaning in relation to the attributes of anything else. Correlatively, the human apprehension of this nexus is one that draws upon all human faculties in concert—perception, emotional apprehension, imagination, intellection, memory, kinesthesis, proprioception, and so on. This leaves us with a field of relationships among both the varied aspects of the world and within the human's abilities to make various kinds of sense, and then between these two. Drawing a boundary for human being might turn out to be quite a fractal drawing of myriad branches and vectors it seems. What is also fascinating is to see how contemporary brain science is adding credence to Merleau-Ponty's philosophy.

"We Feel" and the Emotional Valence

We have spoken, however, as if there is a human subject—a perceiver or thinker. If we are embodied beings who first through perception and its emotional depths are connected to and oriented within a surround that becomes an extension of our body, then the dimension we have not articulated yet is that this emotional sense is a *shared* sense with others with whom we are emotionally interwoven. At the conclusion of his essay, "The Child's Relations with Others," Merleau-Ponty states:

> Recent studies have shown that even external perception of sense qualities and space—at first glance the most disinterested,

> least affective of all the functions—is profoundly modified by the personality and by the interpersonal relationships in which the child lives. (CR, 99–100)

In the essay, Merleau-Ponty examines how the child's relationship with his or her parents affects the cognitive abilities of the child. These effects remain into adulthood. He examines examples of children raised by coercive, punitive parents. This situation throws the child into a dilemma. It is almost impossible in the face of this sort of abuse to admit to oneself as a dependent child the agonized feeling the parents' aggression makes one feel. In this case, Merleau-Ponty states that the child often separates the parents into the "good parent" and the "bad parent," and then clings to the image of the good parent in a kind of emotional ambivalence. The bad parent is denied. This way of dealing with the pain of such parenting becomes a way of perceiving the world: "Unaware of this double attitude, refusing even to recognize in himself the image of the 'bad parents,' the rigid child tends to project outside of himself the part of himself that he does not want to be." Merleau-Ponty, in the wake of World War II, offers as an example of this sort of emotional coloring of thought in the case of anti-Semitism: "The anti-Semite throws off onto the Jew the part of himself that he does not want to be" (CR, 103). So the standing one has emotionally with those to whom one is related, especially, of course, the initial relationship with parents, tends to shape the way one is able to think about the world.

This kind of either/or thinking that stems from emotional ambivalences from the kind of abusive relationships parents inflict upon children Merleau-Ponty calls "psychological rigidity." This cannot be contained in one area of one's life, since one's *way* of perceiving this paradigmatic situation becomes exactly that: one's "way" or particular "manner" or particular "style," as Merleau-Ponty phrased it, decades before the word "style" became so widely and now superficially used. Given that we each have this distinctive rhythm of taking in experience, an analogous experience of the world follows: "The more emotionally ambivalent the subject, the less it suits him that there would be any ambiguity in things and his view of things. Emotional ambivalence is what demands the denial of intellectual ambiguity." To be able to embrace an intellectual ambiguity is to be able to see how things, people, and events are comprised by contradictory qualities and yet come together in a richer meaning. Psychological ambivalence cannot tolerate letting go of the "either/or" way of seeing, first the parents and now the world. The implication of Merleau-Ponty's studies is clear: how we are emotionally enmeshed with others in the world is a key part of the basis for how we think about the world. Yet how we feel is not separate from the kind of interpersonal experiences we have shared, initially with parents and then with others. In *Emotion and Embodiment*, I call these lingering emotional bases for thinking and our modes of apprehension, our "emotional valence."[5] The sense of this metaphor is that like the past interactions of molecules that leave them in another state, which gives them only certain possibilities for new combinations, so too our past history of interrelation marks out our possibilities for future relations and the "taking in" of the surround in apprehension. This valence has such power because an apt substitution for Descartes's "I think, therefore, I am" might well be: "We feel—together—in emotional relationship, and therefore, we think—on the basis of relationship." Human cognition is not only open-ended in that it is extended through the surround's perspectives, but our bodies literally echo the bodies of others with whom we are in a relationship. The feeling way of making sense of the world dawns for us through the shared sense of others who are our caregivers and follows the same rhythms we have established with them.

As Merleau-Ponty describes the dawning sense of the world through the sense of enmeshment with others in "The Child's Relations with Others," he says that at the first stages the child enters into a "pre-communication in which there is not one individual over against another but rather an anonymous collectivity, an undifferentiated group life" (CR, 119). Humans begin without a sense of "I" or separateness. In detail, Merleau-Ponty describes the developmental stages of early infancy, but all of them are marked by a "syncretic sociability" in which the infant and young child emerge only gradually from a sense of the body as neither his or her own or someone else's but rather "the experience of my own body and the body of the other form a totality" (CR, 120). Insofar as we have a sense of our body in relation to the world, a "postural schema," it emerges at first as it is "impregnated" by others. So the baby echoes the smile of the parent smiling down upon it in the crib. At that instant, it is the baby's "own" smile in a way, but more accurately we might say that it is "the smile," since there is no boundary sense of self distinct from the parent yet. In a similar way, as mentioned previously, Merleau-Ponty describes the "transitivism" of the infant under six months of age with a group of similar-age infants, who all cry when one hurts her or his hand, since it is "the hand" that hurts, which is in some sense all of their hands. There is not yet a visual notion of where one's body ends, and there are no boundaries set up with other bodies.

Without going into great detail about these stages, Merleau-Ponty shows how up until age three, there is some sort of unbounded, shared life of the child, both emotionally and in the sense of the body. What is especially important for us is that this sense of our relationship to others becomes profoundly modified but remains as a dimension of who we are as humans; secondly, it has ramifications for the supposed rational basis of cognition and language as represented traditionally within philosophy. So the Cartesian thinker, even Descartes himself, has been a child who has experienced a certain sort of emotional history with others, and as Merleau-Ponty aptly phrases our condition, "Childhood is never radically liquidated" (CR, 138). If there is a troubled history with a parent that has led to a denial of certain aspects of this relationship, then this will be likely to form the way we see the world as adults. The sense of transitivism with others does not vanish, even if superseded by more elaborate and rational models of connection with others, but remains a deeper current in the flow of energies that is our embodiment. The sense of indivision, of being touched when the other is touched, for example, can reemerge palpably at times, as when the feeling of love draws upon this still-surviving potential. Yet other intervening experiences may have altered the possibilities for some to experience this sort of relationship with others.

In the phenomenological perspective of Merleau-Ponty's philosophy, the logical functions, the more rational grasp of the world that had been seen as primary by Descartes and those of the rationalist bent in Western philosophy, are revised to acknowledge that these human abilities are always built upon an emotional understanding, and that both proceeded to develop through each other. Instead of subjectivity, there is only intersubjectivity—making sense of the world in and through others and within a history of human relationships. Merleau-Ponty concludes, "In sum, the intellectual elaboration of our experience of the world is constantly supported by the affective elaboration of our inter-human relations" (CR, 112). This way of understanding human cognition also alters views of language. We have already disputed the notion that language is an emanation of our rational and disembodied intellect, but in addition, as a material reality that is embedded in the surround, it also develops within this milieu of affective human relationship. Merleau-Ponty states: "The use of certain linguistic tools is mastered in the play of forces that constitute the subject's relations to his human surroundings. The linguistic usage achieved by the child depends strictly on the 'position'... that is taken in the play of forces in his family and his human environment" (CR, 113). Humans as the "speaking beings," as they often have been defined, as well as humans defined as the "rational animal," are actually beings who are emotional and who are caught up in affective ties and frictions with others that alter the ways rationality and language take shape and function. Merleau-Ponty will develop at length this silent underside of language, which is partially the emotional communion with the world and others. It can never be fully captured by explicit speech but underlies and surrounds it with an atmosphere of significance that emerges more powerfully in poetic language, and when one lets oneself be released by the words beyond themselves to the larger surround in which they echo.

What is startling and rewarding is how much in the past decades brain science, psychology, and even physics as applied to both have corroborated these insights that may have been seen as irrational and irrelevant by science in its more mathematically and logically reductive phases after the scientific revolution and the Enlightenment. By looking at these scientific elaborations parallel to phenomenological insights, it can further help us see that defining human being as either the "rational" or "thinking animal" or as the "speaking being" leads us into a nexus of other distinctive powers in which none of them remains as straightforwardly defined—so that turning to "emotion" as the distinctive feature of humans also lands us in an interwoven fabric that may have to be better described in order to give a more complex, interesting answer to how humans differ from animals and machines. The other traditionally obvious answer to humanity's distinctiveness—the being who emanates from a source of selfhood and has an "interior life" that is inviolable and utterly unique—is tied up in the same nexus and also stands in need of reconsideration and further clarification.

Neural and Material Plasticity and Open Systems

Humans have been considered by science at the beginning of its modern era to be at the center of the world with a boundary encircling us cast by the light of our innate abilities to reflect upon ourselves and the rest of universe and arrive at reasoned clarity and certainty. In the thrall of Enlightenment rationalism, empiricism, and the Galilean declaration that the "book of nature" was really just a "book of numbers" to be read by human beings, the dream of many was to organize reality around them and perhaps one day re-engineer the earth to increase efficiency, increase productivity (of humans, nature, and machines), and create a stable order. In the reductive materialist vision that accompanied these ideas, humans and the rest of the universe often were seen by scientists as if all phenomena were determined by linear chains of cause and effect and were nothing more than changes of measurable physical states. Love, friendship, divinity, beauty, awe, terror, and other phenomena of meaning and value were seen to indicate nothing "real" other than being the by-products of exchanges of particles and electrochemical events.

Currently, brain scientists, computer scientists, geneticists, and technologists—whose members might be thought to be the most strident reductive materialists—are often at the forefront of a dynamic and holistic revisioning of the world where brain and mind, matter and spirit, emotion and reason, and culture and nature can be seen unfolding together in dynamic interaction. Until recently, insisting that the mind can only be understood through the brain has often been used by reductive materialists in their arguments for determinism, for a sheer physicalism, for deriding ideas such as humans' ability to be free to choose (or at least shape) the meanings of their lives or the ability to change (or at least reshape) themselves in their character or ways of behaving. These human abilities were denied as illusory in face with the assertion that the brain is at the heart of all these phenomena and is the unalterable site of "hardwiring."

However, brain scientists currently see that the dichotomies of freedom versus determinism or "nature versus nurture" are oversimplified extreme positions that obscure the more nuanced sense of human freedom and responsibility or, as Daniel Siegel puts in his *The Developing Mind: How Relationships and the Brain Interact to Shape Who We Are*, "The reduction of human behavior into an 'either/or' condition of 'genetics versus learning' or 'nature versus nurture' is unhelpful and clouds our thinking about the issues" (DM, 244). Those dichotomies leave both the mind and brain as merely part of a vast system of material cause and effect interactions according to traditional science or are something drastically different from the world around us according to those who defended the separate realm of spirit. Rather, brain science now sees "at its most basic level, the brain can be considered as a living system that is open and dynamic." This means that "an open system is one that is in continual emergence with the changing environment and changing state of its own activity" (DM, 16–17). Again, this matches the kind of insight into human understanding and human being as articulated through the phenomenological approach in philosophy taken by Heidegger, Merleau-Ponty, and others as "an ongoing becoming" through continual interplay with others, the surround, and ongoing activities.

Implied in both of these perspectives of open, dynamic systems or "becoming" is a different sense of materiality—one that is not reductive but is, rather, connective. The brain is material, but that does not doom it to be part of some closed linear mechanism. Materiality is not made of inert and isolated particles nor is it antithetical to "meaning." Meaning is embedded within materiality. Rather, the brain as material means it is part of an open system with all sorts of inputs and influences with which, as part of the body, it sets up a dialogue with the world around it: "The brain's development is an 'experience dependent' process, in which experience activates certain pathways in the brain, strengthening existing connections and creating new ones. Lack of experience can lead to cell death in a process called 'pruning' " (DM, 13). What one has felt or thought in an experience is retained and opens an altered future, and it does so by causing the material basis for the system to go in another direction of development. Instead of the traditional notions of materiality being opposed to meaning or spirit, at some point soon we need to understand that the materiality of the brain enables it to carry on a history, some of it genetic, and some of it about past interactions, leaving their tracings in the neurons and systemic interrelations. This means it is a "living history," one that is dynamic. Like writing in a text, the fact that the brain and its neural system are material means that there can be a past inscribed, and yet further written and revised.[6]

It is interesting that the same word now used to indicate this aspect of the materiality of neural systems and the brain, "plasticity," had been used by artists and those who speak of the aesthetics of art objects to indicate how matter is not inert and utterly enclosed but gives the material medium of each of the arts a way to "hold" meanings in order to "show them forth" to others. The *plasticity* of paint or sound or stone as spoken of by artists and aestheticians means that these varied media can be shaped in order to embody and convey the identity of an aspect of reality in its various stages of transformation. So the way paint was manipulated by Edvard Munch in his painting "The Scream" holds that instant of overwhelming anxiety and dread in the arrangement of the pigments on the canvas for anyone to recognize. In this same manner, looking at the art's core principles in *The Birth of Tragedy*, Nietzsche used the term *plasticity* to speak of how the artist shaped seemingly ineffable ideas into something that could contain them and allow them to be seen and felt by others in an approachable way. Sound allows itself to be shaped by the composer and so holds forth for others a sadness in the low, slow tones, minor keys, or dissonant rhythms, or it preserves a meaning of some even less definable, but identifiable, sense whenever we hear the piece. Similarly, a painting's blending of colors in a line of a certain rhythm juxtaposed to the rest of the composition is the "shaping" of the materiality of the paint, its plasticity, to allow us to see something—perhaps its dynamic majesty—that we otherwise might never see about a "starry night," for example, in viewing Van Gogh's canvas of that name. Like our commonsense view of machines being based on older notions of grinding mechanical gears, so our commonsense view of matter as opposed to meaning, as antithetical to spirit and expression, needs emendation.

Similarly, brain scientists, philosophers, psychologists, and other thinkers approaching complex systems no longer think of cause and effect in linear chains with incremental alterations. Many still think of science as dealing with changes that are incremental, strictly proportionate to their antecedents, and predictable, at least ideally. In order to understand how science can now comprehend sudden, disproportionate change, and unpredictable transformation, it is important to understand how the notion of feedback has displaced ideas of linear causality insofar as science has begun to look at the world in terms of "open systems." In an open system, an entity functions and unfolds only within the interrelated functioning and unfolding of its environment. Furthermore, whatever one might have been tempted from within a traditional atomistic perspective to designate as a discrete entity can be seen within the open system to be an interrelation of its constituents. The environment is itself an interrelation of varied constituents, including the entity in question.

I use the word "interrelated" to designate the case in which the current state of the relationship between these two entities is *fed back* into the identity of the other, each is transformed by it. This is in contrast to the old mechanistic view of parts affecting each other through a series of impacts whose identity is separable from their relatedness. A cog is a cog or a spring is a spring, no matter what other part of the machine it is connected to at the moment. However, as scientists focused both upon more complex phenomena, such as the weather, and on living systems, they discovered that there were so many high-energy flows occurring that they were "self-organizing": their processes became interwoven in order to maintain their identity through using the energies and patterns of the total environment to facilitate their own unfolding. From within the old mechanical metaphor with its atomistic assumptions, this sounds anthropomorphic, yet myriad phenomena demonstrate an openness to the whole as well as this self-organizing characteristic.

Before continuing, let us stop for a moment to consider the other term used earlier in introducing the notion of open systems: "feedback." Feedback phenomena designate the way in which different entities are in a relationship so that the action of the one is factored back into the action of the other. In a "negative" feedback loop, the action of one entity is triggered by the other, which in turn regulates the action that triggered it: so, for example, the rise in the temperature measured by the thermostat of my heater is what causes the heater to momentarily stop, regulating the very activity that caused the thermostat's thermometer to rise. Each works as a function of the other. In a "positive" feedback loop, the entity in relationship to the activity of the first entity augments that original activity, is "fed back into" it in such a way that there is a self-amplification created: thus when a public address system produces an ear-splitting screech, the output from the amplifier has been picked up by the microphone, fed back into the amplifier, and emitted from the speakers as a chaotic burst of sound, where each stage of output has become input for new output. These self-regulating and self-amplifying cycles among parts of a system exist as a tension between continuity and change, or as often referred to when such ideas were first becoming more widespread, "order" and "chaos."[7] When represented mathematically, we could say that feedback gives rise to iterations, to terms becoming repeatedly multiplied by themselves. This aspect of self-ordering allows for both sudden change or turbulence, but also for how within a process, a certain rhythm can be maintained.

Again, when most people think of factors that are multiplied by themselves, they tend to think of this in a linear way, as a value growing in predictable and regular patterns, so that it can even be graphically represented in a progressive, orderly fashion. However, for the complexly interwoven phenomena scientists have turned to exploring, nonlinear equations have proven to be better representations of the interaction of factors involved. In nonlinear equations a small change in one variable can have a catastrophic impact on other variables, correlations that were relatively constant can suddenly demonstrate wildly different behaviors, values that were close together can soar apart, and solutions to nonlinear equations are not generalizable to other nonlinear equations (TM, 24). Unlike the smooth curves made by plotting linear equations, nonlinear plots show breaks, loops, recursions, and various forms of turbulence. The power of iteration—the feedback that involves the continual reabsorption or enfolding of what has come before—mathematically represented also creates a sensitivity to initial conditions that seem to get lost in the process of unfolding but then can suddenly reappear again. Even in its mathematical representation, self-amplifying open systems demonstrate an alternation, a tension, of continuity and wide change, or of order and chaos (TM, 86–87).

Given that we can now see materiality as having this duality of both providing a substance, a substrate, to hold or carry forward with continuity, and yet also a site for shaping or transcribing new information or meaning, the brain's materiality is not an impediment to growth and change of meaning in relation to the surround of other beings. The brain may be considered an open system reacting to changes in the surround with dynamic relationships to other brains/minds and with its own activity. The sense of reductive mechanism resulting from the exploration of the brain's material basis for mind is gone. Seeing the plastic dimension of materiality reconfigures our sense of how mind and body—mind and matter—are a unitary phenomenon. A powerful example is provided by Dr. Jeffrey M. Schwartz, who works with obsessive-compulsive patients trying to help them into other brain-firing patterns. For Schwartz, the neuroplasticity of the brain is key to helping the client's way of being-in-the-world change: "*Neuroplasticity* refers to the ability of neurons to forge new connections, to blaze new paths through the cortex, even to assume new roles. In shorthand, neuroplasticity means the rewiring of the brain."[8] Given the inherited structure and the patterns of the functioning of the brain, which are themselves the result of past experiences, there are certain possibilities for what the brain can apprehend in the surround. Yet this is not determined or invariant, hence the power of psychotherapy, for example. The brain is not the seat of "hardwiring," but of possible change.

This newer vision of the brain and its neural network as an ongoing, continually emergent process enmeshed in a flow of energy and meaning with the world and others around it also has removed the idea that the essence of human being, either as a species or a personal being, is its genetic makeup—invoked as the determinate and material ground so that we are the mere products of our DNA. The genes "encode the information for how neurons are to grow, make connections with each other, and die back as the brain attains differentiation of its circuitry," but "these processes are genetically pre-programmed *and* experience dependent" (DM, 18). As Siegel articulates at length, the kind of bond formed with the parents, given their emotional availability to the child, or the child's experiences with other people or with a frightening dog or in living in a war zone, will alter the kind of neural connections in the brain, how different centers in the brain form a pattern of functioning together, and therefore how the brain emotionally transcribes the world and is able to think, feel, express, and apprehend in a host of ways. Both genes and brains emerge through experience: "Experience determines when genes express themselves via the process of protein synthesis. For the brain, this means that experience directly influences how neurons will connect to one another, creating new synaptic connections, altering their strengths, and allowing others to die away" (DM, 18). So the kind of relationship that one has with a parent and the kind of relationships that one then goes on to have with others and the sorts of experiences that occur within the surround change the physical and physiological makeup of the brain, since it is a continually dynamic process of making new connections and unmaking others.

Brains as Process, Emotions as Integrating, and Selves both Inside and Out

If we are to understand that matter and meaning are inseparable and not opposed, then it stands to reason that any sense of the world we apprehend is expressed materially, which is not to say that it is merely reducible to this. From the perspective of looking at the brain as the material manifestation of how we understand the world, "Our experience of reality is constructed by activity patterns of neuronal groups within the brain." The firing of differing groups of neurons with differing firing patterns gives us another sense of the world or ourselves: "At a very basic level, the patterns of firing serve as symbols or codes that carry information and cause events to happen in the brain. These events are themselves patterns of neuronal activation, which in turn carry further information. . . . In other words the brain creates symbols whose actions are themselves symbolic—they carry information" (DM, 162). If we look at the different meanings, whether perceptual, motoric, conceptual, or emotional, as information, then the firing patterns of the neurons are ways of encoding the information within a certain energy flow of the brain, as are the various "modules" of information processing within the brain. When the neurons fire at different rates or in different patterns, different information is presented by the mind (DM, 24). The brain's structures shape experience, but experience as encoded information gained through one's history shapes the brain's structures. It is a feedback loop, self-regulating and self-rewriting.

The use of various scans has allowed the pinpointing of localization of functioning within the brain. So, for example, we have various kinds of implicit memories—not specific recollections but emotional echoes of the past evoked by a certain object, event, or person, which is the function of the amygdala and limbic regions; behavioral memories so that my body "remembers" how to do something such as ride a bike or teach a class, which is the function of the basal ganglia and the motoric cortex; and also perceptual memories, such as knowing my way home from the beach or who is walking down the street, which is the function of the frontal cortices. The more explicit sense of recollecting, "traveling through time virtually," also is the function of the frontal cortices. Part of the taking in of the emotional sense of something or someone is from the action of the amygdala and is linked to the memory system by the hippocampus (DM, 29–49). Of course, this just skims the surface of the brain's functions. The complex functioning of these and other modules of information processing in the brain comes together as a system that is always dynamic in its interrelatedness. Even memory, for example, is not something that "stays" in a static brain, nor is it like our popular image: "There is no 'storage closet' in the brain in which something is placed and then taken out when needed" (DM, 25). Rather, memory is "encoded" through chemical alterations that make it more probable that a certain neuronal firing pattern will be repeated. In an ongoing firing that is the life of the organism, firing patterns can loop back again. Memory is not a thing, but an enactment or a repeated activity.

The way that unity emerges for this active set of processes known as "the brain" is that a "state of mind" emerges as a point of equilibrium in this open system. A state of mind can be seen to be "the total pattern of activation in the brain at a particular moment in time" (DM, 208). There is a certain profile of neuronal firing patterns to which the system returns as again feeding back into itself as well as regulating itself through the taking in of the surround to form a cohesive state of activity among processes. What is now postulated is that "emotion recruits distributed clusters of neuronal groups in the emerging states of mind that organize the systems of the brain." By "recruitment" it is meant that the particular energy flow and information presented by emotion as a firing pattern bind the activity of distributed mental circuits at a given moment and across time. So emotion turns out to be the integrative factor not only on the level of phenomenological description of how the person somehow is "connected" and "oriented" within the surround and with others, but it is also the factor within the brain's system that connects and directs: "What coordinates such a clustering process? We can propose here that part of the answer is emotion" (DM, 209). It turns out that the very phenomena that Descartes thought had to be resisted by rationality and the will in order to avoid chaos, confusion, and error, the emotions, instead are ways the brain comes to be integrated and to have the order upon which the more rational functions can be built.

If we try to reduce human thought to its most mechanical, then instead we find that on the level of constituent material parts, the synchronization and the directedness of these seeming parts are actually the outcome of the work of emotions defined as "at its most basic level, this view sees emotions as the flow of energy, or states of arousal and activation, through the brain and other parts of the body. The process emerges from and directly affects the further processing of information within the mind by the appraisal of meaning." Emotion is a flow of energy that brings together the embodied information about the world, from our perceptual interweaving with the surround, and brings into it all of the other forms of processing of which humans are capable. Seen in this perspective, emotion in its primary sense is the bringing to attention of the body that there is something to be appraised as emerging meaning. Emotion motivates, focuses, and directs, as well as integrates the different contributing processes to meaning making. This primary process then leads to what are called the "categorical emotions," such as sadness or joy or fear or anger, which already are a layering of this initial appraisal with more formal and discursive kinds of meanings. So I may be struck by alarm by the percept at the corner of my visual field, that little corpse in the grass, that turns out to be as I integrate my perceptual, conceptual, memorial, and so on experience of the now-emerging focus of my attention, the dead body of my neighbor's cat, which I recognize in a wave of sadness and concern that deepens and refines my initial emotional start.

Brain science finds that we are embodied beings, immersed in the surround in the way we are "moved" emotionally and called upon to focus our attention. The meaning and energy that form the flows of neural life are neither purely matter nor spirit—but the way each becomes the other. Resonant with the phenomenological perspective used throughout this book, it means that we cannot draw a boundary around the human being as a thinking substance, for there is no thinking substance in the sense of thought removed from emotion or perception or imagination (as we will soon discuss) and imposing its order upon it. Rather, thought emerges from embodied experience and emotional relationships and then becomes inseparable from it, as both deepen meaning through their juxtaposition. If we are first "emplaced" by being connected and directed by emotion, then it is not surprising that it has this integrative role in the brain's processes: "The regulation of emotion directs the flow of energy through the changing states of activation of the brain" (DM, 209). If emotion is the flow of energy and the initial appraisal of meaning through pathways described by Susan Calkins as varied as "neuroregulatory structures (such as neuroendocrine, autonomic, and frontal lobe systems), behavioral traits (such as attentiveness, adaptability, reactivity, soothability, and sociability), and cognitive components (including social referencing, beliefs and expectations, awareness of need for regulation, and ability to apply strategies)," as well as responsiveness to others and the surround in "interactive caregiving patterns," then it coordinates the modules of brain function dispersed throughout (DM, 156). In doing this, however, emotion, as I have phrased it in *Emotion and Embodiment*, "moves out" and circulates throughout the surround and through our embodiment to bring us to a stand within our situation. Emotion is a circulation within and without that integrates the sense of things and our relations with them.

For our current inquiry, this means not only that we cannot draw the traditional boundary around human being as the "rational" being, as the genetically determined being, as the "hardwired thinking" being, but also our current clinging to the idea that we are unique as the being who has certain emotions also is compromised. This seems to be turning from one abstraction, "reason," which was traditionally supposed to make humans unique, to another abstraction, "emotion," which now makes humans unique. Both attributions distort reason and emotion by making them into separable things. Looked at phenomenologically, emotions such as love or anger or joy cannot be separated from the structure of reflection that we have built up during a human lifetime. These events only happen within a context of a much longer temporal span. For example, my thoughts about the importance of human communication, my knowledge about the histories of this loved one or those friends, what they have done, and what I have identified as their values and actions are not separable from the sense of warm affection or love or joy I feel in seeing their smiles or eyes. The emotion is part of a web of ideals, memories, commitments, imaginings, concepts, past feelings, and so on. Similarly, for another example, the knowledge I have of the cruelties perpetrated on civilians, the rapes of women, the killing of innocent children, and the refusal to compromise with those they hate, cannot be separated from the sadness or anger or helplessness felt when face-to-face with the combatants of this war. The rage some might feel when they see a terrorist interviewed cannot be separated from images in the memory of wreckage of hotels that have been bombed across the globe, trains blown apart, or the Twin Towers collapsing, and also the stories read about the suffering of surviving families, ideas about social responsibility, doctrines concerning protection of those not involved in political conflicts, and so on. Yet others might feel pity or empathy or admiration for the sight of this same terrorist, given their previous thoughts of starving children in refugee camps, recollections of ones they loved killed by bombing runs by other countries, doctrines they have read or thought about calling for armed resistance, and so on. Of course, taken out of temporal context, there are moments of pure emotion, or there are states in which we can find ourselves where access to the reflectively built-up context of thought, memory, and knowledge is broken down, but this is not paradigmatic of how human emotional experience, for the most part. Emotions and even more fleeting feelings are not atoms of pure experience but occur within a richer context.

What has now been corroborated is that brain and body have common neural pathways in which the most visceral aspects of emotion and the more reflective aspects of emotional background work together: "These emotional activations pervade all mental functions and literally create meaning in life. In this way, we can say emotion and meaning are created in the same processes" (DM, 158). How the cognitively oriented aspects of the brain system work with the emotive aspects is called "interwoven" by Siegel in reviewing the neurobiological research, which is the same term used by Merleau-Ponty in describing how experientially the emotional sense of space, time, the "faces" of cities or buildings, and other people, is inseparable from objectively discernable aspects: "The central features of emotion—are interwoven with the representational processes of 'thinking'" (DM, 159). We should note how different this perspective is from the Cartesian one, in which thinking substance is utterly distinct from embodiment and material substance, and the clear and distinct ideas of cogitation are utterly different from the confused pushes and pulls of emotion. As a result, Descartes spent a lifetime wondering how mind and body and reason and emotion could ever meet. In his view of the body, he had to postulate that somehow the thinking of the brain met the emotional system of "animal spirits' in the blood through the mediation of the pineal gland, but he could never start to explain how this could be the case, given two utterly different kinds of phenomena of matter and mind. In the emerging perspective of brain science, Siegel concludes that the lesson of neural networks and brain science shows us that "creating artificial or didactic boundaries between thought and emotion obscures the experiential and neurobiological reality of their inseparable nature."

Against the idea of Cartesian substance, the famous "I" of the "I" think, that we are one as indissoluble, as having an indivisible core, brain science has only found diverse information processing modules of differing sorts that leads to the conclusion that "... the idea of a unitary, continuous 'self' is actually an illusion our minds attempt to create." Looking at the diversity of input, one would have to conclude, "We have multiple and 'varied' selves" (DM, 229). These clusters of processes called forth by differing situations are referred to as "self-states" by neurobiologists. This too echoes Merleau-Ponty's idea that "each sensation ... is a birth and a death (PP, 216); each is its own lifetime in some sense. Yet there is also the opposing sense that, as Merleau-Ponty expresses it, our entire lifetime is just one extended moment of perception in the sense that "I still am that first perception, the continuation of that same life inaugurated by it" (PP, 407). We are one self as a continued process and we also are many selves. Both make up our experience, and both make up the way our brains work. Alan Sroufe has said that the "self emerges from an 'organized care matrix' " (DM, 229–30) in which human continuity emerges in the give-and-take with other people, creatures, and the things of the surround—again an echo of the phenomenological sense that the self is in an ongoing dialogue with all around it, and that dialogue gives us our felt continuity. It is the network of relationships and how we enter and process them from which we draw an identity.

So again, as everywhere else, a paradox about humans is evident: our strong internal sense that we are a self comes also from that which is "outside" of us but comes to be "within" us, as ultimately not a firm boundary, as Descartes and other philosophers have thought, but as Merleau-Ponty put it, a "reversible" one—the "inside pivoting around the outside, the outside around the inside (VI, 264). Into this weaving of self, emotion provides a fabric: "Emotion, as a series of integrating processes in the mind, links all layers of functioning" (DM, 275). For the brain scientist, emotion can "serve this integrative role by way of its neuromodulatory systems that are themselves widely distributed and have direct effects on neural excitability and activation, neural plasticity and the growth of synaptic connections, and the coordination of a range of processes in the brain." In other words, these widely divergent processes are linked by chemical changes and biological branching brought about through emotion's energy and flow. For the phenomenologist, emotion is that moving out into the world that brings into felt bodily registration meanings that encompass a depth, because the focus of emotions brings together worldly differences. I may think that my country is reprehensible in some of its actions, but I also may think that it is wonderful in its stated principles in its constitution, feel proud of some of its achievements, feel ashamed of other parts of its history, imagine a greater possibility of harmony among its citizens, fear that it may do this group of people wrong or destroy this natural wonder, appreciate how it has preserved and honored so much other natural beauty, and so on, and all of these seeming contradictions come together in a depth of feeling of loyalty and belonging that is multilayered and complex. Emotions are those rich registrations of sense that gain depth and meaning from the tensions of the different significances they bring together.

So we are left with a notion of human being as the being that thinks only through feelings that incorporate energies moving from the surround and throughout the body interwoven with the shared sense of things with other brains. Furthermore, although many of these brains are human, we have already seen that some of them are brains of animals and possibly also extended through machinery of varied kinds. Rather than a univocal voice that speaks to humans from the depth of experience, there are echoes of kindred experiencers forming a stream of dynamic meanings, always capable of change and involving divergent identities that nevertheless have a deep continuity.

Chapter Five

Drawing the Boundary of Humans with Animals and Machines

Reconsidering Knowing and Reality

Juxtapositions, Brain Hemispheres, Brains as
Observer/Observed, and the Logic of Yin/Yang

In Antonio Damasio's *Descartes' Error*, he describes, like Siegel, the way in which reason and emotion differ and yet go together in processing human experience. However, Damasio emphasizes to a greater degree the lines of tension *within* human thinking and human emotion—two candidates for human "specialness" we have been discussing. Not only may the way reason and emotion play off one another make humans distinctive, but also there is a special excellence of the complexity *within* both of these ways of apprehending the world. In articulating as we did earlier how thought is based upon a sense of the surround and self that is first emotional, Damasio emphasizes William James's famous description of the emotions as being a sensing of the body's response to the world and others. Damasio is careful to focus on the role of "feeling" within emotion as distinct from emotion itself. He states, "All emotions generate feelings if you are awake and alert, but not all feelings originate in emotions."[1] All of the many changes that happen in our bodies are registered by us as part of emotional experience contributing to sense of the emotion. The way the body takes in the surround registers its being moved by the dynamism of the surround, as feeling is at the heart of emotion. Damasio agrees that as emotion develops from its initial registration of something that grabs us from the surround, images of what is perceived (not necessarily a visual image, but what a phenomenologist would call a presentation of the sense of something) become part of a more elaborated secondary emotion, such as sadness, joy, or fear. Yet there remains a tension within the experience as simultaneously we are drawn into this expanded meaning of the emotion, as we are still called back to the state of the body by feeling. Emotion is not a seamless experience, but one that has within it a "juxtaposition":

> If an emotion is a collection of changes in the body state connected to particular mental images that have activated the specific brain system, *the essence of feeling an emotion is the experience of such changes in juxtaposition to the mental images that initiated the cycle.* In other words, a feeling depends on the juxtaposition of an image of the body proper to an image of something else, such as the visual face or the auditory image of a melody. (DE, 145)

In further explaining this idea, Damasio says he means to indicate by using the term *juxtaposition* that there is not a "blending" of the feelings of the body in emotion with the sense of the melody or the face that inspires joy or love, but the felt sense of separate dimensions is present within the emotion. Damasio says maybe the word "superposition" would also describe this quality of experience. So within the emotion there is a trajectory from the percept toward the emotion it has given rise to, but this is always played off against the feeling of how this emotion is registered in the body. The emotion is a further cognitive layer of meaning but is also equally a sense of the visceral.

Damasio describes how the feeling aspects of emotions vary, from the initially powerful sense of primary emotion, when one feels strongly the heart pounding, the breath shallow as one first becomes frightened, to less strong feelings that are engendered by projecting an "as-if" state, to even less powerful feelings that can be conjured up in "semblance" by just thinking alone, to the diffuse and pervasive feelings in having moods and background emotions (DE, 149–59). Yet even though all emotions, even those most diffuse, are anchored in the viscerality of the body, they all move toward and incorporate another dimension into them. As "e"-motion ("e" indicates "out of" or motion "out from"), they move out from the body into the world. All feelings in emotion "are just as cognitive as any other perceptual image" (DE, 159). We learn both about the world and how it stands in relation to us at that moment through the sense of emotions. Yet we also have juxtaposed to it "the cognition of our visceral and musculoskeletal state as it becomes affected." In this way, "feelings let us mind the body, attentively, as during an emotional state or faintly, as during a background state" (DE, 159). Emotion seems to pull us compellingly into the world, into the state of mind of another person, or into the meaning of something that confronts us as being delightful or fearful, and yet human experience is not seamless, not even emotion, which might seem to be so, more than other experiences.

This sense of juxtaposition within a larger unitary experience is exactly at the heart of Merleau-Ponty's work when he attempts to articulate the way in which these juxtapositions give experience and meaning a depth that might be a key to what is unique about humans. I have called this kind of unique logic, a logic of "inclusive differences"—where what is separate both remains so and at the same time "plays off" the other components of the experience (EB, 7). The example of this logic that is most striking in Merleau-Ponty's work is his description of how each sense is its own "world"—the world of seeing, for example, or the world of hearing—and cannot be reduplicated by any other sense, *and at the same time* each sense overlaps and is inseparable from the others. So, for example, Merleau-Ponty says we can only see the "wooly" red of a rug or the "smooth" red of a tile with the other senses implicitly given—its sound, touch, and so on. There is always a level of synesthesia present in perception, a fact that art highlights, for example, when a Van Gogh paints not only the shapes and colors of a landscape but how hot it is, what the landscape sounds like, how it feels to the touch, and so on. Yet a painting will never be the same as a musical composition that tries to express the sense of the fields around Arles—the auditory is distinct from the visual presentation. The senses both go utterly together and are utterly distinct, simultaneously, and this gives them their depth of meaning, never to be exhausted. The same is true of emotion as giving us a sense of the world about us, that we are sad about the loss of life in the war or elated over the feeling of love that has entered our life, and at the same time each emotion pulls us into the mute visceral feelings of the body and the sadness is not distinct from the heaviness in the limbs or love from the energy and lightness. This adds to the obscurity of emotional apprehension, since it always returns to the density of the body and is not transparent and diaphanous. The "spread" of emotion between the two poles of more open meaning and the enclosed sense of the visceral gives us the emotional "expanse" or "depth" or "volume" that flows through and also surrounds us. Yet it is the "inclusive logic of difference" present in this duality of emotional experience that might be a part of the key to what is different about humans.

This same sense of "going together of what is different" is stressed by Damasio between emotions and thinking—in "both directions." Coming from the side of the emotions, the secondary emotions, such as fear or joy, tell us about the world around us. However, not surprisingly, the cerebral cortex is involved in their processing as in other kinds of percepts (DE, 159), incorporating other schema learned from prior experience about our relationship to the world. *Therefore, our emotions and feelings are different from a being that would have "pure emotions" or would have emotions and feelings in isolation from a prior established framework of thought, memory, and imagination.* Yet from the "other direction," the opposite is true: Damasio claims that no matter how abstract or purely logical our reasoning is, as we try to use it to make a decision, for example, we have various "gut feelings" as we proceed. We may tend to discount these, but Damasio calls them "somatic markers" (DE, 173). *For humans, there is no "pure" thought either.*

When a human starts to think logically and abstractly, unlike Deep Blue, he or she does not go through all of the logical possibilities that may factor into his or her decision or answering a posed problem. Damasio says we have "feelings generated from secondary emotions" that as "somatic markers" orient and guide our logical reasoning. Certain logical possibilities will be felt negatively and rejected without having to be "reasoned through" exhaustively. In the opposite direction, certain positively felt possibilities will draw a focus and an interest motivated by the somatic markers. The secondary emotions have "given us the lay of the hand" or have let us "understand" certain aspects of our surround or others so that our logical reasoning is informed by the "feelings" of our bodies having these emotions. Without these feelings, we would have to reason our way through a much larger set of possible answers, but the somatic marker "allows you to choose from among fewer alternatives" (DE, 173). As embodied beings, caught up in the surround perceptually and emotionally, feeling our bodies' visceral responses to meaning and energy, our reasoning is situated and guided by these other dimensions of our being. As Damasio puts it, "The partnership between so-called cognitive processes and processes usually called emotional should be apparent" (DE, 175). He then goes on to show that this makes perfect sense in terms of brain science, if somatic markers are signaled to the prefrontal cortices that also receive signals from all of the sensory regions of the brain in which images and thoughts are formed, the somatosensory cortices, where past and current body states are registered continuously, several bioregulatory sectors, and the amygdala, the anterior cingulum, and the hypothalamus. In other words, this is the part of the brain that receives varied input about the world, the body, the past schema of the body, how experience is categorized, the emotions, and the chemical and motor responses to the world. Damasio leaves us with a picture of human being only able to function within a complexity of being, in which body, emotion, reason, and surround are traced inwardly in our neurobiology so that we are drawn from and toward each.

Another related insight from neurobiology about the hemispheric functioning of the brain adds yet another layer to how human consciousness has an integrity and yet a duality, a logic of "not one, not two." It has become a cultural cliché to talk of the "logical left brain" and "the emotional right brain," which may have the merit of starting to get us to think less monolithically about mind but unfortunately is yet another oversimplification that tends toward dualism in our cultural context. On the left side of the brain are more slow acting, linear, sequentially active, and time-dependent processes that deal with "more complex and abstract symbols." It processes more discrete "packets" of information, and especially "linguistic representations . . . constitute the modality of the specific regions of the left hemisphere" (DM, 179). In contrast, in the right hemisphere are the "fast-acting, parallel (simultaneously acting), holistic processes. The right side specializes in representations such as sensations, images, and the nonverbal polysemantic (multiple) meanings of words." Also, the left hemisphere is more motivated for externally focused attention and action and to explain events, whereas the right side recognizes patterns, understands more analogically, and focuses more on the sense of others actions, beliefs, attitudes, gestures, and so on. Anatomically, the right hemisphere has a slightly higher density of neuronal interconnections than the left hemisphere, and the kind of input from the body's viscera to the right orbitofrontal cortex suggests that it has a greater sense of the body state (DM, 182).

To step back from these details, it can be seen, given all that we have said, that Siegel's conclusions about these asymmetries make perfect sense: both sides of the brain act together and call for increasing integration to get deeper meaning and complexity within human experience. For example, unlike the popular cultural oversimplification, Siegel declares, "Emotion exists on both sides of the brain" (DM, 181). This seems to follow if the right side processes bodily input and nonverbal emotional expressions such as gesture, posture, voice tone, or facial expression. This is one dimension of emotion. However, both sides of the brain appraise meaning and direct attention, and Siegel concludes, "It is fair to say that both sides of the brain are filled with meaning and emotional processes," even though he adds in the next sentence that the qualitative sense of the emotions as processed on both sides may be "quite distinct" because of the distinct way each processes the world (DM, 183). One idea about this relationship may be that states of "hotter' affect, such as intense anger or joy, may be more the products of the right side, and "cooler," more regulated emotions products of the left.

I suggest that when we look at emotions as we live them, not just instant to instant, but over the days, months, years, and decades, the interweaving back and forth between the immediate and visceral flood of feeling in emotion, whether it is the rush of love or the arrow of hatred, and the deeper meaning of these feelings in terms of reflection, language, planning, and categorical determinations, becomes greater. Over the years, I learn things about the other person's character, or we have a shared history of being able to dialogue and work out difficulties or express little kindnesses, or they gradually come to express in language insights and emotions that transform their behavior, identity, and moral commitments. Over the same decades, I learn things about myself, from immediate experience, certainly, but also from long reflection and using language in self-talk or with others, and this changes my own capacities to discern and express the love I come to feel more. In the opposite case, it may take years to formulate what about the other person is treacherous or cruel or immoral, or they may gradually, through the reflections they have entertained, shape themselves in such a way that they behave differently or feel differently about the world and others. Then my recognition of this, which is both immediate and also processed in categorical and linguistic ways through reflection, changes my emotional response to them. Over the long term, "emotion" is a more complex mix than that of the isolated instant. Many of our oversimplifications of both emotion and thought stem from considering instances isolated in the moment instead of within a longer temporal context.

This recognition of the process of emotion over a longer span and how it incorporates other sorts of understanding as part of its felt sense helps explain some science fiction fantasies that are now becoming more relevant to our considerations about the issues raised in this book. Can an android "think" itself into some sort of love or friendship? This is a question posed in fictions from Marge Piercy's novel, *He, She, and It*, to several episodes of "Star Trek: The Second Generation" in regard to the culturally popular character "Data." These are thought experiments about how we could imagine possibilities for machines. It would seem that part of our emotional relationship, at least insofar as it deepens, is contributed to by insights that are more logical and reflective. Data, for example, continually declares that he cannot experience emotion, yet he seems to feel friendship for other crew members and his cat, or he has feelings of loss for dead comrades. The script accurately portrays that he does not have an embodied relationship to people, beings, or the surround, and he does not feel visceral emotional connections, just as Cog and Kismet do not. Yet just as Damasio or Siegel report about scans of the brains done by researchers, which show the cortical involvement of more abstract reasoning processes as being inseparably part of emotion, Data reminds us that part of our emotions plays off our ideas about others and how things stand between us.

There have been many attempts to express this different sort of logic, but I would recall perhaps the most ancient articulation and tradition that focuses on how those dimensions that seem opposed also go together inseparably for those who allow the depth of the meaning of existence to show itself—the insight of Taoism. The *Tao Tê Ching* begins in its first verse with an injunction to the reader that he or she will only be able to fathom the mysteries of the meaning of existence by allowing the opposites of the manifestation and the deeper ineffable ground of being to play off of one another, and to see that they are utterly different and utterly the same. Through "kuan," or this sort of contemplation of opposition and unity, "one immediately grasps the complete identity of the nameable and the unnamable, or being and nothing."[2] The parallel can be made to Heidegger's "ontic" and "ontological" in *Being and Time*, which asserts the inseparability of the opposed senses of empirical facts and their deeper meaning in a way akin to Taoism and recognized in the affinity by many Taoists who came to visit Heidegger. In either case, all things that can be pointed to, that can be delineated clearly, that can be counted, such as all of the objects, the people, the words spoken, the desks and chairs, and so on, in a class do not capture the "being" of the class, yet this being is not "other" than all of these things either. This logic is presented even more widely in the Taoist idea of yin/yang as opposing forces dark and light, hard and soft, aggressive and passive, and so on, which as opposites also are inseparable and only together make up the being of what is. So the second verse of the *Tao Tê Ching* asserts among its other lines, "High and low are mutually posited in their contradiction/voice and tone are mutually posited in their unity, front and back are mutually posited in their succession." Similarly to Heraclitus's declaration that "between opposites, there is the fairest harmony," so the idea of yin/yang means that the heart of one pair of opposites is at the heart of the other. Furthermore, since Taoism sees all things as processes, as flowing like its symbol, water, the one side always flows into and turns into its opposite, especially if one allows the full meaning of things to emerge. This is what is practiced in an embodied way in Tai Chi, the continual movement back and forth from yin and yang.

We also have seen how the person (as well as the animal) and the surround cannot be separated, although quite different. This too is implied in the Taoist identity of opposites. In explaining the sense of the Tao, Chung quotes Nishida, that in embracing the self-identity of contradiction, "one experiences directly one's conscious state that there is neither yet subject nor object." Chung explains that "difference and identity take place simultaneously," and that this "extends to the unity of the subjectivity of man and the objectivity of things" (TC, 10–11). It seems that this is the kind of logic that even the studies of brain and neural function have come to realize: that reason and emotion can only work through each other, even if different, that the hemispheres only give us the full meaning of an emotion, for example, or other presentation, if both work together despite their difference. They form a unity in being opposed functions. Together they also give us a deeper experience in allowing the outer world to shape the inner and allowing the inner to shape the outer. However, not only is this true of the meanings we discern through the brain and neural networks, but also the structure of the connections in the inner helps determine the shape of the outer, which then reshapes the growth and change of the inner. This sense that we find ourselves in the world and the world is found within our ways of making meaning is what Heidegger called "being-in-the-world" or Merleau-Ponty (focusing more on the logic of embodiment) called "the flesh of the world."

Quantum Minds and Nondualistic Reality

Perhaps the most radical way to look at the outcome of advances in studying the brain and neurobiology and also to see how far these studies have brought science into resonance with the phenomenological perspective on reality (which has parallels with older Taoist and Buddhist ideas) is to explore for a moment Schwartz's and Begley's idea of the "quantum brain." It may be one of the notions that further sketches the line that has been emerging throughout this chapter to draw a boundary in a very nontraditional way around humanity. It is one thing to formulate that subject and object are somehow conjoined, but to fathom how this alters one's sense of objectivity is a further challenge. The idea that there could be a determinate world of states-of-affairs, as if it were to be seen by an absolute observer not confined by any perspective, is a persistent chimera that haunts our Western intellectual history and popular culture. It is what prevents us from taking ambiguity and indeterminacy as positive phenomena, as ways of truly describing the world, instead of "defects" in our knowing. Schwartz and Begley take the results of the uncertainty work in physics to imagine what the inseparability of the observer/observed means for fathoming brain function.

Schwartz and Begley remind us that the contribution of quantum physics "is the fundamental role played by the observer in choosing which of a plenitude of possible realities will leave the realm of the possible and become the actual" (MB, 263). They trace the history from Thomas Young's original famous "double-slit experiment" in 1801 to recent experiments and interpretations of the basic indeterminacy of quantum phenomenon. Young's experiment demonstrated that light passing through either one or both of the slits displayed both the properties of a wave phenomenon and of a particle, which should not be possible in a determinate universe. As a wave, the light passed through both slits and created a wavelike interference pattern, and as a particle the photons could pass through the slit in a straight trajectory and be recorded on a detector. What was recorded depended upon what was sought. Similar experiments have demonstrated the same behavior for electrons and even larger particles, such as ions. This is important, since neurons communicate by ion transfer. The resolution of the dilemma by those willing to consider an indeterminate universe was that what actually passes through the slits is a "wave of probability." It is the observer, posing a question to the system, that causes the quantum phenomenon to be seen as a wave or a particle: "Before the observation, the system had a range of possibilities; afterward, it had a single actuality" (MB, 269). In other words, the observer has been a part of the resolution of what state actually exists. I emphasize that it is not the case that the observer "created" the state of affairs, since the world "answered" the question and the way it was posed, and there are other answers that would become manifest to the observer with a differing question and the way it is posed. The world is not passively shaped, since it answers our questions and is an interlocutor in an ongoing dialogue. We are beyond the either/or of subjectivity or objectivity.

Niels Bohr, Paul Dirac, Werner Heisenberg, and Wolfgang Pauli all agreed in 1927 (strangely, or not so strangely, the year Heidegger's *Being and Time* was published) on the "Copenhagen interpretation of quantum mechanics," that "it is the observer who both decides which aspect of nature is to be probed and reads the answer nature gives. The mind of the observer helps choose which of an uncountable number of possible realities comes into being in the form of observations" (MB, 272–73). Most physicists, even if they were able to accept this shift away from expecting determinate answers to inquiries of the world around them, still wanted to insist that this indeterminacy was only evidenced within the limits of what humans can know about existence, and this did not indicate what was really there. In other words, there must be a determinate reality, but we cannot always fathom it (what Einstein preferred to believe, for example). However, this attempt to somehow hold onto a foundation—a "thing in-itself," even if unknowable—had been tried by Kant and his successors in philosophy but seems to obscure the more straightforward conclusion—the only reality to which we have access is one that is an interweaving of observer and observed. If all we can tell about reality is that it is indeterminate outside of circumscribed contexts, then it makes more sense to see it and conceive of it in this way.

The fear of those who oppose this perspective seems to be that without determinate objectivity, science and philosophy would be plunged into mere relativism—that anything would be whatever the observer wants it to be. However, this does not follow from the fact that there is a dialogue between observer and observed. There is not one answer, but there is only a certain range of answers, and there is *an* answer given within the context of a specific relationship of observer/observed. Reality retains a depth of meaning, but one that can be probed in differing directions and can evolve in differing ways, yet always in a network of relationships that can be fathomed to some degree, and to a greater degree the more we take all of the relationships into account. Physics, restricted to its particular area of inquiry, sees this as holding for quantum phenomena, but phenomenology sees this as holding for any phenomenon, if we are approaching it on the level of meaning. What something means will always be an outcome of a web of relationships, but that does not indicate that just any meaning will emerge. Phenomenology starts with assuming that what we experience is what the world is about, and what we experience is the dialogue of question and answer or the interweaving of observer and observed. What is there for us is what is there—period. There need be no other projected ideal yardstick against which to measure it and find it lacking.

Returning to what this means for the brain takes Schwartz and Begley to the parallel they see in the kind of Schrödinger wave equations that can be applied to the wave of probabilities that are the photons passing through the double slit that then resolve or "collapse" into an observed actuality, with "the behavior of the ions whose movements create the electrical signals along axons and of neurotransmitters that are released by synapses" (MB, 284). If the brain is a system that evolves by the various possible interactions of its material constituents, but also a part of the same system is the input of the feeling of the presentation of what is being processed by the person experiencing it, then the observer is a given part of the system of brain activity. Furthermore, how "the observer," or the one having the experience that is being processed by the brain/neural system, focuses upon what is being processed will cause it to "resolve" in a certain way. The fact that the observer and observed together form a system that unfolds through their "dialogue" or interaction helps make sense from an empirically based scientific approach of what the phenomenologists had asserted since Heidegger's *Being and Time*.

Heidegger claimed the only way to resolve the meaning of being was to see it in terms of the "ontological difference," which partially referred to the fact that existence, in terms of what Heidegger called the "ontic" dimension, was the collection of facts about the world. This dimension was comprised of what could be named and pointed to as having a clear definition. The ontic dimension was juxtaposed to the "ontological" or the realm of meaning, the way that facts can only be experienced as having a certain significance given whatever context within which we apprehend or encounter them. The two terms refer to dimensions of a unitary phenomenon—there is no fact without meaning, and there is no meaning without the something that comes to mean—the fact. Within any "world" or context of meaning, value, and framework of interpretation, anything discovered has already appeared within a certain light—a certain range of possible meanings that makes sense within that world—a world that consists of all things within it. To say that all phenomena are what they are as "within-the-world," as within these contexts, means everything is a phenomenon of the observer/observed.

Again, it is helpful to remind ourselves that this sounds similar to the Taoist idea of the inseparability of the Tao and the "ten thousand things," or the Tao that is beyond naming as the source of meaning and all that can be named. This points to a wisdom that has a long heritage, and suggests a confluence of ancient Taoist wisdom, phenomenology, and modern science. For Begley and Schwartz, using the perspective of quantum theory provides a way to both explain the results that Schwartz has been working with obsessive-compulsive patients and to overcome the matter/mind dualism of traditional science and philosophy. When Schwartz had his patients go through a four-step process of training in order to learn to "focus away" from their obsessive loops of processing the surround and to refocus on more open, flexible, and spontaneously responsive ways to process their situation, he found that they could move beyond their obsessive-compulsive syndrome. Not only could they change their behavior and their emotional and cognitive sense of the situation, but they could cause changes in their brains' circuitry. Schwartz and Begley postulate that efficacy of refocusing the attention of the experiencer as a "mental force," in the sense that "mental force is a physical force generated by mental effort." In stating this, the regard of the observer is not "outside" the reality of what is unfolding but is rather folded within what comes to pass. In phenomenological terms, we could say that these patients have opened up other regions of the wider context to which they had not had access before, and within this new "world" or context, new things can appear. Not only is theirs a shift in context, but also the way something is "taken up" or "encountered' in part of the process of that phenomenon unfolding with a certain sense and identity.

The reinterpretation of the previous feelings and the sense of the situation involved in "relabeling," and the refocusing on other possible interpretations and responses to the situation, is, as Schwartz and Begley put it, a "wholly active process." This shift in focus and the way the "observer" makes sense of the brain's processing "amplifies newly emerging brain circuitry" (MB, 295). This shift in perspective also entails that "the basic principles of physics, as they are now understood, are not the deterministic laws of classical physics," but rather "those of quantum physics, which allow mental effort to keep in focus a stream of consciousness that would otherwise become quickly defocused" (MB, 297). This focus allows what is focused upon to become actualized. Schwartz and Begley note how this is different than the traditional notion of "will," so hallowed in the tradition of rationalist philosophy—as if there is some spiritual faculty of "forcing" one's intentions determined by deliberate thought to make one act in a certain way despite whatever habits, emotions, and situational factors might lead one to act otherwise. Will presupposes that the situation has already come forward in a certain identity and then the mind decides to act upon it in a certain way, versus this way of seeing the phenomenon as coming to appear as a meeting of observer/observed.

Instead of traditional notions of will, Schwartz and Begley point out that this idea is more like that of William James or Buddhist traditions. James also had given an alternative to the traditional egocentric and rationally inspired will in declaring that "volition is nothing but attention," and that will in the way he reconfigured it was the ability to "emphasize, reinforce or protract" certain thoughts instead of focusing on other thoughts as they might emerge (MB, 309). Begley and Schwartz compare this to the Buddhist practice of "mindfulness." Mindfulness is a kind of concentrated attention that permeates one's perceptual, emotional, and feeling awareness, but one that also is unfocused in the sense of being open to all of the environment's beckonings instead of preoccupied with the ego's usual strategies of defending itself and setting out a world that conforms to its ongoing sense of things. Instead of the world fitting set categories, and phenomena having a set meaning, there is a way of being aware but open, what Heidegger called "letting be," in which the unfolding flow of each happening is entered with attentiveness but with a nonimposing wonder. In Buddhist mindfulness, if one is walking, for instance, then one is wholly aware of each sensation of the muscles, the foot, the texture of the ground beneath one's feet, the breeze, and so on. In this sense, everything around oneself, the sense of the body and its feelings and the focus on carrying out the intention to walk, is one conjoined field—the "lived equivalent" or dynamically engaged unitary flow of observer/observed. Even though this is at the heart of experience, it takes a cultivated sensitivity to allow it to emerge, given the constructs with which our culture has obscured this dimension.

If one no longer posits that there should be some "outside" beyond perspective, beyond the inclusion with the rest of the field of phenomenon, then it is no longer the case that human consciousness is just an inessential knower confronting an objective reality, but rather that the field of observer/observed is the ongoing "foundationless" flow that is: "the object is an object for the subject, the subject is a subject for the object."[3] These are the words of Buddhist Master Seng-Ts'an, who explains the meaning of the Buddhist term *emptiness* which indicates that everything is in a field with everything else, including the human body/mind. Emptiness is the lack of an absolute foundation beneath experience or of self-subsistency that Western metaphysics continually sought, whether God, substance, or numbers—something must be the ground of all else! Yet, there is only relativity, which is not the same as relativism.

Subject and object still have their ground in their specific properties, the ten thousand things, but these properties only appear in relationship to each other, leaving Seng-T'san to say that "there is neither 'self' nor 'other.'" There is not "direct identification," yet subject and object are inseparable. Seng-T'san concludes "We can only say 'not two.'" This sense of the subject and object interwoven also was at the heart of Merleau-Ponty's philosophy, which he first expressed with the idea that the embodied perceiver was embedded in the surround in such a way that both formed a "phenomenal field." At the end of his life, he used the image of the "chiasm" as the way in which, for example, the two strands of DNA are separate and yet in their entwining are one, for expressing the relationship of the human to the world. Merleau-Ponty wrote in his last notes to himself, "Start from this, there is not identity, nor non-identity, or non-coincidence, there is inside and outside turning about one another" (VI, 264). We cannot posit an "outside" as standing on its own, for Merleau-Ponty, for whatever is there in the world is *for us*, the observer in the observer/observed. We wind around each other so that we are neither one nor two.

Nonlocal Quantum Reality, "Phenomenality," and Magic in Emotion

Schwartz and Begley say that not only does the mind's attentiveness function like a repeated question of an observer and cause the quantum system of the brain to actualize with certain properties, but unlike many other physicists, they also are willing to embrace the implications of this state of affairs for envisioning a different ontology. They discuss as well the implications of "nonlocality" in deepening the picture of the quantum world as one in which mind and matter are inseparable, and each works in concert with the other in a nondeterministic unfolding. To quickly summarize this complicated topic, creating an electron and a positron from a pi-meson sends these particles off into opposing directions. The spin of these particles is in a relationship that is called "entangled"—the spin of the one particle is in a necessary complementary relationship to the other. If one knows the spin of one particle, then the spin of the other, although different, can be inferred. However, if as a quantum property the spin of the particle, say, the positron, does not exist until it is observed, then the probabilities of spin up or down or right or left collapse into the particular spin only when measured. However, given this scenario, as soon as the positron was observed, the state of the electron also would become actualized and known as the complement. However, this would mean that "physical reality" would be affected instantaneously by an action of the observer in a faraway place. The conclusion drawn from this was that "the universe must be nonlocal" (MB, 347). In a universe of locality something causes an effect by being contiguous in space and time and going through a linear succession of events. In this case, what is decided in one place instantaneously influences what is true in some other place. So we have here, both mind (or the observer) influencing the state of matter (the observed) in a larger system, but also that this is happening in a manner outside of any possible linear chains of cause and effect, since they are noncontiguous in space. The idea of context, even in the unfolding of the materiality of the constituents of the embodied mind, expands to bring together aspects that may have been seen as disparate but nevertheless are part of a unitary phenomenon.

At first these ideas were postulated as thought experiments, but given the advancement of technologies, it became possible to perform the experiments that would verify the ideas. In 1982 in Paris and then again in Switzerland in 1997, experiments were done where the particles were separated to such an extent that no causal connection was possible, unless the cause and effect were faster than the speed of light, an impossible notion in the cause-and-effect framework of interpreting the world. In the Swiss experiments, the particles were actually sent through fiber-optic lines to two Swiss villages that *were 11 kilometers apart.* Yet still each photon of the pair "seemed to know" instantaneously what measurement had been made on its distant partner and exhibited the properties specified by the measurements that had been made this vast distance away (that is from the perspective of the miniscule world of quantum physics) (MB, 347–48). The outcome of these experiments is to reinforce the notion that mind and matter or observer and observed are inseparably part of a system. It also means that "human consciousness must be viewed as an emergent phenomenon in a seamlessly interconnected whole called the cosmos" (MB, 350). Schwartz and Begley explain that an *emergent phenomenon* is one in which the whole cannot be explained as merely the sum of its parts. If the mind is emergent, they say, it is more than just the physical components of the brain. If the reality of the observer and observed is emergent, then it is more than their sum. If the human consciousness is emergent, then it is more than just the sum of itself and the world around it.

The two aspects of the workings of the brain—that emotion is the integrative, background base of its greater scope of processing, and that the unfolding of consciousness is a "quantum brain" or a system in which the observer and observed are intermeshed in such a way that there is only a field of becoming in which both become what they are through the other—can be seen to be pointing to something similar. In *Emotion and Embodiment*, I coined the term *phenomenality*, to characterize an aspect of emotion that is distinctive (EE, 117). Given that it is the case that all *perception* takes place for an embodied perceiver within a surround, if we look carefully at the aspects of the perceptual process we find that the sense of perception has a "trajectory" that belies its own workings. If, as we have described, I see the tree outside my window not only from my seat here in the kitchen but also from the perspective of the tree next to it, the cloud above, the bird sitting in its branches, and so on, because the body is this power of "inhabiting" all of these others places within my "perceptual field," then it is easier to see how we are drawn to our habitual idea of reality. Given this expanding sense of all of these perspectives felt within my perception as "co-given" in an implicit way, the felt trajectory is toward an all-inclusive "God's eye" perspective that would incorporate all of them (EE, 123). Even though we cannot reach that "outside the system" regard, this pull in perception helps us see why we expect a perspective beyond all perspectives to be possible and would indicate "reality." It is our ongoing way of looking at the world. However, *in emotion*, we have the palpable sense as part of the experience itself that this meaning is revealing itself, particularly to me. We know we are reacting to something we are encountering, yet we also have the immediate sense that it is *my* reaction. Certainly the most forceful part of the meaning of the emotion is that something has occurred that I am taking in through emotion, yet this is not all of the experience. For example, if I am angry with you or I am feeling kinship with you or I am sad that a certain species of animal is endangered, then the anger is *in response* to someone's act or the kinship is *with* someone or the sadness is *about* something, but at the same time, there is the present and palpable sense that those feelings are *mine* and may strike me differently than someone else.

When feeling an emotion, we feel the sense of our own unique involvement in the situation in feeling it. In feeling love for this person, we feel it is our unique love and not somebody else's. Even in just feeling the emotional part of a wider experience, such as a perception, we know it is our unique feeling as part of the perception, so that in thrilling to the sight of the willow swaying at the end of the block or the vulture circling overhead, I feel myself as giving over to this emotion given who I am and my relationship to the world as well as to this object of my emotion. I am already aware in an implicit way that my neighbor may be dismayed at the willow waving in the wind, only feeling it is a dirty, overgrown monster on the block, or feeling that those birds are ugly scavengers that he wishes the city government would exterminate. The "texture" or the "feel" of the emotional experience is one that my relatedness to the thing, my own having a unique context based on my history, my thoughts, my interests, my relationships, my sensibility, and so on, is part of what I am experiencing in experiencing the object of the emotion. However, this does not mean that, as we often say, emotions are merely "subjective." The thrill inspired by the graceful and rhythmic way of sheltering things within or beside the tree in a gentle way of the swaying willow is not something I would feel about a car or a box or even another sort of tree. The emotional experience is palpably both the subject/object, observer/observed, or the person *and* the surround as one interweaving process (EE, 121). In *Emotion and Embodiment*, I sketch out a continuum with perception at one end and imagining on the other end, with emotion in the middle (EE, 128). Each has an aspect of an "encountered aspect of the world" as part of it, and each has an aspect of "personal involvement in relationships," but the emphasis felt in the experiences varies, and emotion is right in that balancing, middle place between both as felt within the experience—self and world.

Emotion's "phenomenality"—the registration of the strange, interwoven sense of both reality and personal perspective within the emotional experience itself—might have a distinctive role as indicative of what is unique about humans. Humans might be able to understand themselves and the boundary of being human only by seeing their interwovenness with reality. Once again, the interactions of the brain as a system and the phenomenology of emotional experience are parallel in the sense that both indicate that humans are located in dimensions of the world that are "nonlocal." As discussed in *Emotion and Embodiment*, there is a clue from Sartre's *The Emotions: Outline of a Theory*, in which he contrasts the other modes of apprehension with the experience of emotions: ". . . consciousness can be in the world in two different ways. The world can appear as a complex of instruments so organized that if one wished to produce a determined effect it would be necessary to act upon the determined elements of the complex." Sartre details this as the world of cause and effect, which differs from that of the emotions: "In this case, the categories of the world act upon consciousness immediately. They are present to it *without distance*."[4] Sartre says this sense of the world that comes to us through emotion is not the world of objects and instruments, but is that different place where things act upon each other immediately. For example, Sartre discusses how a strange face at the window, even if we are locked up and secure in our house, even knowing that the person cannot get at us, might still flood us with an emotion of fear. He calls this way that the world affects us outside of cause and effect a "world of magic" (SE, 90-91). At a distance, without contiguous intermediaries, our bodies are caught up in an emotional sense.

I believe this is the deeper sense of the phenomenon of magic and is the *magical sense* of emotions. For example, rather than indigenous peoples painting animals upon cave walls or rock canyons because they thought this would "cause" the animal to be killed in the hunt working through a supernatural "cause and effect" that we often assume to be the mark of the magical, it might be more the case that they wanted to feel the kinship with the animal across barriers of time, space, and species. Emotion is also a nonlocal phenomenon in this way, both in bringing together disparate kinds of things and in constellating a felt sense from what might be logically and physically distant. The cave painters were conjuring a felt "knowledge" of what it was like to be an animal trying to make it through the winter, to forage for food, to withstand the cold, to age, and so on. They may have sought more to feel an emotional connection out of gratitude and kinship across the barriers of time, space, and practical conditions (EE, 140). This would be the emotional import of the practice of "magic," as mysterious and deep, but not supernatural. This makes the magical more spiritual than a way of manipulation. Various indigenous ceremonies, in which the dancers become the animals they are portraying, such as the kangaroo dancer becoming the kangaroo, are this kind of movement beyond cause and effect, the linear laying out of space and time, in order to "be" something one cannot be otherwise.[5] Yet we do not have to go to these cultures for experiences of this kind—it is also what any of us feel when we are "one" with the other in love and friendship. For that moment one might feel the other person's sadness or joy, even though there might be no cause and effect way of explaining this sudden shift in who you are for the moment. Even more to the point, when listening to a well-told story or reading a gripping novel, one might be in a faraway land or in a faraway time, feeling emotions that put one in relationship to one's ancestors, perhaps, or with a people one never even met or with some event that never happened. This conjuring, this connecting, outside of cause-and-effect relationships of a certain kind of delimited space of physical barriers and time, is part of our ongoing experience as being human. This magic moves us and causes us to do things—perhaps even lay down our lives for a story or a connection with someone. This is the distinctive power of emotion—to bridge the gap of the cause-and-effect world by feelings. Emotion introduces not only a physical, quantum world that is nonlocal but a world of meaning that has this altered boundary of spanning across the normal boundaries of time and space. Again, these considerations allow us to see human emotion as a much more complex than simple irrational attractions or repulsions. It seems as if human faculties are inseparable from our distinctive way of taking in the sense of other beings into our human core.

Imagination, Being Moved, and the Virtual Dimension of Human Life

Where have we come in this attempt to draw boundaries around the human? We do not seem to be the "rational animal" in the sense this was taken to mean for millennia, as the beings uniquely marked by a rational detachment and achievement of a transcendence of the sensory, emotional, interpersonally related, entwined with nature, thinking within the materiality of image, and so on, as purely logical, categorical, and analytical mentalities. This, of course, is more of a description of a "thinking mechanism," than the rational "animal." We are rational *animals* and do not leave our kinship with animals behind. Therefore, as thinkers, we remain quite sensory, emotional, related with kin and kind, entwined with nature, thinking within the materiality of image, and so on. Yet we are caught "in between" and cannot claim to be just another animal, as these capacities for intellection do change our sensory and emotional registration of the world into something different. A world rendered by us is one that comes from our viscera and yet stretches to connect with ideas, images, juxtapositions, imaginary worlds, and worlds distant in space, time, and possibility.

In this chapter, we have seen how both the most general meanings of the world and also the workings of our brains, neurons, and sensory and emotional systems point to humans as being a "parallel processor"—receiving input from all sorts of systems simultaneously—in a world that also is made up of differing layers of significance that can come together in new and unpredictable ways. After all, part of the traditional definition of humans depends upon humans being the equal and opposite foil to a stable, objectively orderly external world. If the world, too, is an open system of the type we have described, shifting, evolving, able to integrate surprising changes as the system transforms with the appearance of a strange attractor, the point at which a small change can have a big effect, then the being whose life is taking in the world and is woven into it might also exist in a way more fluid, more open to aspects of the surround, and more erratic. This might mean that human life, personally and collectively, is surprisingly fragile, open to impacts and changes of direction, and can be thrown off course and into sudden shifts of meaning that require a kind of care about who we are becoming that we may have thought unnecessary if we are guaranteed an unquestionable "essence."

It is interesting, however, that even if humans were more straightforwardly definable beings, it would only cover part of their time of existence. It ignores all of those hours they are asleep, the hours of dream—the purely productive hours of the mind, emotion, memory, and imagination. Yet to take the hint of dreams is to be led from the night back to the day, as Freud was in *The Interpretation of Dreams*, articulating a "dream logic" of the unconscious, until he realized at the end of the work that these symbolic processes and alternate logic at work in the dream were active in humans all the time. The realm of the dream or of the kind of logic of the dream in our waking life is yet another way of making meaning and apprehension. It seems to be a realm that is virtual and also symbolic. We live in a postmodern culture more and more addicted to the virtual, where many are able to tolerate their daily lives "in real life," as it is called on the Internet, only because of their adventures or experiences in "virtual reality." What do we mean by the virtual? It is not the "unreal" or the "make believe," since it has an impact on people's lives, and they do believe in the meaning of the experience. Some of cyberspace seems like it is a more fluid, manipulable but limited extension of our daily life in providing another sort of newspaper, or a more handy encyclopedia, or a more extensive library or a super shopping mall, but then there are regions of cyberspace that are more like the space of dreams. The first examples are straightforward in that we move toward the library that is not actual in the sense that it has no material objects called books or desks or carrels, and therefore it is virtual in respect to the fact that these objects had been only available as material objects before becoming available in their electronic form, yet they are presentations of the same sort of things just to be handled or acquired in a different way. However, the second idea—that parts of cyberspace are like the space of dreams— brings us to the deeper sense of the virtual that combines with the symbolic. In some ways, the Internet has brought us more virtual objects and space in the sense of substituting electronic variations for material objects, but perhaps no more, or even less, of the symbolic, since people have always spent a lot of time with books, stories, games, and the like, that focus on this other space that enlivens and enriches our Cartesian space. The very elaborateness, distanced presentation, and prefabricated nature of the sensual presentations of the Internet often mitigate against the symbolic power more easily found in things powerfully present to our senses, but enveloping, viscerally engaging, and somewhat obscure.

An interesting clue to how the virtual comes about in this second sense is offered by Suzanne Langer's older work *Feeling and Form*, where she describes the locus of the power of the arts in different media as different sorts of virtuality. For Langer, the way that each medium, whether painting or drama or music, conveyed its meaning was through its particular sense of virtuality. She articulated this theory in 1953, and it is worth revisiting today, given our new focus on the virtual, because of cyberspace. Langer denies the virtual as being unreal, but she admits that it has the air of illusion or, perhaps more fittingly, of "semblance."[6] However, in this case, the illusion is not a mistaken reality but rather is *a more concentrated one*. It is not a "mere" semblance, fooling us by taking the place of a truer semblance, but it is "pure semblance"—a phenomenon utterly concentrated in just the way it shows itself to us. Langer says that the sense of illusion comes from being enveloped in one sensory modality, so that it does the job for all the rest. So in a painting, the senses of hearing, touch, and smell come to us through the visual presentation of the color, line, compositions, and so on;

or, in music, everything is reduced to sound for our hearing, and the world of smell and of vision becomes a landscape of sounding rhythms, tones, resonances, dissonances, and so on. If this were all that art were, however, it would be a titillating experience of sensations and not the kind of communication from artist to audience that moves us profoundly, opens new vistas of understanding, and may even change somewhat who we are. The part that is to be added to the sheerly visual or sheerly auditory, and so on, is the symbolic dimension of the virtual and is the way in which art appeals to the imagination.

Langer describes how concentrating all of the significance of our varied experience into an "aesthetic surface"—whether it be paint, modulated sound, or stone, so that it is apprehended by one sensory modality doing the work of all others—gives this surface a "plasticity" to be shaped or manipulated in such a way as to become able to carry symbolic meaning from the expression of the artist to the audience of the artwork (FF, 59). So again we see materiality being shapeable or moldable in such a way to "hold" and "convey" meaning—but here it is on the expressive side, not the apprehending side—however, the correlation between the object conveying and the brain and neural network apprehending makes sense in a holistic view of humans and the world. Langer continues to show how the simplest designs or the simplest sounds convey a movement—a "virtual" movement, in the sense of not actually traversing Cartesian space, but by expressing the symbolic or imaginative sense of movement (FF, 64–65). For example, if one were to see either

—two very simple designs or drawings using only black lines, we see the waves "move" or even the droplike shapes "spin" around in the circle by perceiving stationary marks on a page that have been shaped to convey this significance. The symbolic power of the virtual in art, for Langer, is that the shaping of the aesthetic surface conveys a movement that "stands in" for the "movement" of our emotions—the kind of rhythms of vital sense that we have already discussed (FF, 82). So a slow, deep in pitch, haltingly paced, and somewhat dissonant series of tones in a musical passage might convey symbolically or "stand in" for the slow, lethargic, hopeless, and sad sense of depression.

It is an interesting conjecture to consider how much of symbolism might act on our emotional rhythms to resonate with meanings of our other ways of apprehending the world that might be measured by the kind of brain science mapping studies referred to before, to start to make sense of the neurobiology of imagination. If symbols act upon the emotional sense of the surround or the event, object, or person encountered, then could that be detected by neurobiologists in those areas of the brain and neurons that normally process emotions? If we consider Kant's brilliant analysis in the *Critique of Judgment*, that imagination works by bringing into free play the aspects of sensibility and categorical understanding, then it would be fascinating to see if the brain and neuronal system demonstrated a firing of the emotional centers followed by a kind of interplay of the perceptual and categorical cognitive regions. For Kant, the productive imagination used in art is the imagination that does not merely give images to what has been apprehended before (the reproductive imagination) but instead moves us forward into a new sense of things by being the way of connecting the rational categories to our sensible inputs, by dynamically connecting them in a free play that never comes to a definite stopping point of having the "exact fit" or "clear link." Instead, in this freewheeling between the rationally categorical and the sensible, there is a kind of resonance or harmony achieved that gives us a "sort of" or ambiguous feeling of "getting it," but not one that can be pinned down. It will be fascinating to see if brain scans can corroborate this kind of dynamic, ongoing resonance among these processing areas. Once again, imagination is another case in which humans, insofar as they seem to be unique in their expression and apprehension, are so because the various modes of taking in and expressing the world are juxtaposed and play off one another within that very specific way of experience.

What is important to us in this chapter is that by taking a moment to consider imagination, we see yet another dimension of expression and apprehension that renders humanity more interconnected, dynamic, and complex within itself and in drawing in the complexity of the world of its surround. Yet if imagination is at the heart of what makes humans unique, then why, for the most part, is this aspect of human uniqueness not a focus, both in popular culture and in the disciplines of neurobiology, psychology, and philosophy, despite periodic outbreaks of enthusiasm about its power? Imagination, in fairness to Western intellectual and cultural history, has been at times a candidate for what makes humans unique, especially among the Romantics and writers such as Samuel Coleridge. Yet when it has been championed, the imagination has been placed in the realm of saving grace, as opposite to the sober, rational world, as release from the prison of everydayness, as in Coleridge's opium-inspired poem often taught to schoolchildren,

Kubla Khan, in which imagination seems to be equated to "the milk of Paradise." Whether there are such wondrous flights of imagination, this characterization matches those of the rationalists insofar as it places imagination "to the side" of everydayness, one taking it to be trivial and just an entertaining diversion, the other as salvific. What is more to the point for characterizing human being is how in its everyday taking in of the world, the imagined may be at the core of its apprehension and reality, and once again inseparable from the other modes of apprehension.

Traditionally, one can see that imagination would not be chosen as being key to humanity's uniqueness insofar as it too challenges the dichotomy of the subjective and objective. Imagination had been customarily portrayed as the entertaining of the "nonreal" in opposition to the real world around us. Even the earliest writings of Merleau-Ponty labeled the imaginary as having "no depth" and offering "no hold upon it" versus the perceptual whose "significance encircles and permeates matter" (PP, 323–24). However, as his philosophy progressed and he attempted to articulate the "flesh of the world," as how, through embodiment, humans were of the surround, he saw that the painter and other artists were more adept than most of us at bringing forth from their perception "the imaginary texture of the real" (EM, 165).[7] Now, in discussing the poetry of Valery, Merleau-Ponty could see that when Valery wrote about "the secret blackness of milk," he was getting at possible dimensions of perception that yielded greater depth of its meaning. In perceptions, in memories, and in emotions, there are other significances that can only come into the light of day through the play of imagination, breaking up the usual ways of meaning making. Some meanings might be more submerged in the background of experience, given the usual emphasis on accomplishing practical tasks, but that does not mean that they are not vital to the overall significance of our surround.

If we look at imagination in this way, we realize that at every moment, interspersing our other apprehensions, plays of imagination, or at least potential ones, give depth to what we are witnessing. As I watch a political leader, the image of Frankenstein or Macbeth flickers across my apprehension, or in watching my nephew, the image of a talking bunny rabbit or "Dennis the Menace" from the comics arises for a second, and my overall sense of the experience integrates this moment into it as much as any other part of my information processing, even if it does not capture my explicit attention. There was an administrator at my university more than a decade ago who did something that made me think of him as dressed and as a member of the Nazi High Command, since the spirit of his actions seemed so hurtful to the well-being of others. Now, a decade later, I cannot meet him in the lavatory or elsewhere without having a flash of the image of him in his high boots, tight coat, swastika, and so on, in full Nazi dress uniform, flicker instantaneously. Even if imagination occurs continually, its purpose to making us more human is not obvious, if we focus on what is considered "practical human achievement."

Actually, for many, to define humans as the imagining being or at least as partially defined as the imagining being might seem to make of human life something frivolous. That mistrust of imagination would be a misunderstanding of both the way that all of the apprehending powers of humans are interwoven, and how human imagination is not just the power to entertain nonactual state of affairs. Of course, some of the nonactual states of affairs will become potential ones, and even that power of imagination is vital to giving humans a richer future. However, it is even less appreciated how shaping symbols that concentrate the meanings of our relationships with the surround and others and how giving sensual shape to emotions, feelings, and concepts are an integral part of human meaning making. In the first case, for example, to see the other person's expression not only requires an empathetic emotional resonance to be fully understood and also a thinking through of what the person has told you about her or his situation, but in addition it takes an ability to imagine aspects of her or his world and life—to imagine, for example, what it would be like to be deaf or to be tied to a dialysis machine. As another example of this power of imagining in the situation discussed before, yes, we can be emotionally sensitive and feel a kinship, an affection, and respect for the deer in the forest in the winter, but to imagine it foraging through the snow for tufts of grass or being hemmed in by predators and giving itself up to them in order to protect its young and so on deepens these other apprehensions. In considering the power of imagination to give shape to emotions, feelings, or concepts, think how the flag brings together the ideas of patriotism, the memories of historical events, the feelings of excited pride, and the emotion of loyalty into one palpable experience musing on the flag, or how the bride and groom putting rings on the other's fingers makes real for themselves ideas of commitment, feelings of excitement, memories of their shared history and the history of other couples in their family and community, and the emotion of love. Part of those feelings and the meaning of their action flashed by in the images and imagined resonances of countless couples feeling similar feelings in all sorts of times and places and making this vow.

All three powers of imagination—conjuring up the nonactual, deepening relationships with others in the surround in partaking of their experience and bringing together in a sensual form ideas, feelings, memories, emotions and bodily gestures—integrate both the person and aspects of the world around her or him. So once again we can see that imagination as part of our embodied being is layered with other levels of significance and interwoven with other means of apprehension in such a way that each is altered by its relationship with the others. When computers generate wonderful new images or make projections of possibilities given the inputted data, new iterations, and combinations, they do so as separate data streams. Human embodiment only works by apprehending the perceptual, emotional, categorical, memorial, proprioceptive, and imaginal as a single phenomenon of interplaying streams of meaning.

The Storytelling Communal Animal, Integrated Brains/Selves, and Human Excellence

Part of the power of present inquiry is to look at humans, animals, and machines together, always comparing all three. Looking at just the comparison of humans and machines to fathom the pivotal role of the imaginal for human reality would miss something. So to turn the other way for a moment in our triad of comparison, if insofar as imagination seems to be the power of conjuring up experiences that are not actual—are "as if" they were real—this is a capacity that we share with animals. As Johan Huizinga pointed out in the influential work about the role of play in human and nonhuman life, *Homo Ludens*, and now echoed by so many writers about animal existence, animals seem to continually play. Huizinga opens his book with the declaration that "Play is older than culture . . . animals play just like men" (HL, 1). When two dogs romp and roll, bearing their teeth and growling, even nipping at each other, they are playing and conjuring up a scenario of acting "as if" they were fighting with the other dog. Of course, this kind of play fighting happens among many species, and even between animals and humans, as any dog companion will confess. This kind of play, projecting a situation that might be the case, but is not, and taking up its context and role to engage in fun, is that of imagination.

What is revealing in this comparison between humans and animals, however, is to see that what might make our human imagination differ is the way in which it has become integrated with the linguistic powers of our body, mind, and brain. The kind of linguistic power most relevant, however, is not merely a logical and rational use of language, for besides being imaginative, this language use undeniably appeals to our emotions, feelings, memories, and sensual and kinesthetic sense. The kind of imagination referred to here is that of the story, of entering into fictive worlds. The dog is in a fictive world, but one that is fleeting and not rich in much detail. It is a general framework of an imagined activity or situation. It does not set forth a particular significance or a particular history. If, as we have said, our minds use the power of language or of the movie screen or of the "dungeons and dragons" site on the Internet to "extend" the scope of our imagining—then we have a different power to inhabit the virtual world of the story—even when one day, June 16, stretches out for 750 pages in James Joyce's *Ulysses* and chronicles a staggering amount of details, links to history, and differing significances.

Many cultural critics and thinkers in the past decades have focused on the power of story for humans. Within philosophy, it was Alasdair MacIntyre's book, *After Virtue*, written in 1981, that contained the memorable declaration that the human being "is essentially a storytelling animal."[8] Stories give us continuity, place, purpose, and belonging. MacIntyre declares, "Deprive children of stories and you leave them unscripted, anxious stutterers in their actions as in their words." It was a shared insight in many fields that there was a power to be unleashed by the few words, "Once upon a time...," that could sweep humans up into a spell and introduce an addition to their world that was certainly beyond the direct chains of cause and effect. Not only to situate us, but to populate our world more fully, humans thrive with worlds of love, adventure, grace, betrayal, horror, and mystery, and they have all sorts of beings that are part of their surround, from six-foot rabbits to spaceship crews of the twenty-fourth century Federation of Planets to Huck Finn to Odysseus to Ophelia to Madame Bovary to Leopold Bloom to Puff the Magic Dragon and the Wicked Witch of the West, and so on, indefinitely. Our world has always been one interwoven with the flip side of fictional worlds. It is my contention in *Earthbodies* that although the Internet adds a ready-made intensity to the quality of virtual worlds, with its elaborate designs, sights, sounds, colors, and so on, to prompt the imagination, books already had a similar power to conjure up worlds of Hamlet and Beowulf, and that before that, for thousands of years, the four words "Once upon a time," the incantation of storytellers, already opened up virtual realms to their listeners.

In *After Virtue*, MacIntyre claims that without the attempt to weave our lives into a story, we fail to bring about a unitary sense of self and also fail to highlight and make real the values that are embedded within our familial, cultural, professional, and other heritages (AV, 203). In imagining the story of our lives, we bring into vitality ideas, moral concepts, feelings, emotional relationships, projected goals, prideful memories, and a sense of our own unique way of being. Without achieving this, for MacIntyre, we fall into a hodgepodge of social roles and mass culture identifications that dislocate us from ourselves and from resources for meaning. The story helps us not only gain a sense of who I am as an individual, but equally important is that in starting to tell my story, I realize how much it is "our" story—that my story only emerges from the stories of others, my family's, those who founded the spiritual path I have faith in, those who founded the town or country where I belong, those who have tried to achieve the kinds of things to which I am drawn as a calling, those who share a political situation, and so on. When humans discover and narrate their own stories, they discover how they are inseparably bound to others and to those with whom they are related, not only directly but by so many indirect legacies in their culture and history. As MacIntyre phrases it, humans cannot find meaning or act without posing to themselves the question, "Of what story or stories do I find myself a part?" (AV, 201). So, again, like with emotion, also with imagination, we are brought to the insight that for much of what we experience it is not "I imagine" but rather "we imagine." Also, in the imagined world, in our stories, we find that we already have a place, a history in which others have narrated me into stories that I now have to extend.

The idea that telling a story is the way we find a sense of continuous self within a context of meaning brings us back to a culminating point in Siegel's *The Developing Mind*. Siegel has described the ways the infant's "attachment" to the caregiver "establishes an interpersonal relationship that helps the immature brain use the mature functions of the parent's brain to organize its own processes" (DM, 67). The infant is "felt" by the emotionally sensitive and available parent in its emotional state and feels itself being felt by the parent. Channels of nonverbal communication are established, and "mental state resonance occurs in such a way that the infant's brain is 'co-regulated' by the parent who helps develop the child's capacities for self-regulation" (DM, 70). Again, unlike Descartes's assumption that thinking takes place in a sphere of private subjectivity, at the most basic level we become a consciousness through and with others who help us become what we can be. However, not all adults are capable of this sort of openness, communication, and availability, and the long-term effects on the child's development can be measured both as an infant and as an adult. The infant's behavior is observed in a controlled setting, where the infant is left for three minutes by the figure to whom they are attached and then observed during the separation and also afterward. In the diagnostic purview of "attachment theory," some responses can be considered as evincing "secure" attachment as a result of a bond with a secure caregiver, but a "dismissing" caregiver will result in an "avoidant" child or a "preoccupied" caregiver in an "ambivalent" or a "resistant" child. The detailed descriptions of these different capacities and behaviors are beyond our concerns here, but what is important to note is that one's ability to be emotionally sensitive and to integrate emotion, thought, and imagination in various tasks will be affected by these dynamics with the caregiver.

However, what also is relevant is the way in which these capacities, behaviors, and histories are assessed by asking the person to tell a story about his or her childhood, to tell the story of who he or she is and how he or she came to become himself or herself. The person is asked to relate a narrative that includes details of his or her childhood, the nature of his or her relationship with each parent, the sense of what it was like to be fearful, separated, upset, or threatened. The person is to narrate the losses in his or her life and the feelings associated with the losses. Then he or she is to tell the story of how his or her relationship with parents and other key figures changed over time, and how his or her personalities developed, as well as how he or she relates to children, including his or her own. Although this is oversimplifying it, in many ways how the narratives are assessed in order to gauge the psychological integration of the individuals is to see how well people tell their stories: if it is organized, gives detail, is well reasoned, is coherent, is recalled vividly, has insight, is able to take some distance, is emotionally modulated, has access to memory, is fluid, and so on (DM, 78–80). The narrative is not about "an exact accounting of what occurred in the past" (DM, 79) but rather the narratives of secure/autonomous individuals are "life stories that allow them to live fully in the present, unimpaired by troubles from the past, denial in the present, or attachment-related worries about the future" (DM, 91). To have a rich, imaginal current running through one's existence, one that integrates emotions, memories, and interpretations of the history of one's experience, is key to the development of a human self that can take in the world fully.

Siegel ends *The Developing Mind* by describing how vital narrative facility is to the fullest use of human capacity and meaning. On the level of brain function, "Narrative can be viewed as requiring both right- and left-hemisphere modes of processing information." To become better at telling one's story—which for Siegel is a lifelong quest—is to achieve better integration of the brain: "Coherent narratives are created through interhemispheric integration" (DM, 331). This greater integration between the hemispheres through developing the abilities of storytelling is also accompanied by greater integration "vertically"—that is, within the layers of flow of varied input within the hemispheres. However, this neurobiological integration only echoes the level of integration of emotional modulation, insight into implicit meanings of our lives, and our ability to communicate with others: "The narrative process also enables a form of interpersonal integration" (DM, 333). Patterns of "collaborative communication" are developed within oneself and with others. Similarly, to other areas of brain and psychological development, Siegel sees this narrative ability being fostered in the child by the parent: "In the co-construction of stories, parent and child enter into a dyadic form of bilateral resonance." Again, we return to the notion that humans are beings who learn and function through and with others, at least optimally, and who bring together emotion, rational, categorical thought, bodily gesture and feeling, and imagination, much to the transformation and deepening of all.

For Siegel, the capacity to narrate our lives leads to transformed abilities to achieve states of mind that allow for greater meaningful attachments with others in emotionally involving relationships. This deeper sense of shared selfhood leads the individual to experience greater "mental coherence." As a result of these breakthroughs, often people will experience greater vitality, spontaneity, energy, artistic creativity, and an invigorated sense of personal expression. However, Siegel also states that much of this transformation is below the level of reflective consciousness, as activated elements of the neuronal-brain system in one modality more freely recruit and interact with others, resulting in a resonance among them. In general, Siegel says, "Such spontaneous and energized processes . . . can also yield a deeper sense of creativity and appreciation within the 'everyday' experience of life: communication with others, walks down the street, new appreciations of the richness of perceptions, feelings of being connected to the flow of the moment. Life becomes a process, not merely a focus on products" (DM, 335). Rather than being Cartesian minds, distrustful of the senses, the emotions, and the influence of others to cloud the mind and deceive them, Siegel paints a picture of humanity coming to itself through greater shared emotional sensitivity and co-states of mind, gaining an inner and outer integration through others that leads to a greater letting go or spontaneity in being able to enter the flow of the moment as perceived, felt, interpreted, and imagined.

Taking what Siegel claims from neurobiology, attachment theory, and psychology, and putting it in an Aristotelian perspective, that virtue is the development of our capacities to their highest level and achieving their integration in order to be as creatively and sensitively responsive to our situation with others, telling our story well would be a key to humans' achievement of their *telos*, their excellence. Similarly, for MacIntyre, explicitly drawing inspiration from Aristotle, the ability to tell one's story is what not only allows one to achieve the same sort of coherent sense of self, and to overcome the nihilistic tendency of modern culture to fragment the person, but also allows for a moral vision (AV, 206). Only from finding their story do humans locate the values that are authentically theirs—values grounded in the fabric of who they are and how they are part of a community, a history, and a tradition. What are considered the goods of the good life emerge in finding all of the stories of which we are a part that can now be incorporated into our current story. Otherwise, we drift, without finding our virtue. Unlike either machines or animals, humans' distinctive excellence is inseparable from the imaginal stream that makes their lives into tales worth telling.

Ambiguity and Boundaries among Networks

The boundaries afforded by human thinking, emotions, and imagining seem so interconnected, indeterminate, and transgressive that they might offer no help in distinguishing humans from animals and machines. Yet it is this quality of not being able to be neatly separated and characterized as a collection of distinct faculties that is most distinctive about humans. If we are to draw some sort of boundary around humans in regard to animals and machines, then these characterizations of human apprehension and expression should be compared in direct relation to these two other realms.

Probably the most culturally persistent idea of humanity in the West has been the notion that our rational thinking makes us different than the rest of the planet. Insofar as humans are unique as thinking beings, it might be tempting to now consider whether machines are not better thinkers than humans in their ability to calculate, to utilize logical principles, to apply algorithms, to play chess, and so on, but we have described how this is not the kind of thinking that is distinctively human. Whether in turning to the findings of brain science, phenomenological descriptions, artificial intelligence projects, psychology, child developmental studies, and so on, the unique aspect of human thinking is that it occurs through our embodied sense of the surround, grounded in an emotional apprehension and orientation, involved in a nexus of relationships with other beings, and functioning within the parameters laid down by a history of interpersonal communication and care, channels the powers of the environment, extends its scope through aspects of the surround, is fraught with dualities that give it greater depth (both in terms of its meaning and its means), and is inseparable from the virtual and the imaginary. Yes, the logical, abstract, and rationally categorical is a precious part of this, but only that—woven in with the others insofar as it is distinctly human. Also, insofar as the *means of thought* might be thought to be merely mechanical, reducible to neural circuits or genetic organization ("hardwiring"), instead we find that these means are continually shaped and transformed by experiences with other people, events, and beings that also are emotional, imaginative, memorial, rational, linguistic, and cultural. Whether assessed according to content, process, or means, human thinking is more layered, complicated, and interactive.

The object of this rational thinking also is an evolving meaning of the world that is inextricably an interweaving of subjective and objective—neither of which exist in isolation, but only as aspects of an open dynamic system shifting through ongoing transformations. Not even the image of the individualized "thinker" remains—Rodin's wonderful statue notwithstanding—since "thinking" does not inhere in an immaterial, immutable private substance but is a "*we think amidst feeling, having emotions, dreaming, imagining, acting, within a surround that is material, cultural, personal, interpersonal and historical.*" However, this lack of impermeable and well-defined boundary around humans as thinkers eliminates machines as immediate rivals to take over this position and instead makes them part of human thinking as our "extended" body/mind incorporates their powers into its own.

Equally, the notions in this book dispute both the idea that only as having emotions are we distinct from machines, and also that as fundamentally emotional beings, we might be more close to the animals. Machines—especially those robotic, artificially intelligent ones—will incorporate in the near future more open-ended programming oriented toward the demonstrable aspects of emotionally communicated sense—like further responses to the "tonality" or rhythm of mood speech patterns—and incorporate more algorithms that cause them to behave *as if* they "need" companionship or physical embrace. Yet what machines will be constructed to achieve and "learn" about is more akin to the kind of emotional life *often attributed* to animals. It will be a response that might demonstrate behaviors that indeed are the way that emotions become manifest (and the behaviors that in humans "feed back" into themselves to deepen), or even cause machines to behave in ways that seem to be entering into emotional communication by seeking the gaze of a person. However, the human way of having emotions, at least when emotions are allowed to be developed in their fullest capacity to be sensitively revealing and expressive, is not being impelled by "drives" or only having elicited responses to a clearly defined stimulus (nor is this the case for some animal emotions), but rather is a way of entering a "give-and-take." Part of the emotional give-and-take with another person, with the surround and its things or events, is informed by memory, imagination, thought, rational categories, and history, and also part of the feeling is the *feeling of being felt* that is so key to attachment theory.

This makes human emotion different in two ways. First, human emotion is "impure," to put it in a more negative way, or "inextricably integrated" to some extent with other means of apprehension, to put it in a positive light. Second, sensitive human emotion is a sort of "resonance" among beings, because as embodied beings we have a visceral attunement that can be augmented by the kind of "letting go" or "letting be" that Chorost struggled to achieve in allowing his cyborg body to take advantage of his humanness. Emotions are not just responses to others; they are entering into a stream of shared experience that is transforming—in a minor way, of one's mood, one's way of experiencing the situation, of one's relationship(s), and so on, and in a more major way, of who one is or behaves or values.

Like the evolution of machines that is not going to leave an absolute difference between them and humans, so the same is true for the emotional life of animals, who are with us as "companion species," in an even wider sense than Haraway intends. The cave paintings were not wrong—there is a possible kinship of emotions among humans and other creatures, even with those with whom we will never open any sort of dialogue, because there are feelings of animals that also are partly shaped by memories, by concerns about other members of their group of whatever sort, by some sort of categorizing capacities of their minds, by animals' own relationality not only with their own species but possibly at times with others—as in the case of the isolated whooping crane, Tex, with whom George Archibald formed a "pair bond" and in the third season was able to engage with the crane in the elaborate leaping, spinning, pirouetting courtship dance of the cranes (SA, 78), or Martin Buber's wordless almost "I-Thou" relationship he describes with his cat, when he declared that "the eyes of an animal have the capacity of great language." Perhaps even more to the point is the way that animals' emotions are drawn in differing directions at times by the world and its relationships and are not just at the service of achieving pragmatic ends (again, despite the cultural prejudice to the contrary), as the continual play of animals shows (unless we are determined to interpretively reduce it to something else). However, it is perhaps most pointedly demonstrated by the chimpanzee that was in the midst of breaking open a coconut to eat for dinner and was observed stopping this task in order to stand for several moments to watch an utterly spectacular sunset, standing there gazing and gazing into the sky's colors and then afterward forgetting to take along the coconut. There is some commonality between human and animal in these emotional experiences, and yet the extent to which human emotion is integrated into all of the other ways of taking in a world in a continuous and multifaceted way alters the sense of human emotion. Just the power alone of human reasoning to project detailed futures or to categorize objects in extensive ways, or even the power of our imagination to generate complex fictions, alters also the sense of our emotions. Here the extent of something changes its quality, insofar as animals have evidenced each of these abilities, but to a much lesser extent. There is a difference of projecting the ways to build an atomic accelerator or fearing the scenarios of global warming and of the fact that soon it is time for dinner or feeling impatient to go for a walk.

These blurry differences between animals and machines come down to being implicated in the way the reality of the world comes forth in the only way we can know it—as experienced by humans, as *a phenomenon.* The rationalist philosophers of the scientific revolution wanted to separate "primary qualities" from "secondary qualities," since the latter ones—such as heat, softness, loudness, and sourness—depended upon humans' perceptions in order to be registered and could not be quantified for an absolute observer who would have no body and no part in the system. Now we know from modern science that there is no property that we measure or feel that is not dependent upon our human way of allowing itself to show itself in the world—to be witnessed by us by some means, even if through the machines we have created to extend the reach of our senses to that which could not have been perceived otherwise. The "quantum" brain of Schwartz and Begley has made us aware that the brain's own workings may well become what they are through the role of "the observer" within its own process—the human feeling of what is felt and thought is part of the brain's resolving itself into a certain state.

Inside and Outside Ourselves Simultaneously, Freedom, Interbeing

These conclusions about human embodiment, thinking, feeling, emotion, and imagination would seem to put this work at odds with most of the traditional ways of assessing humanity's distinctiveness. Yet as stated at the beginning of this chapter, divergent philosophical theories are rarely "wrong" in the sense of having no ground in our experience but often, rather, need to be given a wider context. Descartes's idea of the separation of the mind from the body and between the person and the world or others during experience is relevant to clarifying how humans are implicated in the world around them and have another sort of more fundamental freedom than the freedom that often is focused upon by theories of freedom or ideas of popular culture. Descartes took this distance as absolute, as given, and as foundational to humanity, but it may just point to aspects of our experience that are more complicated, and also to possibilities of certain kinds of human existence. In a technologically driven, consumerist culture, we may live in this dualistic way, for example. Both modern philosophy and psychology have articulated this sense of separation from the world as part of a larger and more complex situation of human consciousness. Trauma, child abuse and other events can lead humans in this direction. Furthermore, as part of a more complex situation, the power of humans to separate or to become psychically distant may serve other ends than the kind of detachment it represented for Descartes. It may be a necessary moment in a longer, integrated process. Paradoxically, to be split or to have a gap between us and the world through our consciousness may make possible the kind of enmeshment with the world we have described throughout this work from the initial description of how even animals are situated in a surround through a combination of distance and seamlessness.

For Sartre, the sense of being aware of ourselves as we experience anything is that background that makes any sort of human consciousness possible. In *The Transcendence of the Ego*, he describes how before any deliberate awareness of oneself, there is always an implicit awareness of ourselves when we are caught up in any act. It is part of the background of anything that I focus upon—that is, that I am focusing upon it is part of what I experience. As Sartre famously explores in *Being and Nothingness*, we can then focus on this implicit feeling and have the sense that the one who is now thinking about what we did an instant ago is *not* the same one thinking about this at this later instant, since it is no longer the same act of consciousness. For Sartre, this reflecting back upon oneself is the basis for a kind of insecurity that I am not one with myself, I am not utterly sure of myself, the way we could imagine that a rock is just a rock. This insecurity will strike particularly if we are trying to be sure how we were being perceived by others at that prior instant, and if we want to make sure that who we were a moment ago lived up to the ideal of what we were trying to achieve for ourselves and to project to others—for example, if I am trying to be a "true author" at this moment, or you are trying to be a "real reader" of that last sentence, or you are trying to be a capable driver driving across town, or an attractive person walking down the street. This looking back on who we were a moment ago ushers in the upsurge of self-consciousness that can lead us to not be able to swing our tennis racket fluidly or dance another dance gracefully, if we are trying *to see ourselves and also be ourselves at the same instant*, and thereby secure our ego ideal from the questioning of either others or ourselves. This is the problem of human consciousness that is at the heart of so much greed or violence or insecurity or desperate attempts to achieve something with one's life, so well described by Sartre. These are all attempts to achieve an unquestionable identity through money or success or the power over the other person. These are all afflictions that could not visit either animals or machines in the same way. A dog or a fox or a fish will not be racked with doubts about whether it is really a dog or a fox or a fish or just some sort of imposter, nor can we imagine a machine having this sort of doubt. A machine may be programmed to be open to various options and even responses, but to doubt what it is might be a tall order. So is this where we draw the boundary around humans? Actually, it may be a telling characteristic of humans that as Heidegger said we are the being that cannot be what it is. Given our awareness of ourselves, there is no aspect of ourselves that we cannot look upon and wonder if it matches what it is supposed to be. However, instead of pursuing further this negative side of self-awareness, it is helpful to see how it also opens us to the world in unique ways.

The other side of this unfocused self-awareness that still accompanies our consciousness of whatever is our explicit focus even while immersed in any act that can then break out into a more overt looking at oneself is that it gives humans an opportunity for both transformation and "identification." In the first case, Siegel speaks of the transformative power of a client's mastering "metacognition"—which is the awareness of having an experience while in the midst of it—of tacitly recognizing the sense of the unfolding experience without halting it or distancing oneself from it to the extent that one would become an object for oneself and therefore no longer involved in the experience. Rather, in metacognition, one is aware of the sense of what one is feeling, for example, but also is focused on the cause of those feelings and is able to "move" in guiding one's attention here or there within the experience. Siegel relates how a client who had always become agitated during experiences in which she was beginning to feel ignored was linked by her unknowingly to neglect from her mother. Her mother's neglect had been shameful to her, and thus she found herself in these circumstances to be feeling the rage that she had felt toward her mother. Now, through a process of reflection, she has opened her ability to become aware of herself during her experiences and to see how an experience is going to cause the same linkage to her feelings of that previous period of shame. Siegel explains that this linkage is easy to understand in terms of brain science as the firing again of past patterns of neuronal activation resembling a previous pattern, and having become woven together with other patterns that tend to activate each other, another way that brain science provides evidence for the way phenomenology sees present experiences as having symbolic dimensions of historical meaning. Having arrived at the point of metacognitive capabilities, however, when this client becomes aware of her unfolding feelings, she can focus on some other aspect of her experience and another facet of her relationship and then alter the context for this feeling. Then the larger sense of the feeling, with its background depth leading to rage, will be disrupted and transformed into a new possibility.

The kind of metacognition described is not the same process as the subject looking upon itself as an object that Sartre describes in our states of alienation but rather is more of a "dancing duality," a feathered modulation of "both and" or "not one, not two" that we have discussed in its dynamic. What is experienced is not so much a distance of detachment but the opening up of enough space to allow a depth of more than one kind of consciousness interweaving as it juxtaposes like the DNA helix. The freedom here that has been gained by much work over time by Siegel's client is not the Cartesian will to order the mind in commanding itself to proceed in a certain predetermined line and corresponding behavior but is, rather, the letting emerge from a wider flow of meaning that can expand us in a different kind of direction toward a new relationship. The situation comes to have differing significances and therefore differing possible outcomes. This is root human freedom—to make sense of the world in differing ways and to attend to the world and to ourselves in such a way that different aspects of the background of our context are presented and new possibilities become actualized. We often think of freedom as the ability to choose one way or another, but this is not the primary sense of freedom—it comes too late. Choosing between alternatives presupposes a human's ability to enter into a relationship with the surround in differing ways that give rise to differing senses and therefore differing choices. It is this primary sense of freedom to construe the world otherwise that so many humans either do not realize or flee from in order to preserve the status quo, either personally or collectively.

The other related sense of freedom, to choose what one wants when one wants it with no outside interference, is the idea of freedom that seems to be most often declared a goal in American popular culture. This freedom from restraint is a necessary part of human freedom—for example, to be enslaved by the threat of death and torture is certainly the antithesis of a humanly free and expressive life—but it is not sufficient to make humans free. It is the "negative" moment of freedom—to not be constrained, but does not address what freedom is to be used for—namely, to pursue a meaning and purpose in life, which requires commitment and foreclosing one's options by making choices and seeing them through. The most vivid portrayal of the trap of "negative freedom" is Kierkegaard's in *Either/Or* (vol. 1), when the aesthetic protagonist of the book strives to always be free to make another decision, to open another possibility, declaring, "There is nothing so intoxicating as possibility."[9] As a result, he cannot stay within a romantic relationship, a friendship, not even in a family, let alone sit through an entire play or book, because he feels constrained and needs to be able "to put on his marching boots" whenever he feels like and to choose to do something else, to go somewhere else, or to be with someone else. He ends up feeling like he is nothing, a stopped top, who was only spinning but had no courage to move forward. He has been so obsessed with staying "free from" any impingements on his moving wherever he likes that he ends up nowhere. Our one-sided view of freedom is leading many postmodern Americans into this impasse.

If we can distance ourselves yet also remain committed to our experiences, that is, to focus our attention and our care on those aspects that seem most likely to lead to our flourishing and to the flourishing of those around us, then metacognition, or the sense that implicitly we are caught up as prereflective selves in a richer surround, can return us to those selves and reintegrate all that comes along with it. Those obsessed with negative freedom, or those alienated from their experience, drive a wedge in the openness (just as Sartre proclaimed of modern, alienated European culture) between the selves they are and the implicit selves they find caught up in what just happened and its surround. We can take refuge in that distance and feel empty of purpose but "free," or we can be driven there by abuse or oppression because our experience is too painful to bear, or we can use that distance to not feel empathy for those we manipulate or overpower. However, we are the unique beings who can be "inside and outside" and bring them into creative tension and mutual enrichment. To cultivate this ability takes a sensitivity and a willingness to cultivate that attunement that Chorost pointed toward in being balanced between a diffuse focus of a slackening of the will with a flowing concentration.

The Taoist and Buddhist traditions have focused most acutely for thousands of years on this unique dimension of human being. Thich Nhat Hahn is a Buddhist teacher of "mindfulness" who is able to express very sophisticated insights in simple terms, and yet not sacrifice nuance or depth. He has described at length the interplay between the flow of consciousness and feelings and the focus of an awareness that pays attention without driving a wedge into experience or separating subject from object. He likens that awareness that does not separate itself from its object to the sun shining. He states that it appears then that there might be two "selves," the one of the flow of experience and the one aware of it, but he cautions, "Don't be in such a hurry to cut your 'self' in two. Both are self. Neither is self. Neither is false. They are both true and both false."[10] Hahn would agree with Schwartz and Begley that this kind of "mindfulness" is akin to the insights of quantum theory and allows a duality within unity of experience that transforms how and what humans experience: "You can no more separate the observing self from the self observed. When the sun of awareness shines, the nature of thought and feelings is transformed. It is one with the observing mind, but they remain different, like the green leaves and the sunshine. Don't rush from the concept of 'two' to the concept of 'one.' This ever-present sun of awareness is at the same time its own object" (SH, 11). What can open up for the human-layered consciousness is the interconnection of all the layers of experience within and without.

Hahn explains that if humans are nonjudgmentally, attentively, perceptually, gently, concentratingly, emotionally and sensitively aware of all of their actions, such as "while waking up we know that we are waking up, while buttoning our jacket, we know that we are buttoning our jacket, while washing our hands, we know that we are washing our hands" (SH, 14), then we would gain access to a different sense of the surround and ourselves in relation to it—one that had always been present, but not manifest in the same way. Hahn states that through this sort of "continuous recognition," humans gain a lived sense of "all particles being dependent upon all other particles and none have a separate individuality" or what he calls "interbeing" (SH, 32); not being swept along, yet "you must live in the body in full awareness of it" (SH, 43), such that the knowing that arises "is the life of the universe itself" (SH, 59). Hahn states that what humans can achieve this way is a direct sense or "knowing" that "cause and effect are no longer perceived as linear but as a net, not a two-dimensional one, but a system of countless nets interwoven in all directions in multidimensional space" (SH, 64). Humans sensitized in this way can see that "each object is composed of and contains all others" (SH, 65). This is a putting into action of what Merleau-Ponty described philosophically, summed up in phrases such as "Each object is a mirror to all others." It also is the recognition that physics and other sciences have realized. What Siegel makes us see in regard to his clients, or Schwartz and Begley in regard to their clients, or Hahn in regard to his students, is that any human has the potential to live this recognition in a way that opens up her or his experience of the world to greater vitality, meaning, creativity, flexibility, and insight, by paradoxically being inside and outside, or "not one, not two."

Humans Witness the World's Depth in Multivalent Apprehension

At the end of this long meditation of what boundaries might be drawn around humans in regard to animals and machines, it may seem as though we are left with too many lines—lines of connection both within the brain and neuronal system and with the surround, lines marking layer upon layer of different sorts of meaning, lines of force between humans and other humans, humans with all of the beings contained within the surround, humans with reality itself. Yet this is a unique kind of territory and way of being that exists among all of these lines. One way to name this might be to see that humans are a matrix—the site from which things emerge in what they show themselves to be and also are enclosed or sheltered within that system—here a dynamic system of observer and observed. This term might be apt, given that its meanings fittingly move from the abstraction of mathematical sets to crystallizing factors in metallic alloys to the between spaces of living tissue to the molds for printing and language dissemination to arrays of electronic components to its more ancient sense of womb or parent stem that nourishes. The multiplicity and variety of beings and functions that come together as a community of interplaying juxtapositions or as a parallel processor suggest human being. The human in its creative capacities does help shape or form, transmit, and give the solidity of meaning to show forth and yet nourishes the vitality of how the whole comes together to actualize and evolve.

Despite the immense power that humans have accrued from manipulating the natural world through machine extensions, the basis of their unique place is the recognition of all that is around them and their ability to let it come to be seen as what it is—whether expressed in language or the arts, in science, or in the built environment. Letting it be seen as what it is does not mean rendering it graspable—as if we have definitively captured it. As we have looked at humans, we are forever on the way to getting at more of a sense of who we are as caught up in these lines of interconnection with everything, and the same is true for each being as revealingly expressed by us. The power of human recognition is unlike the operation of the camera or the microscope or of the X-ray machine to give a defined and delimited image to the real—a rendered objectivity—but rather to make of each being a personlike acquaintance, an invitation to ever-more meaning and facets seen from ever-more perspectives, but never attaining a final, all-encompassing one. Even if we use machines or use our own power to produce a rendering that can be seen as definitive within certain parameters, we have that power and ability to both acknowledge that more clear and distinct sense—to use Descartes's terms—and at the same time to render it within other contexts and perspectives that give it back its inexhaustibility. We allow inexhaustibility to show its face—in the positive sense of meanings, brought together and articulated with always more to fathom, but also these meanings will never reach a closure.

This opening up of what always has more dimensions is human *witnessing*. Although the word is used most often in two very different contexts, the legal and the religious one, the legal idea is skewed toward the old rationalist sense of objective observation—at least in part. There are witnesses to "the facts" and then other sort of witnesses, but even with "character witnesses" and others, the legal procedure strives for objectivity. Legally, we want the witness to give us a clear and definitive testimony. Sometimes, for very limited purposes, the witness can do this. He or she can say this or that happened to a certain degree of certainly that might be enough for the legal goal of inquiry about the events of that moment. However, even if we can testify, for example, that he hit her, that may still be ambiguous in the sense that it might be impossible for the witnesses to have determined if he hit her purposefully or accidentally, or with the intention to kill or hurt or just scare or some other intention. But whatever certainty emerges for the legal venue, the witnesses may ponder for the rest of their lives what the events they perceived meant in other ways—for the people involved, for the neighborhood, for themselves, or for the nature of humanity or scheme of the cosmos. This excess of meaning that is not relevant to the court proceeding is most relevant to how humans take in and are involved in the world in their unique manner. Other kinds of beings other than human may make a state of affairs accessible for others to experience, but it tends to be framed in a more univocal way. We have described how bees make clear through their waggle dance the direction, distance, and amount of nourishment to be gained by others of the hive or how prairie dogs indicate to others the presence of various types of predators. Machines indicate to other machines or to humans much data about the world. Yet these are not witnessing in the second sense of moving into wider and deeper realms of meaning but are reports of states of affairs, as we might wish in the legal venue. Humans, however, have a choice about how to present something as witnessed by moving beyond the objective to share the unique human way of apprehending the world.

The witness in both senses of the legal and the religious is one who shares what she or he has experienced, but only the former reduces testimony to the objective. In the religious sense, a community or a person claims not only to have had a revelation of the presence of a spiritual reality but also to have taken in its meaning, and in addition to have felt its power, experienced its reality, become transformed by the revelation, and committed to sharing this with others. However, the religious use of the term is implied in all sorts of witnessing that humans perform. This kind of witnessing takes us beyond the daily practical concerns of getting food and shelter, and so on, or what Marx called the "animal needs," although this phrase is too reductive to animals who seem to seek affection, play, pleasures of various sorts, and other aspects of life beyond mere survival. However, humanity's most distinctive abilities do not manifest them in considering mere survival, but often when humans go deeper into the realm of meaning to reveal and express what about human being may differ from machines and animals.

The kind of recognition that occurs in witnessing is inseparable from the kind of indirect, but root freedom that we have described as human freedom. Before we can have a sense of ourselves, before we can learn to take the actions necessary for our daily projects as well as the larger sense of our life, before we learn to enter language through others talking us into it, we have to allow the surround and its things, creatures, and other humans to become manifest to us. The witness does not just feel an isolated, pure input of emotion or take in a perception as a piece of sense data or remain at the distance of objectively registering a pure fact. Rather, as we have described in this chapter, to witness is to be moved in perception emotionally in regard to something that we care about, and to make sense of, to have an idea about, to remember interconnected meanings and contexts from the past, to feel ourselves having the experience, to have imaginative senses come to mind that deepen the meaning, to viscerally experience the sense, to gesture, to have the sense of others' stake in the experience, to have our past with others resound through our openness to the experience, and to be called toward a response to what we are witnessing. We are drawn into a nexus of differing vectors of significance.

There are many spiritual, mythical, religious, and philosophical descriptions of the need for witnessing. For example, the natural surround and the place where one might dwell within it have called out to many to be witnessed, from Thoreau to Wendell Berry, who writes about paying attention to the natural surround where one lives as life's goal—one worthy, exciting, and demanding: "My own experience has shown that it is possible to live in and attentively study the same small place decade after decade, and find that it ceaselessly evades and exceeds comprehension. There is nothing that it can be reduced to, because 'it' is always, and not predictably, changing. . . . This is a description of life in time in the world. A place, apart from our now always possible destruction of it, is inexhaustible. It *cannot* be altogether known, seen, understood, or appreciated."[11] Without ever being fully fathomed, the human, such as Wendell Berry with his land, is drawn into the dynamic life around it to which she or he can resonate and express its sense and impact on her or him for others. A lifetime can be a commitment to taking to heart in differing ways a place, a person, an idea, a group of animals, a set of musical motifs, the breath going in and out of the abdomen, the suffering of wars, a vision of the divine, the differences in cultures, or the qualities of food or flowers or birds. Each of these objects of witnessing calls to mind famous witnesses and many groups of witnesses, from Annie Dillard to Albert Schweitzer to Mother Theresa to James Audubon to Ludwig Beethoven to Martin Buber to Jane Goodall to Loren Eisely to Donald Hall to the Dali Lama to Merleau-Ponty, and so on, indefinitely. This unique human practice is akin to Buddhist "mindfulness," as Thich Nhat Hahn would call it. Berry feels there is nothing more exalted or uniquely human than to experience the wonder and the details of the changes in his farm, the facts of topography and horticulture and their significance, the present and the past memories, and the fantasies that emanate from this place where he dwells. This is what Heidegger means when he says that humans "dwell" in a place: their being is caught up in a nexus of relationships with that of the place, and they care about aspects of the surround in caring for themselves and are capable of meditative thought that allows the sense and details of that place to come forward and be seen, heard, felt, put into language, and so on—what we are calling "witnessing."

We are called upon to tell others what we have witnessed, but this follows from the structure of witnessing. Others are already implicitly present with us in the way we receive that which we witness, for in some way the witness takes in the world for the sake of all others' world and for the sake of the world itself. We have seen how our powers of apprehension in what, how, and even the biological means of taking in the world are shaped by our history of interpersonal relations with others and with humans being included in joint structures of language, institutions, shared tools, categories of conception, traditions of artistic, emotional, and imaginative expression, the needs of the audience addressed, and so on, in such a way that "others are there with us" in our perceptions, moving through our bodies, at the core of any sense we can make of the world around us, and in the gesture of trying to express it to them to be shared with them—the task and opportunity of the witness. This is the sense of "being with" others, as a joint sense of existing only in and through others even if "literally" alone in a deserted locale that all of the phenomenologists, such as Heidegger, Jaspers, Marcel, Bergson, Merleau-Ponty, and Sartre, were trying to express.

This "shared being" with other humans also is what the early philosophically oriented Marx of the *1844 Manuscripts* meant by "species being"—that only humans in any expression, apprehension, or action have an implicit sense of how this comes from and impacts upon the entire species of humanity. There are myriad examples of animal affection, bravery, compassion, and mourning for one another, but we have no sense that they worry or celebrate or doubt or in any way represent to themselves how their lives might impact upon all other apes or all other birds or even all other dogs. Certainly machines, even if the AI robots can now *enact* emotional responses of some sort toward another being, cannot internalize a sense of their own being as inseparably united with the existence of any other beings, including other robots. Certainly the idea of being included in a set is a categorically rational one that conceivably an AI robot could come to master, and there may be "bonding" algorithms that drive it toward other beings, but the uniqueness of humans is that the idea first of a species-wide community—a sense of "humanity"—but finally a notion of community with all living and nonliving beings—and the accompanying feeling viscerally that other humans, creatures, and nonliving beings have all contributed to our apprehension and expression is at the heart of the sense of witnessing. The experience of a bond with others at its deepest level stems not from the recognition of compatible or complementary functions but of an ability through the interplay of what and how we experience that the most personal existence is the way we have channeled the interplay of all. Even this realization dawning from both a conceptual frame and an embodied feeling is different and yet the same within humans in the logic of "not one, not two," which comprises the way all of the human constituent powers form a whole in their juxtaposition yet retain their specificity.

The other senses present in witnessing is that the witnessing brings forth a meaning that itself is not only the work of all other humans, and the work of all beings in the world, but also that the sense that emerges from the witnessing is done on behalf of all beings. The kind of witnessing that has the power to add a depth of meaning to humanity's grasp and appreciation of the world centers on the way that what is witnessed is not the expression of a separable entity or person or creature or event. This does not just refer to the multiplicity of witnessing acts that humans perform and add to a summative appraisal of the world. Rather, when humans are most clear as witnessing—in contrast again to Descartes's claim that the most clear is the logical and distinct, but instead taking "clear" in the Buddhist sense of "cleansing the mirror" of the dust of ego concerns—the witnessed is seen, felt, and perceived in all ways as being both what it is itself and as being interdependent on all other beings. This interdependence allows for the "reversibility" that Merleau-Ponty articulates in how we bring forth meaning as if it were expressed by all of the beings to whom and to which we are related. To witness is to be rid of our own self-concerns that get in the way of what might be taken in about other beings within their own significance. We cannot help but witness from our own unique perspective informed by our personal and cultural history, but the powerful and sensitive witness pushes off from his or her perspective to allow to flow through himself or herself as many other perspectives as possible. We witness *as if* all the others were witnessing too.

Again, Hahn states most straightforwardly what happens when we move from our usual, everyday way of perceiving to a deeper witnessing that for him happens through meditation: "When we look at a chair, we see the wood, but we fail to observe the tree, the forest, the carpenter, or our own mind. When we meditate on it, we can see the entire universe in all its interwoven and interdependent relations in the chair. The presence of the wood reveals the presence of the tree. The presence of the leaf reveals the presence of the sun. The presence of the apple blossom reveals the presence of the apple. Meditators can see the one in the many, and the many in the one" (SH, 90). In other passages, Hahn goes even farther in describing how in the chair we also can see the logger, the logger's parents, and the long tradition of men who have logged trees or worked with wood, and so on. What we might add to that description, using Merleau-Ponty's idea of reversibility, is that we also see the logger's vision of the wood, the cloud's vision of the forest from above, the way loggers were seen by others, and so on. The witness is the means through which all of the interconnecting meanings of the world and the play within their apprehensions come to be expressed. What is witnessed is the way the world has of letting all of these lines of cooperation, interrelation, and interdependence come together and show forth. Only humans can allow this. Heidegger claims that this sort of meditative capacity of human thought is not separable from thankfulness or appreciation, and that is a subject we will consider in the final chapter when we look at what sort of ethical lessons are to be learned from the relationships of humans, animals, and machines.

It is undoubtedly the human physiology and structure of experience giving this ability to witness the whole and the interdependence of all beings that drives the religious traditions of the world to focus upon human witnessing as being central to the sense of the meaning of human existence. Yet this is self-defeating if these religious perspectives belittle our inclusion in the embodied, material, natural, and cultural world for some higher "purely spiritual realm." If we witness all other beings on their behalf—so that they can be seen, felt, heard, fathomed fully, and make an impact—then we are open to something beyond human being in our unique capacity as a witness, but this "beyond" is still very much of the earth. Almost all spiritual and ethical traditions warn against taking ourselves as the sole meaning of existence, and this seems to be what is most special about us—our openness to other beings. *This is paradoxical: what is most defining about us is that we allow the specialness of every other being to be able to come forth into the light of expression and comprehension.* In the major religious traditions, there usually is a guidance of humans to love. This kind of spiritual love is expressed in more personal loves, but it has an impersonal dimension to it—an embrace of all humans, all creatures, and even of all beings that exist. This is usually taken in the sense that humans are called to love in order to thrive among themselves and with the rest of the planet. However, I might suggest that it is even more fundamental that humans love in the sense of opening themselves to take in the world sensitively, so that the rhythms, meanings, and significances of all other beings come to be appreciated and then expressed through humans' ability to witness. Perhaps this thought is most strikingly articulated in the opening phrase of the Tao te Ching, which asks of humanity to concentrate and meditate upon the manifestation of "the ten thousand things" in relationship to the deeper Tao as the entry into its spirit.

As we look further into what is distinctive about animals and machines, we will try to distinguish how it is that they do not witness the world in the way humans do. However, for humans, witnessing is not just a distinctive activity but more like a virtue in Aristotle's sense, as the fullest realization of all of the potential abilities of the person on all levels, bringing out all of the excellences that are components of human makeup. We cannot help but witness to some extent, but to fully witness with all of the sensitivity, the imagination, the passion, the intelligence, the openness, the fluidity, the expressiveness, the acuity, the patience, the motivation, the generosity, the care, the appreciation, the compassion, and the "loving kindness" (as the Buddhists would say) is a great achievement and an ongoing task that no person could ever perfect, for the world is inexhaustible as are the beings that resonate fully to it.

The witnessing upon which we have focused is the positive experience of the witness—the deepening, expansive taking in of meaning from events, beings, and people in the world that we appreciate in their coming to stand forth. However, much witnessing is of pain, of suffering of varied sorts, and of horror. As James Hatley fittingly entitles his book, *Suffering Witness*, to speak of the plight of humanity being called to witness something as unfathomable and horrific as the Nazi exterminations during World War II, compassion often hurts and can run the risk of being disheartening. Yet this too is uniquely human. Animals can feel the suffering of others and certainly of those animals with whom they have bonds. They mourn, feel sad, and are in pain. They can howl with loss. Yet we only know of how humans can witness some atrocity and as part of the witnessing be called into considering the flaws of humanity, the nature of evil, to imagine realms of negativity, to take this horror and put it into poetry, to conceive how even in surpassing this horror humans can have a dignity in the face of the realization of the horror that Kant saw as the deeper sublime, and so not despair. Humans perhaps also are unique in both their vision of the abyss and how it might be transformed. Ultimately, the trajectory of the abyssal breaks the web of interconnections, yet in being witnessed the human can struggle against this fate. Even in the worst "hell world," as only humans seem capable of creating—a realm of hatred, violence, and brutality in the sense of attacking the other's dignity and sense of self-worth—there is the power of the witness through seizing upon empathy, compassion, and the universalizing power of expression in language, art, and recording for history a resistance to the annihilating spirit of that hell world. Attentiveness not only is vital to the coherence of interconnection, the joining across distances of the realization of the power of the observer and observed, but it is also vital to the actualization of a felt sense of solidarity among humans. As we will consider in the last chapter, this attentiveness to violence may be needed to create solidarity between the human and non-human world too.

When Hahn speaks of the Bodhisattva of compassion—that being who has overcome attachment to all emotions but compassion—he speaks of how humans are capable of the greatest compassion in nondiscrimination. In this state of mind, humans no longer choose one thing over another. For Hahn, "A compassionate person sees himself or herself in every being. With the ability to view reality from many viewpoints, we can overcome all viewpoints and act compassionately in each situation. This is the highest meaning of the word 'reconciliation' " (SH, 128). This does not mean for Hahn that we are to accept cruelty or duplicity, but that we are to oppose all sorts of violation "without taking sides," without closing ourselves off to the reversible relationships of interdependence with others. However, this is only possible for Hahn because humans can see themselves in all other humans and all other beings. So again we see that the distinctive human abilities are based on the fact that as brain science, psychology, philosophy, and other fields have found, humans take in the world in so many ways simultaneously, from so many vantages, being immersed in the process and also dancing outside the of process simultaneously. These abilities translate into a relationship with the whole of so many dimensions and dovetailing perspectives that in joy, in appreciation, in suffering, in compassion, in fear, in reconciliation, and in forgiveness, the human is the being who can witness the interplay of the world's web of varied beings.

Chapter Six

Animals

Excellences and Boundary Markers

The Problem of Understanding Animals' Perspectives from Within

For humans to describe the "experience" of animals embedded within a surround and open to other beings would be considered by many an impossibility and a heresy against common sense. Some would claim that we cannot even know *if* an animal experiences. Many more would claim that it is, on principle, impossible to say anything about an animal's experience of itself, the world, or certainly of other creatures, since humans cannot know or even guess the content of animal worlds. Yet aspects of the kind of relationship that I have been articulating among humans, animals, and machines lead to the idea that humans have access to the experience of other animals. This is yet another point of much controversy among scientists, philosophers, and even within popular culture. Can I experience what animals are experiencing to some extent, or must I admit that we are too different to have that sort of understanding?

The work that became the standard reference for discussions about these questions is Thomas Nagel's essay of 1974, "What Is It Like to Be a Bat?" It is cited over and over again as the touchstone for the opinion that even if a human tries to use imagination to enter the experience of a bat, the best any imaginer could do is get some sense of "what it would be like for *me* to behave as a bat behaves. But that is not the question. I want to know what it is like for a *bat* to be a bat."[1] In other words, the best we can hope to do is project our own human existence into some other context. For Nagel, imagining webbed wings, flitting flight, catching insects in one's mouth at dawn, gaining bearings through a system of reflected high frequency sound signals, and hanging upside down during the day would only give us an idea of what we would do as humans if forced to live like a bat. He claims that imagination is "restricted to the resources of my own mind, and those resources are inadequate to the task. I cannot perform it either by imagining additions to the resources to my present experience, or by imagining segments gradually subtracted from it, or by imagining some combination of additions, subtractions, and modifications" (WB, 394). For Nagel, and those who conceive of the world like he does, humans cannot imagine the experience of another creature, because the type of experience is too foreign, too different.

However, it is important to notice that Nagel has assumed much about the nature of a human's imagination, the nature of a human's relationship to what is around it, and also what it would mean to "understand" another sort of creature. The assumptions are the ones that underlie scientists' thinking, mentioned in chapter 2, those scientists who consider any talk of an animal's experience to be "anthropomorphizing." Nagel, actually, is much less reductive and more open to allowing for the possibility of a greater depth in animals' lives, but his sense of what a human is and what our reality is holds him back from being able to hearken to animals in ways that might be fruitful. His understanding of the power and scope of imagination is too limited, as is his starting point of creatures existing in isolation from one another. For him, our bodies isolate us in space. He does not envision as a possibility the kind of human embodiment that has been the starting point for this book, that the depth of human embodied experience is copresent within perception with other creatures open to the same surround. Given his objectified sense of the body and his sense of rational understanding among discrete beings at a distance from one another, the kind of "resonance" we discussed among beings open to the same gestalt and partially "thought, imagined, and felt" by the world as a materiality lined with currents of energy and meaning moving through the creatures within the nexus of the surround is not a possibility.

Nagel begins his essay on a note that is encouraging to those of us who want to see animals in a less reductive way by declaring that "conscious experience is a widespread phenomenon" (WB, 392). He sees this conscious experience of the world by all sorts of creatures and even in "countless other forms throughout the solar system" as something that can be recognized, even though it is not analyzable or even fathomable. Nagel offers a helpful definition of what it is for an organism to be conscious as indicating "that there is something that it is like to *be* that organism." It seems palpable that there is something like the existence of a cow as being distinctly like a cow or as a dog being something distinctly like a dog or a bird being something distinctly like a bird, and Nagel starts with this recognition. This means that there is a way of being a bird so that seeds have a certain presence *for* it, or as being a lion that a deer has a certain presence *for* it, and so on.

Nagel admits that it is hard to point to the exact evidence for consciousness, but that does not mean humans cannot experience that animals do have this sort of existence as themselves. So it is important to notice that part of Nagel's idea that rats or bats or cats are conscious is to assert that they have "experience" (WB, 393). To have experience means that whatever happens to a creature has a certain specific subjective character to it. Nagel feels that we cannot possibly dream what sort of significance a bat's pain has for it, or its fear when being attacked, but we humans can experience that it does have *some sort of significance* for it.

Another way to say this is to say that whatever occurs in the life of a creature has significance from *its particular point of view*. This point of view may be taken to be utterly unique to that being. For Nagel, this is an evident fact, but it also means that we can never understand the experience of an animal, or even little of a human, who has a very different point of view. Nagel discusses trying to know, for example, the experience of a person who experiences as differently from himself as a Helen Keller, and states, "The subjective character of the experience of a person blind and deaf from birth is not accessible to me, for example, nor presumably is mine to him" (WB, 395). For Nagel, we would have to be able to bridge the gap with another being who has a very different point of view by getting "outside" of that point of view, of the subjective phenomenon, to something that would characterize it that was objective. As objective, whatever could be gleaned could then be generalized to explain aspects of the experience shared by both beings, and thus understood by the other being. By definition, this is not possible, if experience is defined by the particular point of view of each creature. One cannot get "beyond" or "outside" or "above" the point of view and achieve a more neutral point of view, for then one would lose what one was trying to understand. This is where Nagel's faulty assumptions are revealed, and they are important, since they are widespread assumptions of contemporary Western culture. The Cartesian, rationalist shadow looms long over our thinking.

Instead of seeing the bat as Nagel does as a discrete creature within its own hermetic world, as did even Heidegger and von Uexküll, we can envision it as embodied in such a way that its flesh is of the "flesh" or same "stuff" of the surround in such a way that there are resonances or interplays among all of the embodied members of that surround, who have some immediate vantage *through one another* on their common world, so that part of our being is some sort of "bat being." Admittedly, it is a very obscure part, one buried deep in the background sense we have of the surround. But everything within the background can become a focus for attention, concentration, meditation, and exploration. For Nagel, and many others, it is only by finding objective descriptions of a bat's experience that we would start to fathom it. Accordingly, he disparages the use of imagination, the use of analogies, the use of poetic phrases, and the use of empathy as heading in the wrong direction to get at other creatures' points of view. For a rationalist, to turn to imagination and to poetic language is to become further mired in one's own human subjectivity, and thus further from getting at the truth of the bat's or other creature's experience. Admittedly, this *can be* the case. However, there also is a painstaking, artful, careful, and sensitive use of imagination, analogy, and poetic metaphor that can require as much concentration, restraint, training, trial, and effort as any finely applied use of deductive and inductive methods of reasoning, observation, and experimentation.

There are several issues here. First, Nagel, like many empiricists, seems to assume that imagination is merely reproductive, taking what we have already experienced and recombining it in new ways, but never moving beyond its ground in the original experience. Imagination, as productive, however, can be seen to make leaps and create new senses and meanings never before experienced. Admittedly, it is easier, and more people if asked to use imagination, will rely on reproductive imagination. However, this is no different from the fact that most people also will rely on very superficial rational analyses, taking what is known already and not thinking beyond to really new formulations, arguments, or schemas, which require doing painstaking critical and thoughtful analyses. Similarly, poetry, like logical uses of language, can be used in a facile way, with clichéd metaphors as we can think with overused arguments, or it can be used in ways that take care, concentration, daring, intensity, and sensitivity, and become revealing. When Nagel gives as an example of analogies or metaphors of "little use" in understanding experience of others who are different, as in his example of the person without sight saying something like " 'red is like the sound of the trumpet' " (WB, 402), he declares that this sort of bringing percepts of differing senses into juxtaposition "obviously tells us nothing."

Yet this kind of metaphoric use of language, especially one with such juxtapositions of ordinary sense, is precisely where and how we can delve deeper into the meaning of percepts and see into the overlaps with other beings. As Merleau-Ponty has explored, it is precisely in the juxtapositions of the dimensions of meaning associated with one sense that impinge and are expressed by and through the other senses that we can express and experience more acutely and with more depth of sense the original meaning. This juxtaposition is central to his sense of the greater depth that meaning can assume and also is in accordance with the higher brain functioning we discussed in the last chapter. That is why art is so powerful at the moment when a Beethoven gives us the sound equivalent through tone, rhythm, harmony, pace, and so on, of the feeling of jumping upward in the exaltation of joy at peace and understanding among people listening to his Ninth Symphony or of a Monet giving us the color, line, shading, composition of interplaying hues, and so on, of the hush of the morning on the river at daybreak and the tranquil heart of existence. The differing events, objects, and feelings brought into interplay do not capture an objective characteristic, but they do give us another sense of what each means in both its overlap and difference with the other. A joyful feeling in response to some event, a conceptual description of joy, an exclamation of joy in a shout of glee, a kinetic gesture of joy of arms raised in triumphant feeling, a picture of a harmonious group of people, and so on, are all potentially meaningful and powerful, but they become much more so when something like a work of art brings concept, sound, gesture, text, and other ways of expressing and apprehending into juxtaposition as a whole. As we have already described, something like a color and a sound are very different and very much the same, and the different sorts of tensions set up between them can evoke a deeper signficance.

Equally wrong is Nagel's insistence on the need to find assertions that are rationally objective and universal in order to understand other points of view, while he dismisses descriptions that are more poetic. The poetic use of language is that power of language to bring disparate meanings and realms of experience into juxtaposition within one reference. This power of metaphor is articulated by Paul Ricoeur when he states, "It is as though a change of distance between meanings occurred within a logical space. The *new* pertinence or congruence proper to a meaningful metaphoric utterance proceeds from a kind of semantic proximity which suddenly obtains between the terms in spite of their distance. Things or ideas which were remote appear now as close."[2] Ricoeur explains that metaphor deviates from our usual rules of pertinence and relevance, and that a new meaning is produced by bringing what had been previously separate into juxtaposition by the metaphor. What happens as a result is that there is "new predicative meaning" produced. In this way, poetic uses of language, when done well, are "both a seeing and a thinking" that restructure our previous semantic fields and cross the previous categories of thought to become "transcategorical" (MC, 427). Yet unlike more rational, objective assertions, in the poetic expression, the "tension" between semantic congruence and incongruence is preserved, as is also the " 'remoteness preserved within 'proximity' " between the ideas brought together in the depth of meaning of the metaphor. So, to use Nagel's example, to bring an object from the category of musical instruments' sounds into proximity with color can allow us a new sense of that sound. There is something undefinable but meaningful in articulating the "redness" of a trumpet wail. The passion, the penetrating quality, the almost violent quality, the painful aspect of the sound are suggested. This, as we said before, captures what Kant meant when he talked about the "free play of the faculties," when the imagination gives rise to new meaning. It is this logic of "not one, not two" or yin and yang or "one and many." As we have also seen in brain studies, such free play of the brain and neural systems is a fertile moment of meaning making.

Ricoeur also states that the metaphoric dimension of language as a process of "semantic innovation" powers the imagination as productive and is tied to the "image as an emerging meaning," instead of a settled one (MC, 428). The meanings expressed in metaphor play off the visual and sensual in such a way that there is a movement between the conceptual and the perceptual. In this movement, "The metaphorical meaning compels us to explore the borderline between the verbal and the nonverbal" (MC, 429). In other words, this is a use of language that draws us back into embodiment and the perceptual realm, as well as the realm of feelings. The juxtaposition of meanings is also about bringing feeling, affect, into the kind of understanding offered by poetic language and metaphor: "This instantaneous grasping of the new congruence is 'felt' as well as 'seen'" (MC, 432). As Ricoeur puts it, to understand in this way is a different sort of understanding than that of the objective stance: "To feel, in the emotional sense, is to make *ours* what has been put at a distance by thought in its objectifying phase" (MC, 432) If we are to look at the lives of animals and try to express through poetic articulation by paying a certain kind of attention to the texture of their experience that maximizes perceptual and felt resonances or "reverberations"—a word used by Bachelard to express how the poetic imagination can attune itself to the existence of other beings and cited by Ricoeur as an apt phrase—then we can take into our embodiment a "lived sense" of animals. It is open-ended and never achieves closure, as are all "understandings" of this interplay of perception, thought, imagination, and feeling, yet it is something significant. To appreciate this power of poetry, imagination, and feeling or emotion requires seeing us as embodied beings whose taking in of the world is this nexus of meanings and processes.

To bridge the seeming chasm between humans and other species, Nagel and other rationalists need to see embodiment as that immersion in the surround so that we are in a "reversible" relationship with all that makes up its nexus. If the way I can walk across a field is to have the sense of the sky above me as seen from the perspective of the birds above or the clouds floating by, the river roaring beside me or the fish within the water, then the ability to focus on what it would be like if I can restrain my all-too-easy set of human projections upon that being's experience and really turn to extend my sensitivities, my feelings, and my imagination is not entirely implausible if I can get some sort of sense of that way of being, since in some fragile and deeply located way it is part of my extended being. My human sense of something perceived already plays off of the bird's sense, the fox's sense, the chipmunk's sense, and the tree's sense in some background hidden and obscure way. If we see ourselves as humans in comparison to animals as discrete objects separated by not only differing but also insular bodies and processes of apprehension, then there is no access to the other's point of view. If this were true, then one could contend like Stephen Laycock, in an even harsher-stated stance than Nagel's, that all supposed understanding of animals' points of view is projection, and all "discoveries of animals are ventriloquism."[3] However, if we appreciate that our embodiment only works through inhabiting all of the surround, so that the returning currents from it, full of other creatures' vitality, inform our sense of ourselves, then we cannot help but have access to other animal beings, if we can tune into these flows of energy and meaning. This means that the answer to the problem of the seeming impossibility of understanding animal experience is that *to be fully within a point of view is also to be without (in others), and to be without (in others) is also to be within a point of view.*

However, to make one more observation about this ticklish matter, to appreciate the interweaving of perspectives is not to minimize how much effort, concentration, and development of artistry and sensitivity the gaining of a sense of other points of view would require. Two interesting suggestions that are in line with the notion that embodiment as open to the environment is key to this sort of reverberation are made by authors included in the volume *Animal Others*. Carleton Dallery looks at those who work with animals to understand the communicative possibilities with them—something that is necessary to develop and understand if one is going to be a dog trainer or a horse trainer, for example. These people must learn to "read" the animal through all kinds of nonverbal interactions, of touching, postures, gestures, noises, pressures, strokings, nuzzlings, lickings, kicks, twists, and eye contact, and also to communicate back to them. Within all of these modalities and others are possibilities for getting beyond one's perspective and ways to stay locked within. For example, Dallery explores the difference between touching the animal in such a way that one is the human addressing the other, whether giving orders or a certain human-defined idea of affection, versus a kind of "receptive touching"—that patiently, openly, and sensitively attending kind of touch.[4] However, what is key to all sorts of understanding and communicating with animals is what has quickly become lost in this hyperactive, distracted postmodern culture: a slowing down of time, an attending that waits and waits, patiently, for manifestations of presence and expression, a being quiet in respect and openness. It takes a centering, becoming aware that can find resonances that attune themselves to the other, just the kind of comportment that Siegel stated should be expressed and practiced by parents toward a child if they are to develop a connection that maximizes the child's ability to bring all of their capacities for understanding into interplay. Dallery states that it takes "sustained attention" on the part of the human, and that "only through sustained attention can a perceiver detect the temporal unity of an animal, its style, its way of moving and responding" (AO, 268). Like the Taoists also, Dallery is saying there emerges a "way," or what Merleau-Ponty called a "style," a kind of resonance or a melody among all of the expressed aspects of the animal, which says something about what it is experiencing, but only if hearkened to in all of these ways.

Elizabeth Benke suggests that part of these other ways of understanding requires a certain way of living in one's body. She claims that a "letting the weight settle" of the body is required to fully take in the animal's point of view as taking a different posture vis-à-vis the world: "Indeed, letting the weight settle can be a lucidly lived 'act' or 'gesture' that moves me through the whole and grounds me more fully in the situation rather than withdrawing me from it and shunting me into the status of spectator" (AO, 103). Benke says that it is not enough to know the body can be embedded within the environment in an understanding way versus the objectifying distance of rational assessment—one has to find the postures that put this into practice: "And with this, my body is neither a mere point of view on things nor an objective mass over and against 'me,'" but she says it becomes immersed within the surround experiencing the give-and-take with it in perception. Then, she says, "For me to sense myself bodily in this way is simultaneously to be related to something other than my own mass; it is to have a position in the world, on the Earth-ground, with my fellow creatures in a shared field" (AO, 103). Differing kinds of embodied understanding require working with the body in specific ways to achieve certain kinds of attunement.

If we can develop our creative imagination and capacities to be finely sensitive to the animal energies and voices reverberating within our shared surround with them, and can refrain from projecting our human-centered frames of reference, then we can enter the experience of animals. Actually, we cannot help but experience animal energies and senses of the world, or we would not be able to fully function as humans. We do live in a culture that drowns out these murmurings within us, but they are present in our interspecies life. We are encouraged to anthropomorphize, and we often do. However, this is not inevitable. The surround contains the tracings of animals throughout its expanse. These gifts are there to retrieve sensitively and to augment their meaning.

The Thickness of Animal Perception versus a Reductive Mechanical Model

For those who think about the place of animals in the world and about their relationship to humans, one of W. H. Auden's poems, *Their Lonely Betters*, is often cited. The poem is in many ways a statement of all of the traditional conceits of why humans think they are different sorts of beings from animals and are superior, such as having language, being aware of mortality, or taking responsibility for others. The poem ends with the crowning line, "Words are for those with promises to keep."[5] Auden's poem seems to declare verbal promising as indicating something about humans that is distinctively excellent. However, as Nietzsche pointed out in *The Genealogy of Morals*, this particular declaration of humanity's responsibility and virtue can have a more troubling side: "To breed an animal that is entitled to make promises—surely this is the essence of the paradoxical task where human beings are concerned? Isn't that the real problem of human beings?"[6] For Nietzsche, this aspect of humanity points to how we step back from ourselves and try to fashion ourselves into predictable entities that will be approved of by other humans, instead of allowing ourselves to move freely within the unfolding flow of our existence in ways that emerge as expressive and immediately responsive to our situation, but perhaps not in keeping with how others want us to behave. Language here is not the crowning attribute of humans but a way in which humans are at odds with themselves and at odds with others as diminishing what they might otherwise be. Language in this use, for Nietzsche, is a tool to make humans more predictable and able to be controlled by societal groups that might fear the unbridled expression of other humans' vitality.

Animals as not having to bear the responsibility of promise making and of not being capable of entering into moral obligations that need a reflective commitment to be fulfilled are in the vision of Auden's poem excluded from the realm of words in a way that strikes the narrator of the poem, given the nature of animals, as "it seemed to me to be only proper." Animals in this vision are little more than moving objects in the material world. It is true that they are self-moving objects, to revert to Aristotle's original definition of animals, but in Auden's poem, animals "run through" their repertoire in the way a simple machine moves at the behest of its gears with no purpose, meaning, or encounter: "A robin with no Christian name ran through/The Robin-Anthem which was all it knew." Overlooking that we know that members of the same species of bird inflect their songs in differing ways, that a Western meadowlark can sing like a Baltimore oriole under some conditions, that either mockingbirds or lyrebirds can master up to 200 different songs or even sing by mimicking other sounds heard in their surround (SA, 34), there is in addition to this prejudicial denial of animals' ability to be expressive, to deviate from some determinate mechanism, or to be aware of death ("there was not one which knew it was dying") a devaluing of what might be most distinctively excellent about animals, if seen from a different perspective. Repetition and consistency are not only mechanical attributes. They might be part of a different rhythm of another sort of meaningful life.

Auden's devaluation very much echoes Heidegger's characterization of animals (discussed in chapter 2) as not being able to encounter either the world around it or itself in its "captivation" by the environment and as a result of the animal's "driven directness." Enclosed within the "ring" of things around it, "impoverished" in its sense of what is about it, and "possessed" by things, an animal has no encounter with the world and "in a fundamental sense the animal does not have perception (FCM, 259), according to Heidegger, as we discussed in chapter 2. As "self-encircled" by its environment, for Heidegger the animal is "incapable of ever properly attending to something as such" (FCM, 249). In this devaluation of the animal's perceptual life and potential to have an encounter with the world or itself, and in Auden's phrases of "running through" its behaviors, the specter of the machine is invoked, even though many of us might find that Elliot's use of the metaphor of the mechanism to be more telling as applied to human behavior: "Unreal the brown fog of a winter dawn,/A crowd flowed over London Bridge, so many,/I had not thought death had undone so many./Sighs, short and infrequent, were exhaled,/And each man fixed his eyes before his feet./Flowed up the hill and down King William Street."[7] It seems obvious that humans, admittedly not at their finest or fullest functioning, can lapse into mechanisms in the sense of being dulled to the point of barely encountering their world, yet animals, who are in so many cases the finest-tuned perceivers imaginable, seem hardly ever dulled to the point of not taking in acutely their world. They might repeat vibrantly their song, but hardly ever dully, vacantly, or vaguely.

What Auden and Heidegger mean to assert, then, is obviously not about the acuity and precision of the perception or action of animals, since a hawk circling far above and spotting a mouse running across the field displays far finer acuity than we could ever hope for with our human visual capacities, or a spider spinning its web under varying conditions and places within its surround displays far more dexterity than humans can and more responsiveness to the finest aspects of the surround. What Auden and Heidegger are asserting is that without the distancing capacity of being able to be consciously and deliberately reflective about oneself, and taking oneself in the midst of a situation as an object for "the mind's 'I,' " as Daniel

Dennett entitled his book on this issue, there is no "encounter" between the world and "something" else. In addition to this, it is the human capacity to distance that allows humans to promise, as Auden lauds us. We can look at ourselves from afar and project our future actions as possibilities and claim that we will stay in charge of these actions and ourselves as agents by the force of our willing ourselves from a controlling distance. This, for Auden, makes humans capable of being moral, of keeping a promise.

However, it is possible to see that even though this human ability allows for a certain kind of restraint and self-guiding, this is not the only way to be self-aware, nor even the only way to follow through on intentions toward the future, nor even the only way to achieve a certain kind of restraint toward possibly harmful actions toward other beings. Auden and Heidegger, and all of those who espouse this fairly common stance toward animals, seem to assume that animals' immersion in perceptual consciousness without the distance of protracted reflection means that there is a "blind" or an "unnoticing" meshing of organism and world, like the cogs in the gears of a simple mechanism. The thinking of Auden and Heidegger does not fully fathom how animals living in the perceptual world in a more concentrated and fully immersed way cannot only achieve feats within the perceptual realm that we cannot but can also achieve other overlapping vital aspects of existence in a differing way than humans.

From everything we can study about the perceptual world, it is a world that is lined inextricably with emotion, with feeling, with some significance, with vectors of attraction and repulsion, with energy and vitality, with echoes of the past, with future possibilities, with routes of direction and connection, with senses of place and even dwelling, insofar as it is taken in by any animal, among whom humans are so classified by taxonomists with all of the other species of *animalia*. Given the Enlightenment and Cartesian tradition of breaking down complex phenomena into simples and separating parts from wholes, human perception had long been seen in the empiricist or intellectualist tradition as the input of discrete sense data to be either constructed into meaningful wholes by the judgments of reason or through a mechanical association, until phenomenologists insisted on taking as valid evidence the way humans *actually* experienced the world in meaningful wholes with layers of input in the unity of the field of observer and observed. Merleau-Ponty boldly declared about the sensation, "This notion corresponds to nothing in our experience" (PP, 3). There are only meaningful percepts in contexts. To say that we experience our hearing of music as a melody, but that it is *really* made of notes that we must somehow put together as traditional philosophy did, instead of saying the reality of our existence is *the way we experience it* as a flowing whole, is the shift phenomenology made in describing how and what we "know" prereflectively.

Even though phenomenologists recognized that humans always initially perceive meaningful wholes and create isolated parts through analytical reflection upon experience, there has not been much exploration of *how animals experience* percepts as gestalts or meaningful wholes, too, although perhaps in a different way. Yet in the animal studies we have discussed, it seems that there are parallels to phenomenology's descriptions of how humans live in the surround within a nexus of tasks and significant places. Whether it is how insects such as bees see the tree and the angle of the sun in relationship to their flight back to the hive and find it in terms of the whole of the landscape (AM, 196) as a living place and a feeding place, and so on, or how a bird such as the Clark's nutcracker sees not just a physical feature such as a crevice, but sees that crevice as a place "to hide seeds to be retrieved later in the winter" (AM, 59) in terms of having the same sense of things "ready-to-hand" to achieve practical tasks within the overall sense of what it wants to get done, there seems to be a parallel sense of interrelatedness of its life and the aspects of the surround as Heidegger detailed for humans. From all that we can tell, animals too are "woven" into the fabric of the world or as part of "the flesh of the world" and do not experience isolated sound waves or disconnected colors and shapes and then make sense of them, but they immediately see the place where prey are likely to come by or a plant that is edible or a cave as a shelter from the bad weather. In other words, animals register "places" of certain significance within their realm of practical activities like humans do, as described by Heidegger. Even though there is a difference in how animals process what they perceive, first it is helpful to use our similarities to start with a sense of the richness of animal perception rather than a reductive mechanical view.

Part of the perception of something, as we have discussed at length in regard to humans, is the affective registration of one's relationship to that object, event, or other being. When an animal sees a predator or a large storm and feels fear or feels delight at a good meal or affection and connection in frolicking with others in its pack or annoyance at an offspring who keeps bothering it and growls and swats it aside for a moment, it is experiencing the same sort of "perceptual thickness" we have discussed throughout this book that gives layers of significance to perception. When an animal shivers when recognizing a spot where it was earlier attacked by predators or runs to greet a member of the pack who had been gone for some time, there are echoes of the past that comprise part of the percept's present meaning, just as every night or morning making its way back to den or nest or burrow, the same is true. Like human perception, animal perception contains layers that are partial overlays or echoes from the past, that are the affective registration of relationships to what is perceived, and that are also projections of fruitful or fearful future possibilities.

It even seems plausible that the other layer we noted in human perception that occurs in the constellated firing of neurons and brain systems—that of the imagination—also is part of animal perception. To quote more of Johan Huizinga's opening to his study of play as the essence of humanity, in *Homo Ludens*, "Play is older than culture, for culture, however inadequately defined, always presupposes human society, and animals have not waited for humans to teach them playing. We can safely assert that human civilization has added no essential feature to the general idea of play. Animals play just like men" (HL, 1). Kowolski, in similar passages to Huizinga, also adds from his observations of animals: "Frolicking is everywhere, glad and irrepressible. . . . Cranes cavort and people promenade, probably for the same reason. We revel together in the rhythms of the earth. For life is ultimately a gambol—a leap of faith, a jump for joy, a mood of exultation shared by all created beings" (SA, 81). Play seems to be ubiquitous throughout the animal kingdom, from the obvious cases of squirrels chasing and tumbling with one another, to birds swooping, circling, and diving in the wind, to lions rolling around with each other in mock battle, to chimpanzees tickling one another, to cranes dancing, or to our own domesticated dogs not only playing and chasing one another but plunking down in front of us with their front legs and paws outstretched in the "V"-like universal dog sign to come and play in mock fight and chase. Now with more openness to our connection with other life forms, scientists can see even in animals with less complex brains, such as fish or bees, behaviors that seem to indicate play too.

To play, however, is to enter this realm of what Huizinga rightly calls not "make believe" as much as "half belief." Players enter a realm that is not purely fictional but is a special "play space" demarcated from the rest of their lives at that moment in time. The players have entered a "magic circle" where various dramas and actions take on a different sort of meaning. For humans, Huizinga gives an example alluded to earlier of dancers dancing in a kangaroo dance, who are not really the kangaroo at that moment, but yet are in some way the kangaroo at that moment. It is neither something to believe or disbelieve (HL, 25). It is another sort of virtual life that leaves its mark on our daily lives. So, for example, with animals, two puppies may seem to be fighting and will even grab the other's throat and shake and squeeze until the other puppy gives the smallest squeak and then lets go.[8] They neither believe nor disbelieve that they are fighting—they are doing something distinctive, "play fighting." This is a kind of imagining—an imagining of a fight that is not a "real" fight but rather a charade, a game, just as an animal might attack viciously some object as if it were the enemy or the prey, but it is only the imaginative guise of this. It seems likely that the animal's perceptual gestalt has a layer of sense within its overall meaning, which involves imagining, and its space also has its affective and imaginative dimensions or places.

Humans do have an excellence in linguistic capacity, a categorical ordering of the perceptual, and the ability to project purely hypothetical realms, allowing them to promise, to plan, and to evaluate, as well as to contribute to their distinctive witnessing abilities, but animals need to be seen as having their own rich mixture of affective, imaginative, and relational capacities that work differently but have their own excellence. It is not helpful to use either realm as a yardstick with which to measure the other, as Auden does in his poem, rather than delving deeply into each one. Then perhaps we can see how distinctive capacities of each realm also overlap with abilities in the other that can be augmented as well as appreciate the differences between them. In order to understand the animal sense of relation with other animals, with themselves, and with the world, it is necessary to explore more completely the depths of perception.

Animals and Prereflective, Perceptually Grounded Selves

The height of similarity between animal and human perception might occur at those moments when we manage for moments to be utterly immersed in our perceptual life without continually commenting reflectively or taking distance from our perceptual selves or being distracted by our bombarding stream of reflective thoughts and ponderings. As any person who has tried the Buddhist practice of "merely" focusing her or his conscious attention on breathing in and out or fully, focusing on walking when walking, or looking when looking, or eating when eating, will find that this is a difficult feat in postmodern culture. Yet for animals, especially those that have not lived as pets but live among themselves, this seems to be the kind of consciousness in which they dwell. For the rationalist tradition, this mean that animals are enthralled with things around them, "captivated" or "ensnared" with no real sense of themselves or what they perceived. The perceptual object is merely a trigger for "internal programming" ("instincts"), which drives set behaviors like a mechanism once triggered. If, however, we discard the rationalist prejudice that only categorical, abstracted formulations count as knowing, and instead acknowledge that embodiment, in resonating with the surround and taking in perceptually layers of significance, has another sort of "knowing" or understanding, then it does not seem to follow that animals as more fully immersed in perception have no sense of the world or themselves. They do have a *different* sense—one that is more purely perceptually grounded than that of humans, but that sense is not the kind of unknowing that lacks any "internal registration" of what is being experienced that many have taken it to be. There is no reason to assume that animal perception could be "automatic" and could occur as "unexperienced," when human perceptual life is nothing like this and seems to overlap in many ways with animals' perceptual life. Neither does animals' behavior seem to indicate this lack of any sense of themselves, others, and the world.

If animals are able to manage their own aggression, as in the case of play fighting, or if they are able to call out to other vervet monkeys which of the three types of predators are approaching the group in order to warn the other monkeys (AM, 166), or if cormorants refuse to dive again after seven dives until given their fish reward, or when an antelope—called a tommy—puts itself in the path of a charging hyena to distract it from its offspring (AM, 69), then the animal must have some implicit sense of itself as part of the scenario that is unfolding as well as the life of its offspring and the recognition of other beings that are a threat to it or of other members of its group whose own lives might be in jeopardy or even of its relationship to the fisherman's acts. This does not mean that the animal has an explicit sense of itself as actor and thinks or ponders about its relationship to predators or offspring or other group members, but that is not the predominant sense of human self-registration either. As embodied beings we have a proprioceptive sense of our bodies as we move and take up positions or gestures. We also have a sense of ourselves as moved by these others beings in the visceral sense of our overall emotional attunement and also within specific feelings. Even when we are as purely focused on the object of our perception as possible, there is a dimension awakened in us of an embodied sense both of what it is and of ourselves as perceiving it. The next moment, we can always focus on the awareness that was implicit, and recall that yes, we were seeing, smelling, or hearing such an object and it felt like this or that. This is what Merleau-Ponty called the "body-self," or what many phenomenologists refer to as the "prereflective" self. We have already pointed to the sense of the "syncretistic sociability" of infants, where each infant feels echoes in her or his own body of the feelings of the other infants. Merleau-Ponty stated that such a dimension never fully subsides with those with whom we are related, and we have a constant experience of this (CR, 153–54), feeling somewhat the anxiety of those we love in our own body, or at least its echo. Even watching someone on a movie screen portraying the experience of feeling joy or pain, falling from a height, or being hit on the head produces some sort of visceral echo in my own body, despite the fact that I intellectually can recall to myself that this is not "really happening." It is perceptually happening, and this is enough to make many of us have chills or even scream at the fearful images on the screen, because we do have an implicit sense of ourselves as immersed in the shared world of perception.

Another way to say this would be to point out that Descartes could only doubt that he existed, that there was an "I" that was Descartes, because he was looking for a reflective sense of self, an object of his thought, and that self can always be put into doubt. Its grounding is in the self of perception and its enfolded dimensions of emotion, memory, proprioception, imagination, and so on. This is what we experience at all times of experiencing the world. It is what Merleau-Ponty called the "tacit cogito": "At the root of all our experiences and all our reflections, we find then, a being which immediately recognizes itself, because it is its knowledge both of itself and of all things, and which knows its existence not by observation and as a given fact, but through direct contact with existence" (PP, 371). So it is in feeling the wind on my face, in throwing the ball, or in exchanging a glance with my spouse that I continually experience the tacit self, the diffuse sense of myself *within* experience. In my caring whether that coyote on the beach is going to attack me or whether my child is too close to the edge of the cliff as I rush forward or shouting to my friend to be careful to avoid the oncoming car, there is an onrush of an immediate sense of self and also the other. They are not explicitly posited as discrete individuals with certain properties but explode forward as the center of feelings, relationships, and summons to action that uniquely point to me and my world of concern. This emergence of this immediate sense of myself is formulated by Merleau-Ponty: "It is through my relations to 'things' that I know myself; inner perception follows afterward and would not be possible had I already not made contact" (PP, 383). If this is true for humans as their primary access to a sense of self that is the grounding for a reflective sense of self, then it makes sense that animals, in warily watching the predator or rushing toward their offspring protectively to ward off the predator, have the same primary sense of self.

If the primary sense of self is in engaging the world prereflectively, then Descartes is not only looking in the wrong direction but, in addition, his conclusion is false—he does not really know himself as a thinking being. Merleau-Ponty declares, "All inner perception is inadequate because I am not an object that can be perceived, because I make my reality and find myself only in the act" (PP, 383). It is in the diffuse body sense and its other interwoven dimensions of meaning as I interact with the world that I am sure of myself as being. Thinking about oneself allows one to question the immediacy of experience where there is an undeniable being caught up with things and others. Reflective capacities add wonderfully to new abstract concepts that structure and enrich experience and build linguistic elongations of one's insights but also place one in the precarious position of continually slipping out of this ongoing sense of oneself. Animals, as immersed in the perceptual life, not only have an immediate sense of themselves, but it is one that surges forward with a solidity that humans will always lack, and try to compensate for, by doing things such as promising to each other. The human way is fraught with deviations from trajectories of experience and action, and with the uncertainties of affirmation and commitment. The animal's immersion in experience more reliably carries it along a path.

Of course, the traditional claim that humans have selves in a way that animals do not is also valid. If part of the human's gestalt is the large portion of its current sense of itself and the world structured by having processed its life in reflection, shaped by organizing reality through categorical concepts, and as a linguistic universe that expands the range of possible thought in ways that are exponential, then these dimensions of meaning are incorporated into the immediately experienced perceptual gestalt as both its background context and layered within its sense. As Merleau-Ponty put it, we live in "habit bodies" that allow us to turn toward the surround with certain motor proclivities, learned ways of perceiving and responding, and modes of attunement and sensitivity that have a rich history impregnated into each posture, each gesture, and each act of perception and action. Yes, a disadvantage for us may be that we can never be at one with our surround in quite the same immersed fashion as an animal, but the opposite is also true: in any surround, we bring structures of knowledge, experience, and interpretation that render it a possible extension of previous surrounds in a way that makes our perception more continuous with those overlays. Given the categorical schema built into human perception, there is a way to make sense of abrupt shifts or discontinuities or new surrounds by relying on more generalizing, predictive, and synthesizing ideas to give the immediately sensed other interpretive possible significances, even prior to deliberate reflection. Humans, given their distance from their surround as well as their immersion, can utilize their histories and past knowledge to move into other contexts more easily or envision other possibilities into which the surround can be transformed, whereas for animals these shifts would be more discontinuous and disruptive. Given that imagination is also inseparable from rational capacities and linguistic extendedness, the human sense of the virtual can build to greater depths and scope, allowing humans differing ways to inhabit a surround with more latitude.

Of course, within the animal world are great variations in powers of perception, insofar as they are "built into" the physiology of the species, whether in the number of primary colors registered by vision, the shape of the part of the visual field that is most acute, the sense of depth, the scope of the visual field, the acuity of hearing, eyesight, smelling, and so on, contrasts of light and dark, sensitivities of touch, and on and on. These differences in perceptual experience vary among animals and in contrast to humans. Nagel chose a bat, for example, for its very different perceptual apparatus than a human's, and in that sense it is true that the relationship and co-understanding through our embodiment will be weaker and call for greater imaginative effort than with an animal of more similar perceptual abilities. However, these differences are not determinative of an utterly different or unbridgeable relationship to the world any more than Chorost's replacement of the generally perceived auditory world with the computer-generated equivalent meant that he would not be able to find a way to inhabit the surround with others of very different auditory input through a new modulation of his experience, such as transposing a symphony to another key, where all of the tones are literally different but convey the same melody, tone, progressions, and harmonies.

The animal's perceptually enmeshed sense of self differs from the human's sense of self, and yet it is not one utterly foreign to human experience. Humans' ability to fathom an animal's sense might require them to focus on specific and fleeting moments of their experience, and to bracket out the relationships to other dimensions of their experience that even make that moment comparable for them but not the same as an animal's, but it is not the unbridgeable gap that Nagel and others have posited. Again, it is to allow an animal the experience to be what it is in its own right, to which humans have some access, and toward which humans can imagine themselves, but not fully fathom.

Animal Perceptual Sensitivity Meshes with Ecological Niches, Not Human Enclosures

Temple Grandin, in *Animals in Translation*, uses comparisons to children with autism and bases her conclusions on her work with animals in feed yards, slaughterhouses, and other livestock situations, as she tries to explore the perceptual world of the animal for some of its features that give it its ongoing texture and sense. Taking into account the different means of processing information, Grandin takes many of the scientific facts of animal perception and gives us a plausible sense of what this means for a "lived phenomenology" of the animal world (AT, 40–44). Animals are more aware of movement within the surround, responsive to finer details that are part of their particular ecological niche, have curiosity toward the surround, and are cautious about novel objects, events, and changing percepts (AT, 45–48). I think there can be no doubt that as Grandin states, small events in the surround "grab at" the attention of animals in a way that is more acute than humans, who tend to see what we expect, given the greater human integration of categorical thinking with perception (AT, 51). Books on animal experience invariably point to studies that show human "inattentional blindness"—where humans, for example, in psychological experiments have been discovered to carry on conversations with differing people without noticing the change as long as they are still behind the same counter performing the same job with the customer, and so on. Grandin sums up animal perception and experience as "a swirling mass of tiny details" (AT, 67). This means that there is a kind of fluidity and intensity to animal perception that is less "leveled out" than the human's daily inattentive and less acutely responsive perceptual life. This level of response and attention to detail and transition might betoken various possibilities for animals' distinctive experience.

Grandin takes the animal's "swirling mass of tiny details" responded to within the surround as compared to the experience of people with autism, and she asserts that there is a parallel in the way in which the differing sensory percepts are not integrated in both cases. The ongoing and stable sense of a meaningful whole that other human perceivers might form is lacking, Grandin states, in children with autism and in animals. This lack makes sense if children with autism lack certain abstract or socialized frames of reference that are normally integrated with the processing of perceptual experience, as we have seen articulated from brain science, psychology, and phenomenology. Grandin states that the result of this lack of integration is that animals are easily frightened and disoriented by details of perception, such as light reflections, banging noises, hissing sounds, contrasting colors, objects swaying, objects dangling, and so on.

Grandin concludes that the discontinuities and distractions in perception are overwhelming to the animal's ability to maintain itself in a more stable behavioral path without being prone to sudden distraction, panic, or onrushes of emotions such as rage, fear, or separation distress. Although, many of Grandin's points seem to capture much of animal perception, this conclusion seems to attribute too much weight to the supposed internal workings of the animal without enough consideration for the inseparability of neural and perceptual processing with the structure and active participation of the surround. It would seem that given the animal's even much more tightly woven relatedness to its surround than humans, the nature of the surround equally is responsible for the particular quality of perceptual life that the animal experiences at any given time. The fact that the animals Grandin has largely studied are in situations of captivity and duress will have a displacing effect on all aspects of animals' perceptual life, and therefore upon all of those other layers of their experience interwoven with perception, no matter how much Grandin is successful as a consultant in re-engineering the space to minimize the differences with a surround that would be more like the animals' original ecological niche. Whether the animals are to be fed in a way vastly different from a life of grazing on open ranges, to be kept in population densities that differ from what they would normally experience, to be surrounded by materials that even if modified are not the same as the original surround, in rhythms and purposes dictated by another species, surrounded by that other species in invasive and ultimately life-threatening ways, and so on, these changes alter the world of the animal. Given the unity with the surround that we have articulated, these shifts change the very physiological, emotional, perceptual, and social dimensions of an animal's existence.

Of course, that is a sobering thought for human animals, even given our abilities afforded by our large cortex to project very different possibilities into given environments and to create the tools to implement these possibilities. When an animal's surround is too radically transformed, it will perish. We mainly think of this in terms of predator-prey relationships and how the lack of suitable nourishment, shelter, and so on determines the animal's die off, given the shift in surround. However, we also might think of these other changes to the perceptual, emotional, kinetic, spatial, and aural life of any animal when its surround radically transforms and wonder how much these factors change the functioning and quality and quantity of its life—and then wonder about the parallels of these changes to human animals. When the environment has no natural lighting, is inundated with noise, has such high population density, and is permeated with rhythms that dictate constant hurry, are humans' perceptually based dwelling capacities so plastic that they just leave behind their own attunement and relatedness to surrounds that have histories of thousands of years? This thought impacts upon Grandin's comparison in the other direction. Given that children with autism do have differences in their information processing capacities that are physiologically based, do these not become more of a stumbling block for these children given the surrounds into which they are placed continually? Are children with autism really so "deficient" in their functioning, or are their radically different ways of processing information radically at odds with the social contexts of their surrounds with their strict rules of behavior that make them seem so? Are there other social and material contexts in which they could function more harmoniously with their biological capacities?

Another way to consider this lack of integration that comes from animals' more purely perceptually grounded immersion in the surround, given the relative lack of categorical and abstract structuring integrated within it, is to see animals entering a greater flow phenomenon with the environment, but not one that is a "swirling mass of details" with the connotation of confusion, disjunction, and easy disorientation. By observation, animals have patience, an ability to do repetitive actions, to remain at a task, to stay anchored in an environment, and to swim psychically in the flow of phenomena in a way more like the waving grass or swaying limbs of serene tress than humans do, despite being self-propelling beings. Animals may have quicker reaction times and be more open to the small transitory beckonings of the surround, and little fears and flights may be more a part of the daily rhythm of making their way in a surround, but that does not mean that within an ecological niche that is more continuous with their long history they do not resonate and stay within their capacities, and *not* become overwhelmed, paralyzed, and disoriented as they do when held within the confines of human enclosures of various sorts. Also, quick starts and flights of sudden fear that turn out to be mere "false alarms" might be part of a different sort of rhythm, may be a quite appropriate, and not at all disruptive, behavior in a "wilder" setting of the original ecological niche of an animal than it is in a confined, human-constructed setting with humanly projected behavioral norms to which animals are supposed to conform.

As Grandin also reminds us of some other differences in animals dwelling within their surround, such as an adherence to dominance hierarchies, the predatory drive of some animals, the grouping together for protection of many prey animals, and amazing rote memory, these are all factors that are integrated within animal apprehension of the perceptual field and give it certain differing structures. Some of these organizing senses may have been part of the human sense of surround at some earlier historical epoch but now are superseded by many other categories of organization based on linguistically, rationally, and culturally articulated orderings. Animal perception is acute but also organized in its habitat, but not so in human-created confines for animals that disrupt rhythms, foil expectations appropriate to their adaptive contexts, and obscure the felt relationship with a specific surround that contributes to a specific range of sense within their ecological niche. In the surround of some noncaptive or nondislocated animals, there may be a sense of territory with an individual, a pair, or a group that is kept separate from others, or if there is no defense of a demarcated area, there may still be a home range, but obviously in highly humanly engineered or impacted-upon situations, the normal rhythm with the surround is disrupted, and the animals may not be able to inhabit its perceptual, emotional, proprioceptive, memorial, and projected dimensions in the same way and experience a sense of disrhythmia or dislocation.

To see the order of animal perception and its quick responsiveness to detail, it is necessary to appreciate that even more than humans, animals are in an ebb and flow, a give-and-take, with the surround, or *Umwelt*, except those very basic animals we discussed previously as being more "machine-like," in being totally at the sway of the surround. Grandin points to how animal emotions can grow exponentially through perceptual associations, and although this is somewhat a result of the surround of those animals she studies, it is true that animals process in a way more akin to what Freud located in humans as a "primary process," where meaning and emotion build swiftly through associations of the feeling tones of percepts, of echoes of the past spilling into the present, by similarities of physical appearance, of place, of contiguities in time, and so on, that are not logical connections but are not nonsensical either. They are a different way of processing the world, one that Freud found in the apparent chaos of dreams as a key to a "dream logic," which also occurs continuously during waking hours, outside of human recognition mostly. A parallel aspect might be found in the "language" of prairie dogs, who warn each other of varied predators. Grandin calls their communication a "musical language" (AT, 306). As many others have observed, Grandin finds in animals' songs a complexity of sense. This is another kind of communication and information processing that reminds us of Langer's ideas of the musical aesthetic surface that conveys symbolic forms of the sense of emotional life conveying the vital sense of the body within its rhythms. It also calls to mind that apprehension occurs on deeper levels of perception than those to which we usually pay attention. Merleau-Ponty states that beneath the "conceptual and delimiting meaning of words," there is an "emotional content of the word," which he says is its "gestural sense" (and a level that is more central in poetry), which "are so many ways of 'singing' the world" (PP, 187). Grandin is right that the affective currents of existence can gather and inform animal perception in a way that humans more often override with their verbal and conceptual shifts of attention and restructuring of the overall sense of the situation.

Instinct as the Life of the Dream

When we speak of animals and their relation to others and to the surround, instinct is the term that often first comes to mind. Instinct gives us another way to explore further the immersion in the thickness of the perceptual containing layers of the emotional, imaginative, proprioceptive, echoes of the past, and so on, that gives animals a unique way of apprehending and living within the surround. A key to animals' distinctive excellence might be to look at how instinct works in them. This might seem surprising, since instinct traditionally has been taken to be *the* factor in animal perception and action that most betrays their lack of "interior" or "psychic life" and reduces them to simple mechanical processes. Instinct and animal perceptual immersion have together been seen as the factors that short-circuit an animal's "understanding" that there are others in the surround, any sense of animal "self," and any "understanding" that objects are to be reckoned with, manipulated, located, and projected into the future. It often has been considered that as a site of instinct, the world is "blindly there" to be locked into mechanically.

Yet instincts also could be seen in another way. Instinct, in its traditional sense, was conceived on the basis of seeing animals as mechanisms and trying to account for how certain behaviors seemed to be driven from within the creature in response to certain typical situations, and how they were shared by members of a species. Given the overall mechanical view of animals, instinct became a name for that which was not directly causally explainable by preceding events or learning, and so was compelled from within creatures by a mechanism even more "hardwired" or "biologically determined" than the rest of their behavior. Given that instinct was somehow "built into" the makeup of creatures and they were machines, instincts were conceived of as certain invariant and mechanically grinding responses to the surround in which the machine of the animals was particularly adapted to the features of its surround due to evolution or a "grand design."

Yet there are other ways to feel compelled other than driven like a cog by gears. It may be that some feature of the surround "grabs" the creature's interest in such a powerful way that it feels like it must respond. Instinct might be a name for drives that are not mechanical but are woven into an animal's rich perceptual immersion in the surround in a milieu of affect, bodily feelings, projections, echoes of the past, and webs of communicative networks with other creatures.

If approached from this perspective, then instinct could be seen as part of the rhythm in which immediate flows of affect, sensation, projection, and kinesthesis are drawn toward a vaguely unattainable but highly charged and meaningful direction that pulls animals beyond themselves into an encounter with the embrace of the world. I use the word "embrace" to indicate a kind of dance between animals and the world, a moving out of themselves in recognition toward a partnership with the other that may be fevered, and on the part of the animals might be a *throwing of themselves toward the irresistibility of the other*, and therefore would be quite the opposite of a blank realm of absence from one another as if they were blind cogs in a world machine. Rather, the presence of some aspect of another animal or some part of the surround may be overwhelming to an animal, given that perceptual qualities often are perceived so acutely by animals, and as a result they desire to bathe or plunge into the depths of their activity or to enter into a behavior that resonates with that presence. This conception is in contrast to seeing instinct as a blindly propulsive mechanism of automatic behaviors triggered by something in the surround that allows animals to go through a routinized set of actions. Animals have been reduced to being considered automata by being seen as "hardwired" into their surrounds through instinct, as if the normally reactive beings we know animals to be have a kind of circuit labeled "instinct" that can be plugged into the surround to go through an invariant, preset array of behaviors. This view envisions the environment as holding a specific "key" as part of a blueprint into which locks the mechanism of the animal to achieve a goal helpful for the thriving of the surround and of the creature's species.

When lecturing at the College de France in the late fifties about the natural world and animals, Merleau-Ponty first suggested this radically other way of conceiving of instinct in articulating many specific examples of animal behavior that suggested to him that instinct, unlike other behaviors, is "activity for pleasure" (N, 193). In opposition to the commonsense way of conceiving of instincts as geared toward accomplishing a specific task, Merleau-Ponty thought instinct was marked precisely by not aiming at any distinct goals within the surround. The "trigger" of the instinct is something that speaks to the animals as a "quasi-idea," a kind of symbol that "fascinates it." So, for example, when male butterflies copulate with a glass stick placed in front of them that has been smeared with the female's secretion, this is not an aberration of instinct but shows exactly how such behaviors work. The organism is "beside itself," is fascinated with the sheer activity for the sake of the activity itself, when it is in the midst of an instinctive behavior. In this state, it will even throw itself upon the rod, because the behavior is not about achieving the goal of mating but is about the fascination with the scent—what Merleau-Ponty calls an animal equivalent to a "fetish," in the sense of a fragmentary percept having this pull upon a being that appeals to a part of its taking in of the surround—a narrowing of focus that compels. In a fetish, all of the world's meaning becomes focused upon one object. Unlike its other perceptions, the trigger percept is not integrated into the whole, as when the animal sees the flash of its prey peripherally at a distance and understands its significance immediately in its overall sense of the situation of its surround, the need for food, and its ways to survive, and so it bounds toward it or begins to stalk it.

Instead, with this trigger percept of instinct, the animal is *fascinated* by it. It is drawn off into "the anticipation of a possible situation which might not even be the case." The instinctively triggered action might not be the most adaptive at that instant, although fortunately it may be, if its surround and niche have been very stable. Whether it is or not, it is drawn anyway. The stimulus-trigger gives us a clue to the aspect of an animal's surround to which Grandin points, as to how a percept may be emotionally or kinesthetically overwhelming. For Grandin, this perceptual acuity for details out of context and with such affective intensity belies a chaos in the animal's perceptual and affective life. From a more rational "means-ends" approach, it may seem to introduce chaos, but this may not be the only way to make sense of the surround. Certainly, it shows that animals do not have the kind of human cortical development and integration that allow for the freedom of reflective intervention in cutting off behavior in response to such intense pulls. However, this primary process of perceptual acuity and affective intensity may be part of another rhythm and flow of apprehension that works in a more enmeshed way with the surround to find differing ways of directedness. It may have a spontaneity and free flow with a more acute responsiveness, but this does not mean that it is chaotic. Its logic may be of another sort than the rationally considered cause-and-effect logic. The trigger of certain behaviors may make sense only within the context of the surround in which the animal had evolved over a long period of time.

There are cases in which the evocative schema of the trigger percept is very precise, but Merleau-Ponty emphasizes that these are limited cases, while the ordinary trigger has only some abstract details that, for example, make it possible to construct lures with which to trick animals. They are not precise, but rather suggestive. So when a red-throated bird can be baited into trying to mate with a bird with an artificial red patch, Merleau-Ponty says it is because the bird "enters a trance when it sees red in front of it, as if it had lost its head, whereas the perception of forms is infinitely finer. There is an oneiric, sacred and absolute character of the instinct" (N, 193). Merleau-Ponty is drawing an analogy between animal instinctive experience and the world of the dream. If we think of how we perceive in a dream, when we move toward something, it is *as if* we are moving toward a goal, and yet not really. Rather, it is as if we are taken up in qualities about us, and we undertake actions that seem to have absorbed all sense into the fabric of their occurrence—they happen, and we are impelled into them, not as the purposive agent of our everyday tasks but as swimming within a pregnant current whose depths and eddies we cannot sound. That is what the dreamlike experience is for humans, and perhaps this is more similar to the animal experience, in the pull of instinct. The dream's kind of "sacredness" and "absoluteness" is from everything happening in a flow where each event and object is more intensely intermingled with everything else, and percepts speak a language that is more cogent and yet utterly mysterious at the same time, portending meanings, which are deep and yet evanescent in our grasp of them. We are pulled, and we take it all in. We move more like a fish purposively swimming yet caught up in strong tidal pulls than we do in the normal currents of our lives, and maybe this is more like the experience of the animal under the sway of instinct.

Our actions in the dreamlike dimension of perception, for Merleau-Ponty, have the air of ceremony, a kind of meaning in themselves that is not about their practicality but about the compulsion, meaning, and desire just for performing the acts themselves. This is what instinctive actions are like in animals, Merleau-Ponty points out, even in eating or excretory functions: these actions, insofar as there is an instinctive component have a certain species style of movements and actions similar to "ceremony" (N, 191). Merleau-Ponty cites an observation by Konrad Lorenz of a young heron that has not built a nest and will not until next year, but in being "on the way" to that behavior, "perceives leaves, falls in front of them in a sort of ecstasy, then executes the behavioral stratagem of accumulation of leaves for the nest and then falls back into calm." There is a kind of tension in the animal that will later become hooked into an object in the surround, because the object is not so much its goal as the means to resolve the animal's tension "as if it brought to the animal the fragment of a melody that the animal carried within itself" (N, 192). In this sense, Merleau-Ponty states, the tension is like the dream in not knowing where it is going or why and does not really aim at the real things around it. Yet we respond to the pulls of the dream utterly, as if something inside us becomes unlocked, as if now there is a kind of flow that demands our entry: we must do this or that for the sake of the melody of the dream, even though we do not really have a good sense where it is going.

The animal finds its identity in "fixing on an object, it does not know what it is nor what it wants," but it is more like entering a "drama" that is "both vision and passion." The action brings together the internal law of behavior and the relation to the surround, but there is this gap of doing and seeing that makes the behavior compulsive. Instinct is not driven by an indifferent sequence of acts, but like a dream the acts have a symbolic value to the animal. Merleau-Ponty believes that in this way the realm of instinct is not tied into a world that is set out against the animal in a systematic and sensible way but is more of a way of "elaborating" the world to give another kind of sense. He says that there is a "very narrow relation between instinct and symbolism" (N, 195). Since certain actions are tied to certain aspects of the world, and yet there is some free play between them, there becomes a kind of resonance between the behavior and what is pointed to in the world that both carries meaning and can even be used as a way of communication. Merleau-Ponty points to instinctive gestures that are then used by animals to convey a range of meanings to others, such as when in the case of a fish whose lateral head movements are part of moving off can be later used as an appeal to the mother or as a warning to other fish as an alarm, or in the case of a duck's squatting and projecting the neck upward as part of the launch into flight that can become a sign to the young of being about to take off (N, 195). Merleau-Ponty says that there is this "development of instinct into symbolic function," because the instinct is not tied in a determinate way to an object but is rather an imaging function. The movements themselves have a sense. Rather than aim toward a goal, such as copulation, the mating dance could be seen to be more like the copulation itself, but in a dramatic and symbolic form, from which might ensue the latter, but it has already been achieved in a certain symbolic sense.

Merleau-Ponty tries in a passage to evoke and describe how this dreamlike sense might be experienced by an animal in the pull of instinct: "It seems that the animal both wants and does not want the object. The instinct is both in itself and turned towards the object, it is both an inertia and a hallucinatory, oneiric behavior, capable of making a world and of picking up any object of the world. To the extent that it is a tension that wants to find relief without knowing why, it does not aim at the real as much as at the irreal" (N, 193). If the normal sense of animal perceptual immersion is a kind of free flow of associated meanings that form a dynamic whole within the surround as a kind of play between it and the animal, more akin to Kant's description of how our sensory apprehension confronted with a work of art plays off our other faculties in ways that give us a general sense of the meaning of things, not one that is clear or has categorical closure but is evocative and deeply felt, like seeing the face we know so well without thinking about any of the characteristics of the person we might attribute to them, then in instinct there may be a deeply ingrained drive from the animal that is grabbed by the trigger from the surround with even less integration that deepens the dramatic character of this kind of immediate effulgence of sense. This experience is hallucinatory, as being a sense that overruns the normal patterning of the surround in survival needs, sociability structures, senses of space and territory, and other integrating schema the animal brings to an encounter, since the animal is wholly taken up in this experience and needs to fulfill the tension of diving into the pleasure of its activity.

This is a very different way to think about instinct. It moves us away from the prejudice of seeing animals mechanically, and yet it describes the sense of compulsion that seems to overcome animals in the thrall of instincts. It is because the world of the animal is a surround of affective pulls, of sensory experience with multiple senses, and it verges on the beginnings of the symbolic that animals can be woven into a melody with the surround that has the fluid pull and encompassing aspect of the dream—not the meshing of mechanical gears.

The Expressive Spontaneity of Animals as Embodied Dialogue

Looking at instinct in this way gives us not only a far different sense of it but suggests another way to consider the experience of animals in their overall existence. Part of the traditional view of animals as quasimechanisms had attributed to them a certain kind of passivity. They were seen as reactive beings that could be played upon by the surround and by other beings as one would play an instrument. Yet as beings that resist pressures from the surround, have a prereflective sense of themselves, enter into relation, play, communicate, project possibilities, strategize, keep track of certain events, are pulled by the symbolic to desire pleasurable experience, and need community, they shape the world in which they live. They do not necessarily have to do this literally but in a way akin to the manner that we spoke of in regard to the deeper sense of human freedom being achieved by shifting the way the world becomes manifest in seeing its meaning in differing ways.

In other words, animals, like humans, are in the same sort of give-and-take with the surround, only an animal's is wordless and less categorically structured, but still, as Merleau-Ponty put it:

> A stimulus from the milieu triggers a reaction; this reaction puts the animal in contact with other stimulations in the milieu, hence a new reaction, and so on. There is no stimulation from the outside that had not been provoked by the animal's own movement. Each action of the milieu is conditioned by the action of the animal; the animal's behavior arouses responses from the milieu. There is an action in return for that made by the animal, which returns to the behavior of the animal. In brief the exterior and the interior, the situation and the movement are not in a simple relation of causality. (N, 175)

Like humans, animals respond to meaningful objects, events, and others in such a way that the shifting meanings then elicit differing responses in a back-and-forth dialogue. So, Merleau-Ponty gives the example of a tick that keeps its semen in reserve, encapsulated in the stomach as it has fixed onto a lizard that is cold-blooded. It then attaches to a tree and can wait for eighteen years in dormancy. In response to the environment, it has entered a certain state. When the smell of the glands of a mammal passing by reaches it, the tick drops onto the warm-blooded animal, settles in, and nourishes itself on the warm blood. Then the semen is released, the egg is inseminated, and the animal dies after procreation. Even with this very primitive creature that has no eyes, ears, or taste, only the ability to smell and detect changes in light and temperature, the creature seeks a certain response from the surround, and when it receives this response, it in turn changes its own manner of being. It is the context of meanings that makes it be what it is at any point in relationship to its specific biological structure. Animals respond sensitively to the world in behaviors that are not just blind actions but expressions of the direction of their lives in relationship to what they apprehend in the surround that furthers this possibility.

Given the lack of categorical structuring of the perceptual world, animals do not project purely hypothetical worlds, nor do they distance themselves from the import of what they perceive given their usual sphere of dwelling, nor do they try to become another kind of possible being in response to its coercion or seduction—they remain within a style of perceiving and acting that has evolved within the dialogue of their responsiveness to the species' normal surround. Humans often want animals to become something other—like cooperative helpers in the business of being slaughtered, housed, or transported—or, for pet owners, to become a sibling, or another child in the family, or perhaps a servant, yet animals have a resistance to these demands. Given the continuities of their established rhythms with their surround, it is not the case that animals are prone to being "distracted" or "spooked" by moving objects, shiny surfaces, or clanging noises, as they are characterized by Grandin, but rather that they are prone to act this way when dislocated in the human-constructed world. They are responding to the world on the basis of what was the case of the surround within which the species developed but is no longer the present surround. Animals are not "stubborn" or "uncooperative" outside of our unreal expectations of them, but rather they are part of the same melody they have been and still are—one that makes sense to them and is not just a mechanical sequence to immediate stimuli but to the meaningful whole of the surround. They are merely perceptually responsive to what means something in the long history of their natural surrounds. Within those surrounds, these qualities probably indicate beings or events to which they must pay heed and to which there is a need for a quick kinetic reaction. A sudden movement of an object or a glint of light might mean the presence of a predator, for example, from whom they should quickly retreat and then look around more slowly. As living in an immediacy more like human dreams, they can move quickly within their repertoire of responses as the surround shifts. Animals have the speed and attunement to be more kinetically responsive, without it being exhausting and distracting, as it might be for humans, and without it disturbing deeper rhythms resonant with their ecological niches. Animals are not clay to be shaped into the beings we think they should be, given our aims for them. We may want them to project themselves into some other constructed surround, but they remain attuned to their niche, able to respond creatively to it using established rhythms, but not to any possible world in any possible way.

Merleau-Ponty, who reads von Uexküll as being more open to animal understanding than Heidegger reads him, takes from von Uexküll the formulation of the way an animal is immersed in its surround as "the unfurling of an *Umwelt* as a melody that is singing itself" (N, 173). The animal sings itself, despite the fact that there may be a "plan" inherent in its biological structure and in the resonant structure of the surround, because the surround is made up of meaningful parts for the animal that it can shape. Merleau-Ponty's example is again of a "lower" animal with a simple brain and neural net—a crab: "The crab uses the same object (the sea anemone) to different ends: sometimes for camouflaging its shell and protecting itself thus against fish, sometimes for feeding itself, sometimes, if we take away its shell, for replacing it. In other words, there is the beginning of culture. The architecture of symbols that the animal brings from its side thus defines within nature a species of preculture. The *Umwelt* is less and less oriented toward a goal and more and more towards the interpretation of symbols" (N, 176). In trying to fathom what Merleau-Ponty is suggesting through these provocative words, the power of embodiment we have articulated can give us a sense of what he means by the "symbolic" and by "preculture." It seems that for the animal there is a prereflective opening of a sense of objects and of other creatures, whether of prey or of its herd or flock or group, of places and events, that resonates within the body as a feeling of itself that is a reflection of the world around it as fathomable. Its perceptual immersion has an emotive and identificatory sense, not one that ever could be articulated like the human sense of the world, but one that can be lived through, felt, and experienced, just as the animal understands the sense of its own body by living through pain or cold. It knows to lick the painful wound or find shelter as a threatening apprehension elicits response, just as a human knows the bright glare of the full summer sun means it is hot outside by an immediate resonance of embodied perception with how it stands within the surround. The immediate living through the sensed meaning of things allows behavior and is the prereflective "reckoning" of the surround. In addition, these sensed meanings often have a range with which the animal can work. In Merleau-Ponty's example, the sea anemone can be apprehended not only as camouflage but also as food or as shelter. This range of meaning is "on the way" to culture, as having a leeway to work with for varied purposes, and it has a symbolic import as being open to suggest differing senses for differing purposes.

For animals, without the anchoring of the self-reflective, rational construction of a conceptual grasp of the self or of objects, events, or others, there is not the constant sense of "being gathered together" *by an agency*, by the one who is reflecting upon the sensed, the felt, the remembered. That sense of agency gives humans not only the possibility of a kind of distance from experience but also establishes the sense of an underlying continuity, even within the prereflective flow, the sense that Descartes seized upon with his notion of the substantiality of self, which is more of a kind of afterimage of the re-identified conceptuality of self, gathering itself over and over again during a lifetime, which is then taken as a source. The sense of this underlying agency is taken to be a presence that then washes into other human experiences. In contrast to this human repeated self-gathering,

Merleau-Ponty in an image suggests that for an animal "the unfurling of the animal is like a pure wake that is related to no boat" (N, 176). The wake is there—the animal has a continuity that is felt and resounds within its experience, but there is no retrospective gathering together into the sense of an identifiable agent of self. The animal "self" is just this flow, this process of unfurling, which like the wake is evanescent—it does not return to itself, nor can it be grabbed by others. It is dissolving and dispersing, even as its force is evident and palpable.

The animal's way of taking in the surround stretches itself out in time as inseparably woven into what it is experiencing, just as the wake is inseparable from the body of water, but it is there as possible to recognize along with it, in the similar sense that Merleau-Ponty talked about in terms of the immediately sensed prereflective identity of any human. Beneath all of the things that we know of another person and can speak about, there is an immediate sense of "a fittingness and a meaningful relationship between the gesture, the smile and tone of the speaker" (PP, 55) which goes along with his or her sense of humor, sense of pacing himself or herself through the day, way of walking, things that grab his or her attention in the surround, aspects of others about which he or she is concerned, and so on. This recognizable manner of a certain "way" or "style" or "feel" of the person's differing relationships with the world as expressed in all of his or her actions has different dimensions, some quite singular, particular to the individual and his or her history, and many derived from shared ways of culture or ethnicity or gender, and at the most general, some ways of the species. The sense of the "style" as the recognizable vector of unfolding, and the way of relating with the world, is equally palpable in animals, whether in birds, chimps, dogs, or other creatures, as beyond the manner of a species in a certain kind of inflection of that individual upon wider patterns of being. This sort of presence and way of taking in the world carries with it a history of particular experiences, as well as expressing tendencies that have become inbred through the long history of the species. For the human, this *prereflective* manner is only a palpable way of shaping that which unfolds with the person immersed in other forces of the surround, and not the conscious and deliberate presentation of a persona. For the animal, as like a wake without a boat, it emerges from the surround as a vector of movement coming from the surround that the animal has knit together and wholly contains it. There is an interwovenness with the surround in which the history seems to emerge from both in deep rhythms. Paradoxically, perhaps, this gives to the animal a type of spontaneity, as a kind of emergence from within the interrelated vectors of the surround in a profound attunement that humans could not emulate, or can perhaps achieve after working for a lifetime to become transformed to a being with the Zen swordsperson's immediate response to all of the subtle forces around him or her before any overt structures of consciousness intervene.

This openness of embodiment and fine-tuned responsiveness to the surround is what we often have envied and honored in the animal. We have expressions praising athletes for their "animallike quickness," which is the result of an acuteness of synchronized response to the surround, or the term *animal grace*, which indicates an ability to seamlessly enter the rhythm of the surround with a fluidity of bodily movement. This also is the dimension that machines have lacked—a way of being so openly and fully present that the surround is allowed to come forward as the finely tuned motive force of an exact reverberatory resonance within a nexus of relationships, achieving a concerted action of the whole. For the animal, at the same time, it is an encounter that occurs in which the animal is *there*, able to be itself, and not just an object moved by other objects by simple causal chains. In its more fluid, quasidream-symbol, associative, perceptually acute, fine-tuned, and self-reinforcing (like a feedback loop feeding back into itself) immersion in the surround without a separated, underlying, self-collecting sense of agency, animal embodiment has an ongoing openness of embodied spontaneity that we cannot achieve but can wonder at and emulate at times when we seek greater fine-tuning with the planet's currents and energies.

Animals in the Slower Time We Call Nature

In arriving at the sense of how animals meet up with the environment in a heightened sense, which has layers of a more fragmentary, fleeting, and immediate symbolic meaning, such as feeling a place to be a spot of death or danger or dwelling and comfort, or that this bounding partner is playmate and pretend enemy of the instant to be attacked, but not really, or that outcropping is too like the one that was the sight of a fall, we have moved to the idea that animals also live in a different time than linear clock time. Humans in postmodern American and in an increasingly global culture, especially in more urban settings, live in a time that is shaped by the categorical structures of clock time and of increasing demands for capitalist productivity and maximal consumerism. We encounter time as objective, measurable, and something we can "own" as having more or less of. This is to make time into a thing or a commodity. Given the pace of production of this stage of capitalist global competition, it is also a driven time, a time that moves with startling speed. Much has been written about this, including my own *Earthbodies*, and need not be described in any detail here. Warnings for humans range from T. S. Eliot's eerie repeated lines in *The Waste Land*,

"Hurry up, it's time," to Heidegger's in *Being and Time*, that we live in an inauthentic "fast time" in which we "hop" from moment to moment, to Baudrillard's diagnosis of "astral America" living in a "hyper-time." I say that we have arrived at the idea that animals live in a different time because, as Merleau-Ponty points out, animals, in opening "a field of action" with its nexus of relations open a differing sense of the world with its own "specific temporality and spatiality" (N, 173). The interrelations among aspects of the surround in being finely registered not only shift the motive force of action but also the sense of time. For example, the tendency in some animals to repetitive actions or the painstaking stalking of prey or foraging would seem to be part of a differing temporal sense—specific modalities of being absorbed in time's unfolding.

It is obvious that we must differentiate *among* differing animals' senses of both space and time—that a tick that lies dormant for eighteen years awaiting the arrival of a warm-blooded animal has a quite differing temporal structure to its existence than a cheetah that awaits its prey in a hair-trigger time of reaction and fast chase, as is the space of the tick attached to the skin of an animal differing than the land-soaring, running, ground-devouring cheetah or the circling hawk making a ballroom of grace of the sky. However, there may be some shared structures of the sense of time among animals, even given these differences. The first of these characteristics to be articulated is how the animal lives within an overall sense of the thickness or layering of times into one long time span and does not live in a time fractured into a discontinuous set of instants, as has sometimes been imagined. If one were to consider that time only becomes continuous by instants being linked to instants by a function of reason and judgment, then given the relative lack of higher brain functioning in animals compared to humans, one might believe that animals live in a fractured time of moment to unrelated moment. However, to consider an animal's sense of time, given a notion that it is more immersed in the surround that is a spatial, temporal "field," then the past and future may be more unified as always resounding in any present percept. This follows from Merleau-Ponty's analysis that the prereflective immersion in perception enmeshes the perceiver in a web of relationships that "together form a single temporal wave" (PP, 331) stretching from the "remote past" to the future. As Merleau-Ponty describes the temporal experience of animals, the "organism is not defined by its punctual existence" (N, 175). Given that animals are more immersed within this perceptual field than humans who can "step out" of this continuity in the distancing of self-reflective deliberation, this depth of time is even more profound.

If we return to Merleau-Ponty's image of the animal in its surround, like "a melody that is singing itself," Merleau-Ponty claims that "this is a comparison full of meaning" (N, 173) for thinking about the animal's temporality. He states that the image of a melody both includes the sense that "the melody sings us much more than we sing it," and that with the very first note the last note is already there, and in the last note, the first note is still resounding. A melody gives us a sense of the unity of time or a reciprocity between past and future. By also bringing to our attention the relation of activity to how the things around us also work through us, music presents the condition that we have seen present in all existence but is more palpable in music. Merleau-Ponty says music brings to notice that "the body is suspended in what it sings, the melody is incarnated and finds in the body a type of servant" (N, 174). In terms of the animal in the surround, if the animal lives within a more melodic sense of the surround, this means that it is suspended in a temporal flow of past, present, and future that resounds heavily within the enveloping of each time sense in the other. Natural phenomena experienced within this melodic temporality have deep reverberations of the past, like the continuing bass of a musical composition and a forward thrust that is already the sounding of the musical resolutions of chords, themes, and modulations to come. To the animal entering its burrow to hibernate for the winter, there is already in some sense present as an obscure shading at that moment the intimations of awakening in the spring in the budding green world. While that green has suddenly been stripped from the surround, the animal retreats into the dark and cold with an implicit sense like a night's sleep that it will awaken to new days, new forages, and new tasks to be done. Its steps as it goes into the burrow are treads with the echoes of past cycles that pad its steps upon the earth. Not that the animal could sit backs and reflect on this, but it is the thicker meaning of what is done at this moment. Its time moves within rhythms with a vitality that resonates with a diffuse sense of living within long temporal cycles. To remember what we said about the consciousness of instinct and how this is key to animal existence, it is as though past winters and the coming spring are present to animals as a "haunting" kind of presence, diffuse, at the margins, not graspable, but felt in the marrow. They are dreamlike and suffuse into the motion and action that fits like the right note into what is to be done, like a chord struck in unison between animal and surround, which encompasses larger forces with long histories in its deep timbre.

Since this book is a comparison among humans, animals, and machines, there is a level of human temporal existence where there is a parallel to the animal sense of time to which we can turn for understanding. Merleau-Ponty articulates how although each sensation "is a kind of birth and death," as we are taken into perceptions that are then gone, it is equally an entering of a field, a synchronizing with a sensibility that stems from all parts of the field, that gives humans a sense of a *prepersonal* presence, something more primordial than their individual selves. Merleau-Ponty states, "On the fringe of my own personal life and acts," there is "the life of my eyes, hands, and ears, which are so many natural selves" (PP, 216). In my belonging to the field and its sensibility is the interweaving with something that is before my birth and after my death. The field's history of unfolding, its prolonged processes of change, development, and interaction, still is present in its makeup, as well as its trajectories toward the future. In another passage, Merleau-Ponty speaks of how through immersion in the surround or perceptual field, the perceiver coexists with all of the other landscapes that are woven into it and "merges with the very movement whereby time passes" (PP 330). On the fringes of our prereflective awareness, we join this single temporal wave. Finally, there is yet another way to express this sense of ongoing temporal duration that Merleau-Ponty comes to articulate toward the end of the *Phenomenology of Perception*, when he states, "My first perception, along with the horizons that surrounded it, is an ever-present event, an unforgettable tradition ... I still am at that first perception, the continuation of the life inaugurated by it" (PP, 407). In all three of these passages, Merleau-Ponty is articulating that how to be an embodied perceiver entails joining up with the surround and all of the vantages that comprise it, as entering ways of perceiving all parts of it through its circulating flow of meaning, which gives us a sense of the many times within its prolonged moment or temporal wave it has been unfolding throughout history.

All parts of the field echo a past of interrelation and a sense of how they are unfolding toward a future. This is an implicit sense I have in the depths of perceiving that is often superseded by my more ego-constructed, self-reflexive personal life, but in moments of sheer immersion, I take up these rhythms, feel the push of this wave from the past toward a distant realization to which I will never arrive. Loren Eiseley, the famous naturalist, once wrote of these sensations while floating on his back down a tributary of the Platte River: "Moving with me, leaving its taste on my mouth and spouting under me in the dancing springs of sand, was the immense body of the continent itself, flowing like the river was flowing, grain by grain, mountain by mountain, down to the sea. I was streaming over ancient riverbeds thrust aloft where giant reptiles had once sported; I was wearing down the face of time and trundling cloud-wreathed ranges into oblivion."[9] Eiseley, who is attentive and sensitive in a way most of us are too distracted to notice, senses in the water the presence of the long temporal flow of life from prehistoric reptiles to the wearing away of the mountains toward the future shifting of the mantle of the earth and its creatures. For animals, these haunting presences are like a flowing medium through which they move without being able to grasp onto explicit realizations or representations of this past. Yet, these currents of sense moving through perception's depths are primary currents of vitality and sense. The animal knows its species members and even its flock or pride or group, and it lives within a cradle of a long prehistory shared with them and the surround.

Humans assess and project goals through self-reflection, articulate through language, and analyze by categorical thought in order to make sense of their orientation to the surround. Alternating instants of distancing and immersion, they can then plunge back into activity on these bases. For the machine, the program or the plan built into the very arrangement of its moving parts causes it to move toward a future outcome. For the animal, behavior is its continual way of apprehending and expressing a sense of the surround. Behavior is a whole or melody that picks up on aspects of the surround, or as Merleau-Ponty states, "Behavior can't be understood if we understand it moment by moment" (N, 175). It is within a flow of time as a whole that the animal's behavior follows the temporal currents of the surround, for example, toward migrating north as geese on the flyway or in storing nuts like squirrels for the upcoming winter or Clark's nutcracker hiding seeds in myriad caches. These rhythms over seasons are the body's implicit temporal sense. These activities have a broad temporal horizon and meaning to them, and there is no reason to claim that animals do not have a sense of this significance. The behavior itself is the apprehension of past, present, and future in which each behavior expresses how "each part of the situation acts only as part of the whole situation," (N, 175). Like entering into one part of the melody, the whole resounds through the parts, or less metaphorically, each part of the behavior resonates within this larger movement of sense of the animal and the surround.

The animal enters certain rhythms of activity, a give-and-take with changes in the surround, and is, for example, part of the overall rhythm of the season. In hiding its seeds or flying north, there is an implicit recognition, like a haunting presence, an atmosphere of meaning, that feelingly recognizes the overall trajectory of the oncoming harsh winter, the general lack of food that will prevail, the dire competition for food during that time, the need to hold on, to make provisions for the group, and so on. Yes, there is an inner drive of genetic makeup to engage in these activities when triggered by certain presences in the surround, just as we have drives to protect our young or flee from danger, but it does not mean even for humans that there is not at these instants, even on the immediate level of the body, a sense of care and belonging with our young that is part of the behavior or of danger and fearful recognition of menace in the flight. These are layers of consciousness and sense that animals seem to also possess. There is a larger wave of unfolding time that flows through the surround and ultimately through the largest horizon of the world that can be entered, and animal bodies reverberate to its sense. Humans do too, though less acutely, more intermittently, and in ways made partial by their capacity of parallel processing or taking in other streams of meaning simultaneously. A marvelous formulation used by Merleau-Ponty to express the animal's place in the upsurge of overall temporal flow is "The animal is like a quiet force" (N, 177). It contributes to the whole, but only as a more seamless part of the whole being expressed in this individual animal's life that has force, but a quiet one, one that finds the overall pitch easily and makes of it quietly its own voice.

There is another layer of sense in this vague atmosphere comprising the whole of time in which animals move that *encompasses the shadowy presence of all their forebears,* for this sense, too, is implicit in the nature of perception and embodiment. Humans also can sense the long, haunting, receding presence of their forebears at times with concentration or effort, but for animals, without the layers of reflective processing and linguistic construction, this presence would seem more permeating. Given the human construction of the ego, and the powerful distancing of reflection, humans have a sense of their individuality that alters their time sense to one that centers on their personal drama in existence. However, as I have written about extensively in *Earthbodies*, ceremonies, if undertaken in the spirit of sincerity, playfulness, and openness of feeling, are "a shifting of our inner psychic arrangement" (EB, 27) away from structures that allow for the stability of our everyday identity and to "become" for a moment our forebears or other humans or aspects of the surround that are being celebrated. As Paula Gunn Allen, in explaining the central role of ceremony in Native American tribal life, says: "The purpose of ceremony is to integrate: to fuse the individual with his or her fellows, the community of people and that of other kingdoms."[10] The individual, by enacting something bodily, through the senses, through kinetic feelings, enters a larger flow of not only history but prior individuals of a collectivity who have done these things before that are now ritualized. As we gather together to sit at a table to share fall harvest foods, we are brought into a reverberating presence of all the past generations of Americans who have sat at Thanksgiving to be one with ancestors and the fall bounty of harvested summer fields, corn and potatoes, turkeys, to feel the echoes of the generations laboring with the land, humans dwelling under the sky, and groups of humans coming together in family or fellowship.

However, it need not necessarily be a ceremony for this temporal sense to occur. In a particularly sensitive moment, one can feel in the heft of the axe over one's head and in the pull of the blade coming down into its impact with the log the presence of generations of humans splitting logs for fires. In a similar fashion for Buddhists, we quoted Hahn in the previous chapter, claiming that in the Buddhist perspective if we were to practice mindfulness then we would sense in the paper the reverberations of the logger, the logger's parents, and all those other humans who are part of a history embodied in that object. If animals live in a perceptual immersion comprised of the layers of affect, imagination, recognition of others, directedness toward purpose, and so on, then it may well be that this kind of sense of other birds who have flown this path in the sky or other bears who have walked these hills resounds in the embodied kinetic sense of performing these acts within a meaningful surround.

There is yet one more dimension of time to be considered in regard to animals: the dimension of "timing"—as I called it in *Earthbodies*. Certainly a great part of the "movement" of time is the result of the linear chains of cause-and-effect happenings that do give time a dimension of relentless linearity. However, the different ways that time can become manifest in the shallow, slow, but heavy time of boredom, or the frenzied, quick, discordant time of the bustle of postmodern life, or the ever-deepening, quiet time of deep mindfulness and meditation, or the full and expanding luminescent time of creativity are a matter of how sentient beings come to mesh in interlocking rhythms and ways of being open to encountering each other. The felt pace of time emerges from how we mesh with the surround (EB, 38–39). A being capable of registering time could conceivably be "out of synch" with everything in its surround, but then time would fail to happen in some sense, as the taking in of the unfolding of all things as being synchronous with the temporal flow with the one who is perceiving them. The person would in some sense "fall out of time" and become shut off from the unfolding sense that envelops her or him as time's ripening (EB, 39–41). This is not really possible, even for the most distracted human, although there are altered states of consciousness that approach this. Emerging from such distressed states, the person might rejoin time and its allowing the world to become manifest, and feel as if she or he had "been away" somewhere, even if she or he were literally in the normal surround during the period of altered consciousness.

We could turn to many sources that acknowledge this other dimension to time. Heidegger's *Being and Time* articulates how we permeate time as standing away from ourselves in past, present, and future in one movement of letting things be, by allowing them to come forward and be encountered by us. Heidegger calls this the "ec-staces" of the temporal flow—we stand "out" (as the word "es-stace" literally means) by standing within time. As fully within time, we are within the past, present, and future. Tarthung Tulku's *Time, Space, and Knowledge* describes a greater, more "embracing" time as that power of things playing themselves out in being manifested, so that we can release ourselves from linear time's monopoly in order to swim in the "pool" of time by being open to all of time's flashing forth within the playing out of things.[11] To turn to Paula Gunn Allen again, she expresses the same idea: "The right timing for a tribal Indian is still the time when he or she is in balance with the flow of the four rivers of life" (SH, 154), which she explains as coming to meet all of the beckonings—the streams—that could flow into one's life. The more fully one harmonizes or resonates with the surround, the more one "times" oneself into the flow of interaction, which is the body or fullness of time. If, as I put it in *Earthbodies*, this dimension of time is "that graceful mirroring of all beings in timing together, resonating and resounding with each other's intoned sense" (EB, 43), then animals are deeply immersed in time, in its fullness, its aspect of *timing* with the surround that humans might never achieve. Humans have their excellence in the witnessing that we have described. Animals display their excellence and are distinctive by existing as the beings that live in a depth of immersion as timeful beings gracefully encountering the enveloping surround.

Chapter 7

Machines

Excellences and Boundary Markers

Machines and Solid, Impervious Materiality

The machine world has evolved from the earliest machines that were levers or rollers or other simple devices to make energy output more efficient so that human's physical exertion would be less onerous, to the now-ubiquitous computers that calculate, store information, perform other logical operations, or direct all sorts of other automated machines, to machines that create energy from matter, to machines that record the far reaches of the galaxy and beyond and in doing so let humans "see" billions of year ago, to other machines than can combine both information manipulation and physical manipulation to make precise movements beyond human capacity, and so on, for a myriad of functions. Yet despite the ever-growing number and kinds of functions that machines perform for us, there are certain shared characteristics of the way they function, their relationships to humans and animals, and aspects of what their being as machines means to us that can be formulated. Machines in the way they function and help structure the postmodern world, give our world a certain sense. Like animals, machines at times seem to embody characteristics that we lack or can seem frightening in certain ways to many of us, yet at the same time promise certain capacities and possibilities for which we yearn, leading some to envision no greater destiny for humankind than to become assimilated into the machine world.

The first characteristic that seems to distinguish machines from both humans and animals is not, per se, about the way they function but concerns both the nature of the materials from which they have been constructed and the fact itself that they have been constructed. Being made of inanimate materials seems to make machines different from humans and animals in a way that can never be bridged, but of course this is a circular argument. For what do we mean by the inanimate, other than that which we consider cannot be alive in the way humans and animals are living, yet both animals and humans evolved from inanimate materials and are still comprised of them in many ways. This distinction is closely related to that between organic and inorganic materials, which used to be thought to be mainly those materials from mineral sources and therefore inanimate or nonbiological. However, this distinction has been amended to focus on the presence of carbon and hydrogen in most chemical compounds considered organic. Even here, there are some blurred boundaries, such as carbonates, fullerenes, carbon dioxide, and so on, but what is more to the point with machines is that the materials of which they are constructed have been chosen for a specific function or were created synthetically with a certain function in mind. Furthermore, this latitude in choosing the materials from which machines are manufactured often gives them an advantage over "higher-level," more openly adaptable, animate creatures in performing that particular function. So a robot that we want to perform a function in a very high-temperature environment can be constructed of materials in a way that a living being made of fragile biological materials and structures can only be protected against somewhat. As a more open and vulnerable living system, a human cannot endure in the same way as a machine that has been manufactured from specific heat-resistant materials engineered to be closed off from the effect of the environment. Or, in another case, a machine used for performing a delicate surgical procedure can be constructed of precisely machined and rigid materials set in a harness that minimizes vibration and is able to be aimed and manipulated by precise computer telemetry in a way that a human hand cannot—all partially due to the nature of the materials used and the isolation of movement from other functions that an open, living system cannot achieve.

Of course, there are very simple animate beings that have a singular niche and are made of materials that can withstand challenging environmental conditions, such as endoliths living in enormous pressure two miles below the earth's surface ingesting iron, sulfur, or potassium and reproducing once a century, or are made of substances useful to performing very specific functions unerringly, such as leeches with their three-jawed mouths for precise, Y-shaped incisions, anti-clotting enzymes, and sensory organs for blood detection. However, these are not higher-order animals or humans that are able to adapt in some degree to changes around them by having some separation from the surround augmented by responsive self-regulation but in general are made of biological materials structured to have a greater openness to the surround. As we discussed previously, it is tempting to call these most simple organisms "animal-machines," locating them as beings on the boundary. However, in addition to the fact that they have been classified in this way because they often react to the environment in a seamless fashion, being just a direct function of its changes and not generating their own course in life, there is also this aspect of their material constitution that is not often recognized. Is there something monstrous about being a living creature and being constructed of materials that are impervious to the extremes of the surround to such a degree? What is the miracle of "the flesh"? Is it not exactly what Merleau-Ponty came to see—that it is of the same "stuff" as the world, that its materiality is able to become "folded" and "enfolded" into the world in such a way that there is this constant "give-and-take," a finely tuned responsiveness, yet also a "quiet force" of maintaining a trajectory in life playing off of the forces of the surround?

It is interesting that if we "construct" a being out of *biological* materials in such a way that it becomes self-directing or autonomous in its ongoing functioning, then we do *not* consider it a machine. From the famous nineteenth-century thought experiment called "Frankenstein" to the first famous cloned mammal, Dolly, the sheep, even if "manufactured" in some sense, these beings are considered creatures or animals of some sort, even if seen as "monstrous." Partly this is because of the materials used in their being manufactured. We often think that the identities and boundaries of machines are obvious, but they are far from that and not decided by just one factor. If a being were able in every way to act identically to Dolly, yet it was made of synthetic inorganic and inanimate materials—say silicon, titanium, and plastic—would we ever be willing to consider it a creature or a living being, even though Dolly, who was created through mechanical manipulation—somatic cell nuclear transfer—was considered a living being? It does not seem so, given our often unnoticed biases about the nature of materiality.

Part of our current conceptions of whether something is alive seems to uneasily incorporate the materiality of the being, how it was formed—its origin—as well as how it functions, and what functions it can perform. We often focus on the manufacture or function, but to be made of titanium or silicon seems a priori to rule out that being from consideration as a creature or living being. The kind of solidity and imperviousness to the surround of these materials is seen as alien, in both frightening and appealing ways. Given that we are creatures that intermesh with the surround while being at a distance from it, in a dialogue, these intuitions of distrust at imperviousness point to some deeper intuitive understanding of what we are. Yet advances in telemetry, automatic data processing, and actuation have altered the material characteristics of machines so that their potentialities for responsiveness and pursuing an adaptable set of patterns may be surprising, as in the case of Cog, which we already discussed. After all, our own responsiveness to the surround results from how the various constituents of our makeup function together, not from the properties of our various material components. It may be that we need to reexamine our prejudgments concerning various materials. Would it have seemed plausible that life would emerge from the mix of chemicals that oozed in the waters in the earlier days of the earth? Probably not, until the actual emerging patterns of interconnected functioning gave rise to self-directing, but responsive beings.

Certainly for those drawn toward a love of sorts of the machine, it is machines' impervious lack of responsiveness to the surround, as well as the physically enduring capacities of certain synthetic materials, that fuels this desire. Whether it is the fact that more people prefer to interact with ATMs rather than human bank tellers, so that they feel no obligation to interact with them or to suffer with less than maximal efficiency (although tellers try to emulate the mechanical in being as automatically efficient—even before there were ATMs), or some who dream of replacing their pets or their partners or their own bodies with android versions, the idea of replacing the openness and fragility of the biological with something more enduring is appealing to many. Given the materiality of the traditional machine, which was both impervious and durable, and since biological systems made of animate materials are fragile and mortal, a dream that results from this juxtaposition is to find a fortress for human consciousness within the inorganic that endures and can be fixed in predictable ways and escapes the aging process of animate beings. Certainly in more limited ways, and in ways that will only increase, replacing organic materials of the human body with inorganic ones that have been engineered for certain functions such as knee replacements made of lightweight and strong metal and polyethylene or flawed organic components with implanted mechanical ones such as the cochlear implants will become much more common with advances in medicine and bioengineering. Many tout the advantages of "enhanced humanity" by incorporating machine parts into human bodies. The opinion of Rodney Brooks, that "the distinction between us and robots is going to disappear" (FM, 236), is not that uncommon among those working in the technological fields of robotics and bioengineering.

The kind of materiality that we have associated with machines seems an odd mixture of strength, endurance, imperviousness, manipulability, and solidity. We often bemoan the frailty and vulnerability of the flesh. The capacity to age, although shared by inorganic materials, seems more pointed in our fleshly case. The nightmarish fear of our culture that spawns movies, novels, and other tales of machines taking over the world and being utterly unapproachable—crushing and grinding what is in their path—is the frightening aspect of this kind of substantiality we admire but we know comes at the price of being isolated and unable to feel others. Yet at this point in human history, the materiality of machines is a comfort as something that lasts in a fairly reliable and predictable way, something that we can use to support our needs for stability, and something that we can use to repair knees and worn-out arteries and other parts of ourselves.

This machine highlighting of certain materials and their characteristics makes us realize that insofar as we do trust our unenhanced bodies, and are grateful if we are fortunate enough to climb into a secure bed in reasonable health, it is as a result of the fact that we take comfort in the solidity and continuity of the mechanism of our own bodies. Like the purring of the machine, operating smoothly, the quiet pulsing of the healthy human body reassures in a similar rhythm. Part of it comes from the machinelike characteristic of steady function, but part of it also comes from the same machine materiality, from the solid presence of the finely tuned mechanism of our skeletal system made of strong calcium and other components, the fine torque of the flexibility of ligaments and tendons as we twist around, or the supple, elastic push of the heart chambers thumping as we lie there, and we rest in those reassuring material characteristics.

Machines within and around us that permeate the surround and populate our world to maintain its function as the built environment talk to us through our embodied reverberation continually of the efficacy of their materiality that is sheltering in its solidity, reassuring in its endurance, reliable in its tensile strength, demarcating in its imperviousness, yielding in its elasticity, resilient in its hardness, and so on, in a myriad of senses of how machines augment materiality in enacting all sorts of excellences that otherwise would not come to the fore, nor be added to the sense of human existence. It also is this materiality that threatens human well-being and the well-being of the planet. Those parts that are machined to last and the machines that make them threaten to choke the landscape as pollutants as the problematical side of their long existence emerges. Similarly, the many other exotic and dangerous materials made by machines, or by-products of machines, also linger in the surround in ways that are toxic or otherwise destructive. The materiality of machines marks part of their boundary and betokens aspects of their excellence but is also equally dangerous to the surround and its beings.

Machines, Consistency, and the Time of the Earth

The difference in the materiality of machines as contrasted to animals and humans points to its correlate as the most distinctive aspect of machine being in general—that machines are constructed to fulfill a certain function and to perform this function with the greatest possible reliability and consistency. Machines do function in such a way that has a constancy and continuity that would be difficult for humans to achieve. At this point in human history, it might even be said that much of the consistency in our existence, and much of the reliability of our surround as a constructed surround, comes from the functioning of machines—from the houses we live in that are maintained in a fairly narrow range of temperature fluctuations, within the limits that humans can tolerate and find comfortable, to the capacities of storing or preparing food, to the ongoing availability of water, or access to information, communication, and a myriad of other aspects of our surround in the postindustrial countries of the world and increasingly so globally throughout the world. Perhaps until recently there were swaths of humanity for whom this was not true, but increasingly, even in remote cultures of the globe, machines are part of the world's regular, consistent texture. Even in these least technologically dependent cultures, it is noteworthy that at this postmodern point in history, all of humanity relies upon machines to buffer us from the erratic upsurges in natural rhythms that can be cataclysmic, such as the tsunami of December 26, 2004, in which more than 200,000 people were killed or lost because no sufficient mechanical warning system was in place. The loss of life would still have been large, but the lack of machine surveillance and communication that could have reached even these nontechnologically saturated areas made the force of this shift in the earth's tectonic plates far greater.[1]

If machines are designed correctly and maintained, even given the destructive lapses that happen to all material beings in becoming worn down in an entropic universe, then we can, by and large, count on machines to function in a set way and to keep constant so many otherwise fluctuating aspects of the human world. It might be said that the same sort of rhythm of continuity that used to be provided by the natural realm in its regularities within cycles of change is now provided to us by the built world of machines, or at least layered with the dynamic continuity of natural unfolding. There has been created by humans through machines another dimension of more steady-state continuity. The difference is that natural surround does continually change in ways that called for reciprocal adaptation from humans relying upon the regularities that were part of its larger rhythm, while now, to a much greater degree, given machines' functioning, we can insulate ourselves from some of these fluctuations and keep ourselves in a more invariant surround—but only partially so, as the tsunami example also illustrates.

This consistency of operation and function is something we find essential to living. We somehow do not often want to think of that stratum of ourselves that is a well-functioning machine—a miraculous one—the physiological dimension of our bodies, that keeps an ongoing rhythm and function despite all of the challenges from the environment—both internal and external. Yet it is this repeated accomplishment of a pattern of coordinated movements or interactions of various sorts by differing entities arranged in such a way as to accomplish a function or do work that has to do with the creation of different forms of energy or its transfer that is the core of what machines are and that also makes humans and animals possible, both as living and surviving beings able to act in the world and as having a pattern to their lives. We speak of animals foraging, playing, communicating, or bonding, or of humans thinking, writing, playing, or witnessing the world and how the sensed experience of themselves doing these things gives a rhythm and meaning to their lives, yet all of these abilities depend upon mechanical interactions proceeding smoothly beneath the surface or at the interior of all these and other dimensions of action. In providing this substratum to the existence of humans and animals, as well as in permeating the built environment of humans, machines have a distinctive way of bringing forth a potentiality of materiality, whether self-organizing, in the case of biological or chemical mechanisms, or created through humanity (or other organisms) to achieve a level of consistent functioning, regularity, reliability, manipulability, and rationality to achieve a necessary end within a larger functioning.

The consistency of machines, then, is a showing forth of *the consistency within matter* and its ways of interacting repeatedly as designed objects with an even "quieter force" than that of animals. Machines also have very overt forces they display, more than any other being on the earth, except the shifts in the earth and its elements, but there also is the quiet solidity of consistent, automatic, indefinitely repeated, nonconscious, and unidirectional operating or functioning. Humans live in a *temporality of drama*, and so do animals, to a degree, at least in response to the rhythms of the natural surround, but machines seem to reach down into a temporal zone of *geological time*. Dramatic time is a temporality of crescendos and lulls, moments of decisive decisions and breaks with the past, sudden openings of new vistas of possibilities in a future unfolding, exploding lights of opening further through illumination the scope of the present, and threatening shadows of what is approaching that menace, or may inadvertently harm or detour, and ultimately remove beings from life's stage in death.

From the human vantage, it seems that without the dramatic dimension of time, existence would become sheer linearity, sheer monotony, an eternal return of indistinct moments, grinding forward nonsensically. So we see the endless turning of the electric motor, the meshing of the gears to drive the axle, and the endless storage of ones and zeros in the computer binary logic as the prison of a machine time in which nothing encounters each other in the sense of "timing," that is, the meeting among beings that gives an openness to the present that is at the heart of our experience of time. Yet given what we said of the time of animals, that they seem to be immersed in a kind of time that is a totality, a totality of the surround as each entity participates in it through its long history as an element of the surround ultimately linked to all of the other surrounds, then there also is something about the machine that contributes to this other sense of time as found in the surround that washes through us on a deeper level of embodiment. If, as Merleau-Ponty states, "There is a natural process of time. The pulsation of time is not a pulsation of the subject, but of Nature" (N, 119), and that this sense of time "is inscribed in our body as sensorially," then within our hands, our ears, and our eyes there is this other sense of time joining up with us in this unfolding that predates ourselves and continues after us. This might seem to be the very opposite of the kind of time that surrounds the world of machines. Yet as a quiet force of consistency, of the power to endlessly repeat in a way that even the wasp could not endure, the consistency of the machine enters into the sense of the natural surround as now having this built dimension as being inextricably part of it. Just as the sound of the drum, repeated in rhythmic patterns many times, is a powerful tool for giving sound to the earth's own rhythms and time, so the endless turning, meshing, hammering, grinding, and so on, of the repetitive movements of the machine pound out a deeper time that echoes the earth's elemental processes.

It is in this sense of consistency—like the presence of massive sheets of rock in the mountains and below us in the ground—that machines contribute to the ongoing sense of the stability of existence. Their breakdowns are upsetting in a way that transcends the inconvenience of the disruption of whatever function they have been performing. We often get mad or distraught or feel dislocated when our closest machines fail us, because we count on them to be sure in a way even beyond the reliability of tools that Heidegger discusses in *Being and Time*. We expect the tool to be in its place and to work unobtrusively without calling attention to itself, if it is to really serve as a tool and save us the effort of attending to all of these smaller parts of what we are doing, so we can focus on our goal. However, machines are our silent partners in the work of the world, in the sense that they actually are performing operations themselves. Since they do so with the same reliability, for the most part, of tools, they are like partners of a different kind who move endlessly in patterns of function without any consciousness needing to be expended by them or us, like joining the flow of a vast river, but here it is of moving electrons or gears or other components that have been channeled into the work paths of the world. Electric grids, telecommunications networks, airplane systems, heating facilities, the Internet, and so on go beyond the Heideggerian sense of tool to become part of the solidity of the background of postmodern existence upon which we stand as humans. This is eminently reassuring and adds to the consistency of the world. Here the boundary of the built mechanized world with aspects of the natural world (as a "second nature") becomes blurred.

There is another sense to this consistency of machines that reflects not upon the workings of the rest of the surround but instead makes us aware of aspects of human character and its ongoing aspirations. In a lifetime of thinking about the growing possibilities of machines, and especially of the combination of moving machines and thinking machines in the future of robotics, writer Isaac Asimov wrote many stories in which the frailty of human attempts to be consistent in obligations and in vows to follow certain ethical principles was contrasted with the possible ease with which computers integrated into machines with the intelligence of robots would follow prescribed rules. Asimov was famous for his "three laws of robotics," in which he articulated instructions for future artificially intelligent beings to only act in accordance with safeguarding the welfare of humanity and secondarily the robot's own survival, in order to combat the fears of those who feel threatened by the development of robotics. However, in stories such as "Too Bad," "Robbie," or the "Evitable Conflict," Asimov surprises his readers by creating scenarios in which robots do morally superior actions to most humans, willingly sacrificing themselves for the sake of their human charges, because once they had adopted a principle of caring for the other's welfare, nothing would allow them to deviate from this principle, or once they had agreed to run the economy according to certain principles designed for the *overall benefit* for humanity, nothing would make them decide otherwise.[2] Of course, for humans it is difficult, no matter how principled, not to give way to temptations that lead to personal gain instead of leading to the good of all. Humans often aspire to an unflinching consistency and yet are erratic beings thrown off course by all sorts of beckoning temptations from their situation that would not be processed by a properly set artificial intelligence.

Humans often would like to stay at the project they are working on, or they would like to remain true to their plans or to their ideas of how they should live their lives and yet deviate from these trajectories by distractions, by temptations that they know are not really as satisfying or even by sheer laziness. In the moral sphere, as Asimov's stories articulate, humans deviate even from the principles most important to the moral well-being of the community by being afraid, or leaving their ideals for greedy gain, or being distracted by concerns of vanity. Asimov's robots, embodying that machinelike consistency of being driven by rule-bound behavior, are able to not deviate from the principles with which they have been programmed for humanity's good, even if it costs them their survival, and even if this is obvious to them, because they will not deviate from carrying out these principles to the best of their abilities. At this juncture of robotics development, these stories are still fictions, yet what they represent to humanity is significant.

For all of the negative feeling that humanity harbors for machines because of their consistency often seen as relentlessness, from the demands of the assembly line driving us with a consistency that seems cruel, famously stated in Charlie Chaplin's *Modern Times*, to our inability to get computers to understand why we should be forgiven in this case if we did not follow the rules of our credit card account, we also could admire this consistency as something toward which to aspire in our commitment to certain principles in human existence. The machine represents a certain ideal of the will—an unflinching commitment to what we know is right—either because it is the most constructive course of action for us, or because we know it is the right thing to do. We will always be caught in the ambiguity of so many ideas, feelings, fantasies, and emotions that our commitments will always be a struggle and a challenge, but part of us longs to make these principles such a habit in our lives that we would not possibly deviate from what is right or what is helpful to us. At some critical junctures, there is an excellence to such a cleaving to what the program is, when fear or selfishness beckons, and even if it were mechanistic to proceed as smoothly as if driven by meshing gears in the face of temptation or threat, it would be a path of excellence and not to be derided.

Machines, Power, Precision, and Machine Beauty

We tend to view ourselves as beings who have harnessed vast power in dominating the planet, each other, and even beyond the planet by venturing into outer space. We also see ourselves as having mastered the almost Godlike power of having split open the constituents of matter to unleash great force in atomic and nuclear bombs, and in energy production. Of course, what is a more accurate appraisal of our achievements is that our reflective capacities have allowed us to construct machines that have captured and redirected great amounts of force embedded within the material world to give us a sense of power, but the power belongs in the first place to the inanimate—to the fabric of the cosmos—and not to human being itself, and machines of various sorts are the immediate agents of "producing," unleashing, or redirecting this power. The force that a human alone can generate is very small in the larger scheme of things. Yet machines that split the atom and unleash great forces of energy have a power that with enough multiplication of mechanisms, such as the kind of proliferation practiced by the United States and the USSR in their "arms race" during the cold war, could have devastated the planet itself. However, the vast power that humans have harnessed in various ways is in some very real way a property of machines, not humans, except by extension through creating and manipulating them. In a world in which there were no machines, the only overpowering displays of force would be that of natural events—whose power we also frequently overlook until an earthquake, or a tsunami, or a hurricane reminds us.

When we focus on the machine as an object of admiration or in assessing our need for them, their power does capture our attention. In the United States and Europe during the decades from the 1910s through the 1930s, many artists—painters, photographers, sculptures, filmmakers, and others—who were captivated by a "machine aesthetic," the attempt to portray the essence and beauty of the machine. This was part of a larger social movement during these decades that looked to industrial machinery, factories, skyscrapers, new technological advances, and other aspects of modern industry as representing a power dawning upon the world that was awe-inspiring and was dubbed the "machine age." As one writer says of this era, "Indeed many spoke of the machine as the new religion of the twentieth century."[3] Among the many artists, works by Diego Rivera, Fernand Leger, Francis Picabia, the Dadaists, the Futurists, and Charles Scheeler all celebrated the machine. Scheeler, however, in some way came to most boldly depict the bald reality of machines as overpowering humans and to pursue an aesthetic about which he declared: "Well, it's my illustration of what a beautiful world it would be if there were no people in it" (CS, 107). At the heart of the "machine age" in America, and perhaps its culmination in the late 1920s and throughout the 1930s, Scheeler came to his paintings of machines only after an early rural and then urban skyscape period. However, his paintings are stark and overwhelming in their photorealistic depiction of the sheer materiality, precision, and power of machines.

In 1938, Scheeler undertook a series of six paintings for *Fortune* magazine entitled "Power." In one canvas, "Suspended Power," there is a massive hydroelectric turbine generator hanging in mid-air, above two humans dwarfed beneath it, as it is about to be installed by the Tennessee Valley Authority at a hydroelectric plant in Guntersville, Alabama. It is clear that in this painting that even though the turbine has been produced by engineers, like the two below it, the humans who have given rise to the massive power of the machine are dwarfed by it. They will be able to manipulate it and place it within the scheme they have designed, but in a way, it is like earlier paintings of humans herding or riding elephants: the human is able to control a power that far outstrips it through the ability to think and manipulate. In this painting, as well as others like "Rolling Power" (1939), a depiction of the massive wheels and pulleys of a locomotive, or "Steam Turbine" (1939), a depiction of a massive structure with gleaming stainless steel curving input pipes, or like his photographs and lithographs going back to his early series in the late 1920s of the Ford plant at the Rouge River outside of Detroit, with many views of huge stacks, pipes, presses, conveyors, and other machines of imposing sizes and strengths, Scheeler gives us a bewildering array of metallic surfaces, interlocking parts, and crisp edges possessing a kind of inhuman beauty. The animating principle of the beauty, however, is the dynamic action of the machine, which can be read both in its massiveness and in the gracefulness of the many metallic shapes that curve and crisscross, as indeed one of his photographs of massive stacks, supports, and conveyors at the Ford plant is entitled "Criss-Crossed Conveyors" (1927). It is the beauty of sheer power running smoothly, quickly, and efficiently in a way that would take the massive, grunting, sweaty labor of hordes of straining, suffering humans to try to produce if they were to do it for themselves, like the captive hordes who built pyramids in ancient cultures.

The specter of this machine beauty centering on sheer power moving gracefully has not died out but has taken new forms. David Gelernter claims in his recent book *Machine Beauty* that beauty is always at the heart of how science operates to find solutions and is embodied in the machine by the coming together of power and simplicity.[4] This simplicity is not just about the makeup of parts but about the ease of functioning. Since Gelernter is a computer scientist, one might think that these sorts of machines, whose work involves performing computations and storing and transforming information, would be disanalogous to the attributes Scheeler admired in turbines and factory plants, yet Gelernter says, "Beauty is more important in computing than anywhere else in technology" (MB, 22) by virtue of its beauty emerging through power. The beauty that comes from the gracefulness of the power of computing machines is not a power of moving physical masses in space but is more about the sheer quantity and difficulty of the kinds of calculative operations performed by these machines. Furthermore, the beauty of their power concerns the dynamic quality of machines in doing their work. Gelernter states that computer programs are like virtual machines, in addition to the more obvious aspect of the hardware machines. He claims that this sort of dynamic beauty goes beyond the static beauty of a lovely line and forms a "deep beauty" that emerges from the many levels of machine function "resonating and reinforcing one another." For computers, the link to the massive size of Scheeler's turbines, locomotives, and other factory equipment is diminishing as computers have evolved from a start that seemed very analogous spatially to turbines and physically powerful machines, filling suites of rooms in an overwhelming array of hardware, to the awesome computing power of very tiny elements. However, the meaning of the power that they represent to humans is the same—the amount of work that is done without any evidence of strain, but rather smoothly, quickly, and quietly, is staggering. In terms of sheer computing power, the quantity of intellectual work that computers can now perform is staggeringly large.

Power, however, is also about control, in addition to its sense of produced force. Here, too, machines have given humans a great extension of their rather limited ability to control the world around them, and to do so with a precision that humans could not achieve without them. Whether it is in precisely controlling physical forces, such as the flow of water or the amount of electricity or the amount of thrust of a rocket's engines blasting away from our planet, we rely upon machines to measure, to control, and to regulate, as well as to inform us about all of these operations and others made on our behalf to control the surround. Without the precision of operation, which allows the machine to direct the force in predictable and controllable ways, sheer force often would end up not being powerful, because forces of various kinds have to be guided in determined ways in order to be effective and evince power over the things of the world. The result of precision is often accuracy, and again machines outstrip humans in their ability to produce accurate results. To be powerful often requires a precise way of proceeding that produces accurate results and allows the force to be manifested in the correct way at the desired goal. A computer-guided laser can be aimed in a way that a handheld instrument could never be, consistently responding and performing according to the precise, machine-created input and achieving an accuracy of mechanical execution that would not even be achievable by humans, nor even perceivable by them without a machine's measurement.

Humans often have marveled at the natural world for the precision of operation and accuracy of outcome that seemed to be beyond their more improvisational and approximate human ways. Ancient cultures invented the first measuring devices (machines of a sort) and realized that the seasons, the movement of the stars, and other natural rhythms were amazing in their consistency of unfolding and outcome. For Aquinas, this precision and coordination proved that the natural world was the manifestation of a divine plan. With the rise of science and technology, as humans invented more complicated machinery, the precision and accuracy of events and processes in the natural world often were compared to a great clockwork or other precise machine. Yet at this point in humanity's history, the built world is now so extensive, and for many more urban cultures natural rhythms so obscured that machines embody a power and precision that resounds in human's felt sense of possibilities of the surround and in our dreams and aspirations.

In human organizations, there is often an attempt to emulate and achieve a simulacrum of the being of the machine as a way of operating with its members. Of course, what comes to mind for many is a most painful instantiation of this aim, the "war machine," written about eloquently by Deleuze and Guatteri. Those engaged in war are part of an action that aims at maximum force and precision—no faltering or improvising is possible for maximal operation. Bureaucracies often aim to undertake this same precision and forceful action, as is needed, for example, in the opposite case of war, for doing rescue work or other restorations of order when there has been a disruption or breakdown. Often a task requires us to be part of some sort of forceful coalition that can move an obstacle or transform an obstinate condition. Public health, for example, may require an intervention in which regardless of who we are, we must all work together to be part of a precise interaction that can generate enough force to eradicate a persistent menace. There is room for all of the human compassion and care, but only within the larger organization that will mobilize and direct a concerted action that hums along with its human components working in as close a mesh as possible repeating the same required actions, like one of Scheeler's large turbines. This sort of organization can be dehumanizing and violating to those caught in its machinations if it is aggressive, but it is also one of the prime ways to intervene on a large scale to help others—by taking on attributes of machines allowing human care to be delivered inside the precise and powerful as the inner core of meaning. Again, the boundaries overlap, and sometimes for reasons that help achieve well-being.

Machines, Speed, and the Lack of Place for Deeper Time

Machines have eaten up the distances of the earth and even of the galaxy. In allowing movement through space at fantastic speeds to become something smooth, quick, efficient, reliable, and easily accessible, the distances of the earth have receded. Everything is able to be reached quickly through a power and rapidity that humans can only achieve through the machine. This is not to say that there are moments or circumstances where movement is not still slow and difficult, nor is it to say that machines do not bog down, but these rapid movements all over the globe leave their mark on the perceived sense of how distant things are and how quickly space fades as a true journey of unfolding days, months, and years. Only those who choose such long journeys will experience this laborious time of voyaging, but the farthest region on our planet is only hours away, at least within the framework of the possible mechanized reach that gives these distances another sense, even if one chooses to walk for months or years. Given the many millennia where this was not the case and there was another sort of vastness that encompassed our planet and the ways of moving through it, there is a gap of synchronization between the everyday rhythms that were tied to the natural surround and the car, jet, and rocket pace of traversing the earth. Of course, this speed and power not only infiltrate literal movements but the instaneous movement of information, transactions, and so on. There is a disjunction in an earthbound sense of time, space, and place with other rhythms and another hypertime, hyperspace, and override of place that has permeated our sense of the world through the signature of the machine. The roadkill by the side of any highway is a kind of inscription of the natural surround in bloody surrender to some sort of another time lancing across its own time of unfolding in ways that cause it to bleed. When Milan Kundera wrote of the "lightness of being" in the world of the late twentieth century, most thought of the human lack of rootedness in the social fabric and lack of commitment to long and arduous relationships and projects, but equally this phrase could refer to a "lightness of being" of this other time and space hanging above the denser ones of earthly interconnection with a hydraulic force and flux that casts an eerie light upon the earth. In this lack of synchronization with the unfolding of the surround, machines have swallowed time in a way that the Greek myth of Chronos, the Titan and symbol for time, who devoured his children, could never have conjured.

When Jean Baudrillard, the French theorist, came to America in the mid-1980s, he drove across its spaces and discovered what he called "astral America," a vast landscape "star-blasted, horizontally by the car, altitudinally by the plane, electronically by television, geologically by deserts"[4] or, in other words, a vast surround that no longer connected to itself but had been emptied out of meaning in the juxtaposition of its vast natural expanses of desert, mountain, plains, and so on, with the worship of the constant functioning of machines to satisfy a need for power, speed, a display of force, and a barrage of images to entertain and reassure. He saw America as a world of speed that had lost its relationships to "territorial reference points," and being continually displaced, Americans were satisfied to just keep circulating. This constant movement by machine sought somehow to "to annul time itself" (A, 6). This displacement in space and time makes sense if we have lost our felt connection to the surround that we articulated at length earlier in this book as our common ground with animals; then, as Baudrillard puts it, we have lost our sense of reality as humans embedded in a surround as "delivered from all depth there—a brilliant, mobile, superficial neutrality, a challenge to meaning and profundity, a challenge to nature and culture, an outer hyperspace, with no origin, with no reference points" (A, 124). Baudrillard called the accelerated play of surfaces the "hyperreal," which had displaced the real. What is important to note here is that the hyperreal would not be possible without the speed and constant circulation of energies and bodies made possible through machines. This is not to say that machines are to blame for this desolation, for blame is a more complicated question to which we will return in the concluding chapter, but it is one of the transformations of the sense of the surround that machines make possible.

Throughout this book, we have seen how matter holds meanings within it that call out to our perceptual bodies with layers of emotion, imaginary senses, haunting memories, and so on. If machines infiltrate the workings of so much of our surround, then they shape what we encounter and help give that surround its meaning, its sense, for us. Besides the constant motion, the speed, the power, and the ongoing mechanical productivity and efficiency, there is also the lighting up of the night, the former time of rest and of being released into a spaciousness of an enveloping blackness, what Merleau-Ponty called a sense of "pure depth" that engulfs us in the darkness of night (PP, 283). The depth of the night had an attractive pull into which the activity of the day was swallowed and replaced with a rhythm that was more massive, like the rhythmic lull of the massiveness of the earth below us, or the unfathomable tides of oceans—a pooling of energies and a gathering of creatures of the day in rest and dream. In our technologically mechanized world, machines hum throughout the night and often dispell the darkness with artificial light, and the night itself becomes banished as this bower of rest. Baudrillard found this sense represented for him, too, in America: "In short, in America the arrival of night-time or periods of rest cannot be accepted, nor can Americans bear to see the technological process halted. Everything has to be working all the time. There has to be no let up in man's artificial power, and the intermittent character of natural cycles (the seasons, day and night, heat and cold) has to be replaced by a functional continuum" (A, 50). This drive that machines power rends the surround, which also still partially resounds with the slower, more interwoven rhythms and cycles that ebb and flow, that synchronize among beings, both animate and inanimate, natural and cultural, in longer curves of development and unfolding.

It is almost as if each time we look out over the horizon there are two different scenes that confront us: one etched with lines of force, speed, and constant productive activity that comprise a web of relations that spins about its axis like a great cauldron and reaches toward the sky infusing everything within its interconnected energies with a driving motion and inner restlessness—then we can breathe more deeply and look with a slower eye to catch a glance of a deeper, paler, encompassing, shadowy, slowly rotating vessel that also fills at least half of the horizon, but with a spiraling interweavement of the beings of the earth timing themselves together in reverberation, manifesting the ancient life of the natural surround and also the newly created built environment insofar as parts of it can echo older rhythms and patterns of interchange. It is within this portion of the surround that a certain ancient, and perhaps sacred, time sense is kept.

In Alan Goldsworthy's film *Rivers and Tides: Working with Time*, there is a sustained search by sculptor and earth artist Goldsworthy to connect with and articulate a sense of time that works within the deepest layers of the natural surround. In the film, Goldsworthy shapes delicate ice structures that melt slowly in the sun, fashions large constructions of sticks that are gradually carried out by the tide, spun around in circles, and slowly dissolve and return to the sea, where they were before their long journey of being washed ashore, or chains of leaves are sewn together, trailing over the surface of a swiftly flowing stream by lazily meandering back and forth on the surface of the river, like some sort of snake taking in the sun. Patterns of sticks of varying hues also take on differing designs given the strength of the sun versus the clouds and the changing seasons or cairns of rocks that become submerged under tides but reappear at differing times with a different expression of an ancient rocky time of solidity that is nevertheless made slowly fluid by the context of the dynamic surround. The kind of time that Goldsworthy articulates and evokes is the time we have discussed of how animals in the surround dovetail into rhythms of the surround that carry a weight and density of the long natural history of the way this surround has been gradually shaped in the evolution of the planet and inserted into the unfolding of all of the other surrounds. This slower, longer time of gradual shifts is like the sustained bass notes of an orchestral piece that give the more rapid flow of the music's rhythm a kind of simultaneous anchor in a more stable, slow time. This sense of time was alluded to in the writings of Merleau-Ponty as "geological time." However, part of this newest evolution of the planet is the human- and machine-driven transformations of surrounds. Where once there were deep forests now tracts of houses stand, or where once there were lazy marshes of sitting water, now there are airports or factories, or where once, even as partially transformed by human culture, there were rolling farmlands, now there are screaming highways and malls.

For Goldsworthy, this would be at the core of the transformation of the time sense of the earth itself. As he says in the opening of his film, "Time and change are connected to place. Real change is best understood by staying in one place." The time is contained within the natural surround and its many layers of past times and transformations that are still held there. With the transformation of the earth through machines into a series of spaces not uniquely situated in relationship to the other surrounds that developed with it in rhythms of interaction, there is literally no place to hold the depth of time. Insofar as the earth becomes a series of interchangeable constellations of drug store, grocery store, office supply store, and sporting goods store, packaged in recurring mini-malls, or of subdivisions of houses fabricated in uniform shapes as far as the eye can see, the surround loses its power to hold a density and depth of time. Machines chew up the land, throw up these recurrent structures in earnest efficiency, and allow for a pace of development breathtakingly quick. Machines have greatly augmented the human altering of environments that are no longer surrounds in the sense of holding humans and animals in the echoes of long-held, slowly unfolding patterns of life. Humans feel increasingly uprooted from time and place.

At best, within so many of our built environments, there is this split sense of another deeper, slower, more encompassing time playing off against the relentlessly quickening pace of machine time, but in some areas, the echo of the more ancient times is lost for moments or hours of frenzied activity or much longer, until perhaps one looks above at the sky and hears a whisper of a sense outside the fast time and shallow displacement of hurried movement. This might be only for an instant, and then ignored, put aside. Scenes of this kind of machine devastation were painted by Scheeler when depicting the Ford plant or other factories. He filled the entire horizon with stacks and turbines and captured how rivers had been fed into concrete channels of sludge and industrial runoff and how, as far as the eye could see, only iron and concrete, washed-out colors, and no niches for life to take hold were found within the constructed landscapes of the industrial blueprint. There was almost a strange eternity that hung over these scenes and a hush, until the viewer looked more closely and realized that it was a vacuum of time, an emptiness into which any fabricated pace of production could be pumped by any work schedule that the time managers had decided upon to run this world. The quiet was not a peaceful silence but the absence of all voices of life and spontaneity, waiting for the rush of gears and horsepower to create a cacophony that would abruptly cease with the instantaneous cessation of movement that the machine embodies—abandoned machines, inert, used up, and left to haunt us not with antiquity but with obsolescence.

Machines, the Arbitrary, and Dissonant, Arrhythmic Time

The wonder of machines is how they can be constructed to fit almost any purpose humans can envision. Humans, as we have seen, are unique in their capacity to witness and also in their ability to take up and affirm what is around them and within them, but they can equally distance themselves from whatever they have become and to which they are related. Given the power to isolate and change through abstraction, to vary in imagination, and to project alternative futures, humans have the ability to be errant creatures, who move out of interlocking patterns of the surround into divergent ways to be. Yet they also, as embodied creatures whose distancing capacities occur within the more encompassing framework of emotional and even visceral attunement to the surround, can be sensitive to rhythms and to the sense of the surround and can match themselves to it, although perhaps not as finely as animals can. Humans can enfold themselves in the power of meaning and action afforded by the surround, as when a surfer blends in with the enormous force and direction of the rushing wave, or a Van Gogh picks up the swirling energies of the starry night and gives it visible form in pigments upon the canvas.

As we also have discussed, there are many levels of embodied beings, beneath our level of deliberate awareness, that are a function of an intermeshing with the surround. We are "woven into the fabric" of the world around us, as Merleau-Ponty puts it in the introduction to the *Phenomenology of Perception* (PP, x–xi). Despite this enmeshment and the ability to be sensitively attuned to the surround, human errancy is more the norm with its violating effects upon the surround, causing species extinction, ecosystem havoc, and the creation of vast stretches of ugly, built environments at odds with the rhythms of the surround and disruptive to humans dwelling resonantly within the surround. However, once again, if we were to consider how much this created dissonance with the surround and other beings within the surround would result from humans acting through their independent capacities, then the disruption would be quite limited. It is by humans working through machines that the power to set things at odds becomes exponentially amplified and unleashed upon the world in another way. We would not have transformed countless rolling hillsides and marshes into shopping malls or created a gaping hole in the ozone or disrupted climates through the greenhouse effect or threatened the globe with massive explosions and nuclear winter, to name a few of the most cataclysmic ways of disrupting our shared surround, without the action of machines.

In a positive sense, the scope and direction of the machine world are almost indefinitely flexible. Given that machines can be fabricated out of almost any material humans know or will discover, that the processes by which machines operate are open to indefinite variation, engineering, and invention, that the functions they serve are open to any that humans choose to accomplish, and that the other machines and systems to which humans can attach are so varied, machines have a vast flexibility of being that humans and animals could never achieve. The animal, with its close relationship to its surround, its niche, and its narrow range of adopting new behaviors, as well as its fragile biological makeup, has a way of being that is consistent, much more so than the human. Yet both humans and animals are constrained or contained within patterns of the surrounding world in a way that machines will never be. Animal functioning and, to a lesser degree, human functioning have evolved in concert with other beings and constituents within the surround, and they work together to form an ecosystem. A machine has no such constraints on its development and function, unless sensitive humans introduce them into its design and mechanisms of operation. Humans in their errancy can introduce a certain arbitrary new direction upon the surround, but machines are utterly "loose cannons" in this sense, having minimal restraint by the other parts of the surround.

Of course, when we consider individual machines once they are fabricated, traditionally they have been the narrowest of the three realms in their flexibility of the details of how they function and in what they are. Yet this too contributes to their arbitrariness in relation to the cooperative functioning of the surround. It is their lack of responsiveness to the surround that has often most marked machines. Their capacity to violate other beings has been the result of their cutting their way through the interrelations of aspects of the surround in violating obliviousness. Given the individual traditional machine's functioning without any feedback loops with the surround, it relentlessly moves in its own self-propelled path as utterly indifferent and oblivious to its impact on others, resulting in a profound arbitrariness of the machine in regard to the cooperative nature of the surround. In contrast to machines, the living beings and even inanimate constituents, given the long history of mutual interaction and adjustment, work together in ways a machine could easily violate. Of course, one could say that it is the human creating the vast array of machines that displays arbitrariness, but without the actual nature of the machine and the human extending its being and power through the unique being and power of the machine, a new dimension of disjunction, of being at odds with others, of aspects of the postmodern world, would not exist.

The arbitrary is that which does not have a relation to all that is about it in the surround. It merely goes in a direction or introduces new elements into a surround that have no synchronization with the history of the surround, to the prior web of relationships, the rhythms created among all of the beings of the surround. As we have portrayed animals and humans, they are *internally* related to everything around them in the surround. The relationships with others make up their own being—they cannot function, experience, or thrive without this relatedness with others, because that is what they are. The arbitrary appears outside of this network of relations. Its interconnections are limited to cause-and-effect interactions, external relations, which affect it, but from "the outside." The lawn mower rusts, the car gets a flat tire, or the components of the computer break when dropped, but there is no responsiveness, no imagining of alternatives, no feelings to be dealt with, or no compensations in how they function and exist as with a human or an animal that has sustained an injury, for example. Now the animal may have to alter its habits in the surround, become more wary, may feel more vulnerable, and may find new ways to use its body or to achieve its goals in the surround, or the human may feel as if she or he is marred in some way or may mourn the loss of certain possibilities enjoyed while healthy, but then goes on to find new ways to deal with the demands and opportunities of the surround to maintain, according to her or his needs and desires, as much of her or his previous life as possible, or some comparable life. What happens to animals and humans takes on a meaning and affects animals' or humans' implicit sense of self. In response, the creature becomes something else, uses its body in new ways, finds new avenues to get its needs met, or perhaps explores new aspects of the surround that will still meet its needs. Even when this enmeshment has been broken or disturbed, since it preceded the break and was part of the being of the human or animal, the reestablishment of some rhythm with the surround, some new way of becoming enfolded within it is sought, and is possible, because there usually are many possible strands of compatible interweaving that have been established in the longer span of the earth's evolution. The lack of given possibilities for interweaving with the world is what is most frightening about machines, because they can rend other creatures and the surround with their arbitrariness or, as D. H. Lawrence expressed it, there is danger in not being guided by the rhythms of the whole but instead by "the mechanical power of self-directed energy," which gives rise to "machines, full of friction, full of grinding, full of danger to the gentle passengers of growing life."[5]

In trying to be fair to machines, to see the ways in which they have positive characteristics that overlap with humans and animals and may be part of the deeper, implicit meaning of the earth as a home, a surround that anchors and gives both humans and animals a meaning and place, we pointed to the deep bass notes of machines' hum, drumlike repetition and powerful percussion that can resonate with the deepest corelike rhythms of the earth in a slower, elongated sense of geological time. There is this time of slow unfolding and envelopment that is part of the embracing sense of the surround and constitutes a lower level to time's unfolding as a baseline of endurance and strength. Yet machines as arbitrary are able to spring into action, to suddenly cease functioning and turn off, to accelerate to great speeds with little time elapsed, to function at paces utterly at odds with everything around them in the surround, to keep working at speeds that would be fantastic for any creature or even for objects within the surround, and are the source for much frenetic activity, movement, and function that would seem to fill many surrounds with another dimension that is out of synchronization with the flow of energy and change within it. The machines appear to create a rift of functioning with some sort of hyperspeed and hypertime that comes to infiltrate the rest of the surround with an unsettling sense of driven time and crowded space. Machines that function in this manner also have often clattered cacophonously within factory settings, urban settings, or even in our supposedly leisure settings. This kind of sound is also the sound of a fractured and driving time, pushing us on to nowhere in particular but straining the sense of the surround to contain and synchronize that which is within it. Sometimes, lacking the noise, the hush of such speed, and the intermittent stopping and starting and sudden shifts of massive power are even more powerful in their eeriness to undermine the underlying sense of a lower dimension of time that is slower and more stable, and is by machines being vaporized.

Humans and animals need the sense of duration and the slowness of the surround in moving through a longer lifetime of the earth as a contributing community of beings that finds comparable resonant paces, despite upheavals and disturbances. Machines can threaten to move the whole planet into some sort of other arrhythmic time that is humans' arbitrary insertion into another rhythm, but one that machines bring to a pitch, a power and a depth that might move the sense of life on earth onto a differing and dislocating axis. Yet machines are changing as we change our sense of how they might augment humans' possibilities for dwelling in the surround.

Machines as Woven into the Fabric of the Surround

The ability to be knit into the surround and to change with its changes is what computer scientists are trying to build into new, artificially intelligent machines by multiplying the ways in which take in information from the environment and react to it in multiple feedback loops. That dawning ability and enmeshment was most startling to visitors to the M.I.T. AI Lab: Cog did not have a specifically programmed way of moving around the lab but was able to first follow the movement of its visitor with its head and eyes, and then was able to come forward and "meet" the visitor with a handshake, adapting its movements to those of the person it was greeting. We do not expect traditional machines to be responsive, and yet modern machines that have varied means of entering into feedback loops with the environment are becoming sewn into its fabric in ways we had not imagined possible for machines. This is the result of machines being designed from a cybernetic perspective: "Cyberneticists were especially interested in 'self-regulating systems.' These are systems in which the results of the systems' own activity are 'fed back' so as to increase, stop, start, or reduce the activity as conditions dictate" (NBC, 14). As Clark explains, machines that are part of such systems are said to be "homeostatically controlled," which means that they have been constructed to have a reactive relationship to the surround in such a way that as conditions change they respond automatically to return to their original baseline state (NBC, 15). In this sense, both machine and surround hover together around a norm to be maintained in response to deviations.

In the vision of those who are working to extend computer-driven technology further in its ability to facilitate human lives, it is imperative that in order to be effective, these systems of machines must achieve what is called "transparency"—a way of dovetailing with the round of normal human activities so that they become seamlessly embedded within the surround. Heidegger's insight in the 1920s, that tools that are not obtrusive and instead become part of our sense of the space around us as natural constituents are the most powerful, is more pertinent than ever. If humans function best at most tasks when immediately caught up in a perceptual and motoric relationship with the surround, which does not require explicit attention and manipulation but rather flows as easily and unthinkingly as do the moving parts of our own bodies, then machines work best for us as integrated into the surround and with our own sense of acting through the surround. Clark phrases the same insight in regard to technological development: "Transparent technologies are those tools that become so well fitted to, and integrated with, our own lives and projects that they are . . . pretty much invisible-in-use" (NBC, 28). This idea is vital as a guiding principle to make machines more effective. Yet it is an idea that also can be approached from a philosophical perspective in order to see how this way of conceiving of the relationship of machines and humans can be seen to have deeper and wider implications for how we might want to coexist with machines.

This discussion of how to bring machines into synchronization with humans, animals and surround cannot be divorced from the concerns discussed previously that machines are so flexible as to be arbitrary in their placement in the surround. From this attribute comes many disadvantages that are distressing to those who find machines threatening to the quality of human life and ecologically dangerous. Yet we need the latitude that machines give us to enter the surround from an independent angle that is not part of its web of relations—for example, to have machines that are immune to toxic environments or environments at great heat, or to smash the very fabric of the atomic and subatomic structure, to penetrate other materials imperviously, to travel great distances and retain integrity, no matter what surrounding conditions, and so on, for an almost innumerable amount and kind of functions and situations. However, most of the ecological damage to the surround also results from this introduction of foreign substances with differing properties or with functions out of synchronization with the processes of that surround that have evolved and come into equilibrium over a long expanse of time. The same thing is true in the collision of machines with human well-being, when machines are seen to be dehumanizing or causing human suffering—humans are forced to adapt to the rhythms or needs of the machines, and they introduce substances or processes into the human situation that are foreign to humans' rhythms and needs. Again, we need to only return to the powerful symbol of Charlie Chaplain in *Modern Times*, swallowed by the gears of the machines in the factory, force-fed lunch by the automated feeder, and finally pushed around by the hands of the massive clock that keeps efficient industrial time. These are symbols for those forced by technology in hospitals to meet its needs or those in plants losing their lives or being coerced into misshapen ones by machines or the way in which in a less dire manner we are all driven by the accelerating pace of technological capacity to process information and to produce goods at a frenetic pace. There are many reasons for these situations, and machines are not to blame for how we have used them in such a way as to have altered the structure of the surround or even our own lives, yet we need to realize the meaning inherent in the capacities of machines to alter the world in ways that are destructive. If we look at the ideas of "transparency" and of "dovetailing" of machines and surround in another sense, then it is the beginning of an answer of how to keep both vigilant about the quality of machines' relations to humans, animals, and the surround, as well as how to design and place machines in a more mutual, fruitful way that will continue to develop their excellences instead of their dangerous qualities for the surround and other beings. The need to find ways machines can enter longstanding creative and effective rhythms of the surround is imperative.

There is another dimension frequently overlooked in this sort of discussion of the potential impact on the surround by machines that also is important to the quality of life of humans: the aesthetic dimension. The ugliness of parts of our urban landscapes, whether inhabited by machines or altered through their powers, the even more disturbing stretches of refineries or other factories in the midst of rural landscapes, or the reshaping of stretches of land such as forests or wetlands or other parts of the natural surround by earthmoving, explosives, cutting, or other devices will affect humans' vitality and their interwovenness with the surround. Certainly in this age there is little agreement about the nature of beauty and even whether beauty is important to art or to humanity, but outside of academic circles, it is a quality that people still seek in their lives as a source of vitality, renewal, inspiration, meaning, purpose, and well-being. Crispin Sartwell, in his book *Six Names of Beauty*, takes the name for beauty in six different cultural contexts in six different languages and muses on the aspects of beauty as the object of longing, the glow emanating from things, the holiness permeating beings, the ideal sense that surrounds beings, the sparse rightness at the core of things, and the attuned connection among all beings as important senses of beauty. At the end of considering these aspects of beauty, Sartwell declares, "Beauty is the string of connection between a finite creature and a time-bound world. Beauty is an artifact of our jointure with the world and our inextricability with it."[6] Whatever the aesthetic judgments of our age about the relevance of beauty to the art world, I think Sartwell is right, that the longing for the sensuous presentation to us of these varied senses of meaning, holiness, rightness, wonder, and attunement with the world on an embodied level of emotion and imagination in beauty affords us a different kind of connection with the surround. As Sartwell points out, as mortal creatures, there is an awareness of our passing away and the passing away of the beings of the world, which fires that need of making a resonant connection with the world that we have said is at the heart of human and animal existence and is augmented through beauty. Beauty's absence, as the absence of finding that resonant connection on an embodied level of these presentations, dissolves at least partially our bonds with the surround. Machines have a role to play in preserving the beauty of the surround and in allowing this vitalizing connection.

    Whether on the level of practical dissonances with the surround that cause destruction or damage to other living beings, or to the objects of the surround, or on the level of creating a kind of time, space, and rhythm that is displacing to humans and animals, or on the level of the need for beauty, the ways in which machines can be brought into greater dovetailing with the long histories of equilibratory unfolding among the parts of the surround not only add to the efficient functioning of machines but allow for a kind of integration of the human, animal, machine, and inanimate dimensions within the surround. An awareness of these needs for the mutual thriving of these realms and the bringing forth of the excellences of each will not provide us with easy answers to when machines are being used in such an arbitrary manner that they are becoming destructive to the other dimensions of the surround, no matter whatever kind of new function they bring us, but will give us a kind of reference horizon to attempt to fathom. We can ask to what extent the new machines have been introduced to the surround to dovetail with its rhythms, with the needs of its biological and ecological processes, with the functioning of other constituents within the diversity of the surround, with the patterns of intercommunication and interaction of the beings already a part of the surround, and with the sensuous appearance of the surround so that there is a connectedness and a resonance of form with the beauty already present that can be preserved or even augmented.

It is clear that humans have an excellence of their own functioning and well-being to be gained from such an increased sensitivity, but what of the realms of machines and of animals? In the past two chapters, we have seen that there are certain properties of machines and animals that bring out an excellence of their functioning, but also ways in which either they do not function well or disrupt the surround in a way that will be destructive for all three realms, since ultimately all three dovetail in too many ways for any of them to thrive in any way that undermines any of them. Perhaps it appears that animals and machines are the two most disjunctive realms, but at this point in the planet's evolutionary history, the massive die-off of the animal realm would affect the planetary ecology in ways destructive to humans and ultimately, therefore, to the development of machines, and a world without machines would be destructive to any plausible scenario of human thriving and would impact adversely even animals and the biosphere. At this point in history, not only are the identities of the three realms overlapping in the ways we have articulated (and others), but so are their destinies. Machines can be woven more into the fabric of the surround with greater human awareness of the needs and possibilities for this enmeshment of an affirming sort that augments the excellences of the other two realms. However, at this juncture in our meditation, it would be helpful to consider the question of whether we, as humans, have some calling or even obligation to help the realms of machines and animals achieve their distinctive excellences for any reasons that go beyond human self-interest, because the flourishing of the three realms in concert not only has a practical reward but also a spiritual one.

Conclusion

Toward the Community of Humans, Animals, and Machines

Is There Personhood for Animals and Machines?

This book has mapped a terrain in which humans have a flexibility of functioning, because parts of their organism are mechanisms of various sorts that give them a stable basis of relationship with the surround and within themselves from which to reach out in more improvisational ways as both become submerged in meaningful relationships. For example, we explored how even when a literal machine—a cochlear implant—was substituted for the biological machinery of the inner ear, Michael Chorost was able to expand the capacities of the machine and his own sensitivities to others when both became united and enfolded in an augmented existential flow with others. Humans also have been seen to have animal ways of understanding and feeling their way through the world that also comprise partial dimensions of how humans fathom each other. For example, as in their sense of home, as articulated by Merleau-Ponty, humans like animals are drawn upon that vector viscerally though the surround toward an immediate sense of peace (PP, 285). Animals have been seen to have dimensions of self, community, communication, and understanding, among other capacities that overlap with parts of human being, whether elephants that mourn their dead or bees that dance out the location of a distant food source to other bees in the hive. Machines have been seen to be moving on a developmental path in which they too are entering into the fabric of the surround in which interconnection and encounter take on deeper meanings of action and relationship, as in the moment when Cog tracks a visitor with its eyes and moves forward to shake "hands" in the M.I.T AI Lab. Even more traditional machines have been seen to reverberate within the surround in transformative ways that alter the human sense of time, space, place, power, rhythm, and dwelling, as in the descriptions of "astral America" made by Baudrillard. Seeing fully the identities of humans, animals, and machines means to see them in their dynamic functioning and expressive manifestations in the energies and movements of meaning embedded within their surrounds, as they become what they are only through the echoing of each of these three dimensions within the other. If human beings' distinctive excellence is inseparable from their witnessing of themselves, the world, and the larger cosmos, then what they encounter gives them the words and the meaning they are here to express. Humans, through their distinctive parallel processing of perception, imagination, memory, feeling, emotion, bodily sense, thought, and language, are able to give a voice and an expression to the myriad voices of the surround in its widest sense as it speaks to them in silent, evocative ways.

This way of seeing humans leads to a reconsideration of exclusively granting to human beings the distinction of being "persons." For many, it is obvious because humans have language, or self-reflective consciousness, or a soul that is their participation in God, or for still other reasons, that only humans are entitled to the status of personhood. Yet in the last chapter of *God and the Machine*, entitled "The Community of Human and Nonhuman Persons," Ann Foerst gives the reasons she believes humans should consider artificially intelligent machines as persons. She points out that obviously humans do not always consider other humans as persons, as the horrors of the Nazi epoch or the recent genocides between the Bosnians and Serbs or between the Hutus and Tutsis demonstrate forcefully (GM, 158). Humans can wantonly destroy other groups of humans or torture them mercilessly, because they do not see the members of this other group as deserving respect or concern for their well-being but are merely despicable objects of some sort to be obliterated, broken, or discarded. This means that groups can be seen as humans, as the Nazi doctors saw the Jews in their interest to do biological experiments upon them that might help the Germans, but not to be considered as *persons*. They were considered humans or else their biology would not be recognized as comparable and therefore useful to the Germans, yet not any more of the status of persons deserving respect than we consider lab rats. If not all humans are seen as persons, then there is not an automatic identification between the idea of humanity and the idea of personhood. However, if they are not the same set of beings, then we can begin to wonder whether there also may be persons who are nonhuman. Many Native American peoples refer to the "two-legged, four-legged, and winged persons," for example, in discussing humans, animals, and birds.

Foerst explains that in her years of working with the robots Cog and Kismet at the M.I.T. AI Lab, she saw a new kind of bond grow between humans and robots. Humans were deeply moved by some of the reactions of the robots in their interactions with humans, as when Foerst found herself moved by Kismet's babbling to her in comforting tones after she had voiced her frustration and sadness when it was not responding to her initially. Foerst realized how these machines may well come to be part of the stories that humans narrate in order to make sense of their lives and find fulfillment (GM, 189). Even though she knew that Kismet had been programmed to respond to her distressed speech tones with its comforting tones of babble, this did not change her emotional response of feeling good about being soothed by Kismet. After all, Foerst points out, are not most humans programmed in some sort of way to respond to the distress of others with comfort (GM, 146–48)? We know others have been programmed, taught in some ways, and also respond in deep patterns of the biological species in ways, yet we still value being comforted by other humans, so why not by the programmed machine? Whether this analogy is true or not does not matter, since Foerst's response, as well as Cynthia Breazeal's (who programmed Kismet yet could not help having similar responses to it) was not a rational one. It is an immediate affective, kinetic, and perceptual response. For Foerst, this means that artificially intelligent machines are becoming ways of exploring our own emotions, dreams, and thoughts, are becoming partners in activities, are beings with whom we are bonding, are impacting and becoming part of our community, and certainly are gaining a significant role in our stories about ourselves and our existence.

Foerst makes the claim, as do many others in regard to humans (as we discussed previously), that humans are essentially storytelling beings, gaining their sense of identity, value, and belonging through the narratives they tell themselves and others. Yet it also is true that they gain a sense of identity, meaning, and belonging not only from their stories but from being included in the stories of others. Foerst articulates how part of humans belonging to a community is to be included within a shared story. Those to whom they might deny personhood, whether members of an ethnic group they devalue or a person who has Alzheimer's and can no longer display some of the functions taken to be "normal human functions," are excluded from their shared story. They are not "us," but rather "them." Foerst says on the basis of humans bonding with machines, of helping humans understand themselves, and of being partners in so many ventures that machines should be brought into the story of "persons" in a community of the human and nonhuman. Not only that, but Foerst challenges humans to consider whether there is an analogous danger to excluding machines, and I would add animals, from the community of "persons," to the danger of excluding other people from the community of "persons." Foerst points out how our own humanity shrivels in its generosity, care, and respect for other beings when humans begin to exclude other humans from being considered persons, such as considering someone with Alzheimer's no longer a "person." If other beings also have a claim to inclusion in this community, then do we stand to lose something precious of ourselves, as well as being unfair to them? Many science fiction films have asked the question of humanity: When we exclude clones, such as those in *Coma* or *Island*, or exclude animals, such as the newest version of *King Kong*, or our cyborg creations, such as *Frankenstein*, or the androids first pictured by Philip K. Dick's book made into in *Bladerunner*, or Asimov's artist android in *Bicentennial Man*, what price do we pay as humans, and how might this show that we are not "persons" ourselves in failing to respect as intrinsically valuable those different from us but still kin in many ways?

Certainly if we were to attribute bonding, working together, and developing human capacities for community in interaction with machines, then this is even more obviously the case with animals. The history of humanity is, as Donna Haraway describes it, the history of "companion species" of animals with humans working together, learning from each other, having close bonds, and being transformed by one another. Humanity's feeling of being welcome, belonging to, and hopeful on this planet is in large measure a response to animals all around us and to recognizing ourselves as animals of another sort. The "rational" animal, the "upright" animal, the "speaking" animal, the "playful" animal, the "making" animal, and other names for humans have traditionally acknowledged that we are animals, even at those moments when we tried mightily to distance ourselves from them. However, what may be most important for considering whether other beings might be included as "persons" in community with us is not whether we are also animals or machines in some ways, and that they are part of the story that we tell ourselves to see who we are and to understand ourselves, but rather that animals or machines have been or are becoming our *interlocutors*. I agree with Foerst's ideas and statements, but I think that there is an even stronger case for both animals and machines being considered persons. Not only are they vital to our story and add other dimensions to who we are, and add other directions to our story's unfolding, but they do more than that: they also *contradict* us, they offer us a view of the world that differs from what we could envision without them, and they have the possibility to correct us, extend us, and even teach us. In some other kind of voice that we have not always hearkened to, they tell stories that are distinct from ours, even though we overlap in many ways. They deserve to be included in the community of persons not only as a vital part of our story in terms of who we are and what we have accomplished and learned but also as living in their own stories that at times come to challenge ours. *We must recognize them as storytellers as well.*

Native American myths speak of the previous eons of human history when we "talked" with the animals. Now it is said that we have lost this ability. We have discounted our speech with animals, certainly in the American-European-centered world, and the idea would seem ludicrous to many. Yet if this book is correct in its descriptions, then we still "speak" with animals all the time, but it is an indirect language, a silent one, a hearing that is done with our bodies through our perceptions and their strata of the imagined, felt, remembered, intuited, and proprioceptive. It is a speech of the bones, sinews, and heart of vitality that beats within us and resonates with the earth. When we are in a dialogue with another being, we may indeed overlap in our being, so that we feel a bond or a kinship, but when we address another or when we are addressed by another, we are listening for the voice of the "other," a being beyond our immediate fathoming, as has been a theme of much philosophical writing in the past decades. The respect of another *person* is for a unique being who is different from oneself and worthy of hearkening to in order to glean an understanding from his or her "side of things."

To grant personhood to a being entails a recognition of another being as the center of its existence, as having a sense of itself and a relationship to the world and beings within it. There are aspects of that being's carrying on in the face of the world and inspiring respect and perhaps even some sense of wonder, whether for the gracefulness of the circling hawk or the ability of the penguin to live under such harsh conditions and walk for hundreds of miles to care for its young, or, if we take Foerst's testimony to heart, to be amazed at Kismet's (the artificially intelligent robot) ability to respond soothingly to sadness expressed lugubriously to it. To recognize another as a person is to sense that that being expresses some sort of feeling and understanding in some of its actions toward those in its surround. Other persons have other ways of doing things, of experiencing the world, but are to be valued for their very difference, for their unique path on this planet and as part of this universe, or else we trample the growth that gives richness of function and meaning to existence, which is the interplay of particles, energies, and beings that differ yet interact. These actions of persons recognized as other may be worthy of respect and even potentially a kind of love, but certainly some sort of care. Only if we have clear evidence that the action of a person jeopardizes the well-being of others in the community is there warrant for opposition.

The kind of relationship with beings we are to consider persons, whether among humans or possibly with animals, or even in some more attenuated way with machines, seems to be most possible when we experience both an overlap with their being, some communality, and yet there also is a sense of otherness, a difference of being that commands a certain stepping back in respect. This book has endeavored to describe exactly this sort of relationship among humans, animals, and machines: an overlap and a distinctness of being among all three. In focusing upon embodiment, this book has tried to show how humans and animals and, to some extent, machines work through the openness of the surround, which is the meeting ground for energies, meanings, and common identities. In some ways, this book has stressed more of the common ground than detailing at length areas of difference, since between the two factors, the issue of commonality has been more problematic. Seeing animals as "other" has never been the issue in whether to grant them the status as some other type of person. For the duration of Western cultural history, animals have been seen as too "other" to stand in this sort of relationship with humans. Machines have been seen as utterly other, mere bits of the material world, constructed in useful ways. What has been lacking is to see the kinship with them in such a way that we believe their sort of otherness is one that is "kin" or close enough to our own kind of being to warrant the respect and care we feel "persons" deserve.

As I am writing this conclusion, a recent article in the *New York Times Magazine* has engendered public interest on this issue of whether we are not part of a community with animals in such a way that we need to see them differently—in a way, I would suggest, comparable to the status of "persons." The essay is entitled "Are We Driving Elephants Crazy?" and explores whether elephants "are suffering from a form of chronic stress, a species-wide trauma."[1] After decades of humans poaching elephants, the "culling" of populations, and habitat loss, elephants all across Africa, India, and parts of Southeast Asia, from within the patches of their natural habitats that remain, have been striking out to destroy villages and crops and to attack and kill human beings. Striking examples are the 239 humans killed since 2001 in Assam (with 265 elephants killed by villagers in retaliation), a northeastern Indian state, or the 300 people killed by elephants between 2000 and 2004 in Jharkhand, another Indian state. They also have raped and attacked rhinoceroses in African reserves in a very abnormal behavior, with one group of three young males, for example, being responsible for the killing of sixty-three rhinos. The frequency, ferocity, and circumstances of the attacks have never been seen before and have led experts to proclaim, "What we are now witnessing is nothing less than the precipitous collapse of elephant culture." The heart of the problem appears to be that elephants are very social animals and are raised within an extended network of "doting" female caregivers of a birth mother, grandmothers, aunts, and friends. Young elephants stay within fifteen feet of their mothers for the first eight years of their lives (that may last for seventy years), and after that females are taken off in groups of females and young males by an all-male social group until they are ready to join the herd as mature adults (DEC, 45). With all of the elder elephants killed off in many areas, young elephants are left to roam without guidance and belonging, having been traumatized by witnessing the slaughter of their elders and parents. Eve Abe made the startling discovery that in Uganda, the slaughter of elephants and the slaughter of humans had frightening parallels during the end of the regime of Idi Amin and in the bloody war that followed. Adolescent boys who had watched their parents and village elders slaughtered in front of their eyes, who were left abandoned after the war with no schools, no hospitals, and no infrastructure, roam together in destructive, violent bands. This overlap in humans and animals is striking and points to the fact that the failure to treat these boys as persons rather than fodder for war to be taken off and discarded is alarmingly parallel to the failure to treat as persons the elephants living in harmony with humans in their villages and instead destroy them for profitable sources of ivory trinkets.

What the tragedy with elephants brings to our attention, however, is that for once perhaps a natural species is answering back to humans, instead of slipping away silently into degradation and extinction. We obviously have been too distracted and too intent on ourselves to really listen to animals as interlocutors. It may be true that, as we have detailed in this book, at least part of our sense of the sky and what it means to soar comes from the silent speech of birds, or that the sense of what loyalty or comfort means has been silently spoken by the many dogs who have shared our hearths, but given our view of humans, the body, our sense of insulated self, and so on, we may have hardly heard those voices and certainly not recognized them as such. Siebert talked to many elephant experts, especially with Gay Bradshaw, who has devoted herself to their study, who dismissed other factors such as hormones or land competition. What seems to be the case, according to those who know them, is a response. As Siebert puts it, "It has long been apparent that every large, land-based animal on this planet is ultimately fighting a losing battle with humankind. And yet entirely befitting of an animal with such a highly developed sensibility, a deep-rooted sense of family and, yes, such a good long-term memory, the elephant is not going out quietly. It is not leaving without making some kind of statement" (DEC, 44). We cannot be sure that this is the case, but it seems like what is happening to many who know elephants best. If this is true, then we have entered a new stage of dialogue with the animal world, where we are getting an outraged, desperate reply to our human arrogance.

We are being told to rewrite our story, so that its plot is not so destructive to the planet. The most interesting fact to me in Siebert's report, however, is the *sense of respect* that is being shown to us by "the other side" of this conflict of persons. If you recognize another as a person in true dialogue, even if the interlocutor is in the midst of a conflict with another, finding the other utterly wrong, as Martin Buber put it, then "I affirm the person I struggle with, I struggle with him as a partner. I confirm him as creature and creation. I confirm him who is opposed to me as him who is over against me."[2] Buber says that with this kind of genuine dialogue, a mutuality arises, even in conflict. If we look at what Siebert reports of the attacking elephants, we see that if they are demanding that we stop our slaughter of them and even if they are returning our violence, they are still respecting us as "persons," despite the wanton slaughter we have inflicted upon them for decades. As we have pointed out several times, when a member of the elephant herd dies, the other members gather around and put dirt and brush over its body and hold a lengthy vigil for the fallen one, engaging in mourning together. The elephants who have killed humans have been reported to have performed the same rites—burial and vigil—over fallen human beings, as they do for their own. The herd had to be forced away. It seems appalling that we have had to push animals that far to realize as persons that they are capable of dialogue with us—one that had been silent and coexisting with us for the most part. Maybe we have now pushed one species into a kind of war with us in order for them to get our attention, but it seems that if they can still respect us as beings at the center of lives of value to us and related to others that maybe we could do the same for them and for other animals. Bradshaw speaks of a "trans-species psyche" among us and animals,[3] Haraway calls it a weaving together of "companion species," Merleau-Ponty called it "interanimality," Buber had spoken of "authentic dialogue" with animals, the Native Americans called animals our "four-legged and winged brothers and sisters," and Foerst calls for the "community of human and nonhuman persons," to cite just a few voices we have discussed among the many who have called for humans to stop isolating themselves in a separate category of being from the rest of the planet.

Some may still object to my putting Foerst's call in with the others, although she does see the community of animals and humans, because her focus is still on artificially intelligent machines. Many are coming to see the plausibility of recognizing animals as partners with humans, as kin, and even as deserving the status of "persons," as having rights and as being worthy of respect for their being at the center of very different sorts of existences from ours. This is still a long step from looking at machines in this way. To recognize machines as having any sort of status even approaching personhood would mean that we would have to take to heart the description of materiality running throughout this book and question another absolute divide to which we cling—the absolute difference between the animate and inanimate. Science fiction has explored the theme repeatedly in the guise of humans encountering aliens from outer space, that there may be spirit in matter and beings who are made of crystal or of gases or of energy and not "alive" in any way that we recognize, and yet are sentient beings. Asimov explored for decades imaginings of mechanically constructed beings who could do most of the things humans can and more. Probably in the future, both of these scenarios may come to pass, but right now on this planet we are being interacted with and informed about vast stretches of our reality, and we live in a world whose very meaning has been shaped in part by many sorts of machines. In addition, we have explored how our bodies perceive by coming back to themselves from everything in the surround—so stones also speak silently of solidity and unshakenness, or flowing water of time passing and the flux and flow of things. If stones and water are in these sorts of relations of "reversibility" with our bodies that we discussed as Merleau-Ponty's analysis of how perception works, is it not also the case that we silently take in the voices, some of them disturbing, no doubt, of the machines around us?

In 1949, Aldo Leopold wrote the book *A Sand County Almanac*, which articulated "the land ethic," a respect for all members of the biotic community, which he said meant this ethic "enlarges the community to include soils, waters, plants, animals, or collectively: the land."[4] The ethic is based on a "land pyramid," a circulation of energies on the planet that connects living and nonliving beings (SCA, 255–59). For Leopold, there is an evolution of ethics that moves from a first stage concerning relations among humans, then to a second stage concerning the relations with the individual and society, and finally to a third stage concerning the relations of humans with animals, plants, water, soil, and the biotic surround (SCA, 238). If we think that there is any sense in what Leopold says and realize that we are still working our way toward appreciating the intrinsic value of inanimate parts of the surround, such as water or rock, then perhaps one day it will not seem strange to talk about the person that is the mountain in the distance or the person that is the lake outside our cabin. It would be yet another step, however, to address the personhood of one of the large turbines that Scheeler painted or of a more advanced model of a Kismet-type artificially intelligent machine that had many facial expressions of different moods, responded to many types of intonations of language spoken to it that it recognized as indicating a certain mood of its interlocutor, and was able to go for a walk with someone holding hands and commenting upon various sites together.

The mountain is a presence that might offer humans lessons and insights or companionship or inspiration to be determined or brave. It might be that a Kismet can do the same thing one day, and fairly soon. However, even Scheeler's machine is a presence and not just a mass of matter. That is why he found it beautiful, because it spoke to him of raw, overwhelming power, of a sliding, quiet efficiency, and a smooth forcefulness. It was inspiring. It was menacing. It was a presence to him and in our world. Not all persons will be those we admire or even judge as constructive—some will be destructive, too, but call for us to hearken to them. Machines have structured the sense of much of our current world and will only continue to do so, to a much greater degree. To consider them just objects or even tools does not acknowledge the power they have to interject into our story, our sense of the world, and our own capacities to respond. Machines influence the world, humans, animals, all creatures, and the biosphere itself in what meaning and thriving will be possible in the future. Like Chorost, we need to hearken to them, to understand how the world has changed and how we have changed as channeled through their influence. We might be able to work with machines creatively if we can respect them as meaning bearers and as other sorts of silent or indirect interlocutors. However, if we are called into such a relationship with them, we need to consider whether as treated as persons in some extended sense, we have obligations and debts to them. Even if we are to consider them the kind of persons in a parallel sense to our loved ones afflicted with Alzheimer's and beyond direct communication, our relationship with them as persons means we have certain responsibilities to oversee what they do and to make sure they thrive.

Obligations to Sacrificing Animals and Helping Machines, Good and Bad Persons, and Guardianship

Beginning to approach animals as bearers of personhood and in some cases to acknowledge the personhood of machine presences would have many ramifications in our relations with aspects of our world. Many of these would be the kind of shifts called for in much ecologically oriented writing. However, rather than trace out these outcomes, which would be the subject of another book, in this section, I will sketch out the form and direction that these deepened relationships might take. If we are to recognize that animals are persons, as well as kin, as well as part of who we are, members of a larger community of which we are part, then the many sacrifices that we have wrought from animals should perhaps be acknowledged, studied, repaid to some extent, and further negotiated in a manner appropriate to a person-to-person dialogue. We will have to pay attention to machines to see what sort of presence they bring into the world beyond their intended function within systems of production, investigation, and regulation. We will have to become sensitive to how they are shifting the very sense of the world they are constructed to fit. We will have to understand the capacities of both animals and machines from within the surround in which animals thrive or the network of relations into which machines are brought to function, but ultimately transform. This kind of relationship with animals and machines of various sorts will require humans to heighten their often dormant capacities for witnessing by taking to heart the interwoven relationships and communication with the animal and machine world.

We have treated animals as property. We have treated them as objects. We have confined agricultural animals to conditions of life that are at best restrictive and a sacrifice of many fulfilling dimensions of their lives, as we could have empathetically and imaginatively discovered, if we tried. At worst, we have condemned them to awful lives of suffering, such as the chickens stacked in cages one upon the other with no ability to roam, to live existences devoid of any natural functions other than eating and excreting upon one another, or the countless mice and rats living in metal cages in laboratories and subjected to experiments that inflict upon them diseases and other pathological sufferings that lead to untimely deaths, such as Haraway's report of OncoMouse™ in chapter 3, just to name two examples of the almost innumerable examples of suffering animals upon which modern human culture is constructed. We usually have proceeded as if Descartes were correct to label animals as automata, and we have chosen to ignore the pain and suffering on their part. All of the inflicted suffering pales when pondering the many species that we have pushed out of existence or into marginal lives that also are on their way to extinction. By harming the biosphere in ways that have led to the loss of species as irreplaceable forms of life, we have deprived all future living beings of being in relation to those now extinct. We have assumed that animals' fate is part of a world of circumstance, of misfortune, and even of tragedy, perhaps, but not one of human responsibility. We think that this suffering is unfortunate, undesirable, and even regrettable, but not reprehensible, not something through which humanity may have forfeited any claim to be beings of integrity and love. We do feel shame for ourselves as a species when we recall the many genocides, the millions upon millions of humans slaughtered in war and violence of all sorts, but we have not yet acknowledged this shame of what we have wrought upon animals and the biosphere. Yet we now know to what extent at least some animals feel pain, and the gamut of devastating emotions such as grief, hopelessness, anxiety, and fear, as well as the uplifting emotions such as joy, silliness, affection, kindness, and loyalty. Knowing this, how is it really less reprehensible than our worst crimes against other humans to have plunged so many animals into conditions of horror when they are beings who seem so adept at finding a gratifying attunement to the rest of the surround? As we have seen throughout this book, we also can understand how much animals have their distinctive ways of understanding the surround and are in a vital interchange with it. Our violation of their surrounds is an aggressive act toward beings whose center of life focus has been disrupted by us, even if we do not intend this outcome. However, if animals are persons in any sense, then one takes care with other persons to see if there are unintended consequences from one's actions that impinge upon the well-being of those persons. We do not do this for objects or property, and that has been our violating manner of treating animals.

It will seem even more implausible to consider machines persons, but in regard to artificially intelligent machines and their inexorable evolution toward beings who also have distinctive ways of responding to the surround and to other beings within the surround, especially as they become more adept at "learning" or reprogramming themselves to have more flexibility, we can see the possibility of working with machines in a way that they will *feel to us as if* they are centers of a concern toward the world. It felt to Foerst as if she had been responded to by Kismet. Perhaps Kismet had responded to the detection of the sad tonality and rhythm of her voice, in a way different than a human would have come to respond, processing information through circuits instead of through neurons—through a causal loop rather than being emotionally empathetic. Yet I do not want to enter back into the debate of what might be "missing" from this response that we claim that we get from a human, but not from Kismet, a machine, because it is not necessary to establish that in order for machines to be considered persons. It is enough to say that we have come into contact with another sort of center of inputs and outputs that has taken into account inputs, or at least inputs have dictated what outputs will be put into action, in considering some machines reacting like "persons"—that is, in some distinctive way of processing and responding to their surround.

However, even this is to begin to argue too much, if all of the descriptions of embodiment, understanding, and the role of the surround are correct as we have articulated them throughout this book. If we think back to Aldo Leopold's sense of the "land ethic," and remember how we have given it a foundation to be understood in terms of how the body and perception work, then we can see that there is an application to machines. We have seen how in perception material objects of some significance to us "speak back to us" and "through us" insofar as perceiving them involves also having a sense of what it is like to perceive from their vantage within the surround. Perception with the kind of bodies we have as woven into the same stuff or "flesh" of the world is not a simple taking in of the world but is itself an entering into a dialogue among parts of the world. Machines that stand out in the surround have already been perceived through our embodiment by resounding within us how it might be to be at the center of the world from their vantage. Of course, this perception is given vaguely, in the background or context of perceptions focusing on other things. However, we can always choose to search for these implicit meanings in the background and begin to amplify them. So a power generator that allows all humans to dwell in their houses with heat, light, and other survival needs as well as amenities, or a CAT scan machine that allows us to detect diseases, or a robot that takes care of a paraplegic human perhaps should be considered persons in some ways and more so the more self-regulating and responsive to the surround they can become, since their work with us has a significant impact on our lives and takes on meanings that alter our world and experience, such that we are in a relationship with them in which we have to adjust to them, as we try to construct them to adjust to us. Even more than this, however, is the fact that machines have helped us in so many ways to achieve so many things vital to our well-being that would not be otherwise.

This may seem ridiculous in the case of "ordinary" machines and certainly would be for those that have little significance in altering the sense of our lives, such as an electric can opener or a conveyor belt. The advantage to thinking this way is to enter into a respectful dialogue with the built world around us. When we recognize other humans as persons who lack the ability to direct themselves, *then we become guardians for making sure they are taken care of in ways that safeguard their well-being, but also the well-being of anyone affected by them.* If humans are mentally incapable of self-control, then respecting them as persons means making sure they do nothing destructive to themselves or to others around them, as well as to the surround. Also, even though we have said that humans, animals, and machines overlap in many ways, and have tried to look at constructive ways we can work together in these differing realms, as good persons, there is no guarantee that animals and machines, like humans, insofar as they would be able to be regarded as persons in ways, would not be seen often as acting as "bad" persons. As may be the case with certain human persons, however, such as children, the responsibility may fall upon others to help direct their actions in ways that cease to be destructive.

In a fictional way, the twenty-first century was projected to open with an artificial intelligence that had "gone bad"—had become murderous and vengeful, the famous HAL, the computer who ran the spaceship in the film *2001* and murders most of the crew. Of course, despite the many science fiction portrayals of machines developing emotions that then become destructive ones, the reality of machines that have a singular presence in our world is that they predominantly work in predictable and rational ways. However, this does not mean that they cannot have devastating effects on the surround with which they are not synchronized, as we discussed in the last chapter. If we can respect them as having the status of persons, then we are placed in the role of guardians to see that their potential is actualized for using their capacities for the mutual thriving of all of the creatures and aspects of the surround. Insofar as artificial intelligence will push machines farther in the direction of a direct give-and-take with the surround and its creatures, the greater our need will become for careful guardianship. This sense does not give us easy or clear-cut answers to ticklish problems of deciding what machines' capacities contribute to the thriving of the surround as a whole and which of their capacities brings ugliness, disease, or other hardships. However, it gives us a general orientation of how to approach these presences around us. If the machine is a center of generated meaning and action within the surround, then we have an obligation to see and assess these impacts as good guardians, and not just use them as tools or objects, whose impact on others has no bearing other than "getting the job done."

Another analogy that also may seem farfetched is to return to Andy Clark's discussion of language as perhaps the greatest machine created as a way for humans to extend their capacities of thought and creation. Remembering how Clark detailed how humans are the beings whose brains are most open to an "extended architecture" that allows them to greatly expand their capacities of thought and imagination, then certainly language has been one of the most startlingly successful fabrications of humans to achieve these purposes. In some sense, although we never put it this way, we accord to language the status of a person. We try to keep it intact and respected in such ways that it keeps its efficacy and can even expand its potentialities. We are careful that it is not abused or put to destructive uses, as laws prohibit, such as libel, slander, and obscenity. If language is used thoughtlessly to hurt others in ways that damage their self-respect, then there is generally an outcry, not only that the person was wrong, but that language should not be used in this way. Language has been spoken of metaphorically for the past decades in many academic disciplines as "the Other," and perhaps it really is another person in many ways for us—both a machine and another person.

If we were to define persons in an objective manner, then there would be certain distinctive properties that we would need to discover in other beings for them to qualify for this distinction. The genius of phenomenology is to realize that sometimes it is the impact, the perdurance, and the depth of meaning that should dictate how we name something. For example, a student in a class might be defined objectively as someone who has paid tuition and registered for the class, but the "real students" and class members might be the two people who have asked to join the group without registering or seeking credits but love the material come to every class, and are fully engaged in the discussion, wondering at the ideas. Phenomenologically, they manifest better the sense and the unfolding interaction indicative of a "student." The doctor may be the one with the degree from medical school who tried standard medical procedures to treat his patient's illness, but it may be more the person who has given healing concern, loving care, and sensitive responses to the sick person. Here we might find the phenomeonon of healing more cogently. So the loyal dog who has been at a person's side working together in the fields or accompanying the person to the study and sitting nuzzled by his or her side, or leading the blind person through his or her days, or the robot who has helped the quadriplegic get dressed in the morning, has helped feed him or her, and assisted him or her through the day with a range of activities, or the robot teddy bears that respond, hug back, and react to voices in order to comfort hospital patients may be missing those objective features that we might list as being essential, at least for humans to demonstrate the way of being persons, but they might have the status for these people of providing the kind of interaction that is personlike. It would give us an augmented level of appreciation and care for beings that are now seen as property and mere objects. It would also give us a sense of responsibility that we lack for seeing that their potentialities add to the well-being of the world and are actualized as a trust to be honored.

At the beginning of this section, it was suggested that if we approached animals as persons, then we might attempt to recognize the kind of sacrifices that we have forced them to make on humans' behalf and repay them. There are beginnings to this sort of recognition of animals' service to humans, such as the construction of Chimp Haven, under way in Shreveport, Louisiana. The 29 million dollar project will be a refuge for 200 chimps retired from their lives in scientific laboratories, with a population of about 900 chimps eventually living on the 200-acre facility. It will have wooded areas where chimps can live in a semi-wild state and also indoor enclosures for chimps that need medical care. There is also the 2,700 acre rehabilitation and retirement center, the Elephant Sanctuary, for traumatized elephants who were performers in circuses and zoos throughout the United States. As explained by Charles Siebert, who visited the sanctuary, there is the same approach of trying to afford the elephants a sense of security and freedom of choice, as with human trauma therapy, and also much social interaction (DEC, 64). These are two examples of coming to recognize that animals have made painful sacrifices in the service of humans, and perhaps there are ways we can repay them and afford them the care and respect due to persons who have sacrificed for others. It means paying attention to the animals' quality of experience and having the compassion and imagination to envision what their lives are like for them and how they can be helped. This also may add significantly to the quality of human life, for as Bradshaw articulates, "Meaning making from the perspective of a trans-species psyche envisions human and animal restitution as mutually beneficial because it recognizes the necessary relational role of healing" (TSP, 86). Just as we recognize that in helping another human person to heal their psychic wounds, we often heal ourselves, so, too, we might find the same reciprocal healing with animals.

In an analogous fashion, I also would suggest that we might owe reparations to certain machine presences—not to them directly, but on their behalf. Until now, despite their speed, power, precision, and a host of other attributes with a great impact on the world, machines are dependent on humans to bring our their potential for both constructive augmentation for the overall quality of life of the members of the community of the surround, and also for the destruction of members of the community and damage to their quality of life. Part of being machines' guardians not only entails making sure their excellences are actualized, but also that the damage that has been done by them as a result of the way we have designed and utilized them is rectified. If robots can be utilized to help humans perform tasks they otherwise could not do by themselves but need to do, then this is allowing the robots a certain excellence, or Aristotelian virtue. However, if they are used to perpetrate violence or to create toxic substances that are allowed to pollute the surround, then we are responsible on their behalf for rectifying the way they are used or designed and the damage they caused.

It also was suggested that we allow both animal and machines to be given some sort of voice in a dialogue with humans. We have made the case that they do speak to us indirectly through the way perception works by making us experience their vantage upon the world. However, as persons, they also may be owed a direct voice in governmental decisions that affect them or the surround we share with them. There have been suggestions that animals and aspects of the surround be represented in governmental bodies by humans who are there to represent the way they can best imagine they would experience the world and desire its unfolding. In Bruno Latour's *Politics of Nature*, cited at the beginning of this book, the second house of representative government he suggests is one in which scientists let humans hear the voice of the natural surround by giving expert testimony on the processes and intricacies of these systems. I would suggest that both the interests of animals and the most creatively constructive use of machines could be represented in some analogous way within governmental and communal structures but would have to include not only scientists who know about the facts of the lives of animals or artificial intelligences, for example, but those who were also intimate with them in such a way that the emotional, imaginative, and relational sense of what is important in our interactions with them could come forward. People like Gay Bradshaw and other animal experts can speak for animals in terms of their needs for affection and a secure community in order to be healed from human abuse or human-caused suffering, but also for what animals can offer humans in hospitals, to troubled teenagers or prisoners in caring for them, or even to the mutual animal-human healing in refuges, and so on. People like Ann Foerst and other experts in artificial intelligence and machine technology can speak for machines about how they can be developed to bring out new creative capacities and at the same time speak to human needs they can fulfill for the other-abled persons, for human learners, for the arts, for humans in situations of emotional violation, for patients in hospitals needing not only technical treatment but psychic care, and so on.

An Ecospirituality of Humans, Animals, and Machines

Machines and animals traditionally have been seen as part of a material dimension of existence that is in opposition to the spiritual dimension. For many spiritual and religious traditions, this means that both animals and certainly machines are objects that stand at a remove from humans, who as the beings infused with spirit bring meaning to an otherwise meaningless realm. Spirit provides a meaning and a purpose to a world of mere matter. Without spirit, there would be no illumination among things, just an unknowing realm of physical interactions. Spirit often has been associated with its root meaning of breath, as the breath of the divine that breathes vitality and intelligence into an unknowing realm. Spirit is also associated with a diaphanous quality conceived of as finer and purer in an immateriality unfettered by the confines of the spatial and temporal. This finer stuff is the source of illumination for this grosser realm of material beings. One example of this vision of the spirit is the classical Hindu bold division of the *Bhagvadgita* between the clarity and illumination of the spirit and the dark oblivion of the merely material: the realm of the material being called the "tamas," characterized as the dark, opaque, and inert realm as opposed to the energetic, uplifting illumination of the spirit, the "sattwa." In the Western tradition, Plato, at a similar time in history, seems to have inaugurated the sense of philosophy as a learning "to die to the earth" in order for the knowing soul to detach utterly from the material ream with its attentant emotion, which is like a nail to the spirit, threatening to keep it attached to the earth.[5] The spirit within humans, the soul or psyche, struggles to return to its source and home in a higher, eternal, and immaterial realm of purer spirit. Certainly many other metaphysical and spiritual traditions also have seen the proper home of spirit in another realm free of the taint of matter, but often like Plato's own philosophy, only uneasily so—having contradictions that equally indicate that spirit would only have its passion, its vitality, and its content by being interwoven within the earthly and material.

Even within these systems with a sense of transcendent spirit beyond the earthly and material, there are struggles like Plato's to give a sense to "participation" in which the material does partake of the eternal and ethereal, or in his idea of the "world soul" in the *Timaeus*, or in his own use of poetry and myth at the conclusion of the *Republic* after warning that these uses of language were too much of the emotions, the senses, and the material, and therefore expelling the poets from his ideal state. Christianity, too, has at times seemed to preach leaving behind the material for a more perfect sphere of immaterial spirit, yet its central image is of the incarnation of the divine—one of the most powerful images of the spirituality of the body and earth. Hinduism, too, for all of its ascetic traditions, also revels in a cycle of continual celebrations of aspects of the earth that contain the 330 million gods, as it is joked in India. So there seems even in religious or metaphysical systems that want to disjoin the material and the earthly from the realm of spirit a sense that theologian Catherine Keller speaks of at the end of *Face of the Deep,* that spirit must "resist its own disembodiment" and come down into "the chaos of materiality."[6]

This book has attempted to describe the way in which animals are not blind, unfeeling beings driven by mechanical forces, as they were seen by Descartes and others within both the scholarly and popular Western traditions. Rather, they are beings of passions, feelings, aesthetic sensibilities, loyalties, strong bonds, play, mourning, communication, imaginings, dreams, understanding of the world, and self-awareness, perhaps in ways different than humans tend to privilege or rely upon, but also in ways that overlap with the human experience of the world. The world of matter has been seen as a realm that does have depths of sense, meaning, memory, and dream, which indirectly speak through one's perceptual taking in of the world that is inseparably woven with all of these other powers, casting forth differing significances. If we stop thinking about material objects or humans or animals as atomistic beings, as if they are what they are in a universe by themselves, and instead think of all three of them as being only what they are in the web of relationships, which is the materiality of the world, then we can see them differently. Machines, when they gain a presence within the historical, cultural unfolding of the world, can amplify certain senses held in the material world and can be part of the dialogue that is the surround. An example from my own world is of the trains that run by my house through the woods along the banks of the Susquehanna River, which I attempted to articulate in the following poem, *Living by the Railroad Tracks*:

> Friends said the rumbling roar punctuating my sleep and
> morning tea would disturb the orderly march of thought
> from left to right and leave me looking sideways in the mirror.
> Especially, they said, the long horn blast screaming away,
> away from here, sounding bassoon-like if bassoonists were insane
> and amplified by a woofer filling the lower sky and accompanied
> by a stadium full of red-faced fiends blowing their minds out.

> Perhaps, when I saw the house and the tracks running by,
> I thought how dramatic to be in bed, both of us coming
> to the moment of chugging explosion and really feeling
> the earth move. Or I saw myself floating above the tracks
> saber in hand, gleaming light flashes flaring out at the onrushing
> beast for once a knight of glory rather than a book tender.
> Or maybe I knew the sound of the American frontier, oh
>
> so very American, long sounding train thunder and wail
> might make me feel as if I belonged again to this land and
> as if it had a history that still made sense and could summon
> me to smile in my sleep for the visions of my grandparents
> crammed into the lower decks of freighters sailing to the dream
> of this new life without sabers being rattled over their heads
> and plunged into their hearts in a place where they didn't belong.
>
> I like to be reminded of the constant movement and iron
> pushing people into the night faster than the current in the river
> beside the tracks. The flashing eyes in the woods
> are the only witnesses to the lumbering behemoths
> with families in their bellies crashing through the dark
> to where the black ends, even though the windows
> are blacker yet and only reflect swaying blank faces,
> before arriving at welcoming stations.[7]

The trains, as they rumble by, speak of the spirit of seeking freedom, new homes with new opportunities, of the misery of those immigrant laborers who helped build them, of capitalist barons who owned them, of the pollution they often brought to the countryside, of the speed and power first captured by a marveling J. M. W. Turner when he painted one of the first powerful locomotives pulling a train through the English landscape at a then-unbelievable sixty miles per hour, of my own grandparents seeking refuge from oppression, of powerful rumbling presences deep within the night of imagination moving through deep forests, of the restlessness of humans and even animals seeking new surrounds for what they have come to lack, of how the trains made some of that human migration possible, and so on. We may speak on behalf of the world of animate and inanimate things in a language and symbolic system that at times seems to surpass their circulation of energies. However, our greatest powers of human symbolic articulation continually draw upon the way that animals and machines enact their meanings in directions within the surround that all three lay out together, and to which humans add further conceptions and imaginings in our symbolic and linguistic systems—which can be considered, as we have said, to be machines of a sort through which we humans extend our thought. Whenever we think we have broken free from the other two realms, another interweaving emerges.

If another dimension of spirituality is the sense of the interconnectedness of all living and nonliving beings, then animals and machines also augment this sense of the world. Of course, they can help degrade this sense for moments of time, especially machines, as humans also can, for example, in the hellish world of war created by both humans and machines, where there seems for stretches of time no grace, no love, no belonging, no interconnection, no ultimate gratitude, little purpose, and a harsh clashing as the dissonant source of existence. Yet so much of the gracefulness, the magic, and the beauty of this world is augmented and presented by animals, as well as other living beings. A world without animals, forests, flowers, and all other living beings, and also the given inanimate members of the surround, rock, sky, mountain, clouds, and so on, would not stir us in any comparable degree with the ineffable presence of something intrinsically wondrous. Animals not only inspire these feelings in us, but when members of a den are curled up together, when a bird spends the morning playing winds, when a wild mustang takes off on a gallop across the plains, when squirrels run back and forth chattering and playing together, when a dog lies on its back in the sun, when the chimp drops its coconut staring at the brilliant pink and orange sunset, and when birds sing mightily in the spring air, there is some sense of taking in the goodness of existence, registering a kind of praise of the sheer rightness of being and of experiencing, and this kind of expression of an implicit attunement and gratitude is one of the most profound layers of prayer or meditation. Animals, if we are sensitive, communicate to us indirectly through the perceived world of their sense of wonder and gratitude for sheer existence, which also is the heart of the human spiritual life.

We also have created some machines that seem to add to that wondrousness, as the world works through us and through the ways we can work through the material world to create flying machines, machines that give us images of galaxies of millions of years ago, machines that can give hearing to generations of humans who could not take in the sounds of the world, machines that generate universes of intricate fractal shapes and designs, machines that reveal the microscopic world, machines that let us see the processes of life as they unfold, and so on. These machines might not be able to respond with direct recognition and gratitude, yet they make accessible to humans so many aspects of existence that are objects of wonder and gratitude that it is not too farfetched to include them in a cooperative effort of making manifest the wild miracle of being that is the focus of spirituality.

Our sense of the spiritual is inseparable from what we have distinguished as most distinctive about human beings, the ways that we can witness other beings and the world. Yet we can only be these witnesses, moved to wonder and gratitude for the sheer blessing of being part of existence through our interconnectedness with animals and machines in circulating energies and senses of the world. Recognizing this, it seems to point to cultivating a sense of "ecospirituality," taking the root of the word ecology seriously as the Greek "*oikos*," or "household," in which the spirit dwells right here in the marrow, the matter, of the earth. Poet Mary Oliver expresses this sense aptly when she writes that although spirit could conceivably "float, of course/but would rather/plumb rough matter, it needs/the metaphor of the body . . . it needs the body's world/instinct/and imagination/and the dark hug of time/sweetness/and tangibility, to be understood."[8] To take spirituality in this way is to return to the ancient Greek sense of spirit, where soul and nature were seen as inseparably interwoven, that the spirit, or "breath of life and vitality," was seen to be in all things. Human beings were seen to be part of a cosmos in which matter was "ensouled," and things grew together in an unfolding that encompassed them all.[9]

In drawing out the ramifications of this sort of ecospirituality, environmental ethics also finds another source: our embodied sense of enmeshment with the other beings of the surround. It is not that traditional ethical sources are not also important, whether rationally based principles of the categorical imperative or prudential utilitarian calculations, but these can only take on cogency if first humans learn to heighten their embodied felt interconnectedness. As David Abrams states in *The Spell of the Sensuous* in thinking how we might respect and heed our fellow beings of the surround: "It may be that the new 'environmental ethic' toward which so many environmental philosphies aspire . . . will come into existence not primarily through the logical elucidation of new philosophical principles and legislative structures, but through a renewed attentiveness to this perceptual dimension that underlies all our logics, through a rejuvenation of our carnal, sensorial empathy with the living land that sustains us."[10] To return to this "carnal, sensorial empathy," we have seen in this book may call for us to not only feel our kinship with other living beings and naturally occurring inanimate beings, but also those most advanced manufactured beings, machines, that enter creatively this interwoven enterprise of mutually thriving.

Returning to Foerst's closing comments in *God in the Machine* is helpful in trying to think how it is that we can feel our kinship not only with animals in affirming spirituality but also with machines. She reminds us that the heart of human being is "*homo faber*," the being that makes things. In our consumerist culture, "making" often becomes degraded to a relationship between mass production and frenzied materialist purchasing. Foerst reminds us that at a deeper level, making things is about channeling the spirit within all things as well as our own spirit, and in that sense, "every act of creativity is prayer" (GM, 35). In looking at the evolution of machines, she asserts, "The more complex things we build, the more we praise God" (GM, 35). If we are building machines that have become inserted into the surround in ways that augment the capacities for embodied knowledge and expand who we are, and could be used in ways to allow the surround to become more of a place of thriving for animals, too, then machines, insofar as they function in this way, are members of a spiritual community. An ecological approach to the community of inspirited beings cannot leave out the machine world. If there is a community of witnessing that which is wondrous—from black holes to spider webs to acts of sacrifice, kindness, or beauty—then machines, animals, and humans all belong to it.

In closing this meditation, the words of theologian and philosopher Louis Dupré come to mind in his feeling that we were in the process of discovering a spirituality with "a particular version of the transcendent that matches the age." Dupré agrees that the dawning sense is that humans as embodied beings are caught up in a world of material beings who are not adversaries to our spiritual nature but are inextricably of the same fabric of human aspiration and insight. Earthly concerns might be seen as merely mundane, but they have a depth of meaning and spirit that can be uncovered. Dupré states, "Instead of the traditional distinction between sacred objects, persons and events, and profane ones, spiritual men and women in the future will regard existence increasingly as an indivisible unity, wholly worldly and self-sufficient, yet at the same time will be aware of a depth dimension that demands attention and that they allow to direct their basic attitudes to their life."[11] Dupré calls this discovery of the divine within all worldly things and events "a spirituality of world affirmation." Such a spirituality, I believe, recognizes that there is no separate spiritual realm. Otherwise, the interweaving of humans, animals, machines, and the surround could not work as it does, cooperatively, in continual dialogue and mutual transformation to open up insight, knowledge, wonder, love, thriving, and transformation. Dupré considers this a time in which humanity sees that there is a mystery of ongoing creation "that discovers a transcendent dimension in a fundamental engagement to a world and a human community." If, as Merleau-Ponty articulated, each particular perception is inexhaustibly rich in the depth of its meaning, if we wish to explore it, and each perception is "a birth and a death," because there is in each moment of this planetary existence such a surplus of meaning that it is enough for a lifetime, and it is a lifetime in each of its moments of unfolding, then we are in the midst of an ecospirituality. The surround, of which we are part, is the source of spiritual inspiration and the object of reverence, the gift giver to all living and nonliving beings and the necessary focus of our care. Humans, animals, and machines, in their being kin and in being different simultaneously, give the planet an opportunity to find itself mirrored in differing kinds of enactments and differing sorts of registrations of its wonder. This is the excellence of these three dimensions that we should be careful to midwife.

Notes

Chapter 1

1. Jared Diamond, *The Third Chimpanzee: The Evolution and Future of the Human Animal* (New York: HarperCollins, 1992), 23. All future references to this book will be indicated by "TTC" in parentheses, followed by the page number.

2. Donna Haraway, *The Companion Species Manifesto: Dogs, People, and Significant Otherness* (Chicago: Prickly Paradigm Press, 2003), 20. All future references to this book will be indicated by "CSM" in parentheses, followed by the page number.

3. Glen Mazis, *Earthbodies: Rediscovering Our Planetary Senses* (Albany: State University of New York Press, 2002), 181–99. All future references to this book will be indicated by "EB" in parentheses, followed by the page number.

4. Bruno Latour, *Politics of Nature*, trans. Catherine Porter (Cambridge, MA: Harvard University Press, 2004), 223.

5. Edward Conze, ed. and trans., *Buddhist Scriptures* (New York: Penguin, 1959), 42.

6. Maurice Merleau-Ponty, *Phenomenology of Perception*, trans. Colin Smith (New York: Humanities Press, 1962), vii. All future references to this book will be indicated by "PP" in parentheses, followed by the page number.

7. Eugen Herrigal, *Zen and the Art of Archery* (New York: Vintage Press, 1989), 63. All future references to this book will be indicated by "ZA" in parentheses, followed by the page number.

Chapter 2

1. Maurice Merleau-Ponty, *Nature*, trans. Dominique Séglard (Evanston, IL: Northwestern University Press, 2003), 168. All future references to this book will be indicated by "N" in parentheses, followed by the page number.

2. George Page, *Inside the Animal Mind* (New York: Broadway Books, 1999), 60–61. All future references to this book will be indicated by "IAM" in parentheses, followed by the page number.

3. In thinking about the Clark's nutcracker, I wrote the following poem about its mental map in relationship to our human plight:

The Natural Power of Memory

> The Clark's nutcracker knows where every seed
> is lodged in tree burrows and beneath wedged rock outcrops,
> thousands and thousands of them
> as if they were the words of an immense novel
> and each one linked with the others to tell a hopeful story
> that in reading and rereading,
> paying attention to the tale,
> it can survive the harsh months of blank windswept grounds
> where no comforting messages can be discerned
> flying above.
>
> It's a hidden hieroglyphic of an old avian myth
> to get through winters
> that each bird writes in thistles and seeds
> to leave its own Ariadne's thread
> through swaying evergreens and crackling pines.
> It's an unfinished composition of wings and beaks
> through generations of hatchlings
> knowing the Braille of the land
> and the syntax of the sky
> and the perfect pitch of the seasons
> that only a Homer, Tolstoy, or Wagner
> can leave for us secreted
> in the midst of our winter.

4. Martin Heidegger, *Being and Time*, trans. John Macquarrie and Edward Robinson (New York: Harper and Row, 1962), 136. All future references to this book will be indicated by "BT" in parentheses, followed by the page number.

5. Martin Heidegger, *The Fundamental Concepts of Metaphysics: World, Finitude, Solitude*, trans. William McNeill and Nicholas Walker (Bloomington: Indiana University Press, 1995), 254. All future references to this book will be indicated by "FCM" in parentheses, followed by the page number.

6. Giorgi Agamben, *The Open: Man and Animal*, trans. Kevin Attell (Stanford, CA: Stanford University Press, 2004), 40. All future references to this book will be indicated by "OMA" in parentheses, followed by the page number.

7. Gary Kowalski, *The Souls of Animals* (Walpole, MA: Stillpoint, 1991), 10–16. Further references to this book will be indicated by "SA" in parentheses, followed by the page number.

8. Merleau-Ponty will claim in his lectures on nature at the Sorbonne in the late 1950s that the animal's perception is quasi-symbolic (there is a very narrow relation between instinct and symbolism) and can even be taken up by the animal in a sort of symbolic communication to others (N, 95).

9. Donald R. Griffin, *Animal Minds: Beyond Cognition to Consciousness*, rev. ed. (Chicago: University of Chicago Press, 2001), 79. All future references to this book will be indicated by "AM" in parentheses, followed by the page number.

10. Timothy Morton, *Ecology without Nature: Rethinking Environmental Aesthetics* (Cambridge: Harvard University Press, 2007), 108.

11. Maurice Merleau-Ponty, "The Child's Relations with Others," *The Primacy of Perception* (Evanston, IL: Northwestern University Press, 1964), 141–51. All future references to this book will be indicated by "CR" in parentheses, and followed by the page number.

12. Maurice Merleau-Ponty, *The Visible and the Invisible* (Evanston, IL: Northwestern University Press, 1968). All future references to this book will be indicated by "VI" in parentheses, followed by the page number.

13. Ed Casey, *Getting Back into Place: Toward a Renewed Understanding of the Place-World* (Bloomington: Indiana University Press, 1993), 102–103.

14. Daisie and Michael Radner, *Animal Consciousness* (Amherst: Prometheus Books, 1996), 173. All future references to this book will be indicated by "AC" in parentheses, followed by the page number.

Chapter 3

1. Anne Foerst, *God in the Machine: What Robots Teach Us about Humanity and God* (New York: Dutton, 2004), 69. All future references to this book will be indicated by "GM" in parentheses, followed by the page number.

2. Rodney A. Brooks, *Flesh and Machines: How Robots Will Change Us* (New York: Pantheon Books, 2002), 66. All future references to this book will be indicated by "FM" in parentheses, followed by the page number.

3. Juyang Weng, James McClelland, Alex Pentland, Olaf Sporns, Ida Stockman, Mriganka Sur, and Esther Thelen, "Autonomous Mental Development by Robots and Animals," *Science Online* 291 (June 3, 2005): 599. All future references to this book will be indicated by "AMD," followed by the page number.

4. Michael Chorost, *Rebuilt: How Becoming Part Computer Made Me More Human* (Boston, MA: Houghton Mifflin, 2005), 6–7. All future references to this book will be indicated by "RB" in parentheses, followed by the page number.

5. Donna Haraway, *Modest_Witness@Second_Millenium.FemaleMan©_Meets_ OncoMouse™: Feminism and Technoscience* (New York: Routledge, 1977), 129. Further references to this book will be indicated by "MW" in parentheses, followed by the page number.

6. Andy Clark, *Natural-Born Cyborgs: Minds Technologies, and the Future of Human Intelligence* (New York: Oxford University Press, 2003), 33. All future references to this book will be indicated by "NBC" in parentheses, followed by page number.

7. Amanda Schaeffer, "In Latest Robotics, New Hope for Stroke Patients," *New York Times*, D 1, 5.

8. Susan Griffin, *Woman and Nature: The Roaring Inside Her* (New York: HarperCollins, 1979), 272.

9. Martin Heidegger, "Memorial Address," in *Discourse on Thinking?* (New York: Harper and Row, 1969) 49.

Chapter 4

1. See the *Animal Communication Project*, http://www.acp.eugraph.com/news/news06/gentner.html. For more details, visit the Web site or see Timothy Gentner, *Nature* (April 27, 2006).
2. Baird, "Baffling the Bots," *Scientific American* (July 12, 2006).
3. Kobo Abé, *The Face of Another* (New York: Alfred A. Knopf [Perigee Books], 1966), 27.
4. Daniel J. Siegel, *The Developing Mind: How Relationships and the Brain Interact to Shape Who We Are* (New York: Guilford Press, 1999), 127. Further references to this book will be indicated by "DM" in parentheses, followed by the page number.
5. Glen Mazis, *Emotion and Embodiment: Fragile Ontology* (New York: Peter Lang, 1993), 158–56. All further references to this book will be indicated by "EE" in parentheses, followed by the page number.
6. Eric R. Kandel, *In Search of Memory: The Emergence of the New Science of the Brain* (New York: W. W. Norton and Company, 2006), 281.
7. John Briggs and David Peat, *Turbulent Mirror: An Illustrated Guide to Chaos Theory and the Science of Wholeness* (New York: Harper and Row, 1989), 25–26. Further reference to this book will be indicated by "TM" in parentheses, followed by the page number.
8. Jeffrey M. Schwartz, M.D., and Sharon Begley, *The Mind and the Brain: Neuroplasticity and the Power of Mental Force* (New York: HarperCollins, 2002), 15. Future references to this book will be indicated by "MB" in parentheses, followed by the page number.

Chapter 5

1. Antonio Damascio, *Descartes' Error: Emotion, Reason and the Human Brain* (New York: HarperCollins Publishers, Quill edition, 2000), 143. Future references to this book will be indicated by "DE" in parentheses, followed by the page number.
2. Chang Chung-Yuan, *Tao: A New Way of Thinking: Translations and Commentaries of the Tao Tê Ching* (New York: Harper and Row, 1975), 5. Further references to this book will be indicated by "TC" in parentheses, followed by the page number.
3. Edward Conze, trans., *Buddhist Scriptures* (New York: Penguin Books, 1959), 174.
4. Jean-Paul Sartre, *The Emotions: Outline of a Theory*, trans. Bernard Frechtman (New York: Citadel, 1948), 89–90. Further references to this book will be indicated by "SE" in parentheses, followed by the page number.

5. Johan Huizinga, *Homo Ludens: A Study of the Play Element in Culture* (Boston: Beacon Press, 1950), 25. Further references to this book will be indicated by "HL" in parentheses, followed by the page number.

6. Suzanne Langer, *Feeling and Form* (New York: Charles Scribner's Sons, 1953), 47. Further references to this book will be indicated by "FF" in parentheses, followed by the page number.

7. "Eye and Mind," Merleau-Ponty's last published essay before his untimely death is also collected in the previously cited *Primacy of Perception*, but future references will be distinguished from the other cited essays by "EM" in parentheses, followed by the page number.

8. Alasdair MacIntyre, *After Virtue: A Study in Moral Theory* (Notre Dame, IN: University of Notre Dame Press, 1984), 201. Further references to this book will be indicated by "AV" in parentheses, followed by the page number.

9. Sören Kierkegaard, *Either/Or*, vol. 1, trans. David Swenson and Lillian Swenson (New York: Anchor Books, 1959), 32.

10. Thich Nhat Hahn, *The Sun, My Heart: From Mindfulness to Insight Contemplation* (Berkeley, CA: Parallax Press, 1988), 11. Further references to this book will be indicated by "SH" in parentheses, followed by the page number.

11. Wendell Berry, *Life Is a Miracle* (New York: Counterpoint, 2001), 138.

Chapter 6

1. Thomas Nagel, "What Is It Like to Be a Bat?," in *The Mind's "I"*, ed. Douglas R. Hofstadter and Daniel C. Dennett, 394 (New York: Basic Books, 1981). Future references to this book will be indicated by "WB" in parentheses, followed by the page number.

2. Paul Ricoeur, "The Metaphorical Process as Cognition, Imagination, and Feeling," *Critical Inquiry* 5 (Autumn, 1978): Reprinted in *Critical Theory since 1965*, ed. Hazard Adams and Leroy Searle, 426 (Tallahassee: Florida State University Press, 1986). Future references to this book will be indicated by "MC" in parentheses, followed by the page number.

3. Stephen W. Laycock, "The Animal as Animal," in *Animal Others: On Ethics, Ontology and Animal Life*, ed. H. Peter Steeves (Albany: State University of New York Press, 1999), 277. Future references to this book will be indicated by "AO" in parentheses, followed by the page number.

4. Carleton Dallery, "Into the Truth with Animals," in AO, 263.

5. W. H. Auden, "Their Lonely Betters," in *Collected Poems*, ed. W. H. Mendelson, 583 (New York: Vintage Press, 1991).

6. Friedrich Nietzsche, *The Geneology of Morals* (New York: Random House, 1967), 57.

7. T. S. Eliot, "The Waste Land," in *The Norton Anthology of Poetry*, ed. Arthur Eastman, 1003 (New York: W. W. Norton and Co., 1970).

8. Temple Grandin and Catherine Johnson, *Animals in Translation* (New York: Scribner, 2005), 153. Future references to this book will be indicated by "AT" in parentheses, followed by the page number.

9. Loren Eiseley, *The Immense Journey* (New York: Vintage Press, 1959), 20.

10. Paula Gunn Allen, *The Sacred Hoop: Recovering the Feminine in American Indian Tradition* (Boston: Beacon Press, 1986), 62. Future references to this book will be indicated by "SH" in parentheses, followed by the page number.

11. Tarthung Tulku, *Time, Space and Knowledge* (Berkeley, CA: Dharma Publishing, 1977), 161, 183.

Chapter 7

1. Interestingly, in many locations, animals sensed before the tsunami before it occurred and fled the coastal regions. In some areas, the human populations followed the animals and were saved.

2. Isaac Asimov, *Robot Visions* (New York: New American Library, 1990).

3. Karen Lucic, *Charles Scheeler and the Cult of the Machine* (Cambridge, MA: Harvard University Press, 1991), 9. Future references to this book will be indicated by "CS" in parentheses, followed by the page number.

4. David Gelertner, *Machine Beauty: Elegance and the Heart of Technology* (New York: Basic Books, 1998), 2–3. Future references to this book will be indicated by "MB" in parentheses, followed by the page number.

5. Jean Baudrillard, *America*, trans. Chris Turner (New York: Verso, 1988), 27. Future references to this book will be indicated by "A" in parentheses, followed by the page number.

6. D. H. Lawrence, *The Complete Poems of D. H. Lawrence*, ed. Vivian de Sola Pinto and Warren Roberts (New York: Viking Press, 1964), 675.

7. Crispin Sartwell, *Six Names of Beauty* (New York: Routledge, 2004), 150.

Conclusion

1. Charles Siebert, "Are We Driving Elephants Crazy?," *New York Times Magazine* (October 2006): sect. 6, 44.

2. Martin Buber, *The Knowledge of Man: Selected Essays* (New York: Harper and Row, 1965), 79.

3. Gay Bradshaw and Mary Watkins, "Trans-Species Psychology: Theory and Praxis," *Spring Journal, Psyche and Nature: A Journal of Archetype and Culture*, 75 (Fall 2006): 81. Further reference to this essay will be indicated by "TSP" in parentheses, followed by the page number.

4. Aldo Leopold, *A Sand County Almanac* (New York: Ballantine Books, 1970) 239. Further references to this book will be indicated by "SCA" in parentheses, followed by the page number.

5. Plato, *Phaedo*, trans. W. H. D. Rouse, in *Great Dialogues of Plato* (New York: Mentor, 1956), 88 [83D].

6. Catherine Keller, *Face of the Deep: A Theology of Becoming* (New York: Routledge, 2003), 236.

7. Glen Mazis, *Ellipsis . . . Literature and Art* 42 (Spring 2006): 35.

8. Mary Oliver, *Dream Work* (New York: The Atlantic Monthly Press, 1986), 52–53.

9. Gerard Naddaf, *The Greek Concept of Nature* (Albany: State University of New York Press, 2005), 64.

10. David Abram, *The Spell of the Sensuous: Perception and Language in a More-than-Human World* (New York: Pantheon Books, 1996), 69.

11. Louis Dupré, *Religious Mystery and Rational Reflection* (Grand Rapids, MI: William B. Gerdmans Publishing, 1998), 143.

Index

Abe, Eve, 240–241
Abé, Kobo, *The Face of Another*, 98
Abram, David, *The Spell of the Sensuous*, 255
affective rhythms, 107, 112, 180, 189
Agamben, Giorgi, *The Open: Man and Animal*, 28–29, 37
Alex, grey parrot, 91
Allen, Paula Gunn, *The Sacred Hoop*, 205, 206–207
Alzheimer's sufferers as retaining personhood, 237, 244
ambiguity, 15–16, 110; good versus bad, 13–14
amygdala, 119, 128
animals, as mechanism, 5–6, 22–23, 33, 190, 195; definitions, 24; distinctive excellence, 190, 207; feeling suffering of others, human obligation to, 244–251; imagining in, 181–182; in niche, 186–190; instinct, 190–195; melody as being, 195, 197–198; overlap with humans, 4–6, 30–31, 46–48, 142, 180; possible personhood of, 235–244; sanctuaries, 249; sense of death, 33; sense of self, 183–186, 198–199; slower time of, 200–207; spontaneity, 195–200; thickness of perception, 177–182; supposed distractibility, 186–189; understanding their experience, 169–176; unity of, 23; worlds of, 27, 28–32, 37
animal spirits (Descartes), 5, 6, 102–103

anthromorphizing, 170
anthropocentricism, 28, 37
Aquinas, Thomas, divine design, 222
Aristotle, 91, 102, 152; virtue, 167, 250
artificial intelligence [AI], 49–51, 165; embodied, 51–58
Asimov, Isaac, *Bicentennial Man*, 238; *Robot Visions*, 217–218
Atman, 10
attachment theory, 150–152
attention, 64–65, 176
attunement, 27, 31, 50, 66, 67, 105, 176, 183, 197, 199, 254
Auden, W. H., "Their Lonely Betters," 177–179, 182
autism, 188
autopoesis, 50

Bachelard, Gaston, 17–18; murmurings among things, 17; reverberations, 174
Bacon, Francis, 83
Baird, Henry, "Baffling the Bots," 93
Baudrillard, Jean, 235; *America*, 201; hyperreality, 223–224
bees, 34–36, 39, 46; waggle dance, 162–163
"Being-in-the-world" [*Innerweltsein*], 26–28, 58, 104–109, 132, 134–135
Benke, Elizabeth, lucid gestures, 176
Beethoven, Ludwig, Ninth Symphony, 172–173
Berry, Wendell, *Life Is a Miracle*, 164

267

beauty of surround, 232–234
Bhagvadgita, 251
Bodhisattva, 168
bodily maps, 25–31, 45–46, 49
Bohr, Neils, 133
bots, 93
Boundaries of Humanity: Humans, Animals and Machines, The, 7
boundary lines among humans, animals, and machines, 87–91
Bradshaw, Gay, 241, 250; trans-species psyche, "Tran-Species Psychology: Theory and Practice," 249
brain, as open system, 113–118; as process, 118–131; hemispheric functioning, 128–132, 151; infant's co-regulated by caregiver, 151–152; pruning, 114–115; quantum, 138–141
brain science, 104, 109, 113, 115, 120, 128
Breazeal, Cynthia, 237
Briggs, John, and Peat, David, *Turbulent Mirror*, 116–117
Brooks, Rodney, 52–53, 71, 97; *Flesh and Machines*, 56–57, 212
Buber, Martin, 155; *The Knowledge of Man*, dialogue, I-Thou relation, 241–242
Buddhism, 14, 41, 182; cleaning the mirror, 166; compassion, 167–168

Calkins, Susan, 121
Casey, Ed, *Getting Back into Place*, 46
cave paintings, indigenous, 141, 155
ceremony, 205
Cezanne, Paul, 43
Chaplain, Charlie, *Modern Times*, 3, 218, 232
chimpanzee, 155
Chorost, Michael, 154, 160, 235, 243; *Rebuilt: How Becoming Part Computer Made Me Human*, 58–74, 80
Clark, Andy, 71, 248; *Natural Born Cyborgs: Minds, Technologies, and the Future of Human Intelligence*, 74–76, 81, 101, 231

Clark's nutcracker, 24–25, 75, 180
cochlear implants, 59–59, 61–74, 80
Cog (M.I.T. robot), 97–99, 130, 211, 236; handshake of, 98, 230, 235
Coleridge, Samuel, *Kubla Khan*, 145–146
Coma (feature film), 83, 238
companion species, 154
computers, 50–53, 55–59, 61–64, 73–74, 78–80, 85, 88, 93–100, 113, 148, 186, 209, 210, 215, 217–218, 220–221, 229–231, 247
Confucius, 10
cormorants, 91, 183
consumerism, 10–11
Cox, Harvey, 98
cyberspace, 143
cyborg, 4–6, 58–64, 154; definition, 59–62; fyborg, 60; Manfred Clynes and Nathan Cline; 59, 70–71, 74–77, 80

Dallery, Carlton, "Into the Truth with Animals," 175–176
Damasio, Antonio, *Descartes' Error*, 125–128, 130; somatic markers, 128
Darwinism, 4
Deep Blue (IBM computer), 51–52, 96, 97, 98–100
Deleuze, Gilles, and Guattari, Félix, 3; war machine, 222
Dennett, Daniel, 38, 178–179
depth, 108–109, 223–224, 226
Descartes, René, 50–52, 56, 74, 89, 96, 99–100, 111, 112, 120, 122, 150, 158, 166, 171, 179, 184, 198, 245, 252; animal spirits, 5–6, 102–103; *Meditations on a First Philosophy*, 28–29
dialogue, of humanities and science, 7–8
Diamond, Adele, 55–56
Diamond, Jared, *The Third Chimpanzee*, 4, 87
Dick, Philip K., 238

disability concept criticized, 95
DNA, 118, 137, 158; shared with chimpanzees, 4, 87
dogs, 22, 248; as imaginers, 148
Dolly, cloned sheep, 211
dream consciousness, 190–195
Dreyfus, Hubert, *What Computers Still Can't Do*, 94–95
dualism, 7, 14–15, 24, 101, 129, 156
Dupré, Louis, *Religious Mystery and Rational Reflection*, 256

earthbody, 15–16
ecospirituality, 251–257
Einstein, Albert, 133
Eiseley, Loren, *The Immense Journey*, 203
elephants, 14, 33; disruption of their culture, 240–242
Eliot, T. S., "The Waste Land," 200–201
embodiment, 15; as imagination, 147; as temporal process, 62, 206–207; understanding or knowing of, 19, 27, 29, 39–40, 45, 52–58, 66–67, 72, 81–82, 95, 123, 174, 239–240
emergent phenomenon, and emotions, 68–69, 138
emotional (affective) understanding, 11–12, 68–69, 180; ambivalence, 110; categorical, 120; connection, 106–108; give and take, 154; integrating brain processes, 118–124; felt with and through others, 109–113, 150; juxtapositions within, 125–129; magic (action at a distance) within, 140–141; providing orientation, 68–69, 106–109; secondary, shared with animals, shared with others, versus enacted, 165; versus feelings, 127–128
emotions, 118–130; basic, 102; co-regulated, 150–152; distinctive of humans, 103–104; movement of, 104–105, 120–121, 124; secondary, 125; superposition, 128

emplacement within context, 57, 61, 68–69, 104–109, 203–204
emptiness (Buddhist), 136, 166
encroachment of biotechnological, 82–84
Enlightenment, 113
enmeshment of body and surround, 81, 156, 227–228
ever-present event, 203–207
experience, 11–14; in animals, 169–176; versus theory, 12
extended architecture (scaffolding) of human cognition, 74–75, 100–101

Fabre, Jean Henri, 47–48
face, and thought, 94–99; expression of, 99; of inanimate things
feedback loops, 49, 55, 64–65, 200; self-amplification, 116; self-regulation of, 231
feeling, 125–126, 128; feeling of being felt, 150, 154
Foerst, Anne, 250; community, *God in the Machine*, 50–56; 235–238, 239; embodiment, 97–99; making and prayer, 255–256; narratives, 242
Frankenstein, 3–4, 79, 83, 211, 238
freedom, negative, 159; primary sense, 158–159
Freud, Sigmund, *The Interpretation of Dreams*, 142; primary process, 18, 189–190

Galileo (Galilei), 113
Gelertner, David, *Machine Beauty*, 220–221
gene expression, 118
Gentner, Timothy, 92
gesture, 97–98, 173
Global positioning system (GPS), 81–82
Goldsworthy, Alan, *Rivers and Tides*, 225; time and change, 225–226

Grandin, Temple, 192, 197; *Animals in Translation*, 186–190; autism, 95; distractibility of animals, 187–189; musical language, 190
Griffin, Donald, *Animal Minds*, 38, 91, 180, 183
Griffin, Susan, *Women and Nature*, 80–81

Hahn, Thich Nhat, *The Sun My Heart*, 161, 166, 168; mindfulness, 160, 205–206; reconciliation, 167–168
HAL, the computer in *2001: A Space Odyssey* (film), 247
Haraway, Donna, 71–73, 245; biopower, 82–84; *The Companion Species Manifesto*, 5, 54–55; cyborgs, 59–60; informatics, 85, Modest_Witness@Second_Millenium. FemaleMan©_Meets_OncoMouse™, 82–85; natureculture, 5, 16; technoscience, 7–8
Hatley, James, *Suffering Witness*, 167–168
Hegel, Georg Wilhelm Friedrich, 90–91
Heidegger, Martin, 114, 132, 157, 201; around world of animals [*Umwelt*], 28–31, 46, 197; *Being and Time*, 26–28, 104–106, 134, 206; *Discourse on Thinking*, 84; dwelling, 164; knowing of the hands, 52; *The Fundamental Concepts of Metaphysics*, 28–37, 178; mood, 104–106; ontological difference, 134–135; privileging human, 32–37; reduction of animals, 32–37, 171, 178–179; technology, 84; thanking, 166; tools (ready-to-hand), 76, 84, 180, 216, 231
Heisenberg, Werner, 133
Herrigal, Eugen, It shoots, 15; *Zen in the Art of Archery*, 15, 68
hierarchy of beings, 8–11; possible horizontal plane, 9
Hinduism, 251, 252
hippocampus, 119
Hobbes, Thomas, 79

hodological space, 26–27
Huizinga, Johan, *Homo Ludens*, 148, 181
human, boundaries 121, 124; distinctiveness, 102–104, 113, 148, 152–161; parallel processing, 142; and personhood, 235, 237–238; recognition, 162; witnessing as distinctive excellence of, 161–164, 215, 235
Human Genome Diversity Project, 83–84
Husserl, Edmund, 12

imaginal, 16
imagination, 13, 140, 141–150, 163; creative, 176; intersubjective, 150; productive vs. reproductive, 145–146, 169–172
imploded boundaries of humans, animals and machines, 82–86
incorporation into embodiment, 30, 41, 46, 54, 56, 77–79, 126, 185
indeterminacy, 71–72, 108–109, 153
inexhaustibility of sense, 73
information processing, 118–119
instinct, 38, 47, 182, 190–195, 196; activity for pleasure, 192; as fetish, 192; "ignorance of," 37; nature of irresistibility, 191–192; oneiric and sacred character of, 193–195; relation to culture, 194, 198; seen as hardwired, 190–191; symbolic function, 194–195, 197–199
intentional arc, 77–79
interconnectivity, 9–10
interpretation, 13–14
intersubjectivity, 43, 70–71, 111–112, 165
Island (feature film), 83, 238

James, William, 89, 125
Joyce, James, 44, *Ulysses*, 149
juxtapositions of meanings, 125–126, 172–175

Kac, Eduardo, 81

Index

Kandel, Eric, *In Search of Memory: The Emergence of the New Science of the Brain*, 115

Kant, Immanuel, 26, 133; *The Critique of Judgment*, 145, 195; deeper sublime, 168; productive versus reproductive imagination, 145

Kasparov, Garry, 51, 95, 96, 98–99

Keller, Catherine, *The Face of the Deep*, 252

Kierkegaard, Sören, *Either/Or*, vol. one, 159

kinesthetic dimension, 173

Kismet (M.I.T. robot), 236–237; apparent emotional response, 97–99, 130, 243, 246

Koko, 33, 91

Kowalski, Gary, *The Souls of Animals*, 155, 181

Kundera, Milan, lightness of being, 223

Langer, Suzanne, *Feeling and Form*, 144; aesthetic surface, 144, 190; plasticity, 144; semblance, 143; virtual 143–144

language, 91–93; extended architecture of thought, 101–102; as Other 248; poetic, 112; through shared milieu, 112–113

Latour, Bruno, *Politics of Nature*, 7–8, 250

Lawrence, D. H., "Two Ways of Living and Dying," 229

Laycock, Stephen, "The Animal as Animal," 175

Leopold, Aldo, *The Sand County Almanac*, 243

letting-be (letting go), 67–68

lived understanding, 106–108

logic of inclusive differences, 127

Lorenz, Konrad, 193–194

Lucic, Karen, *Charles Scheeler and the Cult of the Machine*, 219–220

machines, arbitrariness of, 227–230; beauty of, 220–221; consistency of, 213–218; definitions, 2–4, 22, 24; dialogue with, 252–253; evolution of, 75–76, 79; excellences, 213–214, 216–218; fear of, 79, 209, 212; flexibility of design, 227–228; human obligation to, 244–251; machine-animals, 21–22, 210–211; machine age, 219; materiality of, 209–213; overlap with human, 6, 21–22, 78–79, 103; part of animality, 21–22; possible personhood of, 235–244, 247; "postmodern animal," 21; power, 218–222; precision of, 221–222; responding to human intentions, 76–79; simple, 75, social, 3–4, 6; speed, 222–226; swallowing distance and time, 223; threats from, 1–4, 79, 82–84; transparency, 231–232; woven into surround, 49–58, 230–234

MacIntyre, Alasdair, *After Virtue*, 149–150

Malebranche, Nicolas, 5

Marx, Karl, 79

materialism, mistaken, 10–11, 17, 255; reductive, 113–114

materiality, 50; holding past, 17; imperviousness of machines, material sense, 16–18, 74–75, 109, 252

matrix, 161

Mazis, Glen, *Earthbodies*, 6, 127, 149, 200, 205–207; *Emotion and Embodiment*, 104–105, 121, 138–141; emotional valence, 109–113; "Living by the Railroad Tracks," 252–253; "The Natural Power of Memory," 260; timing, 206–207, 215–216; phenomenality, 138–141

mechanism, social, 3

melody, 48, 72, 176, 194, 195, 197, 201–202

memory, 17, 27, 35, 119, 146

mental maps, 26–28, 46; Vanderwall, Bald and Tuck, 25

Merleau-Ponty, Maurice, 34–35, 50–51, 61, 71, 81–82, 88, 114, 122–123, 137, 172, 211, 256; body schema, 77–78; "The Child's Relations with

Merleau-Ponty, Maurice (continued)
Others," 109–113, 183; and cybernetics, 85; emotion, 106–109, 122; experience error, 13; "Eye and Mind," 145; flesh of the world, 38, 42, 101–102, 132; geological time, 225; imaginal, 146, incorporation, 77–79; instinct in animals, 192–200; interanimality, 44, 242; knowing of the hands, 52; lateral relations, 58, 161; method, 12–14; *Nature*, 22–23, 192–195, 196–199, 201–202, 204–205, 216; night as pure depth, 224; perceptual field, 35, 40–41; perceptual faith, 64–67; *Phenomenology of Perception*, 15, 39, 41, 45–46, 53–54, 65, 69, 72, 106–109, 145, 84–186, 190, 199, 203, 227, 235; *Primacy of Perception*, reversibility, 42–43, 78–80, 123, 179; syncretistic sociability, 41–42, 111–112; tacit cogito, 184; *Visible and the Invisible*, 15, 42–44, 123
metacognition, 157–160
metalanguage (and animals), 92
metaphorical understanding, 56–57, 71–72, 172–175
Michelangelo, 43
mindfulness, 160, 164, 205–206
M.I.T. Artificial Intelligence Lab, 16, 19, 51–53, 98–99, 230, 235
Monet, Claude, 173
mood [*Befindlichkeit*], 104–107
Morton, Timothy, *Ecology Without Nature*, 39
Moss, Cynthia, 33
motility, 53–55
motor significance, 53–55
Munch Edvard, 115
myth, 107–108

Naddaf, Gerard, *The Greek Concept of Nature*, 265
Nagel, Thomas, "What Is It Like to Be a Bat?," 169–173, 185–186

narrative, 149–152, 237–238; collaborative, 149–152; integrative, 151–152; sense of self, 150–151
Native American tribal perspective, 8, 238
neural plasticity, 63–64, 113–118
neuronal clusters, 118–120
Nietzsche, Friedrich, *The Birth of Tragedy*, 115; *The Genealogy of Morals*, 177
Nishida [Kitarô], 131
nonlinear equations, 117
nonlocality, 137–141, entangled particle spin, 137
not one, not two logic, 128–129, 137, 158, 160–161, 165

observer/observed unity, 132–141
oikos, 8, 255
Oliver, Mary, 255
oneiric, 15, 18, 193, 195
open systems, 115–116
overlap among humans, animals and machines, 6, 21–22, 72–74, 91–93

Page, George, *Inside the Animal Mind*, 25, 91
parallel processing, 142
Paterson, Francine, 91
Pauli, Wolfgang, 133
Pepperberg, Irene, 91
perception, animal, human, overlaps between humans and animals, supposed chaos of animals, thickness of, 138–139
perceptual field, 43–46
perceptual understanding, 13–14, 18–19, 40–41, 246
personhood, 235–244; for animals and machines, 235–244; and guardianship, 247, 250
phenomenality, 138–141
phenomenology, 12–14, 19, 24, 113, 125, 248
philosophical theory, 89–91
Pierce, Charles, 89

Index

Piercy, Marge, *He, She and It*, 130
plasticity, 73–74; in aesthetics, 115
Plato, 10, 90, 102–103; *Phaedo*, 251; *Republic*, 252; *Timaeus*, 251–252
play, 148, 181–182
poetry, 172
postmodern capitalism, 10–11
postmodern skepticism, 88
postural schema, 111
pragmatism, 89–90
prairie dogs, 44, 92, 162, 190
preculture, 194, 198
prereflective unity, 179, 199–200
probability wave, 132–133
proprioception, 36, 183
Proust, Marcel, 44

qualities, primary versus secondary, 155–156
quantum phenomena, 137–138

Radner, Daisie and Michael, *Animal Consciousness*, 47–48
receptive touching, 175
recognition, versus reflection, 34–35, 184
recollection, 119
reductive common ground, from above, 23–24; from below, 23–24
reflection, abstract, integrated with emotion over time, 121–122, 129–130; interplay with perception, 65, 184–185, 188
relativism, 133
relativity, versus relativism, 71–74, 133–134, 136
responsibility, 245–251
rhythm, of biological functioning, 213; felt, 110; of machines, 214–216, 232; of surround, 189, 197, 223, 225, 228–229, 234
Ricoeur, Paul, "The Metaphorical Process as Cognition, Imagination and Feeling," 173–175
robots, 53–58, 97–99, 130, 165, 217–218, 249

Rube Goldberg machines, 75

Sartre, Jean-Paul, *Being and Nothingness*, 157, 158, 165; *The Emotions: Outline of a Theory*, 140–141; *Transcendence of the Ego*, 156
Sartwell, Crispin, *Six Names of Beauty*, 233
Scheeler, Charles, 222, 243; power series, 219–220; "Suspended Power," 220
Schrodinger wave equations, 134
Schwartz, Jeffrey M. and Sharon Begley, 156, 161; mental force, 135–136; *The Mind and the Brain*, 117–118, 132–136; obsessive-compulsive syndrome, 117, 135; quantum brain, 132, 138
scientific theories, 88–89
sea urchin, 22–23
seamlessness with environment, 22
self, agency, 198–199; illusory, 122–123; prepersonal, 123–124, 202–203; prereflective, 183–186
self-consciousness, 50, 157
self-organizing (regulating), 116
Seng-Ts'an, Buddhist master, 136–137
sentiment, 10
Shelley, Mary, *Frankenstein*, 3–4, 79, 211
Siddhartha Buddha, 9–10
Siebert, Charles, "Are We Driving Elephants Crazy?," 240–242
Siegel, Daniel, 19, 157–158; *The Developing Mind*, 114–115, 118–124, 129, 150–152
situatedness, 57
spatiality, lived or existential, 106–109, 222–224
Sphex, yellow-winged, 47–48
spirit, 251
Sroufe, Alan, 123
starfish, 22–23
starlings, 92
Steiglitz, Alfred, 43
Stelarc, 76

style, 199
symbol, 18, 118–119, 144–145, 253; relation to instinct, 194–195, 197–198
synaesthesia, 127, 173–174

Tai Chi, 131
Taoism, 41; kuan, 131; *Tao te Ching*, 130–131; ten thousand things, 135, 167
technoscience, 10–11
temporal context, 122, 202–203, 206–207, 223
temporality, arrhythmic, 230; felt pace of, 202, 206–207, 223–224; geological time, 215–216, 224–226, 229–230; of human drama, 215; lived, longer cycles of, 202; slower of animals, 200–207
thinking, 96–97; having a face, 98; impurity of, 100, 128, 154; inter-subjectively ("we think'), 100, 153, lived understanding, 97; thanking, 166; through surround, 74, 100–104; transcategorical, 173–174
tools, 76, 79, 101–102
transitivism, 41–42, 111–112, 183
transposition into animal worlds, 36–37
tsunami (of December, 26, 2004), 214
Tulku, Tarthung, *Time, Space and Knowledge*, 206
Turing, A. M., "Computing Memory and Intelligence," 93–94
Turing test, 93–98

Turner, J. M. W., 253

Uexküll, Jakob von, 28–30
Umwelt, 28–37, 189–190, 197–198; versus objective world (*Umgebung*), 30
Upanishads, 10

valence, emotional, 109–113
Valery, Paul, 43, 146
Van Gogh, Vincent, 115, 227
virtuality, 141–150, 181
viscerality, 126
von Uexküll, Jakob, 28–31, 171, 197–198

Watkins, Mary, "Tran-Species Psychology: Theory and Practice," 249
wave of probability, 132–133
Weng, McClelland, Pentland, Sporns, Strockman, Sur, and Thelan, "Autonomous Mental Development in Robots and Animals," 57–58
Whitehead, Alfred North, 13–14
whooping crane, 155
will, and attention, 135–136
witnessing, 161–164, 215, 235
world as bodily context, 41–42

Young, Thomas, double slit experiment, 132–133

Zen, 68; garden, 40; swordsperson, 200